te long expected

d Singapore

e off the enve

d by I ... one Sunday

on the 19 - I could hardl

s had elapsed & consequ

could be stated - the fac

me shed tears of joy &

Rey added to my happi

t ... of your letters h

cannot tell what you

antage for I can turn

as about & what I thought

y - ... referring to my book

what I expected playing

I note your remarks abou

LETTERS FROM CHINA

The Canton-Boston Correspondence of Robert Bennet Forbes, 1838-1840

compiled and edited, and with background essays, by Phyllis Forbes Kerr

MYSTIC SEAPORT MUSEUM, INC.
MYSTIC, CONNECTICUT

Dedicated to my sister
Elizabeth Lee Forbes Titherington

In Memory of my mother
Elizabeth McKean Bourneuf

This book is printed in Hong Kong

ISBN 0-913372-77-3

Designed by Clare Cunningham Graphic Design,
Essex, Connecticut, USA

First Edition

Forbes, Robert Bennet, 1804-1889.
Letters from China: the Canton-Boston correspondence of Robert Bennet Forbes, 1838-1840 / compiled and edited by Phyllis Forbes Kerr. — 1st ed. — Mystic, Conn.: Mystic Seaport Museum, c1996.
p.: ill. maps, ports. ; cm.
Bibliography: p.
Includes index.

1. Merchants – Massachusetts – Boston – Correspondence, reminiscences, etc. 2. China – Commerce – Massachusetts – History – 19th century. 3. China – Social life and customs – 1644-1912. 4. Ocean travel. 5. Opium trade. I. Kerr, Phyllis Forbes. II. Title.

CT275.F67A3

Mystic Seaport Museum
75 Greenmanville Avenue
Mystic, Connecticut 06355

CONTENTS

Foreword 6

The China Trade That Awaited Robert Bennet Forbes 8

Family History Before RBF's 1838 Trip to China 11

Perkins & Co. and the Opium Trade 14

THE LETTERS:

Departure from Boston 18

Landing 54

Commissioner Lin Demands All Opium 106

A Visit to Macao 154

Back in Canton 208

Gales and Squalls 242

Aftermath 266

Acknowledgements 274

Bibliography 276

APPENDIX I: *Maps* 278

APPENDIX II: *Articles from* The Chinese Repository, *1840* 280

Index 312

The Chinese characters blind-embossed on this book's cover read "Keechong" — "flag of American prosperity" in English. This reference to the blue-and-white flag of the firm was the Chinese designation of Russell & Co.

FOREWORD

The correspondence of Robert Bennet Forbes (1813-1889), and his son, J. Murray Forbes (1843-1936), carefully preserved but long forgotten, was rediscovered in the attic of the Forbes House atop Milton Hill outside Boston, prior to its opening as a house museum in 1964. Other family members thereafter generously donated additional papers–notably those of Francis Blackwell Forbes (1839-1908).

Recognizing a wealth of information regarding the varied activities of a venturesome American family much involved in the China trade, the Massachusetts Historical Society undertook to catalogue the entire collection. In 1969, under the auspices of the National Historical Publications Commission, the Society published this material in 47 microfilm reels with an accompanying *Guide to the Microfilm Edition of the Forbes Papers.*

Today, given the uncertain future of Hong Kong and the rocky course of U.S. trade relations with China, eyewitness accounts of nineteenth-century Western merchants doing business in China seem especially relevant and timely. I was delighted, therefore, when my niece, Phyllis Forbes Kerr — a great-great-granddaughter of Robert Bennet Forbes — took on the arduous task of transcribing and editing one of the most interesting portions of the Forbes papers — Robert Bennet Forbes's letters to his wife sent mainly from China from 1838 to 1840.

Whether on board ship or ashore, Robert Bennet Forbes was that rare combination — a man of action and an inveterate scribbler. In the latter role, his letters and journals listed in the *Guide* add up to more than 8,400 ms. pages. He published 60 pamphlets on a variety of subjects, and wrote an autobiography that went through three editions.

Writing to his wife "late in the evening after a busy day...." helped to assuage Forbes's homesick longings; this habit seems to have been as essential to his well-being as eating and sleeping. Although RBF was meticulous about his business correspondence, in his letters to Rose he acknowledged: "I find I am dreadfully careless in my writing & do not punctuate & divide my sentences right...." Mrs. Kerr has wisely retained his idiosyncrasies.

These letters show Forbes to be a man of unusual charm, wit and energy, seldom bored and never boring. Obviously a fine captain and navigator, he seems most at home on the quarterdeck of a ship, waking at least once each night to check course, crew, sails and weather — while the captain, even in a squall, sleeps peacefully below. His evaluations of friends and colleagues are frank and revealing, as when he complains to his wife of a fellow passenger on the voyage home who is "wanting in good manners...par example, he eats always with his knife & half the time with the edge...gulps at table...." His portraits are equally vivid — perhaps none more so than that of the painter, George Chinnery, whom he finds sitting in his studio, with "leeches on his head and blood streaming down his face." The delightful dialogue with the missionary, Dr. Peter Parker, on their return voyage, regarding Parker's choice of a mate, reminds one of the wit and humor of Jane Austen, Charles Dickens or Mark Twain.

These letters provide an important account of the life of Westerners at Canton and Macao and those with whom they interact. We meet the Head, senior and junior partners, and clerks of the several British and American houses.

Compradores, linguists, Hong merchants, including the senior Hong merchant, Houqua–the great friend of Russell & Co. — appear. We learn of exhausting work during the season when ships come and go. And of the luxurious but confined life of Westerners at Canton who try various means to pass the time: card games, sports like leapfrog and sailing, informal dinners with friends, grand dinners at the British factory, and a banquet at the villa of a Hong merchant who begins the affair by throwing fragrant blossoms at his guests. Life at Macao, enlivened by the company of colleagues' wives, grown daughters, small children, and a healthier climate, provides a welcome respite from Canton.

The climax of Forbes's journal is his description for Rose of the day-to-day crisis brought on by the Imperial decision to halt the opium trade. Events leading to the first Opium War will be familiar to many, but RBF's eyewitness account of this woeful phase of the West's relations with China is particularly detailed: British trade at a standstill; Americans virtually prisoners in their own factories; Hong merchants, including Houqua, in chains; Chinese smugglers publicly beheaded.

Forbes expressed his relief to Rose that his fortune during this visit to China was not derived from the opium trade. Moreover, he thought James Innes's attempt to land opium directly at Canton — an act so illicit that it brought the problem to a head — inexcusably foolhardy. Yet he assumed that, once the immediate troubles had blown over, "old custom" would prevail. His letters make it abundantly clear that he sided with the British view that the Chinese, like Europeans, Americans, and other "civilized" peoples, must join the community of nations; if the British had to "bully" the Imperial government to bring this about Forbes, like most other China merchants, favored that course.

Each age sustains institutions and behavior that, though accepted by the majority in their time, may become abhorrent to the majority of a later age. Forbes shared the general view of his age and of his fellow merchants that opium was neither more nor less addictive or dangerous than ardent spirits. Opium, though illegal in China, was entirely legal in the West. Older people used it to relieve numerous symptoms and complaints; small doses of the drug were even used to quiet fussy infants.

A vocal minority in the West, of course, considered opium smuggling as abhorrent as slavery. More often than not, opponents of slavery and opium smuggling were one and the same: Quakers, Evangelicals, and others of rigorous moral stamp. They shared the notion — as universally unpopular then as now — that there is a higher law than that of maximizing profits.

Forbes and his friends believed that these "abolitionists" — whether opposed to the opium trade or to slavery–were seldom to be found among the "best people" — that is, among members of the financial and commercial elite whom they knew. Similar troublesome people later opposed the free-market view that landlords were justified in shipping food from Ireland to the Continent during the Great Famine while the poor starved. Today, similar troublesome individuals may think it wrong for manufacturers to "outsize" their employees by sending orders to other parts of the globe where workers are paid far less than the U.S. minimum wage. No doubt one can even find those today who allege that addiction to cigarettes currently sold by American manufacturers at home and abroad is a far more serious cause of illness and death than opium ever was. These letters of an otherwise decent, generous and kind individual remind us not only that the sensibility of each age differs, but also that there is ample opportunity to judge our own age with candor.

H.A. Crosby Forbes

THE CHINA TRADE THAT AWAITED ROBERT BENNET FORBES

From the time the first European ships appeared in the China Sea in the sixteenth century, they were less than welcome. The Chinese Emperors were fearful of foreign influence and mischief. They thought, rightly so, that if these strange men were allowed to enter China they would corrupt the inhabitants with their barbarian ideas, products, and religions. Warlike westerners might even conquer China or subjugate parts of its vast territory. Although the riches of China, from silks to spices to teapots, had come to Europe for centuries along the Silk Road and its many branches to the North of the Celestial Empire, this southern trade by sea was new and needed not only order but discipline.

In 1760 the Chinese government established a set of regulations to control the foreigners and their ships. Canton was the only Chinese port open to the strangers – an arrangement that simplified dealing with them and also simplified the collection of customs duties. All ships were required to stop first at Macao, a small settlement acquired by the Portuguese in 1557. Located inside the mouth of the Pearl River, Macao was about 65 miles south of Canton and 40 miles across the estuary from Hong Kong. At Macao foreign ships hired a pilot licensed by the Chinese government. Part of his job was to secure written permission – a "chop" – for the foreign ship to enter Chinese waters. This normally took at least two days. At the mouth of the Pearl River each ship was examined. Finally with the guidance of the pilot the vessel could proceed up the river to Whampoa, an island 13 miles below Canton.

At Whampoa all ships were required to anchor. They were prohibited from going further, and it was not uncommon for as many as a hundred ships to be anchored in the waters off the island.[1] Here the loading and unloading of cargos took place. The sailors who were left to tend the anchored ships at Whampoa were not permitted to set foot on the island–but they were allowed to go to nearby Dane Island and French Island for exercise. Occasionally groups of about 20 sailors accompanied by an officer were permitted to travel up to Canton. There in Hog Lane they could buy samshu, a concoction of alcohol, tobacco juice, sugar, and arsenic which enabled them to feel no pain in a very short time.[2]

Meanwhile, "fast boats" carried the foreign merchants, captains and supercargos up the river to Canton where they would reside during the trading season, which lasted from August until March. A regulation decreed that "neither women, guns, spears, nor arms of any kind" were allowed to go with the traders. If women and children did accompany the men to China, they were required to set up housekeeping at Macao and wait there for the men to visit.[3]

In Canton the foreigners had no rights outside the narrow confines of their row of "factories" and its immediate neighborhood along the river. They were not allowed to go into the countryside or into the city of Canton. Four times a month, accompanied by a Chinese linguist, they were permitted to go across the river to visit the Fati Gardens and its immediate neighborhood. They were forbidden to move in groups of more than ten and had to return across the river as soon as they were "refreshed." The foreigners were also forbidden to use the Pearl River for pleasure sailing, and their ships could not "loiter about."[4]

These regulations controlled all trade, and day-to-day business was conducted through a body of Hong Merchants who also served as go-betweens with the foreigners and the Chinese government. The 13 Hong Merchants were first established in 1782, and the hongs, or warehouses, were theirs to rent to the foreign traders. The supercargo from a newly arrived ship–the ship's officer in charge of the cargo and its sale and purchase–would immediately contact a Hong Merchant who would act as the ship's Chinese agent. The co-hong, as this group of merchants and system of doing business was called, was responsible to the Chinese government not only for the foreign vessel and its cargo but for the well-being and behavior of its crew. Although the Hong Merchants paid a large sum of money for their privileges, and made large sums from their ventures, they were looked down upon by the officials of China. The most distinguished Hong Merchant was Houqua, a man treasured by his trading partners for his friendship, loyalty, guidance, and honesty. He was an astute trader whose fortune was estimated to be 26 million dollars in 1834, an amount that one historian has described as "probably the largest mercantile fortune in the world at that time."[5]

The Hoppo, a Chinese customs official at Canton, had each new ship that arrived at Whampoa measured, and levied a tax on the vessel and its cargo. This fee had to be paid to the treasury of the Chinese Emperor before any of the ship's cargo could be put ashore. Then "chop boats" rowed by Chinese men carried each ship's cargo the rest of the way up the Pearl River to Canton where it was stored in the hongs or factories.

A group known as compradors was appointed to handle each foreign ship's supplies and the needs of her men during their stay in China. Members of another group called linguists were hired to be interpreters for each foreign country. Since the teaching of the Chinese language was discouraged by the government, very few of the merchants or sailors were able to communicate in Chinese. Soon pidgin versions of European languages developed, taking the sounds of foreign words and combining them with simple Chinese words to form a very basic mode of expression. This language was described as very comical, and it was hard for foreigners to take anything said in it seriously. Although their services were required by law, the linguists really had little knowledge of any foreign language and relied on fractured versions of European words. More than likely, Europeans and Americans attempting to speak Chinese delivered as ludicrous a performance as the Chinese linguists.

The Americans came late to the China trade. While they were British colonists they were forbidden to sail into the Pacific, and it was not until after the Revolution in 1784 that the first American ship, *Empress of China*, sailed from New York to China and began profitable trade in teas, silks, porcelains, and many other things. After a long ocean voyage of many months, the Americans found a China that was unfriendly as well as exotic. Foreigners going up the river in a "fast boat" had a jarring and crude introduction to China and her people. Leaving the island of Whampoa, where a fleet of foreign ships crowded the anchorage, they soon encountered fleets of smaller Chinese vessels at anchor, under way, and jammed in along the banks. And some large Chinese vessels lined the banks of the river or moved slowly downstream – awkward Chinese junks and 600-ton ships involved in trade with Java. Their elaborately decorated sterns and strange eyes painted on each bow stared down at the anxious foreigners. Long river junks, rowed by gangs of half-naked oarsmen, slid quietly by. Official mandarin boats flying white and red banners patrolled the shores with cannons deployed. Gaily decorated "flower boats" filled with Chinese ladies of pleasure circled and emitted Chinese music that would not have been music to the ears of the strangers.

By the time a fast boat neared Canton, the number of vessels in all directions increased and gave the impression of a town floating on the river. Many of these were houseboats anchored in rows from the middle of the stream to the shores, leaving only narrow lanes of water clear for passing boats. The hundreds of multi-generational families who lived on the water in sampans were a rough breed of people who had no interest in making the foreigners feel welcome. By pointing, making obscene jokes, sometimes throwing garbage, and yelling "Demons, Devils!," they did their best to discomfort the strangers. Their insults were often drowned out by the din of the river's traffic and industry–the pounding of carpenter's hammers, the cries of vendors, the quacking of ducks, the bong of large gongs, the snapping of firecrackers.[6]

The city of Canton was walled off from the Pearl River, leaving a restricted area along the waterfront where the factories or hongs were set back from the water and grouped in a long line for 1000 feet on the riverside. It was here that the foreign merchants lived and did business. Between the buildings and the water was a stretch of foreshore called Respondentia Walk where they could stroll for exercise. This space was usually filled with Chinese who had come to get a glimpse of the strange Westerners, or to set up markets for a variety of services and wares. One could buy anything from pickled olives to paper umbrellas to exotic pastry. Barbers, tailors, cobblers, jugglers, and storytellers offered their services, and beggars cried for handouts. Sometimes the European and American merchants and clerks could barely elbow their way through the crowd. [7]

The bottom floor of each hong or factory was a storage space called a go-down where the teas and silks were kept, and the second and third stories were for offices and living quarters. From the front the factories looked like single houses, but they stretched back about 140 yards and opened onto inner courtyards. Each building kept the name of the nation that had first leased it, but many of these (Denmark, Sweden, Austria, and Spain) were no longer involved in the China trade by the late 1830s. The East India Company, which until 1834 had the sole British right of trading with China, leased the biggest and most impressive factory, twice the size of.any other. The principal product stored in the hongs for export was tea, followed by raw silk, then by sugar, then by Nankin cotton cloth, then by a variety of goods that included camphor. In 1840, *Hunt's Merchants Magazine* in the U.S., describing the China trade, identified opium as "by far the most important" import.

Near the factories were a few streets open to the foreigners. Thirteen Factory Street ran behind the hongs, and the square in front was bounded by three streets – Hog Lane, New China Street, and Old China Street. Overlooking these streets were many small Chinese shops where one could purchase goods and handicrafts: ivory, silk, bird cages, fireworks, medicinal herbs, tea and samshu. There was also one church.

In 1838 when Robert Bennet Forbes arrived in China in the role of a merchant for the first time, the Chinese were still referring to foreigners as "barbarians" or "foreign devils," and the original regulations remained in effect with little change. However, over the years the rule that forbade foreigners the use of the river had relaxed. RBF and his friends were now allowed to use the Pearl River off Canton for pleasure boating. Boating clubs were formed, and sailing and rowing regattas were popular outlets for the energies of these otherwise confined men. Having been in China at various times, since his first trip there as a cabin boy, Forbes was accustomed to the ways of the China trade at Canton in both its obvious and its subtle particulars. By the time RBF commenced his first tour of duty with Russell & Co. at Canton, he was an old China hand. — PFK

FAMILY HISTORY BEFORE RBF'S 1838 TRIP TO CHINA

For Robert Bennet Forbes it seemed only natural to become involved in the China trade. His mother's brothers, James and Thomas Handasyd Perkins, were prominent merchants of Boston who, under the name Perkins & Co., owned a number of ships engaged in trade with China. Of the ten children of Sarah Elliott and T. H. Perkins, eight had reached adulthood, married, and had large families of their own. Perkins & Co. was a family affair. When a position opened up, the brothers needed only to look among their brothers-in-law, sons, sons-in-law, and eager young nephews to find the right man for the job.

RBF's father, Ralph Bennet Forbes, was married to Margaret, the youngest Perkins sibling. Unlike his Perkins in-laws, Ralph Forbes lacked both skill and luck in business. Everything the unfortunate man touched seemed to go bad. Out of concern for their sister's well-being, the Perkins brothers occasionally hired Ralph to work for Perkins & Co. in Europe. By the summer of 1810 Ralph had spent more than a year on such a mission, so his wife Margaret decided to join him in Europe with her two oldest children–Thomas Tunno, age eight, and Robert Bennet, age six. The trip was delayed for six months when the boys' little sister Margaret was severely burned in a fire, and Mrs. Forbes felt she could not leave until the child recovered. By then it was winter and very few ships were crossing the Atlantic.

Margaret Forbes was determined to join her husband and finally booked passage for three on a small topsail schooner. After the sailors knocked the ice off the rigging, the ship left Boston harbor in the freezing winds of 17 January 1811. The voyage began with a severe storm off Cape Cod and ended when the ship was captured by the British, who had established a blockade along the coast of France as part of their Napoleonic War effort. Mrs. Forbes and the two boys were prisoners for three weeks on a British ship. They were finally freed, only to be forced by the French authorities into quarantine at Marseilles for three more weeks. Eventually they were reunited with Mr. Forbes, but very soon the boys were left in a French boarding school for a year and a half while Mr. and Mrs. Forbes traveled to Italy, the Holy Land and Egypt. No one at the school spoke English, so the little brothers quickly learned to communicate in French. When their parents finally returned, they took the boys to Bordeaux, where they delayed sailing home until Mrs. Forbes gave birth to a baby, John Murray, in February of 1813. The trip home proved even more exciting than the trip out. This time the ships they traveled on during interrupted passages from the Gironde in France to Corunna in Spain and then to Lisbon were overtaken in heated chases and amidst cannon fire were captured twice by the English, who were now engaged in the War of 1812 with the United States.[8]

When Ben and Tom finally reached home they were placed in Milton Academy, where they were regarded by their classmates as exotic young heroes. Both spoke French fluently, and each had been through more combat, drama, and travel than most grown men. Robert Bennet Forbes's experience on the high seas, and his independence at such a young age, left him with a thirst for adventure and travel and a love of sailing that would remain with him throughout his life.

In the early 1800s education beyond grade school was a luxury, so as soon as the Forbes boys were old enough their Perkins uncles had jobs for them. Thomas Tunno left Milton Academy at the age of 12 to work in the counting-room of Perkins & Co. in Boston. In 1819 at 17 he sailed to China to assist his much older cousin, John Cushing, who was in charge of the Canton business operations of the family firm. Tom was to be trained so that one day he would take over Cushing's job and become head of Perkins & Co. in China.

Like his brother, Robert Bennet Forbes left Milton Academy when he turned 12 and began to work as an apprentice in the family business. Since the firm was located near the Boston waterfront, when Ben ran errands he often found himself on Central Wharf where his "uncles fitted out their ships."* On one of these occasions his uncle Thomas found him standing on the deck of the *Canton Packet.* Thomas Perkins asked his 13-year-old nephew which ship he intended to sail on. Without hesitation Ben replied, "I am ready to go on this one." To the boy's surprise and delight, his uncle gave his consent and sent him home to inform his mother that he was beginning his career in the China trade as a cabin boy. "[He] took leave of home amidst the tears of the children, and, with [his] mother's blessing, embarked on the 'Canton packet'." This was in October of 1817.

As a sailor RBF turned over his meager wages to his parents. He worked hard, learned all he could about ships and the sea, and rose steadily in rank on each trip to China. In Canton he met and stayed with his cousin John Cushing. Cushing took a liking to Robert Bennet Forbes and was eager to have the boy work for him. But Ben was aware that his brother Tom was being groomed to take over Cushing's position. RBF intended to keep his promise to his Uncle T. H. Perkins, "to stick by [his] ship until fit to command her."

In 1824 at 40, ailing, and a failure all his life at business, Ben's father died, leaving Ben's mother, his three sisters, and his little brother John in a farmhouse in Milton supported by the Perkins brothers. The day after his father's funeral Robert Bennet Forbes, just 20, left once more for the Far East. This was his fifth trip to China, but his first trip as captain of a vessel. He was in command of his uncle's favorite ship, the 267-ton *Levant.* As Captain Forbes, Ben took *Levant* to the East, then sailed from China to Manila and back to China again.

Meanwhile, his brother Tom, still working as a merchant in Canton, enjoyed a life of luxury on land. As planned, he had taken over as head of the Chinese operations of Perkins & Co., leaving Cushing free to return home. Thomas Forbes's promising career as merchant was cut short when he drowned in August of 1829 after a typhoon capsized the topsail schooner he was sailing from Canton to Macao. He was 27 and had spent ten years in China.

The death of Tom Forbes caused a crisis in the business activities of the Perkins brothers, and ultimately it was decided that Perkins & Sons would join forces in China with another New England firm, Russell & Co., which had opened in Canton in 1824. Cushing suggested that Robert Bennet Forbes be sent to replace his brother and represent the family's interests in Russell & Co. Again RBF refused the offer– because he saw himself "as a seaman and not a merchant." Instead he asked his uncle to put him in charge of Lintin Station at Lintin Island. Lintin Station consisted of the Perkins & Sons vessel *Lintin,* at anchor off the island, which served as a supply ship to provision and equip other vessels, and as a storage ship for opium. This was a very desirable command for the young sailor/merchant, even though the ship was at anchor. Once more Ben

* This quote and all further quotes in this section are taken from Robert Bennet Forbes' autobiography, *Personal Reminiscences,* Third Edition, 1892.

sailed to China, this time with his younger brother John Murray, who at 19 was to join the house of Russell & Co. as clerk. For 18 months RBF lived and worked aboard the *Lintin*, "doing a thriving business in storage and furnishing (opium) to ships." In fact, he made a $5 commission for every chest of opium handled, a commission which added up to $30,000 in one year.[9]

When Robert Bennet Forbes returned to Boston in 1832 from his time at Lintin Station, he was a wealthy man. He was generous with his newly acquired money. For his mother, in memory of his older brother Thomas, he built the house which is today the Robert Bennet Forbes House in Milton. It had the newest of modern luxuries – inside plumbing. In 1834 he married Rose Greene Smith and settled in a house near his uncle Thomas Handasyd Perkins in Temple Place, a fashionable address in Boston. Within the next few years a combination of circumstances led to the loss of RBF's entire fortune: he had a hard time saying no when his acquaintances and friends asked him for loans or to invest money; he endured five years of bad luck in various business dealings; and he was brutally hit by the financial crisis of 1837. In fact, despite his success as a trader in Canton, Robert Bennet Forbes seems to have been nearly as unlucky or unskilled in business as his father.

Built in the 1830s for RBF's mother with the proceeds of his first merchant fortune, The Captain Robert Bennet Forbes House is now a museum. The Greek Revival mansion with large cupola was designed by the Boston architect Isaiah Rogers.

Meanwhile, John Murray Forbes took on more and more responsibility in Canton and continued the close family relationship with Houqua, the richest and most renowned of the Hong Merchants. John had an excellent mind for business, and as a young Yankee merchant with sometimes as much as half a million dollars invested in various ventures at one time, he became a respected client of Baring Brothers, the English banking and money-management firm that handled many American accounts. His youth was disguised by the fact that he was almost totally bald at 20 and looked more like a man of 30.

John came home from China with the intention of marrying, and began courting Sarah Hathaway of New Bedford. He married her in 1834, two months after his brother RBF married Rose Smith. Less than one month later John set off again for Canton, leaving his new bride at home. This time he became a partner at Russell & Co., and Houqua agreed to deal exclusively with the firm if John were in charge. As soon as John had completed his term of active partnership, he took his ample earnings and left China for good, reaching home in December of 1836.

John Murray Forbes was home for only a short time when he realized that his older brother was in severe financial trouble. John kindly offered to give Ben his place in Canton as partner at Russell & Co.–an opportunity for commissions on the purchase and sale of goods that would bring RBF his second fortune, this one from trade in teas and silks rather than from opium. RBF accepted and sailed to China for the first time as a real merchant. His brother remained at home to straighten out his big brother's debts and pending bankruptcy.

At the time of his departure for China in 1838, Robert Bennet Forbes began writing letters in journal form to his wife Rose, whom he had left behind in Boston with their eight-month-old son. The trip out took four and a half long months. The letters begin on 11 June, 1838, the day of his departure from Boston aboard the bark *Mary Chilton*, cover his business and other adventures in China, and end with his arrival at New York in early December of 1840. — PFK

PERKINS & CO. AND THE OPIUM TRADE

In 1804, the year Robert Bennet Forbes was born, his 16-year-old cousin John Perkins Cushing was sent to Canton by his uncles James and Thomas H. Perkins to learn the merchant trade. A year later the young man became at 17 the head of Perkins & Co.'s Chinese operations. Like other Americans doing business in Canton, the Perkins brothers, faced with a dwindling supply of animal skins from the Pacific Northwest and sandalwood from Hawaii, were looking for something else to trade with the Chinese. They preferred to trade goods and were reluctant to pay hard cash for the tea, silk, and porcelain so eagerly sought by their American clients. Almost by chance Perkins & Co. found that opium could be used as a substitute for money. The smoking of opium had been introduced into southern China in the middle of the 1600s, and the first edict against the drug had been issued in 1729, when only a few hundred chests of opium came into China each year. By 1796 these imports had risen to some 4000 chests of about 120 pounds each.

In 1815 at the age of 50 Thomas H. Perkins sent his son, Thomas H. Jr., to Canton. The War of 1812 had not yet ended, and when young Tom encountered two British ships at sea he captured them. Both were loaded with opium. Perkins & Co. was encouraged by the seizure to trade the drug in China where it was reported to be in short supply. The knowledge that opium importation was illegal in China was of no concern to the firm in light of the potential profits. A ship full of the captured opium was sent to Cushing at Canton. He wrote eagerly back to his uncles in Boston that the opium "had turned a good profit." Without hesitation the Perkins brothers decided to obtain more of this proscribed product.[10]

Since the English through the East India Company had total control of the most desirable Indian opium, the Perkins brothers, like other Americans, turned to the less-popular, harsh, but obtainable Turkish opium. Frederick W. Paine, a nephew of James, was sent to Smyrna as an agent of Perkins & Co. to buy opium for shipment to Canton.

In 1821, Cushing recommended that his uncles suspend all shipments to China except for opium. That was the only thing selling profitably, he reported. Cushing also advised the brothers to attempt to corner the market for opium in Turkey. Fred Paine bought up all he could, at least half of the opium then available at Smyrna. At one point Thomas Handasyd Perkins wrote to Cushing in Canton, "I have written and thought so much of opium that it gives me an opiate to enter upon the subject." The Perkins brothers, both approaching 60 in the early 1820s, had been merchants for more than 30 years. They wished gradually to retire and turn the business over to their sons and son-in-law, Sam Cabot. Accordingly, in 1821 the name of their firm was changed from Perkins & Co. to J.&T.H. Perkins & Sons.[11]

About the same time changes also came to the opium trade in Canton. One of the Hong Merchants was openly shamed for his involvement in the business. A great deal of publicity followed the incident, and to save face the authorities were forced to carry out more severe enforcement of the opium-importation laws. The Hong Merchants ordered all the foreign merchants to remove from

Whampoa the storage ships that held the "vile dirt" or "foreign mud." It was decreed that ships arriving henceforth had to post bonds declaring that they carried no opium. All trade was suspended until these orders were carried out.

The opium traders proposed an easy, unofficial solution: all the opium ships would simply move down the river to Lintin, a three-mile-long island about 25 miles northeast of Macao on the way to Canton. At Lintin Island the business could go on as before. When Thomas Handasyd Perkins heard about the new rules to control importation of the drug at Whampoa, he took the news positively. With less competition there would be a drop in the cost of the drug at its source. He wrote to Paine that "It is our intention to push it as far as we can." When other opium ships from America began to arrive in China, Cushing to prevent loss of profits came up with several ingenious methods for selling the drug. He decided that the Perkins ships would keep all their opium on board while he made arrangements for customers to take delivery from the ships at anchor. When there was too much opium on the market, Cushing developed a plan whereby some opium ships would dock at Batavia (now Jakarta), and from there a shuttle ship would run between Java and China, supplying both markets according to where the prices were higher. As an extra safeguard, he asked that opium be referred to in all correspondence by a code name– "gum"– and he requested that the ships remain at Macao or the islands to the east until he advised them to come up the Pearl River.[12]

In the late 1820s, when RBF's older brother Thomas Tunno Forbes took over as head of Chinese operations for Perkins & Sons, John Perkins Cushing, a 41-year-old bachelor, in poor health, but very wealthy, was free to return home. Cushing had spent so much of his life in China – 25 years since first arriving at the age of 16–that he no longer felt comfortable in New England. "I feel better satisfied in China than I ever expect to anywhere else," he wrote. On his return to Boston he married and had several children. With his fortune from the China trade he created a grand country estate in Watertown, Massachusetts, that he called "Belmont" (now the Oakley Country Club). The district later separated from Watertown and became the town of Belmont, taking the name from the Cushing estate.

In 1829 Thomas Perkins, age 65, traveled to Europe with John Cushing to outfit the ship *Bashaw*. She sailed to China carrying 830 chests of opium, plus British goods, with the prospect of making $150,000 to $250,000 in profits. This was the lucrative trade that RBF encountered when he began to serve the firm on a ship anchored off Lintin Island. From 1830 to 1832 RBF lived and worked for the first time in China at what was called Lintin Station, managing the loading and unloading of opium for Russell & Co. This brought him his first fortune from the China trade.

The mechanics of opium smuggling at Lintin Island were simple. Chinese buyers placed their order with one of the trading firms in Canton–Russell & Co., for example–and paid for it in silver. When a Russell & Co. vessel arrived with opium from Turkey it anchored off Lintin Island before going to Whampoa. Chinese smugglers quickly recognized the vessel, and on the instructions of the buyer of the opium approached it in boats nicknamed "scrambling dragons" or "fast crabs," propelled by as many as 60 oarsmen. Then an agent for Russell & Co.–Robert Bennet Forbes in 1830-32–standing on the deck of the company vessel, opened the chests of opium, weighed out the fist-sized cakes of the drug, and saw them repacked in bags of matting. Some of these ships carried as many as 100 chests, each weighing about 120 pounds and each containing enough opium to supply 8000 addicts for a month.

The foreigners found another method of delivering opium which proved even more profitable. By going up the coast in their own boats and selling opium directly to merchants in coastal towns, they eliminated the Chinese smugglers as middlemen. Jardine, Matheson, the largest English firm in Canton, regularly smuggled the drug this way, and employed the Reverend Doctor Charles Gutzlaff, a medical missionary, to translate for them. In 1826 Robert Bennet Forbes sailed the Perkins ship *Nile* along the coast with two merchants aboard in an attempt to smuggle opium directly to small towns. This was one of the earliest trips of its kind made by an American ship; it was also one of RBF's earliest experiences in the China Trade. He was then a 22-year-old ship captain.

When he returned to Canton in 1838 as a partner of Russell & Co., Robert Bennet Forbes no longer had hands-on contact with the "foreign mud." No longer a smuggler of contraband, he noted in his journal a certain relief to be free from its taint. Nevertheless Russell & Co. was actively involved with opium in 1838 along with every other American company in Canton at that time (except for D.W.C. Olyphant & Co.). In fact, the firm was the third largest in the opium trade, including both British and American companies. The drug was an important source of currency and profit for most of the foreign houses.[13]

Like most other China-trade merchants of the time, Forbes felt that opium was less harmful than liquor. "As to the effect on the people," he wrote, "there can be no doubt that it was demoralizing to a certain extent: not more so, probably, than the use of ardent spirits; indeed, it has been asserted with truth that the twenty or thirty thousand chests, say twelve to fifteen million pounds, of Opium, distributed among three hundred and fifty millions of people, had a much less deleterious effect on the whole country than the vile liquor made of rice, called 'samshue'."[14]

Besides, RBF added, all the best people and most eminent firms were involved in the opium trade: "I considered it right to follow the example of England, the East India Company, ...and the merchants to whom I had always been accustomed to look up as exponents of all that was honorable in trade — the Perkins's, the Peabody's, the Russells, and the Lows."[14]

Warren Delano, successor to RBF as Russell & Co.'s chief trader in Canton and later in Hong Kong, wrote home that "...as a merchant I insist that it has been a fair, honorable and legitimate trade; and, to say the worst of it, liable to no further or weightier objections than is the importation of wines, Brandies and spirits into the U. States..."[15]

During RBF's 1838-40 stay in China, as the letters that follow make clear, the Chinese government began "vigorous measures to suppress the trade" in opium. "I think the trade will be given up by all but the most desperate," RBF wrote to Rose in December of 1838. In March of 1839, a strict new Imperial Commissioner named Lin arrived at Canton to put an end to the opium trade. By the time of Lin's arrival, estimates of annual imports of opium were close to 30,000 chests. The drug was destroying the lives of many Chinese, and the country was losing its silver reserves in payment for it. Lin ordered that all the opium be surrendered. Captain Elliot, the superintendent of British trade in China, oversaw the surrender of 20,283 chests, and Russell & Co. gave up 1,400 chests. The Chinese destroyed it all. In this atmosphere of uncertainty and hostility, the British withdrew, taking all their citizens onto their ships stationed outside Hong Kong. Elliot urged the Americans to leave as well. Forbes pointed out that the "Americans are under no control, subject to no law, except that of self-interest." And, as he noted in his autobiography, "I replied that I had not come to China for health or pleasure, and that I should remain at my post as long as I could sell

a yard of goods or buy a pound of tea." His decision paid off, and Russell & Co.'s profits doubled because they were able to bring into Canton all goods arriving in English ships, while continuing to trade their regular cargos. Writing home to his mother in mid-1840, RBF explained the new conditions: "We have done no opium business which was before a great resource to the house."

In early July of 1840, Robert Bennet Forbes left for home about a year earlier than planned. His timing was right, because by the end of June a British squadron had arrived and was blockading the approach to Canton. All trade was stopped.

— PFK

Above, Canton bargemen amuse themselves with fighting quails in one of a series of genre scenes drawn and painted by Thomas Allom during a trip to China in the 1830s. This engraving is based on an Allom drawing.

NOTES:

1 Dulles, Foster Rhea, *The Old China Trade* (Boston: Houghton Mifflin Co., 1930) 15.
2 Collis, Maurice, *Foreign Mud* (London: Faber & Faber Ltd., 1952) 45.
3 Hunter, William C., *The 'Fan Kwei' at Canton* (Shanghai: Kelly & Walsh, 1911) 28.
4 Ibid. 29.
5 Dulles, Foster Rhea, *The Old China Trade* (Boston: Houghton Mifflin Co., 1930) 129.
6 Collis, Maurice, *Foreign Mud* (London: Faber & Faber Ltd., 1952) 51.
7 Tamarin, Alfred and Glubok, Shirley, *Voyaging to Cathay* (New York: The Viking Press, 1976) 48-49.
8 Forbes, Robert Bennet, *Personal Reminiscences* (Boston: Little, Brown, & Co., 1892).
9 Ward, Geoffrey C., "A Fair, Honorable, and Legitimate Trade," *American Heritage* (August 1986).
10 Seaburg, Carl and Paterson, Stanley, *Merchant Prince of Boston* (Cambridge, MA: Harvard University Press, 1971) 263-264.
11 Ibid. 284-301.
12 Ibid. 301.
13 Ward, Geoffrey C., "A Fair, Honorable, and Legitimate Trade," *American Heritage* (August 1986).
14 Forbes, Robert Bennet, *Personal Reminiscences* (Boston: Little, Brown, & Co., 1892) 144-145.
15 Ward, Geoffrey C., "A Fair, Honorable, and Legitimate Trade," *American Heritage* (August 1986).

DEPARTURE FROM BOSTON

Robert Bennet Forbes begins correspondence with Rose Greene Smith Forbes in his small cabin aboard the Perkins & Sons bark Mary Chilton *in June of 1838.*

After a melancholy leave-taking, he is cheerful at sea, and busy with writing, hobby work, and finally with doctoring a sick sailor.

Monday afternoon
11 June, 1838
Mary Chilton

My dearest wifee–
This is the first page of my journal, & I will preface it by telling you that I shall write with tedious minuteness, & with supererogation, & if you read what I write to any one all I have to ask is be merciful– cut out any dull & trite sentiments–

When I ... parted with John[1], that seemed indeed the *last link between life & death* – he, poor fellow, was speechless & seemed to reel with agony– the *Breeze*[2] cast off, & our men manned the windlass, & after a heavy heave for the anchor seemed *reluctant to leave its mother earth* we were under sail– I assisted at the windlass, & gave an impetus to the nerves of our men– the wind was light & the *Breeze* did not run far with us...I watched her & the receding shore, with new emotions, for I have never known what it was to feel till now– I watched the sun sink below the horizon & the eternal hills too, & thanked God for the fair wind that was wafting me away from all that I love– I took my tea & my cigar as usual, walked the deck till 9 oclock & then took up your bible & read what you wrote in my bible & prayer book, to which my heart responded–how touching, how beautiful are all your sentiments & your reflections– I shall daily read those prayers–

I did feel as the sun went down as if I should be pleased to think of you somewhere where you could see the sunset instead of blocked up among the stone walls of Temple place[3]– I busied myself fixing my stateroom, but Allen (the steward) had anticipated almost all my wants & had made my *bunk* very comfortable– Flora[4] seemed to be the only one that entered into my feelings– she followed me about the deck & when I came below she whined at the cabin stair–I provided her with a mat & a snug corner on deck, for which she was grateful– the night was fine, & the moon almost at full, the breeze fine, the crew & vessel first rate, & I turned in to think of you– Tears came to my relief– I slept for I was fatigued in body & in spirit–

my window is just in such a position that I can look the whole length of the deck & Flora can poke her nose in & kiss me– when I am not on deck she keeps near the window– I presume I slept much as you would have done under similar circumstances, rather feverish & wakeful, *but I dreamed of you & our darling boy*[5] well & cheerful & looked upon that as a good omen– but to my domicile– its dimensions are ...8 feet broad 6 long & six high– my berth

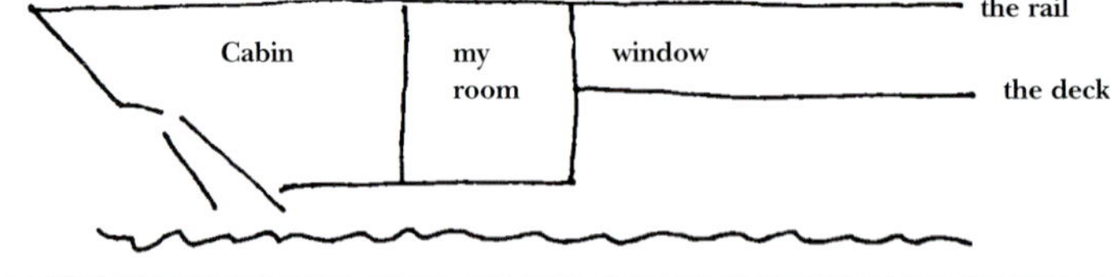

On page 18 is a Robert Salmon painting of a vessel, possibly the first or second Canton Packet, *outbound in Boston Harbor with Long Island to starboard. This painting was first owned by Robert Bennet Forbes. On page 19 is a pastel portrait of RBF, and above is a matching pastel portrait of Rose.*

[1] John Murray Forbes was RBF's younger brother. He had come out on the *Breeze* to see him off.

[2] The *Breeze* was a schooner yacht built in 1837 in South Boston for R.B. Forbes, W.H. Bordman and D.C. Bacon.

[3] In 1834 RBF bought one of the houses next door to the Thomas Handasyd Perkins mansion at Temple Place from his uncle. At the time this section, located between Boston Common and Washington Street, was very fashionable. He lived there with Rose until the loss of his fortune in 1837–8 when they moved to a much smaller house on Mount Vernon Street.

[4] Flora was Forbes' little female dog who accompanied him throughout his time in China.

[5] The boy is RBF's son Bob who was eight months old when his father left for China.

on one side, to which an air of comfort is given by a white dimity [6]– I have not thought of a single thing– ...forgotten, except a bottle of spirits of wine– I got up this morning at 6, drank my bottle of Congress water, shaved & dressed & breakfasted as usual– the breeze still port & fair, & the beautiful little Bark dancing merrily over the waste of waters– she goes well, is stiff & strong & hardy– the mates are good men, having served with the Capt before, & the latter is a careful little man– *I dont think you need have any fears of his frightening one carrying sail,* but he is attentive & kind, & I anticipate a pleasant passage. The cook makes good coffee– I looked for young Geo Winslow [7] this morning when the watch to which he belongs was called : he came up, but apparently sick, pale & trembling– I pitied him, & was glad to see that he went below & probably to bed– I shall visit him before I go to bed–

Allen is also sick, & Mr Cushing's [8] man[9] also– the former has, however, set his table today & goes about, but he puts me in mind of a man who had been broken on the wheel (not on the wheel of fortune as I have been) & whose bones had only partly become knit again– when he gave me my glass of Congress this morning I took the tumbler, while he at the same time, feeling his poor shattered nerves relieved, dropped the plate on which the tumbler had been– the expression of woe & despair on his face as this disaster occurred, was supremely ridiculous & I could not help laughing– Flora takes great interest in all the evolutions, & watches every man that goes beyond a walk or speaks louder than a pig's whisper–speaking of this quadruped reminds me that there is one young belligerent who no doubt is looking forward to getting old enough to having his bristles made into a tooth brush for some fair lady (what a piece of presumption)– this character quarrelling with his other ten or twelve friends, was turned loose on deck & has a laudable desire to come to the quarter deck, but Flora flies at him & drives him forward & seems to have become instantly inspired with a true sense of her dignity, as she takes no notice of the men, except to bark at them & has made friends with the Captain & mates– I shall begin on Scott[10] tomorrow, or as soon as I have read all John's letters to Houqua[11] & others, left open for me to read– I almost forgot to say that the shoe[12] you sent me hangs up at the foot of my berth & reminds me– if anything be wanting to remind me– of our dear boy– poor fellow, little kens the feelings of his parents– ... I shall get my lathe at work in a day or two, when a little more settled– I am perfectly well today– *yesterday the sun shone with such power,* that I had a little headache–

good night, & may the Almighty God above give you resignation & strength to bear this calamity–

---

6 Dimity is a sheer, crisp cotton fabric, usually corded or checked, used chiefly for curtains and dresses.

7 George Winslow was a sailor from Boston, very probably a relative of Winslow the sea captain who sailed many trading ships to China for Perkins & Co.

8 John Perkins Cushing, nephew of Thomas Handasyd Perkins and older cousin of RBF, had been sent to China at sixteen in 1804. When his superior died suddenly, he succeeded as head of Perkins & Co. in China. He remained in that post for twenty-five years and was called Ku–ching by the Chinese.

9 Mr. Cushing's man was a Chinese who was returning to China after working as a servant for the Cushing family.

10 Robert Bennet Forbes was given Walter Scott's Waverley Novels (1814–1832), a set of red leather-bound volumes, by his mother for the trip to China. He read them throughout the voyage. These original volumes are now at the RBF Museum in Milton.

11 Houqua was the most distinguished of the group of Hong Merchants through whom all trade was conducted. He was treasured by the Americans for his friendship, loyalty, guidance, and honesty. He was an astute businessman who amassed a considerable fortune during his lifetime.

12 Rose had sent along one of their baby Bob's little shoes as a keepsake for her husband.

Tuesday PM

... WSW wind...pleasant weather...[but] foggy..all night–...8 miles an hour all day, with *almost all* necessary sail set; the vessel performs admirably, though we have some helmsmen who do not do her justice, but steer wild–

I read myself to sleep last night with the beginning of Scott– had a good night– woke up at 5– this morning I had a little of *dizzy feeling* analogous to sea sickness, which has not gone entirely away– I shall take a nap this afternoon– George Winslow looks better & we are all well except the Chinamen, who are a little blue–... there is nothing wanting to add to my comfort save you– I wish that cook had killed the fowl we had for dinner a week before, for it was about the toughest subject ever I put my masticaters to– I had forgotten that my skill as a barber was brought into requisition this day, for I cut Floras hair close and combed her out smooth and clean, coming once or twice *so near the skin* as to bring blood–...poor unfortunate Pig departed through one of the portholes last night, & will report us if he gets safe on shore–our start is a great thing, & everything looks well for a pleasant passage, though our little Capt *is no driver* & I would give an hundred dollars to have Capt Pearce and $200 to have Dumaresque[13] here, say $500, but I must not be impatient– you may rest assured we shall go safe–...

I have had my nap and feel better– looked over the scrap book and remember the tokens well– I shall paste or tie them on the leaves for the motion else will send them wandering far and wide– I wonder at your parting from these relics– I will keep them for comfort during the voyage, and then return them to you– my headache has almost gone– I wish I could imagine you without one–...I must now go on deck & take my walk, for exercise is the more necessary now that the mind is at rest & there is a repose in this quiet sailing, a comfort in my escape from ledger & journal–... I shall always look back to my last month at home with dissatisfaction, for I hardly had time to commune with thee my love– perhaps it was best, my resolution might have failed had I talked over the matter over much with you– I now imagine you playing with our baby at the old house out of town & in better spirits since you got out–

Wednesday

good wind– 8 miles an hour all day– the deep blue of the ocean is splendid...– a ship passed at a distance this morning, bound towards Europe–

I never had a more pleasant start off–...our China passenger is on the sick list and the only one– we have a crew of good, steady men, & there is nothing so very tough in going to sea under these circumstances, *except perhaps the fowls*–...I have a little lingering headache which will require an emetic before the week is out– I am putting my lathe in order & find I feel better when actively employed– I hate to acknowledge it seasickness, but I suppose it must be of that family– We have in one watch all hands named Charles, & what is more singular, one is C D Cook, so if we call him Cook the cook will answer; and the other is Charles Forbes, so if he is called Forbes, I shall think they are after me– I must now go to work till sunset, & then read & write till bed–

Thursday, 14 June

fine wind.. until noon (then) moderate– 4 or 5 miles an hour– the weather is delightful still– I have been hard at work all day at my turning & have

[13] Philip Dumaresq was born in Maine in 1804, the same year as RBF, and similarly took command of a merchant ship at age twenty. He was renowned for his ability to cut weeks off long sea voyages. Later in his autobiography RBF would refer to Dumaresque as "that Prince of sea captains." Jane F.R. Dumaresq was married to Forbes' first cousin Thomas Handasyd Perkins Jr.

accomplished two small boxes, which I shall send the first opportunity...–I have been on my feet all day, & feel tired enough to prefer to go to bed at 10–

Flora has poked her nose in to say goodnight– grateful creature–I am very glad I brought her, & I shall put a lock of her hair in the box I have today finished– we live like nabobs[14]– our dinner today consisted of fowl soup, fowl, salt beef, potatoes, boiled rice, cranberry sauce & a good plumb pudding– Our cook is a real professor & there is after all more of comfort at sea than I thought before I came–

I wish I could think of you half as happy as I am, indeed I feel a degree of ease & freedom from care which I had long been a stranger to, & if you were only here I should have nothing to ask for, except *wind*– but now that my judgement is clear & defined, I do not regret coming alone– I am satisfied it is best as it is–time will fly rapidly & we shall soon meet again to part no more–you will write me fully by the *F Stanton* & I shall almost wish her to overtake us that I may get letters from you– as our cabin is small & hot, I keep on deck most of the time, & enjoy my cigar– good night

Friday 15 June, evening

Moderate wind...87 miles all day– I have been busy all day restoring my room, taking out new clothes & putting away clothes, getting my guns & pistols in shooting order– various other chores– a flying fish a foot long flew on board this morning– was cooked for supper– the milk is good enough for coffee, but does not improve tea–...this has been decidedly my best day, no headache & but little under the left rib, where the heart is said to be...

I am getting quite reconciled to my fate & thank god half a dozen times a day that here are no carts rattling, no notes to pay, no dust, no child crying! & nothing to interrupt the rising & setting sun from our view– Capt Drew...is a very amiable young man– a very fair sailor, & does all he can to please & make me comfortable– good night

Saturday, 16 June

...116 miles...not bad for the season–...I have been busy all day in making 3 *artificial* flying fish, rigged onto hooks to catch dolphin & Bonitos, & I have with the help of tea chest lead for the shiny part of the belly, pearly buttons for eyes–& a piece of blue silk for the back, made some that would deceive anybody at a distance– the covering is put on first a wooden shape– this is swathed in strips of flannel & covered as above, making an exact imitation of a fish, except the treacherous hook which fishes have not– it looks thus–this thing is put at one end of 20 fathoms of line & a fool at the other, & it is allowed to drag along in the water, skipping it occasionally out of water– the Dolphin jumps at it & is hauled in– we are not yet quite far enough along for them–...

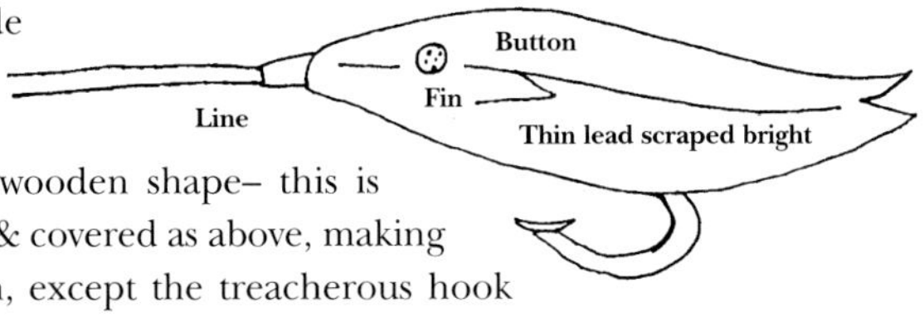

Mr Cushing's cook getting well & today he made a nice potato pudding, while the other docked a Pillau, which is a boiled fowl, surrounded by rice, seasoned with spice & flanked with a piece of pork & sprinkled with raisins– I shall think of you dearest in the morning according to promise[15]– I forgot to tell you that I

---

[14] A Nabob was an Englishman of the 18th or 19th century who returned from India having acquired a fortune. (In Mogul India, a nabob was a provincial governor.)

[15] It seems that RBF and Rose have agreed to think of each other at the same time when they pray on Sunday.

asked Mr Greenwood[16] to pray for me publicly last Sunday– when you see Bacon[17], thank him for the last days work, for I forgot to– I am surprised when I think how little I left undone or unprovided for–what a dreadful morning that was– I hate to think of it– it then seemed too cruel, yet I am already fully persuaded you have begun to rally like a good woman– *oh, I wish I could see that boy, if only for an hour*– I do see him all the time & remember the smile I waited for– *He will be a great comfort to you*– I also think a great deal now I am away, of your Mothers and Sarahs many acts of unrequited kindness– I am surprised at my peace of mind daily– I suppose it arises out of the life of care & trouble I led the last year & a half– when we get a rainy, dull day, I must not feel so well, it would not be proper–

...Flora has found her way into my room & now lies at my feet on the rug, & faithful creature– she is quite well & enjoys all the varieties that we have– Adieu

SUNDAY EVENING, 17 JUNE–

...157 miles...the wind *dead aft*–...we have not had our studding sails[18] in since we left home & only one shower in the night for a short time– I told our Capt that we should certainly see a vessel today– at 12 oclock I went on deck when he asked me where my vessel was– Oh, said I, we shall see her pretty soon, & at that moment casting my eye along the horizon, there she is, said I, & true enough, there she was; at 1/2 past 1 she crossed our bow within a half mile, with all her gay kites aloft looking beautifully– I could read her place of nativity (Dublin) on her stern & thought I could make out her name *Demayara*, but was not sure– as there was no object in speaking her, we did not change our course– we had a excellent dinner as follows: a fowl soup, the same animal roasted brown after– an apple pie– our chickens begin to hold up their heads, & when daylight comes there is as much crowing as would be convenient in a barn yard– we propose to have fresh eggs soon– this Sunday, which always follows Saturday at sea, & last evening I drank a glass of sherry to the tune of *Wives* and Sweethearts, whereas I always used to put the sweethearts first– I asked the Capt which way he toasted, he said he had always had a sweetheart till this time, & now he had so many in view, that there was no particular one in the ascendant: so he seconded my toast– the mate has wife & children, but left them as a matter of course & being a teetotaler did not drink– they are all exceedingly clever people & attentive to all my wants, for which ...the Lord make me thankful– this morning I thought of you at the proper hour, according to promise, which may be said of most any other hour...The sun set gloriously today, & I thought of the last sun which *Rose* upon us together (you see I cant write your name without a capital) & the last sunset within sight of Boston...you are at the panes & saw the sunset tonight & thought of me & probably imagined me tossing about & cursing my hard fate– this is not so, all my thoughts are as peaceful as the ocean & yet they may be made as turbulent–

...keep up a light heart & when the weather is warm, wear a thin pair of breeches– but this writing by candle light wont do my eyes any good & so I will read a little & invoke a blessing on you & our darling *Bob*!!! & go to bed–

MONDAY AFTERNOON

120 miles...fine weather & winds... I have been hard at work all day turning, & feel quite tired– all the better– I have made the most elegant box you ever did see & the top of a second– our little Bark slips along cheerily ... as I wrote considerable

16 John Greenwood was the minister of Rose and RBF's church.

17 Daniel C. Bacon of Boston was Forbes' best friend and manager of most of his business affairs there.

18 Studding sails are narrow rectangular sails set from extensions fastened to the yardarms of square-rigged ships.

yesterday, I will now say adieu for the day & go at Scott–

TUESDAY PM 19 JUNE

...187 miles...– we are highly favored– I have been hard at work writing all the forenoon & as I feel the effects of it in my head, I shall not write you much today– fricassee fowl & beans & cranberry tart for dinner; indeed we live too well & I must cut down my diet– our Capt plays well on the flute, which is something ...god bless you dearest till tomorrow, & ever after sure!

WEDNESDAY 20 JUNE

10 days out– 211 miles...pleasant weather continues to such a marvelous degree that we are as happy as birds...I have been engaged since 10 AM in cleaning my guns & pistols & trying them at a bottle hung under one of the booms, which latter I hit 3 times before the bottle–

I am better today, having acquired a headache yesterday from writing too much– I am too tired to be sentimental tonight, & I suppose you will find fault with my uninteresting details, instead of a constant cry of how I love thee & what is the baby about– Flora was made very happy today by a dose of castor oil– love to Aunt Smith[19] & Sally & kiss the baby; does he curl[20] yet?

THURSDAY 21 JUNE

...186 miles...– took in our Fore Top *mast studding sail for the first time since leaving* the land, which is very remarkable– I am quite brisk today, busy reading, writing & making cartridges for my guns, ready for a brush with anybody that may feloniously dare to cross our path– Your miniature is quite good, now I am away from the original– I wish I had one of our boy– oh how I should like to have him here...there comes the Steward with "Supper lelly[21] sir"–

FRIDAY 22 JUNE 5 PM
12 DAYS OUT, LAT. 30 24 N

Long 35 W– 172 miles...a sail in sight steering to NE for Europe; our breeze has dwindled down to a very soft zephyr[22] & we are now going 3 or 4 miles an hour– dreamed last night that I sailed from New York & that I was there two days & never heard a word about you, & how I reproached you for not writing– this is the only dream I have had which I think betokens a clear conscience to say the least–... when I reflect that it costs us both such a pang to part for a few weeks, I can hardly believe that any circumstances would warrant this long separation– yet it is so & we must make the best of it– I have been at work all day with my pen & this must be my excuse for not writing more now– goodnight & may the Angels of good preserve & protect you & the boy–

SATURDAY 23 JUNE

Our fine breeze has at length deserted us & we have made but small progress today...we shall have this sort of variable, baffling, sultry weather several days, & then the regular trade wind will come–

Finished reading Braddock's Times...a romance partly found on facts, wherein Washington figures a good deal– I dont suppose you would read it, but I

---

[19] Aunt Smith was Rebecca Greene Smith, Rose's mother, who lived with Rose at this time along with Rose's sister Sally.

[20] When Bob's hair is long enough to curl, Rose has promised to have a portrait painted of the boy and then will send it to RBF in China.

[21] RBF is imitating the Chinese steward's attempt to say "ready."

[22] A zephyr is a gentle breeze of west wind.

found it interesting, though *not very* well strung together–

About 10 this morning a cry of Dolphins[23] made me jump on deck, & our little Capt was just hauling in a fine one, & in the course of the day he caught 3 more, one of which was 4 feet long, & 14 inches deep, including his back fin–

They are splendid looking fish, both living & dying, & during the latter process, to which all men as well as fish are liable, they change their spots like the Leopard– I tried, but the luck seemed to be against me, for I did not get a bite– we supped on Dolphin & it was good– I have entirely given up wine & almost given up smoking, & feel better for it, & if I can only bring myself to a strict diet, I shall get over my dyspeptic feelings entirely[24]– I have a little pain in the side, but the pain in the chest & stomach is almost entirely gone– my last month at home it was bad, though I did not say much about it...I have done considerable writing today, & last evening I wrote the date of our marriage & the births of our children[25] in the Bible, & read your last letter, which brought out the salt water in no stinted measure– thinking is bad for me, especially the back thoughts & so I try to think only of the future– tomorrow will make a fortnight since we parted in the body but not in the spirit, for you are always with me in that– good night–

Sunday evening
Lat. 28, Long 33, 48

...little progress today, it has been almost calm with a decently hot sun...– I presume you are comfortably fixed in Mount Vernon St.[26] by this time, & enjoying the pleasure of your smokey kitchen; perhaps you are still at your Mother's, but I hope before this that place is disposed of & the Boston [Temple Place] House too– I never wish to go back there, unless I make much more than I now anticipate– When I get a competency again, I shall think little of style or location, but devote my means to the Boy if he is spared to us– I read the chapter since this morning, & some occasional prayer in the same book, & have had rather a satisfactory day– I took a long nap this PM, just to pass away an hour or two of this tedious calm– we have now a light breeze in the right direction, & I hope it will turn out to be the true trade wind– we can form no correct estimate of our passage, until we are fairly within the limits of the trade...– am reading a very good history of China...it is well I find I have two books on hand at once, one to go to sleep by & one to keep me awake...–

Goodnight

Monday June 25

...at daylight a Sch.[schooner] in sight on our starboard beam (or right hand) standing along the same way pretty much,– a rakish looking craft, & as we are in the way of Slavers & other dishonest people, we naturally felt it worth while to make preparations for action, loaded all the small arms & our two six pounders– during the whole forenoon his motions excited suspicion, & we wished him safe in Africa, yet were not so much alarmed as to prevent the Captain & myself from trying to catch fish off the bowsprit, in which we were not successful– about 10 AM a fine easterly wind sprang up, which we took to be the true trade wind, the

---

[23] These dolphins were not the mammal dolphin, but the fish dolphin as the picture shows.

[24] It seems that RBF may be troubled by a stomach ulcer.

[25] Family report has it that Rose had two babies before Bob was born. Both died soon after their births.

[26] Due to financial reversals, Rose had moved to 38 Mount Vernon St., a much smaller house than the one at Temple Place. It is still standing today.

stranger gradually gaining into our wake (or path) astern, & when directly astern about 3 or 4 miles, we made up our minds if he bore away directly after us he must be a pirate or a slaver, which is little better– but to our great relief, he kept his luff, that is, stood in more close to the wind, & at noon was 4 or 5 miles on our weather quarter (or left hand a little behind)– he showed himself to be a fast sailor at any rate, & as he is not entirely out of sight now (2 oclock) I will not feel too secure, only make up my mind if he comes aboard it must be at a cost of several lives, for I am armed to the teeth– we ate our dinner with much better gout than if he had given direct chase to us–

Thursday 26 June

...214 miles...the greatest day yet...– our little Capt carries the canvass better than I expected, & his mates, honest souls, are too lazy to take it in, so we get along quite fast– The "Long, low, black pirate," probably the one that captured the *Susquehannah,* was lost sight of about 3 PM yesterday, & has not since been seen... – I should like much to know exactly what you are about now– let me see, it is half past 12 with us, & about 10 oclock with you– you have just finished dressing the baby, & are busy making him cut monkey shines– here is where I have the advantage of you, I always know what oclock is it with you, whereas you are in doubt about me ...– I am quite well today, & have no doubt I shall be always when she goes 9–1/2 miles an hour as she does now– adieu dearest & to dinner– love to Bob–

Wednesday 27 June

...223 miles & *took in our top gallant sails last night for the first time*– our little bark behaves very well, & all goes on smoothly; adieu–

Thursday 1 oclock PM

...221 miles...– *not a squall since we left home*– we are now up with the Lat. of the Cape de Verde Islands, & are at 5 this afternoon *18 days out,* which is *very* quick– we are very grateful for our good wind & weather–

Friday June 29
Lat. noon 15? N Long 28? W

204 miles, fine, pleasant trade wind & good weather– look on the chart & see where we are– I have been busy all day turning & putting my tools in order & repacking my butter, which is in a good state yet, & shall expect to eat it when we get the weather a little colder– I am clearer in the head today than any day yet– we live better than fighting cocks, for I believe they are kept short– we may expect decent winds two days more, & then comes a spell of calm again, until we get the S E trade wind– supper *lelly* Sir– Aye, Aye– we eat all the time–

Friday Evening

I have been reading over some of your old letters written to me from Nahant[27] &c when away at Naushon[28], & when I think of the tender affection

---

[27] Nahant is a peninsula north of Boston. T.H.Perkins bought land there in 1819 and two years later built a waterfront house. By carriage the trip to Nahant took an hour, but the new steamboat service which left from Boston regularly made this attractive resort even more accessible.

[28] Naushon Island, seven and a half miles long, is the largest of the Elizabeth Islands that extend southwest from Cape Cod. It was made accessible to the Forbes family by the marriage of John Murray Forbes to Sarah Hathaway in 1834. RBF, John, and their friends often used the island for hunting deer. In 1843 John Murray Forbes purchased Naushon from his wife's uncle, W. W. Smith, and it has remained in the Forbes family ever since.

breathed in every line, & the longing desire to get me back from a *long* absence of a week or two, I feel that I have done wrong to leave you & a momentary remorse cries in my soul...– This reading old letters, & thinking over old times, gone for a long time will not do, I must banish these intruders & seal them up to lie awhile snug– I have also sealed up John's letter to you & his to me wherein he speaks of his motives, &c– depend on it dearest he has acted for the best, & without his aid or interference I should not have opened my eyes to the true state of our case till involved in desperate & irretrievable ruin...– We ought in reality to feel as if we had escaped alive out of a great pestilence, or from an earthquake that engulfed every one else– think how many high, rich & gay have had their heads laid low & their bread cut off forever, while my head is erect & my *prospects* better than they ever were before at leaving my home,– think of these things & be consoled– good night dearest–

Saturday last day of June

141 miles... Our fine trade wind almost deserted us last evening, when it became baffling with light rain squalls, but soon cleared away again ...latter part of the night & all day fine pleasant weather & smooth sea–

Saturday at sea is a great day for cleaning up the arms & the ship generally when the weather is good– Captain Drew had loaded the muskets the day the suspicious schooner was in sight, & he tried to draw the charges, but could not, when he concluded to fire them off, so he took one & holding it up over his head, he fired & it burst, wounding his hand considerably, partly tearing the little finger off near the hand, & making a gap in the hand between the thumb & forefinger– I was near him & went directly to his assistance, bathed the hand in warm water & washed it clean & found it not so bad as we at first feared– he suffered a good deal, & almost fainted– I was surgeon, & directly sewed up the wound, & put on some Friar's balsam & gave him a dose of salts– he has been about ever since, with his arm in a sling, but suffers considerable pain, as independent of the wound the jar to the nerves & tendons was terrible– I suppose some of the small ligaments are cut away–lucky he did not put the gun to his shoulder in the regular way, as in that case he might have lost his hand– I suppose in trying to draw the ball he had started it & not rammed it home again– I shall take the observations for him & assist all I can,...– I have consulted the Encyclopedia, under heads Medicine & Surgery, & think if he has no symptoms of lockedjaw, he will do well enough–

Sunday 1 July

137 miles...– looking out for a sail & for fish– yesterday a school of porpoises came round, & I expected to distinguish myself by striking one with the harpoon, but did not succeed– Capt D. has been suffering considerably with his hand, but is rather easier today–

Read in the prayer book about church time Per agreement...thought about you a large quantity–

As we approached the Lat. where we may expect to find vessels bound to Rio de Janeiro, &c, I will close up all I have written & direct them so as not to lose time–

Am quite well today, unless a too hearty dinner off of a Fowl "omnium gatherum," such as I used to talk about, & a potato pudding has made me heavy...– I take a salt water bath every other day & administer the same to Flora, who I believe is in that way in which coming events[29], &c &c–

[29] Forbes is hinting at the fact that Flora is expecting puppies.

We shall be three weeks out today at 5, doing well, though not extraordinarily– Lat. 11–1/2 N Long 27 W– kiss the boy two thousand times more or less–

MONDAY 2D JULY

100 miles...rather variable winds, with occasional showers...– sealed up the three ivory boxes, putting a small piece of grey hair in the smallest, which is for *bob*– I beg his pardon *Bob*– lazy today as usual when calm, & shall read myself to sleep this afternoon– reading History of China by Davis– very good...–

TUESDAY 3D JULY

only 20 miles...this day's work is hardly worth recording, as it has been almost a dead calm...– cleared out my *stateroom* & had it thoroughly cleaned & restowed: the space on the floor is now nearly a yard square, & I have ample room for all my necessities, so do not complain of your small rooms– our Captain's hand is much better & I expect he will be entirely well in a week– it is too hot to write much, so good night– love to Rose & Sarah & the young Gent–

JULY 4

Much like yesterday– hard at work all day tinkering– we celebrate the day much as we do the six other days– I do a good deal of work at pulling ropes for exercise, & to try to put a little quicksilver into the mates, who are *among the most deliberate of their species*– they live upon two legs all the time, whereas I think mates, as well as men should keep one foot going all the time– had a fine shower this afternoon, caught some water & had a good scrub in the rain– Flora overcome with heat; a dose of castor oil will put her right tomorrow...– a shark has been following us all day & would not take the hook, which is contrary to their usual ravenous custom, so I loaded my rifle & had a shot at him– I *frightened* him considerably...– I shall feel much happier when I get my first letters, for I am anxious to hear of you & how you sustained yourself, how you like your new quarters, & how Bob & your Mother & Sally are...– I hope we shall get through this calm Latitude soon, for it is excessively tedious to be rolling about in a calm under a broiling sun– our thermometer has not however been above 75° in the calm...– it has been too hot to turn, & almost too hot to turn in– I suspect that our little Capt writes some long closely written pages, wherefore I suspect he has a female correspondent of more consequence than a mother or sister...

THURSDAY 5TH JULY

All day variable & baffling winds, & rainy & pleasant weather occasionally; sundry squalls, &c– at 1/4 past 12 (midnight) the 2d mate came to say there was a sail in sight ahead– got up my spy glass & soon made him out a bark standing the other way– it being almost calm I suggested boarding him to put letters on board, but did not urge the matter as I knew he was bound to Europe, & the weather was not very suitable; yet I should not have hesitated had I been in command...– at 1/2 past 12 spoke him & had time to ask a number of questions & to repeat the request to report our name on arrival, but he was a Dutchman from Batavia[30] bound to Amsterdam, & I doubt if he will give you the first intelligence of us– reading Scott today– yesternight read Grace Seymour– rather an indifferent book– but then all things are indifferent in a calm

---

30 Batavia, or as it is now called, Jakarta, was founded by the Dutch in 1619. It is located in the northwest corner of Java on Jakarta Bay, an inlet of the Java Sea. It became the headquarters of the Dutch East India Company and was a major trading center.

July 6
Made a little more progress, but have had a variable disagreeable day; the wind not steady, & the sea quite the reverse–...calms & head winds are bad for the bile & our wind is just so that it is doubtful whether it is best to go east or S W– whats all this to you? I am digging away at Scott, & now that his troubles (in which I can heartily sympathize) have begun I am taking some interest in the work & his letters to the Balantynes about the affairs are much like mine to W L about nail works[31]...– If Scott gets into jail, I shall be quite interested, & if hung I shall be in raptures– this sort of weather & wind prevents my enjoying my exercise, & I am in consequence a little headachy– Kiss the dear Boy a million times for me, & your Mother & Sarah about 500– expect to see a sail every moment–

Saturday 7 July
...not wind enough to keep the sails from flapping against the masts, & what wind there has been, dead ahead– part of the time rainy, & I am getting as cross as a bear– nobody in sight– we have lost ground as well as patience, & if we do not get a wind soon, I shall get out & walk...– here we are, 27 days out, & in the Lat. of 7–1/2 N– in the "*Lintin*[32]", we were nearly 40 to the same place, & yet made a good passage to Java...– tomorrow will make four weeks– the three first went off well enough, but this last is a trial to any one– However, I must endeavor to exercise a little philosophy & patience– if I were in command, it would be another matter, as I should let off my steam & ill humour upon all hands, but now I can only enjoy a quarrel with Flora–

Sunday July 8
20 miles only...– Eight years yesterday since I departed in the *Lintin* to seek my fortune– hope I may find it as easily as I did then– my prospects are better, & my courage & skill better, & I have as much at least to look forward to on my return...– The first peal of rumbling distant thunder was heard today– hope it indicates a change– let me see it is about 1/2 past 1 with you now, & I conclude you are just finishing your roast beef, or your bread & molasses, reserving the roast for Monday, Tuesday & Wednesday, & are about to begin your siesta, which I have just finished– shall pray fervently & sincerely for a wind tonight– Our Capt's hand is much better, & all hands are well– kiss the dear Boy for me & keep up a "good heart– "

Thine ever

Monday 9 July
The same story as yesterday ...20 miles, part the time rainy– whipped Flora for eating the best part of a fowl hung up under the boat which spoiled our dinner–

Good night, it is calm & hot & muggy & I expect to be mildewed if I stay below a moment longer– wrote a long letter to Sim Forbes[33], & one to Bacon today, & shall do one to Copley[34] tomorrow–

---

[31] In 1826 Walter Scott, a partner of James Ballantyne & Co., lost much of his fortune (over 114,000 pounds) when that firm became involved with a bankruptcy. Forbes had invested over $100,000 in a nail manufacturing company in Pennsylvania. When the commercial crisis of 1837–38 hit, RBF lost his entire investment, and this proved to be a major factor in his decision to recoup his fortune by going to China.

[32] The *Lintin* was given to RBF by T. H. Perkins when he sailed to China in 1824. On this trip he was in charge of Lintin Station, the Lintin Island anchorage. For 18 months Forbes lived and worked on vessels anchored off the island "doing a thriving business in storage and furnishing (opium) to ships."

[33] Paul Seiman Forbes was the son of John Grant Forbes and a first cousin to RBF. In 1846 he was in a state of near-bankruptcy. Taking RBF's power of attorney, he went to Canton to represent the Forbes family in Russell & Co. and became head of the house.

[34] Copley Greene, a Boston lawyer, was Rose's first cousin. He was named after their grandfather, the artist John Singleton Copley. He was a close friend of both Rose and RBF.

TUESDAY 10 JULY
30 days out, & still *6 degrees* to the *North* of the *Equator*– we have squally rainy weather with thunder & lightening part of the time, & a rough sea, with the wind *dead ahead* all day...– the rain has given us all our casks full...– I had almost forgotten the beautiful moon that has been a comfort to us these calm nights– I dare say you have looked at it many times, & thanked God that it was lighting our path...– I wrote a little in my life,[35] & shall have it brought up to present in a month more to the present time– we see no vessels, which is extraordinary, & I fear this epistle to my kinsfolk may not find a conveyance short of Java– I shall try hard however to make an excuse if we see a vessel– you cannot expect poetry, or sentiment out of me till we get a fair wind– in these variable times I seldom go to roost till 12, & generally get up about 4 or 5 & take a look on deck for a sail, or for fish– I have not caught a fish yet, & am so stupid I will not inflict any more on you tonight–

WEDNESDAY 11 JULY
Half the day head wind like yesterday, & in the night rain like large guns– latter part dead calm...– if we dont get a breeze today, I shall begin to think we shall have a long passage...– hard at work all day on the boat; cant read while there is no wind– a gale on a lee shore infested with cannibals would be better than this– good night–

THURSDAY 12 JULY
Latter part of the day we are blessed with a steady trade wind, & pleasant weather, which makes all things go cheerfully again– I have been thinking *how strange it is that I do not know your birthday*; I beg you will let me know it first opportunity– I fear we shall have no chance to forward our letters home, as we are past the place where opportunities occur– I regret this exceedingly, on your account, as you will be very anxious to hear how we get on– we have seen no sail since the Dutch ship...– I think I have gained flesh since I left you; the dull, stupid feeling that haunted me for the first few weeks has departed– I live very regularly & drink very little wine– I have said nothing my dearest Rose about the pain in your chest, which however I think about often– do not fail to let me know fully about your health at all times, as I shall inform you about my own– our beautiful boy is now 7-1/2 mo. old; he will begin to say Papa in two or three more I suppose– oh how I long to get your first letters to hear all about you & him & how you relish your new location–

Flora is quite well & a great pet with all hands– I shall save one of her pups for Bob if they survive, & if she does well I shall have her painted for you in a recumbent position nursing her 10 little responsibilities– hope to see a sail tomorrow, for it is pleasant to see a vessel, even if the wind is too high to communicate– good night & God bless you–

UNDER THE TRADE WINDS

FRIDAY 13 JULY
A fine steady trade wind all day & very pleasant weather; a cloth jacket begins to be agreeable in the evening...– I worked rather too hard in the sun this morning,

---

[35] RBF wrote his autobiography, *Personal Reminiscences,* when he was in his seventies. The references to writing about his life in these journals lead one to think that he was compiling notes even then with the thought of someday producing an autobiography.

& ate some pea soup & *cheese* for dinner, the consequence of all which...is a sick head ache this evening– not one of my real bad ones, but disagreeable enough, so I will not make it worse, but take a pill & go to roost– good night–

Saturday 14 July

...making good progress– head better, but did not feel like working; read considerable in Scott...– when I enjoin on you strict economy, & promise the same to myself, it is only to get wherewithal to enjoy life when God pleases to let us meet...– we shall probably cross the Equator about this *time tomorrow (8 oclock PM) just 35 days from Boston*– the average of seven of Capt Drew's voyages has been 38 days, the shortest 32– I have done it in 25 & have been 44, so that our passage thus far has not been very long, & only appears so from the expectations founded upon our good run for 18 or 20 days–

Sunday 15 July 4 PM

We have had a beautiful day with a pleasant trade wind... we passed (the Equator) at 1/4 past 1 oclock...while digesting a good fowl stew ...– the old–fashioned custom of shaving on the Line seems to be entirely abolished; perhaps a description of the ceremony may amuse you, as I have heard tell of it, though I never saw it carried into effect– on approaching the Line, all those who have never before been in South Lat. are kept below, while the rest of the crew dress up an Old Tar as Neptune, with flowing locks of Oakum[36], & a swab[37] for a tail, while his body is covered with some old mat, representing a skin of hairy texture; he is armed with a pair of grains or a harpoon as a trident, & his face blacked so that his mother (if he had any) would not know him– a tub is prepared as the boat filled with water, on deck with a seat so fixed that the novice is precipitated into the water with a given signal– all being ready, one of the unfortunate victims is brought up, when Neptune appears over the bow hailing the ship to know if there are any green hands on board to be initiated into the mysteries of his craft– being answered in the affirmative; the poor youth is blindfolded & placed on the aforesaid seat, when Neptune seizes him by the neck, while his Satellites besmear the face & head with tar & slush[38] &c, & then scrape him down with a piece of iron hoop, & whenever the poor devil attempts to remonstrate, he is let down into the dirty water, or if he opens his mouth a brush full of the lathering mixture is thrust in; finally he is called upon to swear through a trumpet in a loud voice that he will never eat brown bread when he can get white, never will leave the ship till she leaves him, never kiss the maid when he can kiss the mistress, never tell the truth when a lie will do better, &c &c, & ever & anon while he swears, a dose of water is soused into the trumpet, & so they go through with the while & end in a jollification with a due allowance of grog; in old times it was ever customary to take in sail & make a day of it, but the barbarous custom is now nearly obsolete, if not quite– the most critical part of our passage is past, & we may now calculate on being in Sunda Straits on the 15 Sept...

The weather is now luxurious in the extreme, say like our best June days, only the temperature is very equal, about 70? which with the fine breeze constantly blowing, makes it very pleasant– I need not tell you that Sunday is a day full of painful recollections, which I trust will be dissipated when I get your first letters–

---

[36] Oakum is loose hemp or jute fiber, sometimes treated with tar, creosote, or asphalt. It is used for caulking the seams of wooden ships.

[37] A swab here is a mop, especially of yarn, used for cleaning the decks.

[38] Slush refers to refuse grease or fat from a ship's galley.

we are now in the direct track of vessels homeward bound from China, & I dont see why Dumaresque, or Pearce or Pearson[39] should not be coming along here just now– shall look out sharp tomorrow–I am surprised in looking over old letters in 1835 & 36 to find how I always predicted another visit to China; I really do not think I ever feel settled at home for good, though I did not say much to you about it– I must now go on deck & walk till tea time at 6– good night to you & to my darling boy, who I see constantly before me thumping on the little table– I suppose the poor fellow is suffering with his teeth now, or some other of the many ills to which young flesh is heir to– love to Mother & Sally–

Monday 16 July

Lat. 2.18 S, Long 28? W

We have had a fine steady wind all day...– we consider ourselves very fortunate— hard at work reading Scott all the forenoon & carpentering all the afternoon, & am quite smart...

Tuesday July 17 7 PM

37 days out Lat. 5? S & Long 28–1/2? W which is of course not very interesting to you, but I write what interests me, & you must take it as I took you for better or for worse–...

160 miles nothing in sight, & we begin to think all the vessels are sunk...– we live very extravagantly, & I will give you a bill of fare for the day; Breakfast, tea & coffee, the cow kicked the pail over, so we have no milk– hot bread of good quality, sea biscuit & cold water crackers, ditto– rice, & tripe fried in butter, ham, baked beans– dinner, pork & beans, ham, codfish & potatoes, boiled rice, cranberry sauce (of which my Ma sent me four or five jars of large size) apple pudding made with dried apples & very good, bread, cheese, pickles– !!!– spruce beer made by me !!!– claret–lemon syrup, &c &c &c– supper; excellent tea with best crushed sugar, broiled herrings, ham, various biscuits, excellent toasted bread & decent ships butter, *cranberry sauce* & cheese if wanted– to show you how prudent I am, I took at breakfast, rice & molasses with a leetle dust of tripe, & one cup of tea; dinner, rice & molasses & apple pudding, & ditto with but little crust; Supper, 1 cup of tea & toast, with a leetle butter, & no more; this is little enough for a *ship carpenter*...– I must not write any more, for the postage will ruin you if I do[40]...– Flora sends her best love

Wednesday 18 July

All day a fine strong breeze & good weather, except a few rain squalls; a high sea causes the bark to pitch & roll about considerably, & prevents my doing much work on deck– I find many passages in (Scott's) diary which could very appropriately be put into mine– I have marked them & beg you will do the same, & we will one day compare & see if we estimate my feelings & character alike– I have I think a good deal of the same sort of Stoicism & the same sort of feeling also...– hope you will feel the absolute necessity of *thinking* little & *acting* much, & do a good deal of walking & as much riding as you can at other people's expense; dont for God's sake shut yourself up, but keep the run of my friends as well as your own...good night–

---

[39] Captain Charles Pearson was for many years in command of the *Bashaw*, one of Perkins & Co.'s merchant ships.

[40] At this time instead of the sender, the receiver of mail paid the postage.

Thursday July 19

...190 miles...– *took a reef in our top sails for the first time*–...I have eschewed business altogether of late, & have not even looked over my list of notes payable, to see when they become due–I hope John will get through with them without *failing me*, if money should be *very scarce*, he may have to...– When I dont allow my thoughts to revert to you & our Boy, I am happier than I have been for a year & a half...look ahead, is my motto, & let bygones be bygones–...good night my dearest & love to all your household–

Friday July 20

...200 miles...some squalls...– our Capt is too careful & when a squall comes, he turns his ship tail to like a whipped cur, instead of keeping up to it & braving it out...– I have written today 3 sheets of the history of the lost portrait[41], & shall make a good thing of it– you must correct the English & add something before it goes to print; being Bean day, I dined on simple rice & lasses,though tempted by a good apple pudding & a dish of cods tongues & sounds; began on my butter, which is good, though salty...– Flora quite well today– *she knocks about so I cant write very straight– good* night– not Flora but *Mary Chilton*–

Saturday 21 July

180 miles fine winds & pleasant– some squalls in the night, which I slept through–...– overhauled my trunks...packed all my cloth clothes into one trunk & got out flannels, &c– in a few days...it will be cool enough to wear a cloth jacket all day– Capt's hand entirely well– got my first Christening by a spray this evening...– Love to Bobby–

Sunday 22 July 7 PM

186 miles...Twelfth sheet...what a bore it will be to read such a mess– I concluded today that my history of a portrait is so good that it will bear writing into such a book as this, so I fell to & wrote nearly *24* close pages...– Caught Flora trespassing in a manner too unsentimental to relate– gave her a gentle castigation, & a tremendous scolding, & forbid her coming into the cabin again, which I shall insist on, for when she pups it would not do, & therefore it would be hard to enforce the law at that delicate crisis– she amuses me much by keeping two small pigs in their proper places that are allowed to run about decks– whenever they come on the quarter deck she goes at them & drives them forward– I have been so busy today writing that I have not been to church yet, but shall before I go to bed...– we had 72 fowls at starting– deduct for deaths 6, leaves 66– here then are 66 dinners– 8 pigs 2 days each, 16 days– 66 & 16 are– let me see, about 82– passage to Anjier[42], where a supply can be had 95 days, which leaves 13 days only without fresh something; then we catch fish...– aint I great at figures? no figures of speech say you– I suppose you expect me daily to recite my feelings, hopes, fears, anticipations, dreams, &c &c, but this wont do, it is not good to dwell on the vanities of life– love to your Ma & Sally, & give Bob 999 kisses for me...– good night...

---

41 RBF's "History of a Portrait–By Itself" is a detailed, witty account from the painting's point of view of the loss of Forbes' oil portrait which disappeared in Boston.

42 Anjier or Anjer was a seaport on the West Coast of Java in the Straits of Sunda. It was totally destroyed in 1883 by floods after a great volcanic eruption on the neighboring island of Krakatoa.

MONDAY 23 JULY

...150 miles & symptoms of a calm at noon, but this evening there is a fine little breeze, though not quite fair, & a splendid little moon...– I dare say you will go to Nahant for a few weeks in August– I have been hard at work all day on my boat, & it suits my gizzard much better than writing, because when I work I do not think, & thinking is bad for the inward man– read in Scott till 11 last night & buried him...– I have pretty much given up the idea of falling in with any homeward bound vessel, as we are entirely out of the track; it is a serious matter for you, & I regret every day that I did not insist on boarding the Dutchman– no use, however, crying for split milk– good night–

THURSDAY 24 JULY

102 miles only– wind ahead...– this afternoon saw a brig 4 or 5 miles off standing N E ward– probably bound for Europe, could not have spoke him without going much out of our way– hard at work all day, at my boat...cut into the end of my right thumb, which renders it painful to write– good excuse say you for so short a page...–Symptoms of a riot among the winds & waves tonight; now reefing top sails– she kicks about as bad as the *Sylph*[43] did during your trip from Naushon in her, but then we have a tremendous head swell on, such as you never saw– love to Bob–

WEDNESDAY 25 JULY

134 miles...& pleasant... am very well– began on Waverly (1814) last night & soon got asleep over it...– shall see Cape Pigeon tomorrow– this is 45 days– hope to be at Anjier in 45 more, but hardly *expect* it– am not fond of writing after a hard days work, so with love to all I bid you good night...–

Mary Chilton

JULY 26, 1838

LAT. 28? S LONG 34? W

My dearest & best:

...at 1 oclock today... we saw a sail ahead coming towards us, & the moment I put my glass to her, I made her out a whaler, & also made up my mind even if not bound direct home, to board her & dispatch my budget, so sealed up in haste a quantity for you in one package & two or three ivory boxes in another– also a journal for John, a letter for Mother, Bacon, Hooper[44] & at 2–1/2 oclock hove to, lowered the stern boat in which I went on board the American whale ship *Chariot*, Capt Champlin, bound direct to Warren[45]– we were extremely fortunate in good weather & a good hour, & such a chance as I could wish in all respects– I sent our boat back to be hoisted on board, telling the whaling Capt I would return in his boat when one of his sailors was ready with his baggage, whom I had engaged to go with us to China– notwithstanding this crew had been at sea two years, there were three who volunteered to go with us, so I took my pick & returned after a half hour's chat with the Capt about the times, &c, in his boat to the *M Chilton*,

---

43 The *Sylph* was a schooner yacht of 70 tons. Built in 1833 by J.P.Cushing, it was later sold to RBF and Sam Cabot.

44 Samuel Hooper, who was four years younger than Forbes, lived in Marblehead, Massachusetts, and was in charge of the importing firm of William Appleton & Co. He had married William Sturgis' daughter Anne in 1832.

45 Warren, Rhode Island, was a shipbuilding center from about 1800. It is located on Narragansett Bay above Bristol.

sent him a lot of papers...a box of cigars & a handful of thanks, & went on our way rejoicing, & I shall continue to rejoice for the next twenty years that you will get letters from me about the 10 Sept, & let me know when you did get them– I was on board the ship long enough to hear that the Capt saw the *Rose*[46] on the stocks at Warren & knew Mr. Lee [47] very well– I dare say every man on board of her are now reading the news, & the meeting was no doubt mutually agreeable— love to all & good night–

Friday 27 July

127 miles...– this morning at sun rise it was truly splendid & this is the most perfect evening I ever saw at sea– the water like a lake, the moon bright & a host of stars also, not a cloud as large as a pea to be seen, & a little breeze that wafts us along about 4 or 5 miles an hour– I watched Venus till she absolutely touched the horizon, & never remember to have seen any star set to entirely, for there is generally a haze about the horizon, that causes the brightest star to be lost sight of when within a few degrees of the horizon– I am satisfied I shall never be a poet, for if such a night as this will not inspire me, nothing else can...– we have just been taking Lunar to get the position & find our chronometers are very correct– I will venture the assertion that we know within 5 miles where we are, & have seen no land since leaving Boston– sailors ought to be good Christians, for no class of people have half so many evidences constantly before them of the beautiful mechanism of this "work–day world," every star speaks of a great ruler, & yet those who are manifestly so dependent on him & have so many tokens always at hand are as careless & unthinking as if they were buried in a cotton mill, with nothing around them but the jarring & perishable machines of poor man, which like himself are likely to get out of order or be entirely broken to pieces in an hour...– I hope the *Chariot* will have good winds & give you speedy tidings of us– good night–

Saturday 28 July

...I have been at work all day on my boat *under the awning*, for it was so warm that it was necessary...– this has been a busy day with Flora, for we killed a pig yesterday, & she has had fine pickings...– I hope we shall get a good breeze before long, for although this weather is pleasant to look at, it is not at all profitable...– love to all & good night–

Monday 30 July

50 days out this evening; it seems hardly possible I have been seven long weeks away from you, for I have been so busy that the time has gone fast– yesterday was

[46] The *Rose* was a 150-ton clipper schooner modeled by Joe Lee and built in 1836 by Mason Barney in Swansea, Rhode Island. She was owned jointly by Sam Cabot and RBF. Because of her small size, she was at times used to take opium up the coast of China in search of new markets for the direct sale of the drug. William Hunter, representing Russell & Co., was used as interpreter.

[47] Captain Joseph Lee, born in 1745, first went to sea at the age of thirteen. Soon he became captain and then engaged successfully in the West Indies trade. He married Elizabeth Cabot and settled in Beverly, Massachusetts. He became a ship owner and foreign merchant in partnership with his brother–in–law, the Honorable George Cabot. During the Revolution the firm prospered in privateering and Joe Lee acquired a considerable reputation as a naval architect. He designed a number of vessels used in our early navy and merchant marine. In 1800 he retired from active commercial life and eventually moved to Boston where he became prominent in the banking and insurance business. In 1838 Rose Forbes lived near the Lees; the families attended the same church, and often walked home together. In her letters to RBF in China, Rose referred to "Old" Joe Lee, since he was 83 at that time.

the first day I omitted writing– we had a splendid breeze & fine weather, & I wrote a good deal in my life– I have got as far as the loss of my Brother[48] & my preparation to go in the *Lintin*– at my usual time of writing, the wind was fast increasing, & I remained on deck till late, to see how things were managed– at midnight double-reefed top sails–throughout the day strong breeze & high sea, the bark knocking about like a drunken man– the wind continues fresh with clear October weather...– adieu till tomorrow–

Tuesday 31 July
Lat. 33–1/2 S & Long 23 W
...this evening the wind has entirely left us & we are now rolling & tumbling about in a calm as the sea still continues: the flapping of the sails against the masts, the creaking of blocks & bulkheads, & the expensive reality that we are making no headway, added to all these, makes it vastly more tedious than a gale of wind ahead– I shall turn in & try to sleep it off– finished Waverly & began on Vol. 2d, Buenos Noches–

August 1
52 days out– we have now a fine breeze, going right before it 8 miles an hour...but she rolls about like a pig in the wind, & one can hardly keep still even in bed; hard at work all day on the boat & shooting birds for practice, which is rather cruel divertisement– but then I had some hopes that one would fall on board, in which case I should stuff him for Sam Cabot[49]– reading Guy Mannering (1815) last night– sleeping is comfortable business this cool weather, & eating by no means disgusting– I have lost my appetite, & found that of a horse...– twas devilish cruel & unnatural to come away– thats a fact, & it will be equally so to stay away, but what can a body do else for bread– bread– bread?...– went on deck at 3 AM & found a fine little fair wind & no light sails out, so as I had no authority to set them, I called the Captain & requested him to have them set, which he did– the mates are very good men, but altogether too easy, & too slow in putting on the muslin...– good night dearest, & love to all–

Thursday Evening 2d August
200 miles on our way...at this moment are going 10 knots...–I expect to make our greatest days work these 24 hours...– we are now approaching the island of Tristan d'Acunha, which, if this wind continues, we shall see tomorrow night about midnight, if the weather is clear...– my...general health equal to the three days of the hunt at Naushon– God bless thee & good night with love to Bob–

Saturday 4 August
...*240* miles before a high sea, the bark rolling rail under now & then...– Last evening...we rolled about merrily– the steward in coming aft with a saucepan of rice in one hand, a pan of baked beans in another– lost his footing & so our dinner was in great danger, when the fellow righted & recovered the most of it–

---

48 Thomas Tunno Forbes, RBF's older brother, was sent to China at the age of 17 in 1819 to assist his cousin J.P.Cushing at Perkins & Co. It was thought that he would take over Cushing's merchant duties and become head of the firm when Cushing retired. This did not happen, because in 1829 Thomas Forbes drowned when a typhoon capsized the schooner he was aboard for a trip from Canton to Macao. He was only 26 and had spent 10 years in China.

49 Samuel Cabot was married to Elizabeth Perkins, the daughter of T.H.Perkins. Originally he had been a partner in James and Thomas Junior's firm, and then became a partner of Perkins & Co. in Boston. He also owned a large interest in Russell & Co.

the Barometer indicated a gale, notwithstanding one had just done blowing...it was nearly calm, at sundown, after a dirty rainy day– a light streak in the West which was reflected through the dense clouds all round gave them a pink or purple tinge of a peculiar & strange kind, & everything looked unearthly...– through the night– I was up & down often, for she rolled about so that I could not sleep, particularly as I felt anxious lest the inexperience of the Captain & mates in these latitudes should cause them to get caught in one of the sudden squalls that sometimes begin a hard gale, & yet I was afraid to say much, as they are disposed to be easily alarmed when they know of any unfavorable symptoms– at 5 in the morning it looked threatening, called all hands & close reefed our sails & made all snug– at 6 a fresh gale from the SSW & thick rainy weather, but in the course of the morning it cleared off & at 11 I went aloft & gave the heartcheering cry of "Land ho" which we had been expecting to see in the course of the morning– one of the Tristan d'Acunha group, which we passed within 8 miles at 4 this PM– it is cheering at all times to see land & particularly so to the sailor who has not seen any for 55 days, & it is gratifying to an old sailor, a passenger too, to find the Capt's observations are correct...– too rough these two days to work–finished Guy Mannering & began on No. 3, the Antiquary [1816]...Buenos Noches...

FLORA DELIVERS TWO PUPS

Sunday 5 August

...152 miles– clear & cold weather 8 weeks out this evening– ... finished the history of a portrait, which would make a first rate article for a magazine– read my bible & your letter in it today, like a good boy, & shed a few tears (whether salt or not I did not taste) as I always do over it– Flora was allowed to come below last night, & partly tore up my rug, which I should not have scolded her for if I had been aware that her time was so near, not expecting it for 2 or 3 weeks– this morning she got *into a hen coop & snuggled up between the pigs of which honorable mention* has been made in this journal, & this was such a want of good taste & imparted such a flavour of live porker that I went to work (Sunday) & cut a hole in a dry tight barrel, made her snug house & put in some clean straw; she immediately took possession & did not come out all the afternoon...– good night–

Monday 6 August

...144 miles, not very good for this Lat.– this morning found only two pups; one I fear will die, the other feeds well with a little assistance, & as the Mama has plenty of milk I contrive to get enough to put into the other's mouth, but he is puny & has a defect in his hind legs which are very bowed, so I do not care to have him live, except long enough to take his mother's milk away– I expect more tonight, for she has always been more literary– the good one is black & white & very handsome– a shemale– I have removed them into our cabin by the side of the table, so as to assist in the nourishing process...I shall make great sacrifices to save one...– Hope the *F Stanton* will catch us before long & give me letters from home– good night–

Tuesday 7 August

... only 124 miles– pleasant weather all day– one pup died last night, the other doing well by dint of feeding– Flora very well; have great hopes of saving this poor devil– hard at work all day on the pilot boat–

WEDNESDAY 8 AUGUST
...nearly calm, only 62 miles– the Capt caught a porpoise this afternoon with harpoon & I superintended hauling him in– I have an appetite like a shark, & have not been so well for two years or more, but I will not boast for fear of punishment– good night–

THURSDAY 9 AUGUST
...the weather has been rainy with a good wind, & we are now making good progress– This is the anniversary of the greatest misfortune that ever happened to our family[50], & the cloudy rainy weather which keeps me below & prevents exercise, helps also to make me feel gloomy– Sat up late last night & wrote several sheets of a tale entitled "The Escape"...it is well done and will please a seaman...–

I shall do all my romance writing before I get to China, for there will be no time after– 60 days out today– we may be in China in 45 more, but more likely 50 or 55– The time has not seemed so long as I expected...I have a new source of occupation, in acting doctor– one young man, a namesake, nephew of Forbes the stable keeper, has been falling off even since we left home, & has but a scant attention from the Capt– indeed did not seem to have any defined complaint until within a few days it has assumed the character of dysentery– after proper cathartics, I have put him under a rice & sago[51] diet, with three wine glasses of old Port mixed with a strong decoction of black tea, & a little bark– Flora & pup well– oh, if I could only see you & that Boy well for a minute–

RBF BECOMES SHIP'S DOCTOR

FRIDAY 10 AUGUST
Fresh wind and rainy weather with a high sea all day, which has confined me most of the time to my cabin, except when I took the helm, while the man reefed the top sails...– Just finished the Antiquary (1816)...– I wonder if you are keeping a regular journal for me, like this; you have much better materials than I, & I merely write a history of my daily vocations that you may see how an India passage passeth away as a dream– this has been rather a long day though, and not having had any exercise, I am a little headachy today, partly owing to eating porpoise perhaps– my boat makes no progress– finished my Escape– only nine pages– think it is good, just the article for a magazine– Good night and God bless you all–

SATURDAY 11 AUGUST
Our fine breeze died away last night, & left us rolling about merrily, but has again sprung up from the North and we are now (about 10 oclock evening) going 9 knots...damp & foggy all day– our poor young man Forbes...gets no better & his spirits begin to fail him, and the Captain has very humanely concluded to bring him into the cabin in the morning– A crowded ship's forecastle with no conveniences ...is no place for him, & although it will be a great inconvenience to have a dying man in our small cabin, I can attend to him & regulate his diet & medicine much better here than while he is forward– the ship's medicine chest is much on the scale of the little one I took from you, & I have consulted & studied the encyclopedia in vain to get at his disease– it is like consumption, only he has no cough or fever...– as the Capt has little or no experience in medicine, I shall have to take the responsibility of doctor as well as nurse– I have nothing better to

[50] Forbes is referring to the death of his brother Tom on 9 August 1829.

[51] Sago is a powdery starch obtained from the trunk of an Asian palm.

do & shall not flinch from the duty accidentally imposed on me–poor Flora has lost her last pup today, & it is pitiful to see her cuddling up the poor thing & whining over it...– May the kind angels guard & bless you all– good night–

Sunday Evening 9 weeks out

Strong gales & dirty weather, with a large sea, & I am glad such nights as this that I am only a passenger– we have only seen the sun for an hour these three days, yet I am as snug as a bug in a rug in my little room, reading Rob Roy (1817) or the Chapel Service, & taking a good nap in the afternoon, so as to be up till 12 tonight– I believe I keep the run of the ship as well as the kitchen, with more regularity even than the Capt, who is very fond of his berth; but he is very kind & attentive to me as are the mates– we got young Forbes into the cabin today; he is not so sick as I expected, but...is *very* thin, no pain anywhere & I cannot make out his complaint– I am giving him bark & port wine three times a day, one of Dr. Jackson's[52] pills at night, & if it not too rough, I shall give him an emetic of ipecac[53] in the morning– I thought I would let him alone at tea time & see what he ate & drank; he took 5 or 6 crackers, being prohibited any other food, & 4 mugs of tea– I then gave him a lecture to this effect: "as Capt Drew has placed you under my care, I now wish to state to you that I am no Doctor, & I have neither a good supply of medicines, good medical books, nor a knowledge of your particular complaint, but if you will trust to my general experience & obey my orders implicitly, I will do all I can for you & leave the rest in the hands of God; you must on no account take more than two cups of tea & three or four crackers at breakfast, & tea & a bowl of broth or a plate of rice or sage at dinner– I shall watch your diet as a cat watches a mouse– " he promised obedience– I have given him some books to read,– if I cant keep him along until we get medical advice from better hands, it will not be for want of trying– I believe I like the responsibility on the whole– if you could look in upon us you would call our situation "horrid", a small cabin occupied by two mates (one at a time) two Chinamen, Capt D., Flora, the sick man, all our stores...– so entirely is comfort comparative, that I presume the poor devils in the forecastle think I roll & revel in luxury– I had rather be in Temple Place or Mount Vernon St., or at the Morlands[54] to be sure, & would not object to your sweet society at either, but here I am bound on a pilgrimage for bread for you, & the bairn [Scotch for child] or barins, & what have I to do but to content myself & make the best of circumstances ...– God bless thee dearest–

Monday 13 August

228 miles...– finished Rob Roy just now (11 PM)– my patient is not half so sick as he thinks or pretends he is; indeed I cannot find out what ails him, except extreme leanness & weakness...– we shall be up with the Cape of Good Hope tomorrow morning, if the wind continues– Flora seems to have got over her loss entirely– we are now out 64 days, hope to be at Anjier in 30 more...from thence to Canton 16...good night and turn in–

---

[52] Dr. James Jackson was an eminent Boston physician who was a leader in the movement to provide expert hospital care for the working class. Along with T.H. Perkins, he would be one of the founders of the Massachusetts General Hospital.

[53] An emetic treatment of ipecac would cause vomiting.

[54] "Morlands" was the name of a cottage on Jamaica Pond in the Jamaica Plain suburb of Boston. RBF and Rose had spent summer vacations there for a number of years, but were forced to give it up when hard times hit. Their son Bob was born there.

TUESDAY 14

Only 157 miles...– this forenoon was very warm & pleasant... drove my patient on deck to sniff the air– I rule him with a rod of iron & he improves under it– at noon it began to threaten from the NW with distant thunder, & in half an hour all our sun was gone & all our light sails taken in & the top sails reefed– it soon moderated however, & after a flash or two of lightening & a crack or two of thunder it cleared off...but as she is right before the wind she begins to roll about considerably...– Reading Black Dwarf (1816)

WEDNESDAY 15 AUGUST

...239 miles today before a strong gale...– this evening more moderate...– I have just been steering while they made more sail & hope to get a good day out of this wind yet– we had a rich mock–turtle soup today...made of pigs head...& soured pigs feet and bread plumb pudding !!!!!!!!! & claret half a bottle !!!!!!!!! made such a hearty meal that I turned in like a pig & read myself to sleep in Old Mortality [1816] (having finished the Bk. Dwarf this morning) & I am a little stupid, say more stupid than usual...– I will now make a plan of my stateroom for your amusement:

GROUND PLAN 6 FEET BY 8.

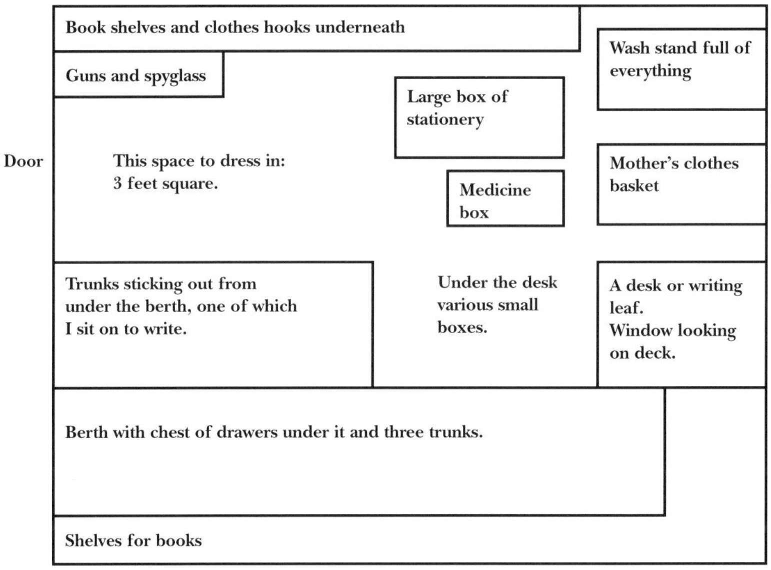

Book shelves and clothes hooks underneath

Wash stand full of everything

Guns and spyglass

Large box of stationery

Door

This space to dress in: 3 feet square.

Mother's clothes basket

Medicine box

Trunks sticking out from under the berth, one of which I sit on to write.

Under the desk various small boxes.

A desk or writing leaf. Window looking on deck.

Berth with chest of drawers under it and three trunks.

Shelves for books

(This drawing, and those previous, are taken from a typewritten copy of the RBF journals, which is all that remains of the original letters that cover from June 11, 1838 to September 15, 1838.)

...its dimensions are...say 8 feet broad 6 long & six high– My berth (to which an air of comfort is given by a white dimity curtain) is about 2–1/2 feet inside, to keep myself steady– a double run of good books, my pistols & sword at hand on my right–I have my gun box & spy glass case on one side & the berth board on the other, my pillow which you came near forgetting, is made high enough by a large package of newspapers directed to Russell Sturgis[55], at the head hangs the

[55] Russell Sturgis was a contemporary of RBF's and a son of his first cousin. He had graduated from Harvard with the class of 1823 and married his first wife Lucy Lyman Paine in 1828. She died that same year. He then married Mary Greene Hubbard, who died in Manila in 1837, leaving him a widower with three small children. Russell Sturgis lived in the Far East for many years as a member of the firms of Russell Sturgis & Co. and Russell & Co.

Madonna & the Mother & little child which I pass off for you and yours– the cover of my rattan basket suspended by the four corners inverted makes a place of deposit for my hats & caps in use & other trifles– in one drawer of the washstand are my journals & writing tools, & all around the walls are coats, pistols, sword, so that there is scarce a square foot of wall or floor not occupied– I can sit at my desk & reach gun, sword, pistol, writing tools, books from encyclopedia to penny almanack, jacket & coats of all degrees– I have contrived *the haul out part* of my great chair, so that it answers for a seat for me lashed on the trunk– the said chair is in the cabin, & has a soft pine board which when placed across the arms forms my solid & comfortable seat at meals– the space remaining on the ground floor of my stateroom is covered by that *leetle* green rug when *end* is doubled up a foot– on the side of my room from the berth sleep the two Chinamen, abaft me, or in the rear, is the Capt's room, 6 feet by 4, opposite to this is the sick man, forward of him the mates and forward of them the pantry & crockery closet store house, &c, all comprised in a space 4 feet square, most of which is taken up by drawers, shelves, barrels, &c– the Boy's shoe hangs in its old place just over my desk...– there are hooks all round for clothes, & by hook & by crook I think there is nothing wanting as you go up the cabin gangway, 3 steps, you come under a small house open in front, but affording shelter in most winds for a passenger to look out & see what is going on, & here you will find me quietly watching the weather & the progress of the ship, oftentimes in the night as well as the day–

our Capt is not constitutionally anxious, for he goes frequently to bed at 8 or 9 and does not move till 7 AM– I could never do this, but always made it a rule to go on deck several times during the night in all weathers, for I never had officers who were disposed to push on & make & take in sail, as I would do myself; they cannot be expected to show great anxiety to get to the desired port, unless the Capt sets the example– The cook & I cut my hair yesterday– good night...& last, but not least, your miniature with the lock of hair are at hand in the top of the washstand, & which is resorted to occasionally (the portrait I mean) but I dont like it altogether– I am a little sorry it was not done in one of those net fly caps, with dandelion & butter cups round it, such as you used to wear in the house– I must have the Boy's miniature, "coutequi coute" [56] as soon as he has a curly brow– well, she rolls about so that I must finish for tonight & beg you not to think your rooms small or your comforts few, when you think of me & my dormitory–love to all and good night–

Thursday 16 August

206 miles...– I have been reading Old Mortality today & shooting *at* the sea fowl which are numerous in these parts– I have committed murder on several but have not been lucky enough to have one fall on deck– my patient took an emetic today; he is quite weak & getting lower in flesh...– I cannot for the life of me name his disease– I have been rather cross today, because they do not set sail enough in the night & I fear the other ships will beat us...–

Friday 17 August

212 miles...– we are getting on bravely– at work turning all the forenoon...– my patient droops & I fear he will never see land again; its distressing to find ones self involved in this responsibility, without knowing what to do– I stick to simples & nursing & leave the rest to fortune– I wish for his sake as well as my own, that he was safe at home– Kiss Bob (B O B) and good night–

[56] "Coûte que coûte" is French for no matter what the cost.

Saturday 18 August
199 miles...& we are now almost becalmed...– reading all the morning & shooting all the afternoon, brought down one bird on the wing with my rifle & winged two or three out of a dozen shots, & *came very near* catching one with a hook; my patient a little better today, but quite weak– tomorrow will complete 10 weeks– I am getting anxious to hear how you were after the first day or two, & would willingly have the *Francis Stanton* catch up with us to get a letter from you, but I fear I shall have to wait patiently until the *Ariel* arrives in China– I often look back & reproach myself for having thrown away so much time (to say nought of money) while I should have been providing for a rainy day– but a truce to discontent, let bygones be bygones– trumps will come again– Adieu

Sunday 19 August
103 miles...but...we are now (10 PM) going 10 knots with good weather...– the last 20 days we have averaged 7 miles an hour; it is now three oclock PM with you, & you are probably on a visit to Nahant for benefit of Master Bob's teeth– I suppose the poor child is suffering sadly with them– I have just finished Old Mortality (1816) & shall read "twal [to all] hours or so" before I go to bed...– I have read my bible like a good boy & my prayer book– my patient feels better than when he came into the cabin, but is gradually getting weaker & I fear his complaint is a galloping consumption...– George Winslow is afflicted with boils for which I have prescribed; he is a good fellow & will make a man– we are on our last legs for cranberry sauce, after having eaten it 70 days its hard to go upon the apple– I have read so much by lamp light, & none of the brightest, that one of my eyes is a little inflamed, otherwise I am quite well– good night, & may the Angels of content & resignation flap their wings about you–

SQUALLY WEATHER

Monday 20 August
...220 miles– I did not go to bed till near 1 oclock & hearing them taking in sail went up at 3 & found the main top galt yard broke & a squally morning; helped take in more sail– wind then came to WSW & cleared off; it is now (11 PM) dying away & is clear & cold, & although I have taken a nap this afternoon, I am going to bed as early as Jennie Deane (1817) will let me...– my patient is pretty much the same, he is unfortunately devoid by nature of all energy & spirit, though his name is *Forbes*– Give my love to Mama and Sally; tell the latter her sewing materials come in play– I keep my clothes in first rate order– Kiss Bob & good night–

Tuesday 21 August
...we have made a grand day's work– some hard squalls with thunder &c today, & this evening a good breeze again at SW & going along merrily...I shall finish (Jennie Deane) before I go to sleep, though it is now 11 oclock–...good night

22 August
...210 miles with decent weather, till this afternoon it came on to blow pretty hard, with a tremendous ugly sea– about 4 oclock I was just waking up from a nap, when a huge wave came curling over the stern & broke on board, a good deal of it got into the cabin & some into my room– the two Chinamen & I were pretty busy picking it up; the only tools I had were a clothes basket & a bag full of dirty clothes, which I poured out & caught as much as I could, & then rung them into

pails; the Capt, mate & man at the helm were completely drenched & poor Flora's house filled, & she came tumbling down into the cabin half drowned; this accident was entirely owing to taking in sail so that the sea caught us, for we have been going well ever since...– but she rolls about & I cant write with any comfort– good night–

Thursday 23 August

200 miles– We had a rough night of it, but did not take on board any more water...– I was up a good deal in the night too, to see that all went well...– this evening we are almost becalmed & the swell makes us roll about almost as much as last night, & the sails are thrashing the masts merrily– finished Midlothian (1818) last night & began Lammermoor (1819), but I have been busy most all day hanging the wet clothes out to dry & restoring & drying my room– my patient better– I have besides Forbes, Winslow...the cook almost "hors de combat" with a scalded hand– I act as MD for all hands– as I did not sleep much last night, you will excuse my stupidity & consider this day as a blank–

August 24

...made but 83 miles... I hope yet to make...150 miles– I have been at my accounts today– this evening the decks have been dry enough to walk, which has not been the case for a week or more– I shall now take a good stiff glass of port wine Sangree & turn in, so good night–

Saturday 25 August

Only 139 miles...– I have read the whole of the journal today!! barring tedium, it will do to curl your hair with, or make lamp lighters– however, I dont think I shall get a longer journal from you– as it will be Sunday tomorrow & I shall write more steadily when the wind is more aft, I will say good night & read till 12 in Lammermoor– love to Bob–

Sunday night, 11 oclock

...210 miles, with rainy cloudy weather... I have finished Lammermoor & began on Montrose (1819)... read your letter today, a chapter or two in the Bible & the service for the day in Chapel Liturgy, & then took a nap, which I do every afternoon, when the weather prevents my working on deck, so that I am less inclined to go to roost till midnight– it is now just 2 oclock PM, with you & you are probably composing yourself for a nap– my patient I fear will decline gradually for our remedies are scant & my experience small...– give my best love to all hands & good night–

Monday

Another grand day's work, with the same wind & decent weather till tonight we have rain & an increasing wind– I have been turning all day & having a new location for my lathe under cover; shall continue to work more & read less– have just finished Montrose & like it much...– God bless you & kiss Bob–

Tuesday 28 August

...226 miles & tonight the wind has got to SW & clear, pleasant weather, which will carry us up with *St. Pauls Island* by noon tomorrow– we are singularly blessed with winds...good night–

Wednesday 29 August

...*216* miles & at 1/2 past 11 AM I went aloft & saw the land which we passed at 4 oclock this afternoon...– I have been on deck most all day, looking at the land, & running aloft for exercise; reading Ivanhoe [1819] busily... we are 80 days out– Pearson was 88 to here in the *Luconia*– good night–

Thursday 30 August

...only 150 miles, but...tonight we are blessed with a fine fair wind, going 9 knots– I have been turning all day & got heated & then went to shooting birds, which was imprudent, & I am now undergoing a slight headache for my pains– *I hit in succession with my rifle & a single ball of course* three birds on the wing; two fell dead, the third a broken wing; it is true they were as large as large gulls, & flew pretty fair, but then the ship was rolling gunwale to...The birds I shot were what we call Molly–hawks– chocolate colour all over & about 6 feet from tip to tip, with a bill like the Albatross in shape– I wish Sam Cabot was here, not only on account of the birds, but to stand Doctor to poor Forbes, who is drooping though a little better than yesterday– the cook's hand much better & the young Winslow afflicted as Job was has got about decks again, but lame–

Friday August 31

...200 miles–...I expect worse weather before morning– we have sailed 12,078 miles...in 82 days– about 6 miles an hour, which is doing pretty well; but with the same chances Dumaresque would have been a week's sail ahead of us– reading Ivanhoe all day & have finished it– like it much– my patient no better, & I only pray he may last to China–

Saturday 1 September

212 miles & are now (10 PM) going 9 knots with a fine breeze at SW & all sail out, except our wings– During the night a real gale of wind with a very large sea running & tremendous hard hail squalls, the bark scudding before it perfectly safe; sometimes her head reared up to the clouds & then running down a huge wave like the boys coasting down the Common[57]– the ocean was truly sublime this morning, with a bright sun between the squalls...– we have now a fair prospect of getting to Java Head in 94 days..– I shall then begin to realize that I am really on my way to China, for I often find myself asking these questions: is it possible I am on a pilgrimage of years to the most distant land under the Sun? Is it I thats forsaken wife, child, home & all for filthy lucre? why not have staid at home & got merely bread? and then comes my good (or evil) genius & says: Tis only for a short time, all will go well at home, & you will gain an independence–hope I may– think I shall– 12 weeks out tomorrow...

Sunday 2d September

...my poor patient & namesake began to spit blood last night & to complain of weariness in his chest– I think he will get worse very fast, being now so weak he can sit up but a little while– had him up & washed him in warm water & cologne, & changed his clothes, &c– he is just in that state where one fears to do much, & yet must do something– I shall put a small blister on his chest tomorrow I think– he has not complained of any pain till today– I wish he were safe home– I have read my bible and prayer book as usual, today, & just finished the Monastery,

---

[57] This reference is to the Boston Common which today is located between Beacon and Tremont Streets in Boston.

which is the most inferior of Scott's works so far– as it is now half past 11, I will say my prayers in which you & the boy are always remembered & with a glass of Port Sangree as a night cap, I will turn in– this is a bad habit, but it makes me sleep well, besides tasting good– I am quite well, or should not indulge in it–

Monday Eve. 3 September

Another grand day, & a good prospect of another...– I have been turning all day & as usual worked a little too hard & having a slight headache– I shall now go to roost though only 9 PM– I seldom go to bed till 11 or 12– in another week you will have my letters from *Chariot,* & will henceforward be a new woman– am reading the Abbot [1820]...– I should like much to see that Boy, if only for a minute– it is very strange that I do not remember to have dreamed either of him or you once since I left you– I suppose this may be accounted for by the fact that I think of you so often waking that I have no leisure to dream sleeping– but then I dont dream at all– I rest well, eat well, feel well, & *look well*– the Capt says he thought me a *very lean man* when I came on board, & thinks I have gained flesh– I cannot realize yet I have pulled & hauled ropes & turned so much that I am sure I am stronger– my old enemy in the side holds his ground & admonished me to be careful...– God bless & preserve you–

Tuesday September 2

217 miles– better than we expected, & as good as we prayed for– got up entirely free from headache & turned half the day, & read the rest...– my patient now complains of a constant pain across the chest...& as he raises a good deal of mucus, I fear he is on a rapidly declining road– he is not conscious of his danger & I have not thought it prudent to tell him what I fear, lest it might through an increased despondency accelerate his disease– I write this particularly about him, because he has a Mother, & she may call on you to know more of his sickness than I shall write to any one else– from Anjiers I shall write to William Forbes, stable keeper, Sudbury Street, Uncle to this young man, & tell him within the limits of a sheet about his case, & refer the Mother to you if anything more is desired– his blister did not draw, though put on properly, & on all night, & today I have put on one of the Burgundy pitch plasters, sprinkled with Tartar Emetic...– all I can hope for is to keep him up now that his bowels are in order again, by gently nourishing food & cordials like red lavender & ether, until we get somewhere– you may well judge I have no pleasant task, but nothing else could be done...– good night–

Wednesday 5 September

...140 miles...– hope by tomorrow night to have a steady breeze again...– I have been at my boat all day & have just finished an hour's walk, & shall take my night cap (Port Sangree) & turn in–my patient much the same, cut his hair today...

The 18 September is not far off & our boy will be a year old in six or seven weeks– I can hardly realize it is so long since I galloped after the Dr.– I trust in God he is well & with love to your Ma and Sally, good night–

Thursday September 6

88 miles only...the moon is at full; I wish it were just beginning, so that we might have the benefit of it in the China Sea...– I should like to have you here now the bad weather is over,– with certain reservations– I must soon get up a letter to Mother, & Copley, & half a dozen other people, to despatch from Java– I should much like to look in upon you & see what you are at...– buenos noches–

Friday September 7
...113 miles...but this evening we have a fine wind again, & are getting along 7 or 8 miles an hour– I have been working on deck all day, except when attending to my patient, who dont require much nursing– I have all but finished the Abbot, but as it is now near the witching time of night, I shall leave it for the morrow and go to roost– with love to all– good night–

Saturday September 8
...155 miles...– the weather is getting warm fast & an awning will be necessary in a day or two– no change in my patient– good night

IN THE TROPICS

Sunday 9 September
...203 miles...– Our climate changes fast & thin pants are the fashion today– I have been writing letters today to Mother, Bacon & the Uncle of my patient...– pork for dinner, & writing without any work have contributed to give me some headache tonight– as the weather gets warm I must reduce my diet & eschew wine– I began on Kennilworth (1821) & read in my bible & prayer book as usual...– it is about church time 10 AM with you now & I have no doubt but you are just trying to pull on a pair of gloves, which are too tight, or are detaining Sally to button them, or perhaps you are at Nahant...getting clear of a sultry week– I hope and *believe* our boy is well– tomorrow I calculate you will get my *Chariot* letters, & about New Years day you will get this– I have not mentioned Flora of late; she is quite well & much devoted to a stray rat that has been about the decks & long boat ever since we left home– she has hunted him as yet to no purpose– sorry we have no pups to amuse us– kiss our dear boy for me & adieu–

Monday 10 September
...171 miles...– my patient seems to revive a little today, & has more appetite but I fear it is only a transient flickering of his dying lamp– having a slight tendency to headache, I will bid you good night, & God bless you all–

Tuesday 11 September
...only 159 miles...– I never had quite so unfavorable a wind along here, but we must take it as it comes, & no grumbling– at work on my pilot boat all day, which is now painted & looks well–headache all gone– page done & sleepy– good night–

Wednesday 12 September
188 miles...shall *if the wind continues* be in the Straits of Sunda the day after tomorrow– I have been at work as usual all day on deck & got the pilot boat's masts in...– too warm for a great appetite & it is lucky we are not troubled in that way for our live stock has dwindled down to one solitary pig– but we shall get a supply at Anjier...– remember, dearest wife, the trouble & misery of that last year & be sure another like it would have killed me; it is true I left my affairs far from settled, though in a good train & in good hands, but I sometimes feel as if I ran away from trouble instead of facing it, & I may have left John more to do than he can get through; but it was his own choice, & perhaps I have taken the only flood tide that presented or might present– I should like *mighty well* (as Joe Lee says) to look in upon you today reading my journal from *Chariot*, & wouldnt mind your ridicule at my egotism– my page is out & therefore I will say God bless thee–

Thursday 13 September

Fine day's run, & are now only 60 miles from Java Head– I have been busy all day getting my guns cleaned & in order...– some tropic birds came round & I shot two, one of which fell on deck, & I spent an hour or two in skinning & stuffing him for S Cabot– it is a beautiful bird (*or was*) the ground a fine straw colour, with shades of bird of Paradise tail & some black intermixed– we shall make the land about 2 oclock I suppose & I must get a nap before that, as I shall be called on to stand pilot...– I have recommended (my patient) to write home, but he says he dont wish to alarm his mother, who is in poor health...– Flora pokes her nose into my window & asks me to remember her– I will skin her and stuff her & send her home to you, if she dont prove more literary in future–... I shall write you a separate letter to send to Batavia, so that in case of a ship's going home from there, you will still hear of me though the journal will not reach you by the same– I did think of sending this whole copy book, but I want it as a reference when I come to get your first letters, written after receiving mine, & that is another consolation for having written by the *Chariot*, as your letters will be *more interesting* to me after receiving my journal up to that time, as you will doubtless comment severely on the same, and now as I have several letters to write tonight I must say adieu again–

Saturday, 15th [harbor at Anjier]

Dear Rose:

We have got all our supplies, but the wind does not come and we are still detained for want of it– I went on shore last evening & devoured all the news– I find old Pearson is daily expected from Manilla, & as he was expected home by his wife in all this month I had no letters for him– I have written to him as well as to Dumaresque, who will be along here next month– I have left one letter for him from his pretty little wife, & some newspapers– from all I can learn, the times in China are dull, & there were no teas in market in July, but we shall have a change by the time we get there– on the whole, the aspect of things is better than I expected there, & as Mr. Green[58] has not yet left, I shall meet him there– I met here an old friend, Capt Engle, in the Brig *Richard Althorp*, who knows Tom Smith[59] well– I have written to Tom care Capt E. who is bound for Valparaiso– *the Vanceuose passed day before us, beating us one day*!!!!!– the *Omega* sailed 3 June not yet come– on the whole we have not done *excessively* bad & that is all can be said...– I hear James & Russell & Harry Sturgis are all well, ...– another American ship, the *N Gossler*, passed yesterday; sailed from Gibraltar 20 June, about equal to our passage...– I have put up 3 snuff boxes directed to you to care of Dumaresque or Pearson, to be sent by private hand to you, one, the best, is for Doctor Holbrook[60], the other two for you to do what you please with; ...I must now write another letter to John & one to Bacon...–

Adieu once more & believe me,
Yrs. devotedly,
RB Forbes

Sunday Sept 16, 1838

We are now 11 PM nearly up into the Strait of Gaspar[61] it is a place that requires

---

[58] Mr. J. C. Green was the head man at Russell & Co., the firm in China where Forbes was headed to become a partner.

[59] Tom Smith was Rose's brother. He was in California selling flour.

[60] Dr. Holbrook lived next door to Forbes' mother on Adams Street in Milton.

[61] The Strait of Gaspar or Gelasa Selat (2.40 S– 107.15 E) is located between two islands off the coast of Sumatra in the Java Sea.

great care & the cabin is too hot to sleep in– I shall not probably go to bed to night, but stay up & help the Captain into the straits with my experience–

Every time I dispatch a package, I feel as if we had separated again– but my spirits are naturally buoyant and do not give way– my poor patient looks very slim & his feet begin to swell– I could get no advice for him at Anjier & did nothing save to buy $6 worth of seltzer water for him– I am wilting with the heat tho perfectly well– when we anchored at Anjier I had a head ache but the moment I found some one to give me the news & listen to my thousand questions I was perfectly free from headache–

Monday Sept 17–

Up most all night sounding & attending to the ship– at day light found ourselves in the fair channel of Gaspar Straits & made all sail with a fine fair wind which carried us rapidly through & did not leave us until this evening when it deserted us & left us drifting within 6 miles of a bad shoal but we were only in suspense for a couple of hours for now 9 PM we have a fair wind again & will be past all danger of Gaspar which I dearly hope nere to see, but once more & that homeward bound– I am a little foggy with an anxious night & a hot day– I have *more pain* on the side than normal as I used to have after a club dinner– Good Night

Tuesday Sept 18

– my birth day– age 24 years [62]

It is now 11 oclock & about 11 in the morning with you...– My dear Boy is also near a year old & probably says Papa by this time or walking alone or from chair to chair– I know he is well for the almighty is too good to make it otherwise & I am not good enough to deserve so great a chastising as his being otherwise–

We have made a good days work– crossed the Equator at 4 oclock this PM & are now in North latitude, passed the island of St Barber at 5 PM & the sun set splendidly behind it– We are now nearly up with the Tambelang Islands [63]...– the suns rays are nearly vertical & it is hot–I am better than yesterday not withstanding a dinner of real Turtle soup & meat & a plumb pudding or "poudain de plomb"– We shall not be clear of all danger till 2 am & I shall not go to bed until then– Good Night dearest & God Bless thee

Wednesday 19 Sept

– good little wind until this afternoon...– the weather is excessively hot & I am almost drowned while I write–...hardly a drop of rain [for a week]...– we ought to expect some bad weather soon...

Thursday 20 Sept

– made only 80 miles...– there is one comfort however & that is the Typhoons will be over before we get in the location of them–...finished painting my gig– we finish the spruce beer & claret in this weather I assure you– the sea is as smooth as Jamaica Lake [64]...– Finished Kennelworth last night...– it is too hot to write for I am absolutely melting–

---

[62] Born in 1804, Forbes was 34 on this birthday; this must have been a joke.

[63] The Tambelan Islands or Kepulauan Tambelan (1.00 N– 107.30 E) are a group of islands off the coast of Borneo in the South China Sea.

[64] Jamaica Lake is now known as Jamaica Pond in Jamaica Plain, Boston. Forbes would have passed it often on trips between Milton and Boston.

Friday 21 Sept
about 20 miles– The worst day save one since leaving home...– in sight of the Grand Natuna[65] all day & this evening at sun set within 7–8 miles– My patient stands the heat better than I expected, but he is a mere shadow– hope he will last as it is disagreeable burying a fellow creature at sea...103 days out today– hope to be safe in China in 12 more

Saturday 22 Sept
...only 70 miles...– my poor patient failing– I have just been dressing him & never saw such a sack of bones– his mind begins to wander occasionally & he must sink very soon...– good night

Sept 23 Sunday
...100 miles...– our fine pleasant weather continues– we finished painting ship inside today–...I expected dirty weather along here & more wind...– Even now while I was writing I heard (my patient) trying to get up...– this is near the closing scene we have got him up & clean dressed & made his bed on the cabin floor & I have just now felt it my duty to tell him before his wind is entirely gone that I think he must soon render up his account to his creator & asked him if he had anything to say– he only asked if I had written about him– indeed he is so weak that he probably does not realize the fact or understand how it is with him– Good Night dearest– I am not in trim to write much & must watch by this poor youth– no headache in spite of hot–

Monday Sept 24
...only 75 miles...nearly half way from Anjier up to China & hope to get a breeze soon– I went to bed on deck under an awning at 1 AM after putting a watcher with my patient & slept enough in spells & was never better than to day...– Thermometer 80 in the shade– my patient seems to be alive by tea & seltzer water– I dreamed of you & the boy last night– the thought I had been much taken up with tending my sick man & upended myself for not having seen you all day for you were on board I thought– I met the nurse at the after hatch– I asked her about Bob– she laughed & said he had grown so that it made her arms ache to carry him– I was then on the point of going down to see you when the d– d mate called the watch & woke me up...– all our meals on deck under the awning– we might have come all the way from Anjier in a small sail boat– so smooth has been the sea..– good night...

RBF'S FO'C'SLE PATIENT DIES

Tuesday 25 September
hot 4.50 N long 109.45 E Lat–
...at 1/2 past 6 this eve poor Forbes breathed his last without a groan...having been speechless all day– I am glad he is released though he has not suffered much pain– we shall commit him to the deep early in the morning– Good Night

Wednesday 26 Sept
...about 100 miles...at 1/2 past 7 this AM all being ready– the ship was hove to

[65] Great Natuna, about forty miles in length, is the largest of several islands off the N.W. coast of Borneo in the China Sea.

(stopped) the body of poor Forbes laid ready for the last plunge– all hands maintained at the gangway where at the request of the Captain I read the following prayer which I wrote last evening while filling up my journals sitting at the foot of the poor boy...–

"Almighty God who hast made the universe who controllest the sun, the moon, & the mighty ocean look down upon this handful of thy sinful creatures performing the last duties to a fellow mortal, teach us Oh God to consider our lives as well as our fortunes in thy hands impress us with a clear sense of our entire dependence upon thee, let this token of frail mortality now before us be a warning that though now in health & perhaps vain in our strength it is in thy power to cut us off in an instant; impress us with the necessity of calling on thy name in thanksgiving & prayers & not in blasphemy, let it not be said because we roam on the ocean & depend upon the winds & waters for our progress that our hearts are waiting in gratitude for thy many mercies– Oh God we have constantly before us especially on the ocean the eternal evidences of thy power, wisdom, & love– We cannot look upon thy works & wonders of the deep without saying in our hearts, man, frail short sighted man had no hand in these things if we acknowledge as we must that they are thy handy work we should also believe if thou canst guide the course of the planets and the whole creation thou surely canst regulate the destinies of thy creatures according to their merits, continue then thy Fatherly care, Oh God & give us proffering gales to waft us to our desired haven, but if it shall please thee to cut us off in our career, teach us oh God to say thy will be done– Amen"

After this I read a part of the chapel services for the burial of the dead & committed the body to the deep– My voice faltered & a sensation of choking (Probably well known to you who have in your day sacrificed so much salt water to the genius of feeling) almost prevented me from getting on– I made the prayer for my audience but I did not trust myself to look at them to see its effect– such a scene could not but be impressive to the most hardened Tar[66]–I have not felt so sad these 3 years as this week past & it is surely that the Lord gives us strength when we most want it...– We have had every thing out of the cabin to day & a thorough wash & scrubbing– We are only about 800 miles from our post– or four days sail yet...– if we get in without any bad weather it will be wonderful– the last 25 days free from rain & all sail spread to gentle breezes– You will think that I have had a "horrid" time lately– but I assure you I have been as happy as possible & as an evidence of my good health I enjoy my 3 cigars a day more than I remember to have done for a long time– You will recollect for months before I came away I used to imagine I could smoke, but before I had used an inch of my pipe I threw it away in disgust... Bob & Sally & Rose for me & Good Night

THURS 27 SEPTEMBER

162 miles...– we are nearly becalmed with thunder, lightening some rain– hardest part of our passage is to come & I expect to be a week or 10 days doing what we could do with first rate wind–I begin to feel tired of the passage as the weather is hot & the bilge water smells something of the strongest & when it rains I must either endure it below or go on deck...– I now pray most devoutedly for a good wind to carry us in since one of our best men is attacked with a sort of bilious fever Good Night my darling ...

FRIDAY 28 SEPT

...129 miles– now 500 miles south of Islands off Canton– a distance we can

[66] Tar, short for tarpaulin, is slang for sailor or seaman.

accomplish in 2 1/2 days with a fine wind...– gave new patient a large dose of Calomel Ipecac [67] which had a very good effect– but did not reduce the pain in his head or fever so this morning after some persuasion I got him into the cabin & bled him to the extent of a pint & then gave him emetic treatment reduced his pulse from 120–95 in a very short time & drove away the head ache, he is now forward again with penny royal tea[68]...– There is no pleasure in being Doctor though it is satisfaction to do good– It is queer what childish creatures some men are– This fellow, a tall, young man with a frame of iron & a hand the size of a leg of bacon (not Daniel C's) made more faces at taking a little ipecac than you would at having an arm taken off & almost fainted at the sight of his blood & could hardly be persuaded to drink warm water during the operation of his emetic because it tasted bad– You would have been amused to have seen me holding him & bathing his temples with cologne– there is a good deal of selfishness in all this for he is one of our most efficient men & I wish to cure him specially that he may resume his duty for we are short handed– another fellow came to day to have a broken tooth pulled that had troubled him two years but having no other tools than a pair of pincers & a bullet mould I told him he could stand it a week more having endured it two years– & so I did not try– but recommended him to fill the cavity with powder & then put a coal of fire in his mouth & blow him up– it is very pleasant this evening but the wind tho fair is very light– the moon at the quarter & a great blessing shines upon us & I hope to get in without any more bad weather– love to all & Good Night

SATURDAY 29 SEPTEMBER
...only 39 miles...– It is now 10 PM a dead calm– the day has been the hottest day– I could not stand it on deck, but with my head out of the cabin window on a pillow I continued to keep cool in a duress to read the end of The Pirate– my patient better– adieu

SUNDAY 30 SEPT
– 9 PM– 16 weeks from Boston...but 40 miles– I am getting especially tired of seeing the same faces–...time always hangs heavy when one is 400 miles from port– Flora stands it well– I have read a good deal in the good book today but shunned your letter which can only be read when we have a fair & fresh wind– it is now about 9 AM with you & you are just preparing to go to church to pray & think more of me than of the sermon– I prepare to read the chapel for the day before I go to my roost so as to beat it the same moment you are– I have been overhauling my papers & reading old letters to day– there is no question that I have a ready pen & with material can write a good letter– Oh vanity– vanity– It has been too hot to think or do much about eating & drinking but we bought at Anjier some 15 fowls & plenty of turtle, sweet potatoes, yams & eggs & have lived better than we deserved–my butter still holds & though rather thin is not yet rancid...– Good Night and may Heaven return your husband to you with a decent Competency [69] in two years–

MONDAY OCTOBER 1
...only 50 miles...I feel in better trim now that we have some wind– My patient better, bleeding from the nose which I don't understand takes Port wine without

---

67 Calomel ipecac is a white tasteless compound used as a purgative.

68 Penny-royal is an aromatic plant with hairy leaves and bluish flowers which grows in western North America and in Europe. It yields an aromatic oil and may be made into an herbal tea.

69 Competency means sufficient wealth for a comfortable existence.

At left, the Perkins ships Levant *and* Milo *are depicted at Lintin Station in a painting by a Chinese artist.* Levant, *on the left, was Robert Bennet Forbes' first command. The lighter being rowed, and the rakish schooner, are opium-smuggling vessels.*

a murmur– I wrote most of the forenoon, read Nigel part of the day & rigged my pilot boat mast to wind up– feel a little sore under the ribs probably in consequence of sleeping in too much draft last night– Our little Captain fidgets me by always saying Sir– whether he hears what you say or not– & this obliges me to repeat which is a great bore & deprives him of much of my valuable conversation & when he sits to read to himself he *snuffles* continually as though his nose wanted wiping & I am almost tempted to say "Why the d– l dont you blow your nose–" thus you see that the smallest things are contorted into sources of great annoyance after one has been cooped up on board ship an hundred odd days– then he paddles about deck barefooted & out at elbows which I should never allow my mates to do–but we shall soon part I trust– he has been attentive & kind to me too & I have nothing to complain of for he takes my advice about the course & lets me take his observations–

Tues 2 Octo

...103 miles...– we are now (8 PM) 269 miles from the islands off the river & the breeze seems to increase a little so that I am really sanguine that we shall have the pleasure of seeing the Lintin[70] squadron on Thursday night...

3rd Octo

...90 miles...– fine weather all day & have now a pleasant little breeze & hope to see the land tomorrow evening– yet the winds & weather are so variable that it is useless to look forward with confidence...– adieu

4 Octo

...122 miles...– I calculate to go to bed perhaps to sleep till 2 AM & then go up to see land at a 1/2 past 2 & at day light to be among the islands...– Good Night

70 Lintin Island, only three miles long, is located in the center of the Pearl River estuary about twenty-five miles northeast of Macao. Opium was stored here aboard anchored American vessels; from these ships it was transferred to boats owned by Chinese smugglers who took it ashore to their agents who distributed it over the countryside. Although opium was illegal in China, the trade continued at the Lintin Island anchorage.

LANDING

Robert Bennet Forbes arrives in the Pearl River estuary aboard Mary Chilton *early in October of 1838, and shortly begins his business and social life at Canton, Macao and Hong Kong, describing its routines in the letters he writes to Rose. Two months after his arrival, the opium troubles begin.*

Whampoa anchorage is shown above and on the fan that decorates page 55. On page 54 are the hongs at Canton and Respondentia Walk crowded with Chinese.

5 Octo

– at 2 AM saw the land just where we expected to find it– at 5 took a pilot[71]...– went on deck in the moonlight & saw the pilot look at me rather hard & then with a broad grin said he "Aya Missier Foxe came again" &c...– he told us on the 28–29–30 Sept there happened a hard tyfong[72] in which an English ship foundered with all her crew & one large junk besides several minor damages & its uncertain my dear whether we are going too slow or too fast in this world– if we had got along as well as I expected & wished, we might have suffered–at 11:00 anchored near the old *Lintin* & had the pleasure of meeting several of my old friends...– at 1 oclock embarked for Macao[73] with Capt Howland of the

---

[71] Pilots were licensed by the Chinese government and were required to register each foreign captain and vessel with the officials. They then secured permission for them to proceed up the Pearl River.

[72] Tyfong is the word Forbes used for typhoon from the Chinese (Cantonese– tai feng or Mandarin– ta feng). A typhoon is a severe tropical hurricane that occurs in the Western Pacific and the China Sea.

[73] Macao is an island about 60 miles south of Canton opposite Hong Kong at the mouth of the Pearl River. It had been settled by the Portuguese in 1557. All foreigners accompanied by their families established residences at Macao. Since Chinese regulation prohibited women and children from going on to Canton, the foreign men left their families in Macao while they proceeded to Canton for business. They then returned to Macao for visits and vacation.

Horatio & his wife a very pretty little woman & at 8 last evening walked into Uncle Jim Sturgis[74] parlour where he was smoking his cigar– says I– any entertainment for man & horse here– the old man jumped up & tried to look cool but the colour came into his face & his veins in his head swelled & he gave me a great shake– I had already met Russell at the landing he came to meet Mrs Howland– he looks quite well & in good spirits– I asked for the children & they came running in muslin night gowns Lucy a very pretty girl now 5 & Johnny about 4 not so good looking...– I shall now return to the Lintin fleet with Capt Howland & go up[75] in the *Horatio* or get a Sch[ooner] from here & go direct, there seems no great reason to hurry up & yet I am somewhat impatient to get there & locate myself as Mr Sturgis has requested me in his house– I am excessively grateful for our arrival & for the good night out I had last night in same room with Russell & whenever I awoke I asked some new question & continued to talk all night– I must now bring up my journal to John ready for a ship...–

Macao– 6 Octo 1838–

My dearest wife–

...You have no idea how pleasant it is here & I heartily wish you were here with me with plenty of money to certain the establishment then it might be not only tolerable but delightful but with the conscience up that I was working only to find money to live here forever– it would be irksome & hard– as it is I think I have done right (if I must have come) to leave you at home– Russell did not like your miniature– he said it would be known by any intimate friend that it had none of the expression which always might be found in your animated face & he said it looked too old– I shall not show it again to any one–

I was up most of the night– I hear Dumaresq is just leaving Manila for home & that he has not done badly–& Pearson too is on his way home & with a good freight & Pearce in whom I am interested has done a safe business...the vessel that takes this to Manila is off soon & as I have other letters to write I must say adieu & with much love to mother & Sally & the young un I am ever thine– Bennet

9 PM 8 Octo

perhaps 9th at any rate its me thats writing though I feel as if my head belonged to some body else for it aches merrily in consequence of my steering the boat most all night– We started at 4 pm yesterday in the Sch *Union* for Canton & are only half way 28 hours out & now at anchor waiting for the tide– on Saturday several people called & yesterday I returned some, among others an old Lintin friend Capt Perry just married to a widow & his partners Messrs Jardine & Co[76] have sent out invitations for a grand ball in honour of the occasion– I was invited of course & had I leisure I should have gone– tell John I met Mrs Mclane at Mr Howlands & she asked after my *elder brother* meaning him of course– I find he has generally been accepted as my senior– Mrs McLane said she heard a Mr Forbes had arrived & supposed Mr John Forbes had come to give the ladies another fancy ball so I asked her if she intended that as a hint for me if so I

---

74 Uncle James Sturgis was a relative from Boston who for many years lived in Macao and was in the employ of the Perkins brothers. RBF later refers to him as "Uncle Jimmy."

75 "Go up" refers to going up the Pearl River.

76 Jardine, Matheson & Company, established in 1832, was the largest and most influential British house in China.

would give them one by proxy after my departure from China– called on old Chinnery[77] & found him sitting on a dirty old settee under fed with half a dozen leaches on his head, the blood flowing down his naturally picturesque countenance, the dirty old brute was glad to see me & I stayed long enough to tell him the story of the lost portrait –Flora is coming up with C Howland in *Horatio* with my traps– a curse on these cockroaches which fill the boat– I have been reading Mary of Burgundy to day–the weather is now fine & after a blue pill at Canton I shall be in good *trim* not having yet got over the excitement of arrival–

George Chinnery is shown above in a self-portrait. Chinnery was the principal European artist in China in the first half of the nineteenth century, and a colorful character in the community of traders.

I saw Gilman[78] at Macao– totally dismasted in a Tyfong last July & was tossed about at the mercy of the winds & waves for some time before he could get command of his vessel & get her in to one of the ports– he has abandoned her to the Insurers & will take command of the *Lintin*– Capt Macondray[79] going home with 60 thousand dollars Good Night

TUESDAY 9 OCTOBER

After a calm night found ourselves several miles below the ships at Whampoa[80] at sunrise & obliged to anchor till about 9 AM a little breeze came to our aid when we got under weigh & soon passed the Canton cutter which left Macao on Sunday morning with Capt Elliot[81] coming up to look into a meeting at Whampoa steered alongside of him to take some letters for Canton when he asked me after my Brother &c– we are now half way from Whampoa to Canton & with a change of tide or an increase of wind shall be there in half an hour– I hope I shall have leisure to keep up my journal on shore as faithfully as I do afloat– adieu dearest–

SETTLING INTO LIFE IN CANTON

11 OCTO

...3 oclock arrived after having got becalmed...– I invited an English Capt– who was passing in a pulling boat to come on board & take some refreshment & rest his men which he did & of course could do no less than return the complement when the wind died away & ask me to come up with him which I did just in time

---

77 George Chinnery, although British and a member of the Royal Hibernian Academy, had lived in India and China since 1800. He was the most distinguished British artist who had ever lived in China. He drew and painted both portraits and landscapes, and he is ranked as a minor master among English artists. In 1838 he was sixty-four and had the reputation of being an amusing, spirited storyteller. He died at Macao in 1852.

78 Gilman would serve as an aide to Forbes during his stay in China.

79 F. W. Macondray was left in command of the *Lintin* for six years when RBF left Canton for home in 1832.

80 The island of Whampoa lies thirteen miles below Canton. Here all foreign ships were anchored and allowed to proceed no farther up the Pearl River. Loading and unloading took place here, and cargoes were discharged onto small river vessels which brought the merchandise to Canton. It was not uncommon for as many as a hundred foreign ships to be anchored in the waters near Whampoa.

81 Captain Charles Elliot was British Superintendent of Trade with authority over all English ships and British subjects in the region.

to get my dinner with Mr Snow the Consul[82] who has a corner in Mr Sturgis' factory [83]– after dinner sent to Mr Hunter [84] one of Russell & Co young partners for a change of clothes– called on Green the head man of same house who (after 5 minutes of general talk) said he supposed the subject of my future movements was the most interesting topic for me– to which I replied I wished first to shake hands with my friends & to see what was going on–took tea with them– called on Russell Sturgis' partner (Delano)[85] & on Wetmore & Co[86]– went to bed at 11 in good spirits– yesterday morning went to see Houqua– read John's letters to him as well as Mr Cushing[87]– very glad to see me– paid me the compliment to offer to secure my ship– asked me & advised me about my future plans– thinks while Green stays I had better take John's share & go into the house– seemed very friendly– quite angry with BB&Co[88] London– said not a word about bad voyage home– went to see Green by appointment at 5 yesterday pm– entered directly on the subject of my future plans & *here let me beg you to keep all I say about my arrangements entirely to yourself & John– I forbid your telling your mother or Sarah or anyone else & I consider it an evidence of the greatest confidence in your discretion that I write to you at all on these points*– you can merely say what every body will know that Green remains here & I have made arrangements as I wished to enter Russell House– you may say this when I tell you such arrangements are made– well to the point– Green advises me to take John's share less than a quarter for the present time up to 1 Jany 1840 & to make a new arrangement at the end of that time leaving out Mr C[oolidge][89] – I will not do this as Green will not stay over another summer– if he were to stay I would do

[82]Peter W. Snow was the American Consul at Canton at this time. It is interesting to note that on September 23, 1839, he reported in the *Chinese Repository* that no Americans were in the opium trade, despite British activity with the drug.

[83] Factories or hongs were a row of buildings side by side, about fifty yards back from the Pearl River, which housed the foreign merchants during their stay in Canton. Each country leased a factory from the Chinese. In the bottom floors teas, silks, and other goods were stored, while the second and third floors were used for living quarters. The American hong provided storage, office space, and housing for half a dozen American firms and the U.S. Consul. The factories were about a hundred and twenty feet deep and were separated from the city walls of Canton by two hundred yards. The foreigners were restricted to the small area between the city walls and the river.

[84] William C. Hunter, born in Kentucky in 1812, was twelve years old when he managed to secure a job as an apprentice to the Canton agency of Thomas H. Smith & Son of New York. He sailed for China almost immediately. He prepared for his work in the Far East by spending eighteen months studying Chinese in the Anglo-Chinese College at Malacca. When he reached Canton, he continued his studies with an eminent English Protestant missionary, Robert Morrison. Hunter earned the distinction of being perhaps the first American to devote himself to a systematic study of the spoken and written Chinese language. When Smith & Co. failed in 1827, Hunter returned for a brief time to New York, but by 1829 he was again at Canton as a clerk in the firm of Russell & Co. Ultimately he became a full partner in the house.

[85] Warren Delano was born in Fairhaven, Massachusetts, in 1809. His father and grandfather were both sea captains. He was educated in local academies and then went to Boston where he worked in the counting room of Hathaway & Co., merchant bankers and shipowners. Several years later he moved to New York City and was briefly employed by the mercantile firm of Goodhue & Co. In 1833 he sailed as supercargo on a ship trading to ports in South America and in the Pacific Islands, and reached China after a year. In Canton he became an equal partner in the firm of Bryant Sturgis & Co., and when the firm merged with Russell & Co. he continued as partner.

[86] W. S. Wetmore Co. was another American house or firm.

[87] This was John Perkins Cushing, formerly head of Perkins & Co. at Canton.

[88] Baring Brothers & Company of London was one of the most important banking houses in the world.

[89] Joseph Coolidge was a Boston commission merchant who went to Canton in 1839 intending to be accepted by Russell & Co., and apparently intending to take RBF's place in the firm.

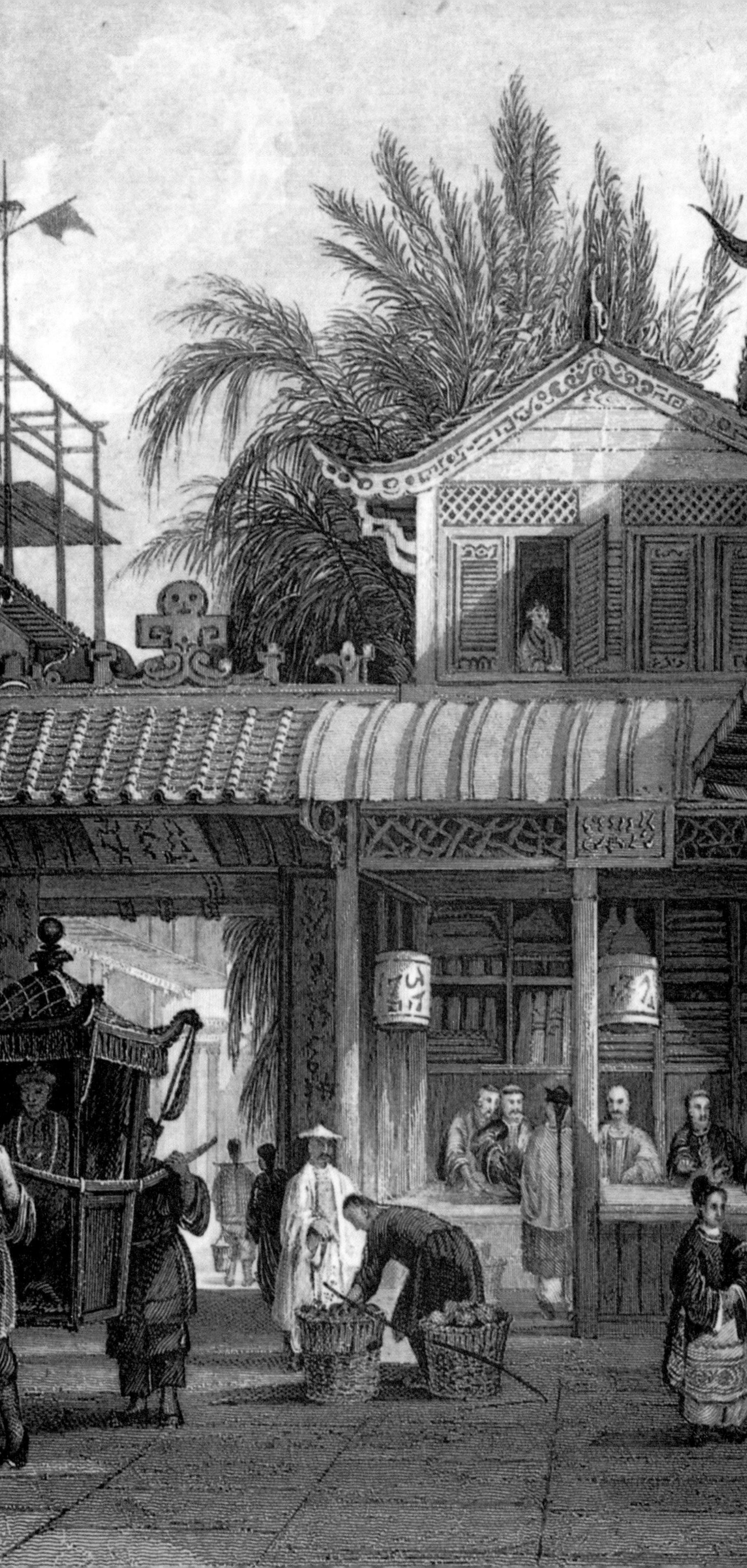

A busy street scene in Canton is the subject of this engraving based on a painting by Thomas Allom. During Robert Bennet Forbes' time in the Canton hongs, the Western traders were rarely permitted to enter the city.

it– I now offer to join them– this giving me a quarter & all the Coms [Commissions] on those vessels that I now have consigned to me & I to have the management of all vessels to RBF– if I please sharing the Coms on such with the house always excepting the three vessels just named–This arrangement to last till a year from 1 Jany next– then to form a new house leaving out C[oolidge]– which all the present members will now agree to not having the power though they have the will to do it now– Coolidge has written from England objecting to my being admitted– I like that, because it is decided & my course is plain before me– my great objective is to get regularly into harness to do what I do *well*– the great changes in the manner of doing business here make me just like a cat in a strange garret & if I was to undertake to do my business alone I should do it at the expense of some of my present constituents where as it is my desire to please & satisfy them above all others & to do them ample justice– I might no doubt join Russell Sturgis & Delano & make an efficient house but they have been unfortunate...– I have not had a word with any one except Russell Sturgis, Houqua & Green– my intention is to ascertain from Houqua what would become of his business & influence were Green to leave this year– if he would give it to me either as a member of R&Co house or any other I might then make a better bargain with the first than I can now do– but I shall not stick out for a great share the first year but shall insist on it when we form a new house–

Houqua has just been here & thinks Green is going to stay & as I am tied up in that respect & cannot undeceive him he prefers having his business in the same old channel & thinks I had better go in–

12 Octo

– Yesterday called on several residence & received calls dined with Frank Hathaway, Mr Nye & Mr Everet [American merchants] & had a hearty meal, mutton &c– passed the evening at home– Wetmore here most of the time very civil & have been kept at home all day by visitors– going by appointment in a few minutes to see some of John's English friends with Delano–

13 Octo

– Made calls till 2– mostly on English people– dined at home– went to sail with Delano in #1– becalmed & had to get back with oars– took tea at home & walked in the evening– to day began morning with cold bath breakfast of rice & fish...– Evening went to see Green at 5 & in a few minutes agreed to my terms saying the younger members would submit entirely to his opinion– my interest beginning 1 Jany next & John continue until that time it being a matter of little importance whether Peter or Paul gets it except that my share is to be more than Johns was up to January 1...– I take up my quarters there as soon as I please but as I have the whole side of this house to myself I shall only take up my desk there at once– the Coms of the house have been greater than ever the last year while the business of all other houses fell off...–Mr Coolidge not having assented or rather having dissented to my coming will be dropped at the end of the term to which I have agreed to stay to 1 Jany 1840...in short I have done *all* I wished & *more* than I expected & far better than I deserve & with the only alloy that you my dearest wife are not here to share my satisfaction– I am quite happy–

14 Octo Sunday

– callers all the morning prevented my going to meeting– then dined with Delano with Hathaway, Howland, Nye &c– walked & wrote till 11 PM after taking tea with Green where I made them very merry with my Portrait Story–

I have written you a yarn via Bombay to go across the country & shall lose no opportunity of keeping you furnished with *curling* papers– so do not fail to send me *shaving* papers in return–

Canton Oct 14, 1838

My dear Rose–

I am writing by the way of India overland I must make a compact epistle as postage is ruinous that way– ...(I wish) to stay only long enough to get my Competency– whether that can be done in one or two years after 1 Jany 1840 remains to be seen & the period is too distant for poor humanity to look forward to– of one thing you may rest assured I shall not stay an hour after I can see my way clear to have enough to live upon in a very moderate way at home...– as for asking you to come out–I dread the thoughts of such a trip without me & as I will not sacrifice health for money & may get sick at any time if I were to recommend you to come out I should feel that I must stay lest I might miss you on the way– in deed all the objections to your coming originally are likely to exist except that of our Boy being then too young to travel– & yet it is hard, very hard to be separated for so long a time– however the moment I begin to get letters from you I shall feel that we are much nearer to each other– Write me a compact letter on *strong* paper for overland mail at the times when ships are not coming direct– John will advise you about this– & pray keep up a journal from day to day of all you *do say or think* as I shall to you to come per ship– for my happiness will be in your letters...–I am now living with Mr Snow for a little while until I get fixed at Russell & Co– he Mr S has grown very old & is not well, has a cough all the time & is out of spirits–as he has nothing to do– I find Canton itself but little changed but there are as many new people as customs & I am like a cat in a strange garret– this is rather fortunate for I knew but little of the detail of Canton business before–

16 Octo

– Yesterday writing , calling & receiving calls all day– got my baggage up with Flora &c &c dined at home & employed all the afternoon & evening with the younger members of R&Co discussing the question of Mr Green retaining an interest & leaving his funds in the house or leaving entirely taking them with him...– I am to dine with Dent & Co[90] to day–have been writing to you via St Helena– shall keep this for first direct home ship–

16 Octo

My business is not yet definitely settled with R&Co for Houqua has raised some difficulties as I insisted upon Green telling him plainly that he was going in February or March & not leading Houqua to suppose he was to stay & then have him hear suddenly that he was gone– I preferred dealing candidly with Houqua who would like to have Green remain in the house even if he goes away especially as he has large funds say $150,000 which he will leave if he retains our interest & will take away if he goes– to have in the house & keep his money & influence I have no objection to valuing it higher, provided my share is not reduced to keep him– the matter rests just so– I can go in at my terms– Green going out– but we all wish to satisfy Houqua & I may have to give way a little for a year– I am quite easy about the whole matter & on the whole am pleased that Green is willing to retain an interest & leave his funds include him on any terms

90 Dent & Co. was the most important British firm after Jardine, Matheson.

as it shows confidence in the concern– for he says the house would have dissolved long ago if he had not stood– Russell Sturgis is up from Macao quite well...— thine ever Bennet

18 Octo

I dined with Dent accordingly a party of 25– & as I was placed on the right of the host I conclude the other guest & dinner were for my a/c [account]– eat & drank a good deal & staid to Whist until midnight– sick all day yesterday as usual after a debauch– & am under the influence of medicine to day– serves me right– however I have not been regularly well since I came on the coast– rather bilious– I shall not accept invitations to dine after I have seen all the people– but one must make sacrifices when coming into a new society– ... went on the river yesterday in my new boat (the "not half so green") & with 3 oars each beat the "not so green" the inferior boat heretofore–

22 Octo 1838

Dear Rose

...I have not been quite right in my inward manner...– you may imagine I am not very ill when I tell you the Dr recommended only 2 to 3 glasses of sherry at dinner! why Dr said I never take more than two in perfect trim except at a party & if you approve I will take none to day– Oh very well just as you please I have ordered a complete Chinese dress for Bob to day ...– I have also got a painter making a copy of you without the bonnet & putting the child in engraving into your arms– will see his sketch first if it will do shall have it painted–... if the house does as well as the last 2 years I ought to get 25-30 thousand at the least for a year besides what I brought out & a much larger share– after 1 Jany 1840– adieu for today

23 Octo

– much better today indeed well except weak– dined at 1/2 past 6 with a party at McLanes say (Maclean) & drank toast water & eat mutton & feel perfectly well to day– except Russell Sturgis there no other Yankee– took a sail before dinner & landed up river & had a walk with Flora distinguished herself by running through all the mud she could find–

24 Octo

– birth day of our young hero– whose health will be drunk by Mr Snow & myself to day– I am having the things prepared for Mrs Hammond & shall send them per *Francis Stanton*– MacLean says his children have been perfectly well at Macao & that it is considered a good place for them– R Sturgis says it costs double to live there than at home & that he necessarily had 15 servants– went to see RS the other night & Flora in chasing a rat ran into his well headlong– I heard her & after a good deal of trouble got her out– when Russell remarked "I guess she'll let *well* alone next time"– pretty good–

25 Octo

No arrival from US which I am impatiently looking for & nothing new here– wrote to Copley, Hillard,[91] W Sturgis, the Col[92] & Mr Cushing & shall write

91 George Stillman Hillard (1808-79) was a graduate of Harvard College and Law School. In 1834 he began to practice law with Charles Sumner in Boston.

92 The Colonel was Thomas Handasyd Perkins. He was referred to by Forbes as his uncle and patron.

some more letters to day to people who have no commercial claims on me...– I shall always tell you how I am & wish you to depend solely on my reports of myself for health is considered as capital here– if my rival imagines his neighbor unwell he writes home making him out very bad– dined at Russell & Co to day & on coming home received 2 invitations for Saturday but declined both determined to be prudent...– adieu–

26 OCTO

Nothing very interesting to day– kept on short diet & walked quantum sufficit– sailed boat this afternoon & walked in front this evening– I take Flora out to sail everyday she enjoys the air– goes home very quickly when I order her– had a rat caught & shut up with her which she soon dispatched– There is but little doing in Canton at this moment the Tea market remaining quiet & the bad news about prices from England keeps purchases back & prices down here–

SUNDAY EVENING 28

...today staid at home after visiting the Hongs & looking at some Tea, & I went over the river to visit Puankheguas[93] house & garden covering space of several acres– partly new & pretty with fish ponds & rural seats & pavilions & partly in a state of dilapidation & decay– saw some of the female women at a distance & while eating sweetmeats the young kids were sent with their nurses to look at us– gave them 5 cent pieces, but they were afraid of us so that I could not take the youngest in my arms– probably not half so pretty as Bob– dined at home & took Tea with RS & canvased over all the news gossip at home &c– think he has a particularly imaginative eye to the growing generation especially the female portion & imagine if he were to go home he would marry very soon–...I have not read my bible since I left the ship for the very good reason that all my books are on board the ship yet– neither have I attended church– I think closet devotions are adopted to this market–

TUESDAY EVENING 30 OCTO

Busy writing all day yesterday– sailed & walked in the evening–wrote till 10 PM– same all this forenoon– weather delightful & health good– this afternoon went to pull in the six oared boat "not so green" manned by RS, Delano, myself & King &c– had a good pull & came back at sunset quite refreshed– played whist all this evening with Delano, myself & Mr Snow– Am chosen a member of the Canton Regatta Club & have put my new gig which I brought out from home into a regatta to take place about the 5 November under the name of "The not half so green" & am to exercise every day so as to win a *silver cup*– went to a *Portrait painter to day* & made Flora sit for her portrait, to fix her in one position I procured a cockatoo which she gazed at fixedly for half an hour & I think the fellow has hit her exactly...–

NOV 1

sailed yesterday & pulled today & got beat– played whist at R Sturgis till 11 last night & went to bed on mulled wine which did no harm *to speak of*– Getting very impatient to hear from you per *Asia* or *Fr Stanton* & must have letters in a few days I think– the ship *Omega* that left New York a week before us & is not yet in– but as she can bring nothing from you I care not whether she sinks or swims...tell your Ma & Sally that I have the greatest respect for them–

[93] Puankhequa was another one of the Hong Merchants.

Sun 4 November

– since my last day we have no arrivals & nothing in particular to notice– the China dress for Bob has come & consists of the following– white shirt & Trousers to go next the skin– over the trouser put the green leggings to come down to the knee– over the white shirt the long blue jacket– over that the orange vest in cool weather, the purple crepe jacket over all– shoes & stocking on *the feet*, the cap & tail on *the head*, you must comb all the *golden curls* up under the cap so as to show only the tail– cost *$10*– this is the only present I shall send him by the *M Chilton*, if Floras Portrait is done I will send that– as Flora & the Chinese know no Sunday– I am going to day to have the last sitting– I have entirely got over the sore pain in stomach I used to have at home– I got up my books & papers yesterday & felt bad when I read your letter over again– I hope you have followed out your intentions of bearing up– I am very anxious to hear of you for it is nearly five months since we parted & time will begin to work off faster when I get your letters regularly– I have written a long letter to Mother, but not a line to another member of the family except John– some how or other the "dear Sister" sticks in my throat– I cant write as I ought that is with any show of affection without playing the part of a hypocrite or appearing cold– perhaps I shall write to Emma– but I don't know...–

Canton Nov 5, 1838

My dear Rose

I had begun to be a little impatient when this morning the long expected packet from the *Francis Stanton* at Singapore made its appearance I greedily tore off the envelop & found your three letters one dated 14 June– one Sunday a week after I sailed & one on the 19– I could hardly realize that only a few days had elapsed & consequently only the state of feeling could be stated– the fact that you were alive made me shed tears of joy & the well being of our dear Boy added to my happiness...– I note your remarks about prudence, liberality misapplied &c & will try to be discrete without meanness, sharp without dishonesty, & at last rich without ostentation– but my dear you cannot change a man's nature– I will however try to be all *you* desire but I am not ambitious to be all John would have me...– went out to day to try & beat all the rest in hope when the day comes to win the cup– value *$65*– I write this by way of St Helena by an English ship– in a week or ten days shall have a direct opportunity per *Mary Chilton* going to New York– I shall send you by her 2 boxes sugar costs 14 cts per lb– 1 portrait of Flora is for you & one is for Sally– We have had a French frigate here & her Capt & officers have been dining & feasting until they are tired– I kept aloof & shall do so of all large parties– but R Sturgis, Green, Delano, Hathaway, Nye & James Price dine with me day after tomorrow– I pay for the marketing here & live free of rent until I take up my quarters at R&Co which is not so pleasant as this factory... a kind letter from Bacon wherein he offers to do every thing for you & I beg you will command him freely as he is one of the best of men & I believe a sincere friend–

Be particular to date your letters & mark the name of the vessel on them & do not think any thing too trivial to mention– adieu my dearest be content, take exercise & believe me happy & satisfied Thine ever– Bennet

Tuesday 6 Nov

...although your letters are only a few days later than I left yet I cannot get over the idea that they convey intelligence five months later– I have sealed your letters together in order & shall preserve every page– so mind your ps and qs–

RS comes to me for family news & you will be quoted often (rather doubtful authority)– it is very pleasant to get later dates from home than anybody else has–

...I trust nothing will come between you & John– however right you may be to throw any cold water between us– for he has given up at least $15–20,000 per annum to put me in the way of getting home again without feeling it a burthen & he has the feeling though he may keep it back from you because he knows you are overflowing with it– If you should have any unpleasant discussions with him believe me I should support you right or wrong & this might put myself in a position to quarrel even with a brother– this must not be–

As for you & mother I have no fear but you will get along like two pickpockets & I care not whether you fight with the sister or not–

10 Nov

– The last few days have been taken up with preparing the *Mary Chilton*s Cargo, boat sailing &c– we have had a regatta in which we Yankees appeared as competitors...– since I got over my little ill turn I have gained four pounds of flesh, indeed I am quite well & need only to abstain from Beer, wine, & hard eating to be very well for a hundred years to come– You can tell Dr Jackson– I left off smoking on reading his letter & did not begin again till next day– but I have serious designs to give it up altogether for it is only an idle habit with me & I can give it up without making any sacrifice–

Friday 16

– I(t) seems an age since I wrote last & can hardly believe it is so long– on Monday 11 I went to Whampoa partly to see how they got on in the *Mary Chilton* & partly to visit Handasyds[94] grave which is beautifully situated on the side of a hill commanding a fine prospect– Russell Sturgis was with me & we had not much to say–I plucked some wild flowers from around the grave which is still as it was before the remains were taken home, Dumaresq must have had a most memorable task to perform in carrying Mr Cabots desires into effect which he was obliged to do in person with his own hands as the superstitious ideas of the chinese prevented them from aiding– I have sent the flowers to Sally Perkins, Flora was also with us– I have been busy writing every day only excepting Thursday (yesterday) when the sailing match came off– a fine afternoon with the wind just strong enough– it fell to my turn to start second, I ran down before the wind about 2 miles turned the boat at that point & beat back against wind & tide– 4 other boats in Co as competitors & many others pulling & sailing as spectators– although one boat which toward the end of the race before the wind had some advantage once I got in ahead of all & won the cup in an old boat, in bad order by superior skill doing the distance in 4 1/2 minutes less than the next boat & 16 minutes less than the worst of the five, a deafening shout of applause from the members of the Regatta Club finished the act– came home quite elated & dined with the other boat sailors at Mr Ebushis & consoled with them & received their congratulations– the boat I navigated came out last at the last sailing match & the one that got the cup then came out No 3 yesterday– it was a beautiful sight I assure you & gave more satisfaction to the public than all the rowing matches–had a good dinner & played whist until 12 oclock did not smoke...–god bless thee my love & Bob too–

---

[94] Thomas Handasyd Cabot was a cousin of RBF's, one of Elizabeth Perkins Cabot's and Sam Cabot's eleven children, and the Colonel's grandson. He had gone with John Murray Forbes to China at the age of nineteen. He had died from smallpox and was buried in China at the age of twenty-one.

CANTON NOV 20 1838

My dear Rose

The *Mary Chilton* has departed & I have now leisure to take up read attentively consider & reply to yours per *Asia* dated June 24 & Monday 25– Yesterday morning I had just finished my breakfast & with a sigh given up smoking my cigar when in came a china man (sweet creature) with a goodly sized package of letters which I instantly untied & not seeing any in your hand & one in Charles Greens I was immediately filled with apprehension & for the first time in my life I realized how I suppose you had often felt– I opened Greens letter which ran thus–

"The *Asia* is off & I write a line to say how are you– I hear Rose is in great trouble but I hope she may soon be more tranquil &c &c"– this did not make me feel easier I immediately concluded the child was sick or your Mother or Sarah– I looked among the letters & could find nothing from you, tore open Johns letters & saw nothing to alarm me, yet they were short & primarily on business & he merely remarked he had seen you once but as you had now gone into Town he hoped to see more of you– I imagined this was rather cool & then the thought came God forgive that you been quarrelling with Milton folks[95] about the baby or with John about house either out of Town or in Town– There was a letter from Sarah John in which she spoke with great interest of you & the child– what the devil could be the reason I knew not– there was a package from Emma which I came near throwing into the drawer unopened but think I Rose missed the ship & perhaps Emmas letters will give me an account of the fight & it must have been with her– after all I sincerely hope they may not have demolished the baby– I tore her letters apart one of yours was stuck fast to hers owing to the wax of one or the other being bad– I opened it with trembling hands & throbbing heart swearing eternal enmity to Mother, John & all the rest– I glanced hastily over it without reading a line & came to "never saw Bennet out of temper" oh then the quarrel has been with John– so I set my teeth & began coolly to read every line & I found nothing new & the passage above quoted was part of your kind note to Mother & Green alluded merely to your grief at my departure...– you may judge from this little incident how sensitive a man becomes when away from all he holds dear– I received many letters & had to reply to most of them in haste as the *M Chilton* was just being dispatched & I put yours & Johns off till I had only time to write a line in acknowledgement as the tide served & the Capt was waiting...– write when you feel most like it– do not wait for the vessel to be named when per chance you may be engaged or not feel like writing– for you must have days (as I have) when I can't write a reply to an invitation to dine– while at other times when the digestion is good I can write with ease & impunity–

But to your letters– In the first place they are satisfactory because they give good accounts of our dear Boy & of your being not only reconciled to your change of location & circumstances but even pleased to show that you can endure & I am sure that no false pride will ever lead you to throw away a dollar– I am aware that all causes & services of grief are swallowed up in my going & that you cannot be deprived of any thing to trouble you in comparison with my absence, but the trial is nothing compared to what you may witness daily around you & to me it is much less than to you– I am situated here at the Top of the ladder, living as well as any body else necessarily & if I dont give parties & receive

[95] The Milton folks refers to RBF's mother and sisters who lived in what is now the Robert Bennet Forbes House in Milton, Massachusetts.

comp[any]– it is merely because I am a stranger entitled to receive rather than give– then I have sail boats at command & servants at the ring of a bell in abundance & as far as living goes I am just as independent as I ever have been at home– I like your description of the house & I have tried to think of something unpleasant about it & can only remember that it had old brass door handles– Your theory of economy is admirable & with your Ma's aid & Sally's your practice will be equally so– I regret to hear that your Mother was still ailing but cannot believe that her good constitution is in any danger– you enjoin on me prudence & I will tell you how far I produce it– in dress– I have bought 1 pr shoes 1 cloth Jacket & have had a dozen fine dinner jackets made costing only 90 cents a yard, I wear Johns old cotton shirts with the collars up thus

thats me!!–

I live at Mr Sturgis' free of rent but sharing table expenses with him or Mr Snow– I do not go to Russell & Co to live– first because no good vacant chamber, second because I shall not take my place at end of the table till 1 Jany next, third because they feed too much & sit too long at table & I am tempted to eat fruit & last because I am valuable to Mr Snow as a companion– We sit down to dine on a cold chicken & without wine or fruit & get up again in 20 minutes & to conclude Mr Green dont like dogs & I do not wish to subjugate Flora to ill treatment or *insulting looks* & to sum it up I have here a quiet desk & a parlour to receive a visitor in & as a *PS*– I have my bathing room here & *moreover* I can look out upon the river & *besides* there is nothing to do that can't be done here– I have committed little extravagance in necessaries but...I have entered a Regatta Club, entrance fee $5–cost of boat race $15– gain a cup worth $75– deduct $20 as above– $55 gain by boats thus far–& I have bought a sail boat !!!! costing something over $200 but worth $300– gain thereby $100 hey !!!!!! here comes the cloven foot say you, theres the sock he has already split open– but this is not so– ask John and he will tell you that health is capital here & health can only be retained by a relaxation from the desk for an hour or two *every day* after dinner– therefore the boat is my capital– I had very good letters from Mr Cushing taking more pains to say some thing than I expected & telling me he had ordered Barings to send anything to me belonging to him & recommending me to them– I also received a good letter from Bacon he ends thus "I intend to call on Mrs Forbes as soon as I think she will wish to see an old fellow like me who will always take pleasure in doing any thing in his power which he thinks will add to her comport or happiness & oblige one whose friendship I am in hopes always to retain" I believe I named to you in my sea journal that Emma had sent me a bible with a very affectionate & feeling letter & I thought it best to start fair with her & to let her know my feelings exactly I cannot copy the letter at length (which has gone) but will extract from my letter book the sum & semblance as follows–

letter to Emma

...I can never feel as I ought to do or as you expect me to do while you talk of your affection for me & my child & say not a word of Rose or hurry over her name as if a pestilence were connected with it...I have been ready as has Rose to meet you at all times half way, you have been willing to meet *me* upon my own terms but as you have never cultivated any thing but feelings of common civility towards Rose you cannot expect me to be to you what I would be under other circumstances...you could expect nothing but coolness, for my love for her is such that in the first place I will not believe her wrong & if I did I would support her in it so what can you expect from so obstinate a fellow– The whole matter resolves itself into this I cannot love those who do not love her, I cannot respect those who do not respect her & I cannot be civil to those who are not civil to her & I can see no better reason for you not hating my son being also her son, than that you should hate her being part of myself...– I shall always write to you while you write to me & I am so far selfish as to wish for good letters in every day subjects & yours are always interesting as they contain family details & as Mother does not write much I shall expect to hear from you more fully– I believe we now understand each other & I feel relieved for if I had not written this letter I should never have written at all...

I have done pretty well for one sitting and must go to work on business details– I shall continue to write every day or two–

Dr. Peter Parker, shown in the portrait at right, was an important medical and missionary presence in Macao and Canton during RBF's 1838-1840 residence in China. He accompanied RBF on the voyage home in 1840.

DOCTOR PARKER AND HIS HOSPITAL

22 November Thursday, 1838

Yesterday I went at 12 to the Hospital which has been got up here by Dr Parker[96] an American missionary under the patronage of the residents for the purpose of relieving Chinese patients by subscription– there are always a considerable number of Chinese in hospital mostly for disease of the eye– Dr Parker receives no pay except from the society at home– he is a most amiable man, a very skillful surgeon & is looked up to by the Chinese as little short of a deity– He likes to have foreigners go to the hospital on Wednesdays to see the operations so I went & stood by while he operated upon six patients for cataract– a line forms at the hospital when he opens– so I stood by 5–6 cataract operations– one totally blind for twenty years with this disorder– put an instrument a little larger than a needle & crooked like the bowl of a spoon just under the ball of the sightless orb & turning about it the film which had shut out the day was displaced– the eye was covered for a moment & then he told her to look into his face which she did with great joy which she expressed in a lively manner– I had looked on without flinching while some who came were obliged to go out for air– until this

[96]Dr. Peter Parker was born in Framingham, Massachusetts, in 1804, the same year as RBF. In 1834 he became the first Protestant medical missionary to China. His activities were restricted by the Chinese, and he was allowed to pursue his vocation only in Macao and in the "factories" at Canton. In 1835, assisted by British and American merchants, he opened a hospital in Canton where he specialized in diseases of the eye, particularly on the removal of cataracts, but also performed other operations, including the removal of tumors, and began giving instruction in medicine to Chinese. By 1838 Parker had opened a hospital in Macao as well.

moment & then I felt the tears come to my eyes as they do now at the recollection of the feeling expressed as well as those which I conceived for her– After the coaching for cataract I saw a number operated on whose eyelids turned in– the process to cut out a piece of the loose skin above the lid about an inch long across the eye & then to bring the lips of the wound together & with silk thread put in 2 or 3 stitches & plaster the thread to the forehead so as to keep the lid out-turned– A boy about 12 years of age was operated on his eye having become ulcerated & sticking out an inch from his head– he was lashed down to a table & cried lustily– I helped hold him & he was kept in fear for a very short time for at one stroke of the knife the offending eye or what remained of it was gone– after this a tumor of small size was cut from a man's head in one minute– there are many dreadful cases of tumors– where they have been allowed to grow to 10 & even 20 lbs weight & in no other country has the same number of operations of an interesting character been done because in no other country are they allowed to go on at all– I shall go every Wednesday & assist if necessary & if the description makes you sick you need not read it–

I will describe a more pleasant operation performed last night–namely dining with Dent & Co– twenty two present– myself on the left of the host indicating no 2– the custom here is for the host to sit at the middle of the side of the Table– the next partner of the house opposite & the two younger partners at the ends– the most distinguished guest is put on the right of the host the next on the left, the next on the right of the second partner & the next on the left– We had a splendid dinner– I took my decanter of Tea & eat & drank sparingly– the dessert was very splendid & a profusion of fine flowers were strewn among the fruit– the grapes & jellies were good– played whist till 12 & came home & feel quite lively to day having indulged in only two glasses of wine...

Sunday Nov 25

We have got winter upon us at one step & a fire is quite agreeable to day...– yesterday went to Whampoa in my boat with Mr Delano & brought up a new boat of Mr Sturgis...– I am preparing a chamber at Russell & Co with carpet & other comfortable things– the bare appearance of most of the sleeping rooms is unpleasant to me & I am determined to have my comfortable bed, sofa, table, bookcase, & all in good order so as to feel at home– when I go there & to feel that I have a home to retire to which by its comforts may remind me of my real home– I see a good deal of Russell Sturgis every day– he is much liked both by the English & Americans & I shall miss him particularly for he is the only one here who knows you & to whom I can talk of home with any satisfaction– all the rest are strangers– if he goes home he will marry in six months & not come this way again– he is a good fellow–

Thursday 29 November

...I am nominated for the Union Club a social Organization of some 15 to which the best people here belong– rather a given confidence that I shall take Russell Sturgis' place here in a club as I did at home– adieu–

TROUBLE BEGINS

Dec 1, 1838–

...I have arranged to take a sleeping room in Russell Sturgis house being the same house my Brother Tom occupied last & shall soon eat and drink at

R&Co...– I shall visit a place of execution which is preparing for some unfortunate Chinese perhaps quite innocent– to give you an idea of the manner in which the laws are administered here I will relate a late incident– A young man in R Sturgis employ Mr Tessender attempted to smuggle two cases of Silks & was caught in the act– The goods were of course seized & the report of the affair went to the Hoppo or head man of the custom house, he tried to fix the blame first on Houqua because he owned the factory or Hong whence the goods were carried out, failing in this he ordered the Silk man who sold the goods to Mr Tessender to be seized but he stripped his shop and decamped, the Hoppo then ordered the Compradors[97] or head servants who keep the accounts of Cash & furnish provisions to us to be arrested, they also ran away & the matter rests thus now– the Silk man will probably pay two or three thousand dollars to get back & thus the innocent suffer, the ships boat is waiting to receive the goods being under the security or guaranty (as all are) of Mingqua a Hong Merchant– he was also called into the City & all his cargo boats stopped from going in bound– the Chinese never disturb foreigners except through the Chinese & these are often made to suffer (innocent as they may be) for our misdemeanors– Very strong measures are taken every day against the Opium trade & I think it will be stopped entirely– I have arranged to admit Mr Delano into R&Co in 1 Jany 1840 & he is to be here ready to help next summer– I make this early arrangement that our Constituents may know the future parties entrusted with their affairs & also that I may not be pressed with work– he is a very clever fellow & a good worker & now a partner of Bryant & Sturgis Co which hence is to be dissolved–

Indies to St Helena
Canton 2 December 1838

I am well superlatively– received your letters per *Asia*– happy you are not disgusted with the new location...– I do not write to John by this conveyance so if per chance it should get home in quick passage you can say– the market not open– Raw silk ditto–*Asia* & *Vancouver* arrived, *Fr Stanton* not in and next dispatch the *York* in a week or 2– *John Gilpen* here 60 days from the Continents ...– no demand for exchange– all imports dull

Monday– 2 Dec

– Have not been to church yet but I read good books at home every Sunday– yesterday I went to Tingquas (a deceased Hong merchant) house & saw him lying in state– first the street was ornamented with large lanterns & glass lamps painted blue & white which colours are mourning colours here– we were well received all the attendants being clad in long white robes & the relatives in sack cloth garments & caps– we were ushered into a sort of room at one end of which a band was placed which struck up discordant sounds on our entrance intended to be complimentary– at the other end was a sort of altar having a picture of Tingqua before it, on either side were curtains drawn hiding the female members of his family assembled there to mourn, they looked out shyly to see foreigners probably a great curiosity to them & I got sight of several very decent faces & sundry very small feet– The son and grandson came and shook hands with us & were pleased at the holiday they were enjoying– directly behind the

97 A comprador was a member of a group of Chinese whose job was to handle all foreign ship's supplies as well as the needs of the foreign factories in Canton. They were required and appointed to each house by Chinese regulation.

altar lay the coffin a huge wooden assemblage of logs painted black and covered partly with scarlet satin and perfumed with Camphor– after looking at this we were shown the gardens & walks & the rooms ornamented with a sort of tapestry consisting of cloth tablets hanging to the walls embroidered in different coloured devices in praise of the departed & which are presented by the friends & are preserved as tokens of affection– in one corner of the garden the wall was painted with characters describing the early career of the rich Tingqua his virtues, talents &c & it stated among other things that he first came to Canton with only the dress he wore, his pipe & his fan & had risen to wealth & fame by his industry & good conduct–

After this visit we accidentally stumbled upon a theatrical corps in full performance, we ascended a ladder sans cere*monie* or any other *monie* & found ourselves behind the scenes, we were well received & excited a good deal of curiosity– our party consisted of Mr Hunter who speaks Chinese, Sturgis & Delano– the actors were deplorably ill clad & dirty under their tinsel dress & we only staid long enough to see one act, from there we visited the Buddhist Temple of Longevity which commands a view of the city walls & some of the distant hills– here we paid a small fee & eat some from dried fruits & returned home with a good appetite for dinner– Last night our Comprador "Amoo" was seized & taken into the city with a chain about his neck, he was taken from his own home and family with only his under garment on– I went this morning to Houqua to try to have him cleared & he promised to do something– he is not accused of any crime that I know of but unfortunately has a Brother who has dealt in Opium & the mandarins have probably taken him & will keep him until the Brother gives himself up– the government are taking vigorous measures to suppress the trade in the drug which is no doubt demoralizing the people & I think the trade will be given up by all but the most desperate–dined with Sturgis & Delano, Capt Macandray & Green a Brother to David & quite a clever fellow– seems to know you– it is late & I must say good night...–

WEDNESDAY DEC 5

– The Community was thrown into a state of excitement on Monday evening by a seizure of Opium which James Innes[98] was trying to land packed in dollar boxes in the middle of the day– he had *fed* the local mandarin but there happened to be some of the government troops at hand who seeing *one man* carrying off *two boxes* of specie when one is normally a load for *two men* pounced upon them & made a seizure of 12 boxes– the Hong Merchants were yesterday morning called into the City & examined– The coolies or chinese porters who were carrying the Opium were seized & probably put to the torture & rather than implicate Innes they said the Opium came from an American vessel, the Hong Merchant accusing that vessel (the *Tho Perkins*) Puankhequa was directly arrested & the "Keang" wooden collar put round his neck[99] – the Hong merchants were ordered to stop all the cargo boats & to go to Whampoa & examine the *Tho Perkins* and another ship & Puankhequa went with them last night to search with his collar about him which I believe is

98 James Innes was a Scotsman who had worked for Jardine, Matheson & Company since 1832. His job was to smuggle opium up the coast of mainland China. By 1838 he was working as an independent merchant.

99 The keang, or cangue, was a long flat board that prisoners were restrained with. It had a space for the prisoner's head to fit through, so it was a bit like stocks except that the prisoner carried it around with him. Because the cangue was wide and long, the prisoner's hands could not reach his face; unless someone fed him he would starve to death.

a board a yard square or more with a hole just large enough for his neck thus– 
it is said that two ships are ordered to leave Whampoa & James Innes is to go in four days or there will be great trouble & it is said as I know while I am writing that Mr Talbot the consignee of the *Tho Perkins* is also ordered off– both he and his ship are perfectly innocent– to make the matter worse our poor Comprador's imprisonment is a secondary matter & he is still in confinement– his Brother has been arrested & will be executed to day– The government are determined to put down the Opium trade & I think will do it– James Innes is a madman & I should not care if he were caught & hanged– but the Chinese in all these cases let the foreigners alone, stop the trade & squeeze the Hong Merchants of large sums & then all goes on again as before– they never attempt to touch us–

Thursday 6 Dec

Went to a boat Race yesterday PM– Gipsey against the Franny– one pulled by Chinese the other by English sailors– the latter won the race easily– dined afterwards with a snug party of 8 at Mr Lindseys & played whist till nearly midnight– am a little sleepy to day but have got to dine with Mr Wetmore at 1/2 past 4 to day have just returned from presenting a petition at the City gates about the innocent ship accused of smuggling & remonstrating against the trade being stopped– the city wall is about 20 feet thick in the middle is a large gate lined with iron & beyond that a wicket gate, foreigners are prohibited from entering the city but when a petition cannot be presented through the Hong Merchants as in the present case the party desiring to present his petition assembles his friends at a given hour & they walk as fast as they can to the city gate & the moment those on the lookout give the alarm the petitioner & party must run & get in first or they are excluded, to day Mr Hunter & two or three more had quite a run for it they got inside the great gate but the wicket closed just as they got to it– Mr Green and Mr Wetmore with myself & some 20 more got there a moment after– the place inside the wicket was filled with soldiers prepared for our reception & to keep off the rabble which they did with rattan whips without any ceremony– after a moments parley through an interpreter four were admitted inside the wicket & presented the petition– but it was not received by the Quong–keep but Houquas son being there received it & said would be put in a fair way of being received– before this we had met the Hong Merchants at the Consoo house which is a public place of meeting for foreigners & the merchants– they stated the smuggling transaction & said the Vice Roy had ordered them to send away James Innes within a few days & if the order was not complied with the said Hong Merchants would have to wear the wooden collar–they accordingly said Mr Innes must go & if he did not go within a certain number of days his house would be unroofed & foreigners were forbid harboring him– we listened to this & the meeting ended after half an hours session by telling the Hong Merchants that it would not do to enter any foreigners house to do violence– that the other residents had no control over Innes & that the government must take its course–& so ends this day– The Chamber of commerce meet this afternoon to give an answer to the Hong Merchants letters to that body– You must know the Hong Merchants are responsible for the good conduct of foreigners, they own the houses we live in

& let them to us & if any one does wrong the Hong are called to account– notwithstanding all this responsibility– the Merchants have no power to enforce their orders therefore when they have any thing to complain of they talk to us & we obey or not as suits our convenience– for instance the Hong Merchants have repeatedly prohibited all decked boats form coming up to Canton & it is only within a few years that they began to come up & during the last year they have not only come up openly but bought Opium at all times & smuggled it & other goods too– now the Hong Merch[ants] tell us they must not come– but they do come & they poor devils have no means of stopping them except by stopping all trade & thus cutting off their own noses– but I must dress for that important matter of dinner & will only say I have just lent Ahoo Two hundred dollars to get Amoo our Comprador out of prison & we hope to have him back to night –

FRIDAY DEC 7
Nothing new today except the arrival of the *Fr Stanton* at Lintin from Manila bringing no important news – I am off in the morning for Lintin to examine into the repairs of the old ship & intend to go thence to Macao & come up with Mr Sturgis by the inland passage – I believe the Hong Merchants have abandoned the idea of demolishing the house of James Innes but they insist on his removal– I have seen Houqua today & he looks ten years older being very much harassed by this affair – I hope it will be settled in a day or two but it may not –...I shall be gone a week or ten days I suppose – so with love to Bob & your mother & sister *Sal* I am dearest ever thine – Robert

AT HONG KONG AND AT MACAO

HONG KONG BAY – BARK LINTIN
DEC 12 1838 –
My dear Wife –
I came here two days ago to see to the repairs to the old *Lintin* –I find she requires less than was expected & is the best ship on the station –... I now write by a vessel going to Manila thinking there may be a chance home from there before one from here – There are several vessels nearly ready but the trade is suspended at present...it is said...[the] rascal [Vice Roy Lu] having been in the habit of winking at the opium trade – receiving large fees for the same has been reprimanded by the Emperor for want of vigilance in suppressing the trade & he [the Vice Roy] now makes a great show to do away with the opium he has incurred – some people think the trade will be opened again soon – & that there will be no unusual impediments to smuggling opium – others say the vernment are determined to suppress the latter & doubt if the legal & regular trade will be opened for some weeks perhaps months – it is certain that Houqua & the other merchants of standing are very much frightened –...

Yesterday I took a long walk on shore with Mr Delano & amused ourselves with rolling rocks down the precipices – Green (David's brother) is here & appears to be a very clever fellow –I am delighted with your account of your house & require only a continuance of letters to make me perfectly contented &... I shall write to Sally & your Ma for first direct ship – give my best to them & tell Bob to write to me – for he improves so fast that I suppose he will be able to write when you get this, he will make his mark at any rate – I'm thine ever Truly Bennett

Thurs 18 Dec 1838
(Macao)

Dear Rose

I will now give a sketch of my proceedings since leaving Canton on the 8 Inst[ant] in the good sch[ooner] *Alpha* in which we proceeded to Hong Kong the anchorage of the stationed fleet where we spent two days on board the old *Lintin* raining most of the time – went to Macao in a Lorcha[100] – were all night going over & arrived there very hungry just in time to enjoy a good breakfast at the Tavern (Thursday 13) then invited ourselves to dine with Uncle Jimmy – ourselves consisting of Delano & myself – I forgot to say that I received your letter of 30 June while on board *Lintin* – it came to Batavia per *Arabella* & up from there per an English vessel & I wrote to you from Macao in reply via Manila – On the morning of our arrival at Macao a boat arrived from Canton bringing an account of a serious riot at Canton – it seems the authorities undertook to execute a Chinese Opium dealer in the square directly under the American Flag – a thing never before attempted & tried no doubt on purpose to insult the foreigners – as soon as the apparatus say a cross to which the native was to be tied & strangled appeared the foreigners collected & remonstrated in such terms that the thing was removed to the water side – great numbers of Chinese had collected & were evidently opposed to the execution & disposed to aid the foreigners in putting it down – unfortunately some drunken sailors were present & were disposed to kick up a row – as soon as the foreigners had done all they intended to do namely to stop the execution in that place they would have retired but owing to the sailors getting in to a row with the lookers on some stones were thrown & in a few minutes a general battle with sticks & stones began but as it was in vain for forty or fifty unarmed men to continue with five thousand of the mob moving – they retreated to their factories pelted with stones & banged with sticks – they closed their gates & for two or three hours sustained a regular siege with out making any resistance, the local mandarins with a few soldiers tried all they could to put down the mob but did not succeed till a large force arrived from the city who instantly restored order & encamped in the square to protect the foreigners from further insult – before the row ended all the windows & doors in the front factories were broken & Mr Sturgis front gate entirely demolished with a brick wall in front of it which was used as it was pulled down to pelt the houses – the mob also broke into the factory next to ours but perceiving several armed Gent inside ready to fire the moment they entered – they did not think it prudent to go in – during the evening the square was more quiet than usual & no further trouble occurred that we have heard of – I am surprised that some of the Gent did not fire upon the perpetrators of this outrage – it is fortunate for some of them & perhaps for me that I was not on the spot – Delano & myself had taken away almost all the guns & ammunition expecting to have some shooting before our return – I could never have stood quietly & seen a mob tearing down my doors & I believe the vernment would have borne any one out in defending his house under such circumstances – We dined on Thursday with Mr Sturgis & the children John & Lucy – played whist after a walk till 11 oclock – dined next day Friday with Capt Howland & his pretty little wife & Mrs Cole (Capt Coles wife of the *Asia*) a stiff & uninteresting woman – Mrs Pierce & Mr Pierce sister also dined there – the two last very pleasant women – Miss Pierce – half an inch shorter than you & consequently not very handsome– after dinner Gents of the party walked

[100] A lorcha is a light 2- or 3- masted vessel used in China, Siam, and the Philippines which has a hull built on the European model and rigging like that of a Chinese junk with battened lugsails.

& returned to tea which is the custom here – we had among other good things a Yankee *minced* pie made by the fine hands of Miss Pierce & I eat of it to such a degree that I dreamed all night of the devil &... all sorts of demons – after tea we got up a round game at cards with Coffee for money & played till 10 oclock when we went home to our solitary pillows "not so solitary nuther" for I had some Fleas & Flora to boot –

SATURDAY

– breakfasted at home & were about visiting Mr Sturgis to inform him that we would not refuse an invitation to dine with him – when we came from Mr Pierce & we again had the pleasure of dining with our country women – walked after the same & I dis*persed* & went to take my Tea with Mr Sturgis then went with him to Sandy Robertsons & played whist with him & *Old Chinnery* till 11 oclock losing $3.75 it being the custom to play for 25 cts per point short whist – you must economize my dear & save this $3.75 – made arrangements on Saturday to start next morning & accordingly at 10 AM started on the boat in which my numb fingers are now trying to write – a chop boat by the inner or legal passage is a thing of great comfort & small speed with a head wind but there is no danger of molestation & some prospect of game – we began our voyage with a fair wind & warm weather all the sides of the boat open, but at 12 the wind came at NW with rain & at 8 we anchored for the night only ten miles from Macao during the whole of yesterday we combatted a North gale & clear cold weather also moving very slowly & only arrived at Hongsham about midnight – here we were obliged to stop to be examined by the custom house people & did not leave the said place till 9 AM – at Macao I fortunately fell in with Copley Greene *Ashew* [101] wanting a master & as I wanted a man I hired him & a cook the latter for the voyage only – we replenished our stock of provisions at Hongsham & here we are pushing the boat along with Bamboo against wind & tide – through a flat but rather pretty country, many pretty views peeping out from under the distant hills – we are scarcely half way to Canton at this time (Tuesday 11 oclock) our other passenger is Mr Allport who is in Dent & Co house & has a wife at Macao – he drinks all – port – Delano & myself go upon Beer, Tea, Sherry, chocolate &c&c&c I never was in better trim, am hungry all the time – but I must go up & get a walk for my fingers will neither write nor spell –

THURSDAY 20 DEC

arrived here (Canton) yesterday at 3 just in time for dinner which I eat at Russell Sturgis' find all quiet here – Innes the bone of contention having departed for Macao – the trade is still stopped by the Opium business & the Hong Merchants declare they will not open it until the foreign Schooners & Sloops engaged in the trade retire from the river – the British Superintendent of trade Capt Elliot seems inclined to *back* the Chinese authorities in getting off the sail boats & I hope they will drive them away as it is unfair that the innocent & guilty should suffer together...

SUNDAY 23 DEC

...no arrivals from the US – I am now established at Russell & Co excepting my sleeping which I do at J P Sturgis till he comes up – Mr Snow is quite unwell & I do not like to leave him alone – dined yesterday with Sturgis, Delano & a few

101 Ashew was a Chinese servant who was brought to Boston where he worked for several years for Copley Greene, Rose's cousin.

friends – eat prudently, played cards till 10 & went to bed after a walk –

I am sitting for a miniature for you with Floras head on my knee & I think it the best likeness that has ever been taken, Russell Sturgis also thinks well of it – I shall send it to you for yourself on first ship – perhaps it will not be quite black enough for I began my sitting before I went to Macao – having got burned a little & wishing to make a small allowance for that I fear he may go too far the other way – No boat sailing lately for want of wind, neither have I pulled for I do not feel the necessity of exercise –I am now of opinion that this climate is better than yours certainly during six or eight months of the year & *as good* the rest – I wish most heartily you could be transported to Macao on a sunbeam without incurring the *discomforts* of a voyage (the *dangers* are nothing) but as this is improbable I have made up my mind to grin & bear the separation...it is expected of any Lady established...[in Macao] that she should entertain all transient visitors of her country women, imagine yourself living at Macao & obliged to take in all the Capts wives & other loafers... Then you must see all Americans & even English Gentlemen who visit Macao, they go there as a matter of course must visit all the ladies & if you dont see them they talk, it is a place of much gossip – it would also be a serious interruption to my business & would I think influence people to send consignments elsewhere, then in the end – exposure & risk of frequent voyages to & from Macao would – cost time, money & health & give you as much cause of anxiety as if I were at sea – on the other hand if you or the child were ill I could be with you in a day or even half a day at this season & I should have regular advices & the eternal anxiety to get home would not be gnawing at my heart strings...if my health were to be as it now is I might regret that you could not be here so that I might stay 10 years or more until our child or *children* were ready to be educated & go home with a large fortune – I now look to health first, *Competency* second – one of the inseparable obstacles to your coming would be the impossibility of your being separated from your Mother & Sally and the cruelty in bringing them particularly the latter to such a place as Macao – No No No it wont do – the three years are *one sixth* gone & time will pass rapidly when I begin to be actively employed –

Write me fully, keep a journal, remember you have much more leisure for this than I have & infinitely more material, any thing will be interesting – leave a margin on the left side of your pages of an inch thus so that I can paste all your letters as received into a sort of book & have them before me – this plan I will pursue in future myself & recommend you to put all my yarns together instead of bundling them promiscuously into your drawer – Flora is lying on the rug before me with her nose almost in the fire as usual– I dont think she is very well– she was sick at her stomach yesterday forenoon but as this is not uncommon complaint for females I am not very anxious –

HOLIDAYS AND DINNER AT A HONG MERCHANT'S

Thursday 25 Dec

– Christmas day...Last night I read an hundred pages to Mr Snow in Bancrofts US & then went into Russell Sturgis' & played whist till 11 oclock then three Gents who were there & good singers began & sung out the Christmas eve over a supper – We had a good deal of fun & it reminded me of some of the evenings we used to spend in Temple Place, we finished by sundry speeches made to another persons motions which you have seen, we had a merry evening & I did not get to roost until 2 AM –

Am engaged to dine with Wetmore & a large party to day – should like to be released but as the young members have invited friends at home I should get out of the frying pan into the fire – The trade is still stopped & it is reported to day that an Opium smuggler a foreign boat has been seized at the entrance of the river – I fear we shall have nothing to do for a week or two longer – the trade has been suspended so long that we shall be overhead in work when it opens – I suppose you will eat your Christmas dinner quietly at home perhaps at Mrs Greenes[102] at all events I shall think of you & drink absent friends – I have not begun to school you how to educate our boy but will ere long – there is only one thing to guard against at once namely spoiling his stomach, *dont give him sweets* –

Thursday 27

– We had a party of 26 at Wetmores & I drank Tea instead of wine – among the guests were the two Rev seniors who *dispersed* after a song or two had gone round – we had rather a stupid time got up from table at 9 & played whist until 11 – when I deserted – two invitations to dine to day which I declined – the report of a boat seized was not true – trade still shut up – went to the hospital yesterday but saw nothing more interesting than a stump of an arm healed which had been cut off only a week before & a woman almost well who had a cancerous breast removed the same day – I have got a set of paintings for young Dr Warren[103] representing some of the enormous tumors which Dr Parker has removed with entire success –this is to pay Warren for advice which I got of him on one occasion – yesterday Houqua sent me seven boxes of fine Tea which I will send per first opportunity – I am getting anxious to hear from you again a ship leaving the middle of August ought to be here now – This putting off the trade is a grand thing for me as it throws all the business of the year into 1839 – most of the Commissions are usually earned in Dec – the devil always helps his own – Good Night

Sunday 30 Dec

– Friday dined with a small party at Lindseys who gives a capital dinner in the best style every dish as well as the soup Tureen of beautiful plated ware as well as the dish cover rich in the extreme, glass and silver to match, he is a remnant of the East India Company & keeps up the style in which they lived here, he is a man of extensive information & has travelled a good deal in India & been all over the coast of China – we had a pleasant evening – a game of whist to wind up with –

Last night I went with J C Green, Greene of Manila (your cousin) R Sturgis, Delano, Mr Price, Capt Howland, Mr Everet, Mr Bradford to dine by invitation with Mingqua one of the Hong Merchants & we had a Chinese chop stick dinner preserving the Chinese Etiquette all of which I will try to describe – We were first received in a large hall well lighted by Mingqua & his cousin & partner Qunghing – seats were arranged for us one half on one side of the hall & the other half on the other the etiquette being for the most distinguished guest to sit in the left hand & the host at the extreme right, a small teapot on the right of each chair – after passing enquiries of health the tea was brought in the small porcelain cups with covers & stands which we sipped a la chinese without sugar

[102] Mrs. Greene was Rose's maternal grandmother.

[103] Dr. John Collins Warren of Boston would gain renown for performing the first public surgical procedure using sulfuric ether at the Massachusetts General Hospital in 1846.

At right, an engraving based on a Thomas Allom drawing shows the richness and ceremony of a Mandarin's dinner party, here with toasts being given.

or milk, in about five minutes dinner was announced & we marched into the dining room, our hosts *following* – on either side of this hall were chinese chairs covered with scarlet cloth richly embroidered in colours – near the centre two tables about 6 feet long & 3 wide with chairs covered with the same surrounding the same – the tables were placed thus –

the hosts seated themselves at the right hand corners & the guests to the left leaving the further ends unoccupied; at this point were dishes of fruit & flowers fancifully blended & having a beautiful appearance –

on the side of the mark were about 20 different dishes consisting first of small pyramids of fruit seeds fancifully arranged tapering off to points with a flower, the variety of colouring in this arrangement was particularly pretty – they

were for ornament exclusively, the other dishes consisted of dried fruit & fruit in syrup, roasted almonds with the shell & skin off, water melon seeds & various other delicacies with here and there a little plate of orange cut up into mouthfuls – each person had a small porcelain saucer highly painted about 3 inches in diameter, a spoon of same material, a small shallow cup & saucer & a porcelain cup for a stand to rest the spoon in – a pair of chop sticks being two ebony sticks the size of a pipe stem, square at the handle & round to the other end, shod with silver at the end – these are held between the thumb & fore finger same thing as a pen is held & must serve to pick up what food you require – The spoon being held in the left hand & much as a temporary receptacle for the food on its way to ones mouth & to dip up the liquid of which there is a good deal in all their dishes – the first step was to fill up our cups with a warm liquid distilled from Rice & commonly called sam–shu which is taken warm – We drank health by raising the cup with the left hand holding the fore finger of the other hand to the bottom of the cup & after emptying the same the inside of the cup is turned towards the party with whom you are drinking to show that none is left it being orthodox to drink bumpers on all occasions – after this we nibbled a while on the comfits when a cup to each appeared (about the capacity of the coffee cups at home) with cover filled with a mixture of several bits of ham, garlic, onion, &c&c&c– then another of birds nest soup which is very palatable –I forgot to mention that each person was provided with a small triangular piece of red & white paper in which a tooth pick was stuck – after drinking three or four cups all round & eating about four courses – the two hosts took off their caps of ceremony & their outside habits of rich silk & their string of beads & exhibited beautiful silk gowns with a belt in which a pen case was stuck & a watch with key and seals ensconced in a case like those you hang up at the head of your bed only richly wrought with an opening showing the face of the watch – after eating of about six courses of mixed boiled meats all cut up in small bits – & of which it is usual to taste, I began to flatter myself it was almost over as the servants continually changed the cup with new liquor – after these six courses we got up & walked around the room took a whiff at the pipes or cigars if we liked them better – in about 15 minutes we were requested to be seated again – the tables had been cleaned of all except the ornamental fruit & flowers situated on the end of the table which is fixed – the other part this side the mark is a double leaf & moveable so that when the table is to be cleared the whole board without any cloth is taken up by four men & carried off dishes & all & a new board deposited which has been previously laden with some twenty new things – there was this difference however in the second load or table namely – that each one being provided as before helped himself out of an octagon porcelain giant bowl to what he wished – the said bowl No 1 being a boiled duck done to shreds requiring no carving & surrounded with bits of ham, small bits of pork, onions, carrots &c– after tasting this all round no. 2 came containing fish & shark fin all in small pieces with a good deal of liquid & so on with different things for about 5 bowls – then came little octagon carved cups with roasted bits of birds & fried pork done brown & such things about 3 courses – drinking with this health frequently in a very strong distilled wine tasting like a decoction of dried raisins – I now began to feel that I could do no more & could not conceive of more being required – when lo– a chafing dish of a porcelain construction was put in the centre of the table with coals in the centre & a space round the fire filled with bits of everything among other things fried frog which was very good – & surrounding this principal dish were 7–8 bowls of hot boiled *something* say everything – we could only *look* at all this pretending however to taste all which is the fashion – just as we were congratulating ourselves for the third time that nothing more could come – a bowl of Rice to each was brought – then the whole was cleared away except the apparatus to each person & in came a large tray filled with a whole roast pig, a leg of mutton, several ducks, fish &c &c – Mingqua announced that this was a present from his Father prepared for us by the family cook – I wished the Father & the cook in the red sea – these viands were all placed on two tables fronting our two tables, then a servant took each thing on a dish separately & walked up to our tables, held up the dish & making a graceful bow, presented it & returned with it to the other table – now a couple of servants probably cooks in clean drapes & red caps, cut up into small pieces all these things & by this time empty dishes being placed before us – these were loaded with the new meats – here ended the eating I confidently hoped & expected –We got up & walked about as before for a quarter of an hour smoked & were walked back to another course of oranges, pears apples, dried fruits & fruits preserved in syrup – just after we were seated a large waiter of beautiful flowers was bought to Mingqua, Jessamines, Roses, &c which he took by the handful & promiscuously threw all over us & our tables filling the air with fragrance particularly of the Jessamine & pink or Carnation – we eat of all the fruit & drank Mingquas Fathers health & many others, your cousin Green sang – several songs winding up with Auld Lang Zyne & finally we took a bumper at my suggestion to absent friends, & departed home – being followed to the door first where we shook hands, then to the stairs where the ceremony was repeated, then to the outer door into the square where we finally bade adieu to our hospitable host & his partner at 11 PM – heartily glad to get away pretty sober, yet much pleased with the dinner which was done in the best style of Chinese Gentry – –

Thursday 3 Jan 1839

– Took my New Years dinner at home & my place at foot of the table which place I shall fill till Green goes when if Mr Coolidge dont come I will assume the head – Green is after all a wonderfully good man of business & I would give a good deal for his head – The Trade still continues suspended so far as the prices of Teas are concerned but ships are allowed to discharge cargo & business is going on again amicably – My miniature is done & is thought by those who are familiar with my face to be a good likeness but R Sturgis, Delano & Green complain of a scared look a raising of the brows not natural to me – the fact is my eyes are a little weak & the strong light made me stare to keep them open – I think it very good & all agree that it is a good painting & that it is too old –besides I am sure it cannot have a very amiable expression because I was kept waiting every day by the rascally painter – this made me feel cross besides which I had no one to talk to – I shall send it however & if you dont like it I will send another & you can give this to Mother but you will be the best judge after all & if you are pleased with it...I am now overhauling the papers & accounts of the home & gradually qualifying myself to take the lead – I trust Coolidge will not come out for we have hands enough without him & as he has pocketed over One hundred thousand dollars out of the home he ought to retire & stay at home –

My health is unexceptionable – weight is 160 lbs which is only 2 pounds less than my maximum at home – Love to your mother & Sally & all friends – went to meeting on Sunday – the Episcopal service used –

BUSINESS AS USUAL

Sunday 6 Jan 1839

Went to church like a good boy & heard an excellent sermon from Dr Parker on the subject of the instability of life & the certainty of death & using other forcible reasons for keeping in new eternity & a due preparation for it he said "How ardently the sojourner in a foreign land away from all he loves looks forward to the day when he shall again be united to the friends of his bosom, how much more important then is it for you my friends to look forward to a reunion with the dear friends who have preceded you to another world, we are here but for a day compared to the endless residence in a place of eternal bliss or punishments" &c &c – he understands the soul as well as the body & I have seldom listened to a sermon with more pleasure to any sermon at home –

We have had no arrivals except from Manila & I am getting impatient to hear from you how you got through the summer in Town which is always trying to young children – I presume you are not suffering from the heat at this moment – On Friday I sailed down to Whampoa some 14 miles dined, visited old Stetson the mate of the *Vancouver* under whom I served two voyages before the mast in 1819–20– I went in a sail boat with no crew but an English Captain but shipped Capt Macondray to come up with us – was seven hours afloat in the cold yet am perfectly well – Mr Wetmore chief of the next house in consequence to *us* told me he had received letters from Mr Alsop recommending him to make terms with me which he says he would have wished to have done had I not arranged with Russell & Co – the business of the latter has been enormous – *say the nett gains of my share* for one year *of the house does as much as last two years* will give me near *$40000* Forty thousand dollars I calculate for only half the business but the second year my share will be nearly double – I tell you these things only for yourself & your mother & Sally & furthermore I say a continuance of the business depends on my staying my time out & you are bound to contradict anything which goes to say I am to leave sooner – which I shall do if I get enough of the *ready*[104] but there is very little prospect of my having enough while such a prospect & such small additional time would give me more than enough...– my Taylers bill since I arrived 3 mo is $15 & all for jackets – my boat bill _______ half a loaf of bread & a gallon of saki – J C Green will retire with *$300,000* Three hundred thousand at least, John with one hundred & sixty or more, Coolidge one hundred & twenty – you see dearest my prospects are most flattering & I cannot be too grateful for the privileges I enjoy –have patience then dearest console yourself that I am not exiled for nothing as Tom has been – my spirits are always good, full occupation keeps me happy – I have the sort of business I like the accounts & hard work being done by the clerks & the younger members – keep up a cheerful heart then & write often by the direct & indirect – our latest letters say to 15 July come through England & lastly 15 July by a ship bound to Calcutta – I am expecting daily to hear you have my letters in whale ship *Chariot*

Tuesday –

No news from home or any other quarter – I bought to day two pieces of Silk one blue Black & one Quaker brown or faun colour – your Mother & Sally are to have their choice & the other is for you, the drab can be dyed they are both very good quality – I have been out sailing these two last days fine weather – I took a long walk in the back streets to day & had a good laugh at the expense of a poor boy about 8 or 10 years old – who saluted me with some billings–gate[105] & as I turned at that instant to go homewards he thought I was after him & he began to hobble off with a large basket every moment looking round very much alarmed & supposing his time was come– I walked fast & kept up with the little urchin who finding the chase becoming desperate stopped & pulling off his thick shoes started again with renewed rigour but having a heavy load I gained on him when the poor little devil stopped in utter despair & began to bawl holding up his hands for mercy & he was much relieved when I passed on without taking any notice of him – they have such an instinctive fear of foreigners that he would have died of fright if I had stopped even to comfort him – I send you per *York* a few late numbers of the Chinese

---

104 Ready was short for ready money or cash.

105 Billingsgate refers to coarsely abusive language or vituperation and gets its name from the Billingsgate fish market near a gate called Billingsgate on the Thames River below London Bridge. As early as the 17th century the Billingsgate market became notorious for foul and abusive language.

Repository[106] which will tell you something about China & about the late troubles – the medical parts will be interesting to Dr Bigelow & Jackson & you can lend them to them – I shall send two bound volumes of 1837 & 1838 by a more direct opportunity – I forgot to tell you that I was vaccinated according to your *orders* some time ago it did not take – I hear to day that little Lucy Sturgis has symptoms of small pox in a mild form which may be fortunate – Flora quite well & sends her love –kiss Bobby an hundred times for me – Good Night

11 JANUARY –

Got some cold & took a "purification" last night – am better to day though the skin of my head is a little too tight – shall not give up my dinner nor my sail this afternoon – my coffee Pot is made & is a beauty will go per first direct ship with two little filigree baskets & a card plate which I merely send to you to *look at* & will write about them when I go – they are for Sale as an adventure for *MY SON* to be kept going until he is 21 – so you will be prepared to effect sales promptly & at high price & return the proceeds in hard money with a Mercantile account – of the whole transaction – dont let him know about it for fear of making him speculative –!![107] we are rather busy at this moment preparing for the *York* to go tomorrow – so adieu for to day

JANUARY 12

The *Yorks* letter bag is about Closing – I have none of yours to reply to have been hoping something would drop in – my cold is a little better to day but not improved by a walk yesterday Now that our work is over till next ship I shall attend to it – I wish you to send me a real good thick flannel gown made in form of a surtout only loose & not open behind with a pocket in the bosom & buttons in front – get a tailoress to make it – also send me a dozen linen cambric Handkerchiefs large size – this is all I want in the way of comfort – Remember me to Mary Motley & her husband & to Copley & all other friends who think me worth inquiring after – perhaps I shall write to Mary when she answers my letter – I hate these dispatches for every time a ship goes I feel as if I had again parted from you –

these are the only moments I have when my spirits flag at all – Mr Snow our Consul says any man who might be well would get ill under his circumstances & any man being ill who would not get well under mine ought to be sick – he has been working hard all his life is now 55 years old & gets hardly enough to keep life in him & is partially supported by Mr sturgis who gives him house room free –he is quite sick all the time with cough & pain in chest – yet he is as well as he was three years ago – I have written a very stupid letter to your mother & shall write a very stupid letter to Sarah per next ship –& hope to get something in return – I have sent the miniature to care of Cary & Co to be sent you by private hand & I have no doubt you will find it quite good –

Adieu then dearest...ever affectionately Yrs, Bennet

CANTON 18 JANUARY 1839

My dear Wife –

...the only occurrences of note are first my dining with the *Union* Club for the first time as a member last night – at our own house – had a very good time,

[106] The *Chinese Repository* was a quarterly paper published in Canton and Macao during this time. Its editors were Protestant missionaries. The greater part was made up of essays on Chinese history, literature, and travel. The rest was saved for current events with comments on them and transcriptions of documents, both English and Chinese.

[107] This is the first of many hints sent in the letters to Rose that she is expected to sell goods sent by RBF from China to various friends and relatives.

played whist until 12 oclock – won $3 – the club is merely a social circle of the elite of Canton we are by rule all hosts & all guests wherever we go, have a supreme right to find fault with the wine or any thing else & to call for whatever we want; this abuse of constraint makes it pleasant, they meet weekly, go or not just as you please – my next great thing was a visit to the hospital on Wednesday where I saw an operation for cancer, my nerves were not effected in the least though several spectators nearly fainted – the poor woman bore it like a heroine & is now very comfortable – I suppose you think me a fool for witnessing these things but I think it does me good & gives me confidence in the use of the Knife & one can hardly say that he could see such things done till he tries...I have given Capt Macondray a letter of introduction to you he has been here ever since I left in 1832 & is a very good fellow – I have also given a similar letter to Mr Hooper brother to Sam Hooper who is supercargo of Capt M's ship – I have seen a good deal of him & he will tell you that I am not labouring under a great depression of spirits, he appears to be a good natured wishy washy sort of body – I shall not do these things much because you are so apt to play the part of the "spirit of the water" undone[108] & at such times you are not so interesting – Capt Mac[ondray] goes home to a wife & children & has some $60,000 which *marks* stand for Sixty thousand dollars & which I helped him to as much as any body

Canton 18 January 1839

Mrs R B Forbes

Dear Wife

...all is now going on however as usual but Teas are high & the prospect for profit to those engaged in the trade is not very brilliant – Every ship that goes makes me think of home & wish I was the happy man embarking...I am quite happy & only require some good letters from you to make me satisfied – Russell Sturgis is about at Macao & we have consequently one man less in our society – As the chances are very small that this will reach you before letters leaving a week or two hence by a direct ship I will only say Love to your Mother & Sally & Bob

Monday 21 Jany

No letters from home yet – went to church yesterday like a good boy & heard a very good seminar from Mr Dickinson – among other good things he assured us we should meet our friends in Heaven & that there were various grades of happiness there, so I have made up my mind that I *may* go there though I cannot expect to enjoy a high station – I have accepted an invitation to a large dinner at Jardines tomorrow & am going to a great public dinner on Wednesday – both given in honour of Mr Jardine[109] who is leaving the country after 14 years residence he is very rich & I suppose very happy –Thursday is club day – I expect to get sick by so much dissipation

---

108 RBF refers here to Rose's propensity for crying.

109 William Jardine (1784-1843) was born in Scotland and entered the China trade at 18 as surgeon's mate on the East Indiaman *Brunswick* in 1802. During fifteen years with the East India Company he established connections in India and China that helped him establish a strong business shipping Indian cotton and opium to China. In 1825 he joined Magniac & Company, and one of his partners was James Matheson, another Scotsman with business experience in India and China. In July 1832 the partners established Jardine, Matheson & Company, and when the East India Company's monopoly on the China trade was abolished in 1834 the new firm was well positioned to serve as agent for much of the business from English merchants and shipowners. The firm's connections in India, and its large role in the opium trade, made it the richest and most powerful of the British houses in Canton in the 1830s.

JARDINE'S FAREWELL DINNER PARTY

FRIDAY 25 JANY –
on the 22 dined at Jardines with about 8 people, dinner cold, crowded & uncomfortable, a good deal of toasting & cheering & some wine drunken – got home at 1 AM quite sober & had little or no head ache next day the 23 when I dined at the companies Hall[110] with a public party of 140 who gave a dinner in honour of Mr Jardine – The Hall is about 100 by 60 feet (I guess) & opens into a handsome verandah some 50 or 60 feet square paved with large marble tiles & looking out upon the river – this Verandah was closed in with cloth & ornamented with evergreens round the pillars & flowers in pots all round the balustrade & some drapery between the pillars & the letters in different coloured lights W J (Will Jardine) at one end – So fitted up for dancing – the

The ornate house and water garden of a Chinese merchant is shown in this engraving made from a drawing done by Thomas Allom during his time at Canton.

[110] Company here refers to the East India Company, which had an absolute monopoly on and control of the English trade at Canton up until 1834. Its building, twice as large as any other, had a wide veranda supported by pillars and was the most imposing of all the factories.

music came from one of the ships at Whampoa & was very fair – the compy were seated round a table forming a hollow square thus

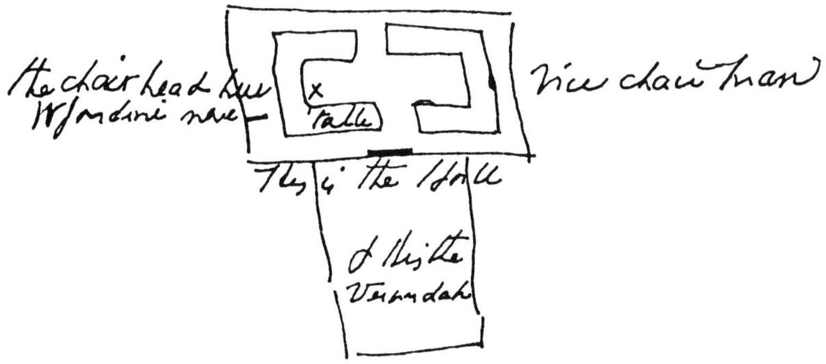

I sat at the cross & directly opposite to the gent & with my back to the whole Compy [RBF's abbreviation for Company] nearly – we sat down at 1/2 past 7 to a splendid dinner – I took my decanter of Tea & drank nothing else till it was all gone say about 1 oclock by which time all the regular toasts & some of the regular songs were disposed of & volunteer toasts were in demand – after various speeches from the guests & a dreadful blundering one from Mr Turner the President or "the chair" as he is technically called – the little spectre looking Mr Bridgeman the parson got up & said he had a sentiment to offer which he would "premise" by a few words – he said he hoped the name of Mr Jardine would not only be transmitted to posterity through the well known virtues of our guest but through another medium – before this can be effected there is an important ship to be taken – hear hear hear! shouted the Compy – Mr B went on to say he wished Mr J a pleasant passage & hoped on reaching his native land he would meet the fairest of the fair who would listen to him & smooth his path through life – I give you then the future Mrs J – then followed a great shout of course –& music to the tune of Willy he'd a peck o malt &c – Mr J got up & thanked the Co – doubted the expediency of an old man who had seen China in 1802 marrying one who must be very young to deserve the title of the fairest of the fair & he also doubted whether such a step would be likely to answer the end of sending a representative to China but if he could find some dame 'fat, fair & forty' he thought he might be disposed to put his neck into the noose – it is said he has his eye on a widow lady who was out here – We then huzzied louder than ever & my Tea being out I took to sherry –& being called upon for a toast I got up & gave, Scotland – we have done honour to England & to America I now give you Scotland – I am proud of my birth right as an American but having some Scotch blood in my veins I give you Scotland – may it *never* be said –

Old Caledonia's hills are bare
Land barren are her plains
Bare legged are her maidens fair
And bare breeches are her Swains
I give you Scotland – huzza huzza huzza huze –

I however left out the last line – As Jardine & full half the Co were Scotch it went down very well & was succeeded by a Scotch song – by this time the wine began to have its effect on many but as I had taken but little I was as fresh as possible – I eat but little as I had partaken of a large dinner the day before – Dr Parker spoke feelingly having been assisted much both in money in attendance at the hospital for Jardine was formerly surgeon of an Indiaman & still retains his love for the sea – the guests then departed quite full of good time & soon after the "chair" cleaned out & the vice chair Mr Lindsey took his seat as I had been just opposite the chair the latter Gent nominated me for his vice & I could not say no though I should have been very glad to have retired about that time, we had now become somewhat thinned owing to a large part of the Co dancing in the Verandah & the shouting & singing was beginning to be very uproarious – at this crisis Lindsey who had given us strong & hot punch in bumpers got away say about 3 AM & I was called on as his Vice to take the chair I accordingly walked *over* the table as he had done previously & presided much against my will & I ordered silence in vain, I appealed to them as gent, as Englishmen, as friend to come to order & the more I shouted order, the louder they responded, order, order, order, sport the chair, chair, chair, chair, hear hear, hear at last a moment of comparative silence allowed me to give a sentiment –

Union – not merely political, not merely commercial *union* but the *union* of principle, the *union* of the heart & soul for good purposes without which all other *unions* are as a rope of sand – Gent – may the *union* I speak of be perpetuated between our honoured guest & ourselves *forever*

during this short speech the cries of *Union*, principle, heart heart, soul, soul, forever &c &c were almost enough to have set a sober man crazy – I was now determined to quit – but at that instant a young Scotchman cried – "let us clear the table & send those d__d Parsees [Indians] home & then we will have supper!!!" the Parsees alluded to took up this insult warmly & a scene of confusion was likely to have followed if I had not insisted on my authority of chairman entitling me to put this misunderstanding right – I cried out order & stood up on my chair & demanded whether I should be supported or not, support the chair, cried twenty voices, twenty more cried supper, as many more cried chair, chair, & two or three who were very *far* threw themselves on me to support me as they said – at last I got a hearing & brought the only two remaining Parsees one on each side of me & explained to them that Mr ___ did not intend to insult them & I made him confirm this & shake hands it was of course imperatively necessary then to have a parting glass by way of good fellowship & reconciliation – All the lamps had gone out by this time & there were only three or four stumps of candles left in a silver branch candlestick from which I had removed the glass shades to prevent them from sharing the fate of the glasses which had been broken in great numbers – so I seized the branch and walked to the other end of the hall & took my seat (all this time assuming the most grave & dignified face & action) but being quite merry – We then called for champagne & had a glass all round & dispersed in good humour – among a great many funny things that happened Mr Hunter one of our younger members who was very drunk, asked me with a most ridiculous attempt at gravity in the middle of my toast if I was acting the part of a representative of Russell & Co or in my individual capacity of RBF – he was afraid the dignity of the house would be compromised I suppose – after leaving the hall we marched in a body & gave three or more cheers under Jardines window & various others elsewhere & at 4 AM I bolted from the *very* small remnant of the riotous party & got home – first calling into Mr Snows room & *awaking him up* to enquire how he was & if the noise had disturbed him!!!

I must confess in dust & ashes I was quite high & in proof of it was made entirely sober in half an hour after I got home when I was sick at my stomach –

I heard of many queer things I did & said which I had but a faint recollection of among others my taking an Englishman Mr Thorn by his red beard & telling him if he would only shave it off & get a new hat (he wears a wonderfully old straw one) he would be quite a decent looking man – I was only pretty well yesterday & did not go to club which met at Mr Artells – I eat my broth & took two blue pills last night & am now quite well again & trust I may never have to go to such another dinner – you are aware that I never go half way in any frolic but I committed myself much less than many who retired or were carried home earlier – Green went at 2 having declared he would not stay after 12 – Delano in waltzing was *let go of* by his partner & tumbled headlong against a flower pot & cut a gash in his head an inch long – but he came home in better order than I did – in short it was just like all great public dinners which may be called great bores – I never went to a public dinner before that I recollect – We are dispatching the *Westminster* to day for England & I must go to work & write some letters so adios...

TRADE CONTINUES SLOWLY

Monday 28 Jan 1839

On Saturday night we heard of the arrival of the *Niantic* below & yesterday got our letters as well as some others which came from Batavia by an English vessel – I have all yours from July 5 marked No & July 29 to Aug 4 – the intermediate ones are in the *Roman* not yet in & on the way to Calcutta I will take them up at the first moment which I have time

– July 5 letters contains your expressions of determination to be hopeful, industrious, economical & I have no doubt but you will carry out all these good intentions – I have often trembled to think of your state of feeling after my departure – yet I always felt that our dear Boy would be all in all to you to make up for my absence more than anything else could – I feel that it depends on him for if he should be taken away I could not stay my term to leave you alone, but I cannot believe such an infliction is in store for us...I saw a notice of Mrs Cabot & Miss Warrens presentation to the Queen in our English paper & the account of the coronation which you propose sending me has been here these three months – You must not think of tiring me by any little thing that occurs, every item must be interesting to me in my exile & I hope you will keep up the journal form –...you should write weekly at least – I write to you oftener –

July 29...announces the birth of young Mr Motley weighing 8 lbs – I congratulate my friend Mary upon her happy deliverance – Boy just learning to say Papa & Mama...

July 30 Hale came to dine...Park engaged – Mrs Prescott dying – this I regret very much – Mrs S R Mellon very ill – now *dead*...

Aug 5...plan of reading & instructing our boy – your plan in this is capital & you will be able to instruct me too for commerce will absorb all I have learned of history – I notice what you say in regard to the management of our young rascal... *you* may indulge him too much –

August 4... Charles Green called – I am much obliged to him – Copley gone to Halifax what for you dont say & you are driving about in his carriage & quite proud I dare say –

I think it will be a good thing for you to keep a memo of letters dispatched – say their dates or numbers & by what vessel & route & when you write put down occasionally a list that I may know if I get all & always *direct* the letters in your own hand for it sometimes happens that a clever fellow will deliver private letters & I have sent a muster [sample] of your writing to the Consignee of the *Roman* requesting him to send me any letter in that hand as they cannot interfere with his business – it is often necessary to detain letters a week – so tell George not to cover your letters by an envelope –

...No 5 is of 8 Sept from a hot August day you had jumped into a cold September one – in your former letters your nurses child was sick & in your last you had got a Mrs Flinn...some fine lady who volunteered to nurse Bob for the pleasure of it – I am glad you thought of sending Bob to Milton on the 18 Sept & my letters from Emma & Mother give good accounts of him...I see Temple Place is still vacant John did not say a word about it – I have only one long private letter from him – he must have had an anxious time of it & I feel almost guilty that I did not stay & see matters settled...I calculate you have just now got my letters from Anjier – having now acknowledged all letters up to 8 Sept – that I have received I will go a little into general subjects – the *Niantic* came consigned to J C Green above Wetmore & Co shewing that Russell & Co are considered much better with him than without – We have a prospect of several more ships soon – all goes on well – I have a cold & am out of order in consequence of my debauch at the Jardine dinner & shall not expect to get round again for a week – Emma gave me a very good account of the Abbot[111] jubilee & sent me the odes &c- she is a very good correspondent – I had also a letter from mother in praise of the Boy & a long one from Mr S Cabot very kind & feeling in answer to me... got nothing from Bacon – tell Hillard he must write to me – I had begun to get very impatient for letters from you & was much rejoiced to get these per *Niantic* – You know I am not fond of enlarging in the feelings but you are equally aware that I do feel as deeply as any one can – You did not say a word of Heard[112] & John says he had hardly seen him since I sailed – I fear he & Coolidge will hatch up something to the disadvantage of the house – I committed a great piece of extravagance in buying $25 worth of china such as the Chinese have themselves in rich homes – some of the china is superb – the 10 cups one within another – cost 2 1/4 dollars – there is a waiter of plates which I think are very handsome the six large cost 3 1/4 the six small 2 3/4 for the six – There are ten sets of dishes – one of 4 & one of more the latter all match together, that is they fit together & make one large dish with compartments for different kinds of fruits or sweetmeats – the 6 bowls & saucers cost only 1.50...I thought these things would do to distribute very sparingly among your most attentive friends – There is one thing you neglected in your letters & I am grieved thereat namely Flora – not a word of Flora – !!!!! Only next to Bob she is my affection – she will be confined[113] in ten days – hope she will have better luck than she had last time...John says he has wished for me a thousand times to assist him & he speaks with great affection of his visit to Naushon...good bye for to day –

---

[111] Abbott refers to RBF's aunt Mary Perkins Abbott. Forbes referred to her in his autobiography as "Aunt Abbot" and described her as his "admirable counsellor." She lived in Exeter, New Hampshire,with her husband, Dr.Benjamin Abbott, who was head of Phillips Exeter Academy, and had three children.

[112] Augustine Heard was born in Ipswich, Massachusetts, in 1785. He sailed as master on the brig *Caravan*, acting as both captain and supercargo. In 1812 he became a leading captain in the East India trade. He sailed for Canton in 1830 and became a partner of Russell & Co. Ten years later he formed his own company and returned to China to assume charge. At home he incorporated the Ipswich Manufacturing Co. and founded and endowed the Ipswich Public Library. He died in 1868.

[113] Being confined was a term used to describe the time during which a woman was giving birth to a baby, in Flora's case puppies.

Jany 30

was literally done up yesterday with a bad cold & stiff neck brought on by imprudently bathing in the morning after a sweat – think of such imprudence! I however worked at my pen all day & lay down at intervals – to day the pain in neck is better but I have had a busy day writing & this afternoon have had occasionally a sharp chronic nervous pain shooting like a hot knife from my neck up to my left temple & I cannot now write half a page without being seized I then lay down & it goes off in a few minutes but it is so severe when it comes that I can't sit up a moment – it is really muscular – I am well enough otherwise for my cold has all gone into my neck & I can not bend it any way – You always found me rather stiff necked – alias obstinate didn't you...Another ship announced to day the Rob Fulton suppose she will bring something from you –letters not yet up – there comes the pain & I must wait a little –Its all over again but that twinge reminded me of the vice & the one screw more I had once a time like this at Nahant when I was vaccinated but not equal to it – As here – formerly Copley's man is now with me & when I scold him for not rubbing my neck well with liniment he says "Suppo you stay home, Missi Foxe maker do more better for me, my no unstand" – you did not tell me how your Mother was in health nor how you was yourself nor if you had heard from Tom – I must beg you to write me on all these points – you did not name T P s family nor Sally Perkins who I am sure is good to you – curse this pain – it gives me no peace– I wish you were here to hear me scold & hold my head when I had done – What a queer devil he is says your Ma – well why should I prolong my suffering & us by *writing* (not writing) being too stiff to writhe in agony –I wont & so with a great deal of love & much kisses to our dear Boy that is if he has not grown above that I subscribe myself most excruciatingly Yr Bennet

Canton 1 Feb 1839

My dearest wife –

That was an infernal pain to be sure with which I wound up my last lines of 30 into – I went to bed soon after however & slept it off & got up yesterday quite recovered stiff neck all gone, my cold still lingers about me & I fear Dr Cox will insist on my taking some of his vile pills – while writing he has just come in he says take two blue pills to night & I will give you a draught to take several times a day – your late debauch has upset your biliary organs you must be content to diet & take pills a few days – he recommends a glass of wine however & this part of his advice I shall take – We have been so busy for a week that I have not been to sail, indeed walking is best for me when I am out of order – The *Roman* is in & probably has rest of your letters but I have received nothing from her yet, confound the Consignee I say

Canton February 2 1839

...My dear Rose

No 5 came first & gave me an account of your well being & the progress of Robertino & I cared little for the nurse until I got No 3 which gives an account of your nurses *going dry* & your efforts to replace her, pendent I suppose he was quite unconscious of all the trouble he was giving & I can readily conceive of you running around Town like a hen with one chicken full of business & now that it is all over & Bob is probably crying for more pudding you can laugh as well as myself about it if you should have any more children in my absence you *must* nurse them yourself like a good wife that you would be under such circumstances, & then you will be perfectly independent – I received a very good letter from Hillard who came out in praise of our young man & says he is the noblest fellow & winds up by saying how much he resembles me – this I call comfortable, he says your domicile not only neat & comfortable but elegant & the very height of his ambition is to live in a house equally good he says you would throw a charm around any cabin or barn...the China new year holidays begin in a week when there will be nothing doing & I think I shall take a run down to Macao for a week or two & change the scene – it did me so much good when I went before that I like the prescription pills than standing at a desk all day...I should like much to see Bob in his china dress screwing up his eyes – I beg you wont let him get any of your tricks (making up faces I mean) I have hardly had time to read over fully your letter rec to day per *Roman* to 6 Sept but I am rejoiced to see you begin to write in your naturally witty style & I anticipate many of the letters I used to talk about – how little did I think I ever should hang my happiness on Rose Smiths letters received in China – Tell Sarah I will never send her anything if she dont write to me as your Mother seldom writes to any one I cannot expect it of her – you must tell her however that I have the "highest respect for her" – give my regards to C W Greene when you see him & thank him for advising you of a chance to write to me which is the highest favour he can do me – Adieu dearest Keep up a cheerful heart & believe me faithfully Yrs RBF...

Mon 4 Feb –

Went to Church yesterday & heard an exhilarating sermon from Mr Dickinson on the subject of conscience – I am glad that we have decent preaching here for nothing carries one home more than to meet in church & if we had not good preaching I should not go – I have not got entirely over my cold & have an excellent appetite again – yesterday after dinner took a pull to the neighborhood of The Fatee Gardens & visited an establishment for the education of geese & pigs – The entrance is a shop for the sale of rice and liquor distilled from rice called Samshew – inside is a large space roofed in where men are employed pulling – the rice & paddy, others removing the chaff from the seed, others distilling Samshew, the fuel being the hull of the rice, & the ashes from the same carefully saved in large baskets, on one side of the distillery are several large pens filled with hogs of different sizes – each class by itself the floor of the piggery of *clean* tiles in the centre an ingenious tub around which a dozen or more could feed the swill being passed into a fixed tunnel in the centre of the tub – sleeping places to each pen & a separate location for the manure which was strictly respected by the pigs – on the other side were immense coops of geese about 20 feet square or rather elevated pens with boxes underneath to catch the dirt & surrounded with a trough filled in one side with chaff in another with grain &c – each goose & pig pen contained different classes of critters that is those which were not to be sold soon for market were fed more sparingly – then a second class fed a little better & a third who were stuffed with bran & grain & good food to be ready for market & finally a hospital for the lame & sick & in the rear a pond of artificial manufacture for a bathing place – these pigs & geese were kept here merely to consume the spare grain & the chaff &c being secondary to the Rice establishment, in the rear of all was the great granary full of rice in the hull – the whole space enclosed was about half an acre all covered with a tile roof & clean in every particular – I was much amazed with it – the Chinese are very economical people & also very ingenious – but this is not to the purpose I read over your letters again yesterday & do not find any thing in particular that requires reply – yet every line is interesting to me – I enter fully into all the little details about our boys progress & according to all the accounts I hear he will be a prodigy indeed – I fear he will be made too much of between Sally & Grandma & you – on no account let him get into the way of stuffing cake, pies & sweets of any kind – remember his Father has suffered more or less these last twelve years – I expect to suffer an hundred years more on account of a weak stomach which became so on account of want of care in eating as much as from any other cause – I sent his first adventure per *Trenton* a few days since consisting of a filigree Card Plate & two baskets of same the whole cost about $50 you must make some of your friends buy them the duty will carry the cost to $70 – I also sent you a solid silver coffee pot won at the regatta & at the spring meeting I expect to win the sugar bowl & cream pot to match – you will then admit there is some virtue in boating after all –

Thurs 5 February –

no *Robert Fulton* letters yet though that vessel has been in more than a week – I suppose one of your missing numbers must be on her...– went to sail this afternoon but there was no wind & we had to pull home – I have written to Charles Greene, to Copley, Hillard, Aunt Abbot, Aunt Jas P[114] & Sarah & I believe every body to whom I owe any thing but I shall give up all private correspondence except to you, Mother, & John for I find myself often scratching letters which will probably be considered giant bores –

There will be no further opportunity for the sea for two or three weeks before which I shall have your letters acknowledging my letters per *Chariot* up to 26 July...One day is so much like another here that there is little to say & I will not trouble you with my oft told talk of how I miss you & how I wish you were here or rather how I wish I were with you – the man for closing the dispatches has come & I must say once more adieu – kiss our dear Boy an hundred times for me & believe me ever Yrs Bennet

Saturday 9 February 1839

My dear Rose

I resume my journal having just received a dateless letter from you per *Robert Fulton* but as it says something about my having been gone 11 weeks I presume it must have been written in the latter part of August – it was short & sweet & acceptable – I received letters from John & am now looking forward to further letters from you per *Morrison* which ship was to sail about 10 October & would bring me letters written after my *Chariot* letters were received – I have a long letter from Joe Lyman[115] to 31 July which was very acceptable as it gave me good accounts of Brunswick – I also got a letter from P S Forbes dated at Rio Janeiro acknowledging receipt of mine of April announcing my intention of embarking for China in June...*Not a particle of interesting news since the Gopler* & the approach of the China new year prevents all business negotiations –Floras single pup born two days ago died & I fear she may get over the literary propensities of her former days – she is very well & as reconciled to her hard fortune as any mother could be under the circumstances

[114] Aunt James P. refers to the wife of Uncle James Perkins.

[115] Joe Lyman was a cousin and good friend of RBF's.

THE CHINESE NEW YEAR

4 February & China New Year –
the incessant firing of crackers & guns has kept me awake the last two nights – I have been out of sorts for several days – on the 11th we had cold rainy weather which kept me within doors & I got a severe cold & bilious head ache & having nothing else to do staid at home & took the prescriptions of Dr Cox & am perfectly well again...I have now determined for the millionth time to be regular in my diet – to eschew fruit & to chew only of one dish – R Sturgis has come up from Macao where he left his children well – There is one good thing about me I am easily frightened about my health & so shall be more prudent –

15 February –
Having little to do to day & being well I started at 10 AM in a sail boat with Sturgis (Russell) Delano, Hathaway & went to Whampoa say 10 miles working the boat ourselves & returned by an indirect route some 12–14 miles more arrived here at 4 PM – staid at Whampoa just long enough to get a snack of cold "vittles" –

dined with Delano on our return & have had hot damp weather for four days thermometer at 75 to 78 whereas it is generally at 40 or 50 at this season, to day it was beautifully pleasant with a fine south wind & I enjoyed the excursion – we are all somewhat burnt with the sun which is not usual in February here – The new year holidays are celebrated by a continual firing of crackers & guns & beating of gongs & all the river craft as well as the people are rigged out in their gayest dresses – every one having the least semblance of a claim on you demands a Cumcha[116] & the dollars walk out of ones pocket very fast – I have received some 20 & odd boxes of Tea which I shall send for first ship for sale after selecting a box for Hillard, C W Green, Dr Bigelow, & sending you one or two to distribute where you please – I have also received one of those pieces of beautiful Mandarin Silk of my favourite colour dark purple or claret or mulberry like your figured Setting gown *in colour*, this will make you a handsome new pelisse – I shall send no Tea to any of those who are able to buy or who have proved themselves too selfish *to give* – Flora quite well & sends her love she is deplorably lazy here & as Mr Green does not like dogs & always scowls at her she keeps clear of him & pays long visits to Mr Delano & Mr Snow where she is made much of...

Sunday 17 February –
Our hot muggy weather has been succeeded by a cold rainy North wind very much such a day as you have at the moment likely enough – went to meeting this morning & heard an excellent sermon form Mr Dickinson...the Tea market was in a bad state, here every thing is in the worst state for our constituents & we as the agents naturally feel for them it being very unpleasant to be identified with bad business even though we get our Commissions for doing it – all imports are unsalable & Teas & Silks high –& under these circumstances people will always be dissatisfied even though you do your best under their orders...good night

Friday 22 February 1839 –
The disagreeable weather continues & I have not had my boat sailing for a month – on the 20 we got letters of business from the US to 27 October per *Panama* – but her owners ordered the Captain to leave all letters outside until we had a chance of doing something for them – so I have none of yours to

116 A cumshaw is a gratuity or tip.

acknowledge & shall not get them for several days this is a state of suspense which makes me very cross & if I had any cause to feel anxious about you and our boy I should go mad – luckily my last letters were good though only to 5 Sept or there abouts – we had the unwelcome & distressing intelligence to communicate to Wetmore (head of our rival house) of the death of his wife which the Capt of the *Panama* reports, she had been confined three weeks before he sailed of her first child & had got pretty well – but the Captain knows no particular & could not say whether the child was alive or not – Mr Green communicated this intelligence to Mr Wetmore – before I knew it & he is of course very much distressed – I wrote to him a letter yesterday telling him that no unmarried man could appreciate his feeling that having seen a beloved wife brought to the brink of eternity under similar circumstances to that which had deprived him of his best friend I could sympathize with him &c&c – he replied & expressed his gratitude for my letter – I really pity him though I am inclined to think he is not over sensitive – His wife was an own cousin of his, & you will remember having seen her at T H Perkins – I look upon this as a misfortune to me personally as Wetmores house & ours have always been rivals & some of our friends would give their business in Greens absence to Wetmore & Co if Mr Wetmore was here –

As he intended to go home this spring we expected we should retain all our business – but I fear this event will keep him out here & if he stays he will get some of our constituents away from us – I am excessively anxious to get your letters as they would contain the acknowledgement of my first letters from sea & would be in consequence more full– however there is no remedy but to wait patiently – the ship *Moroccan* that sailed a fortnight before the *Panama* is not yet in but must come daily & by her we shall also get letters – the *Panama* was consigned to Wetmore House the two last voyages – I think from Coolidges last letters to the house that he will on finding how the land lies come out here perhaps with Heard & try to *oust* me & get up a house which he will want to call Russell H – time will determine – on these subjects remember *you are to know nothing* even in talking to *John* – I give you my fullest confidence relying on your discretion & knowing you will not abuse it – the present members do not want Coolidge or Heard in a new establishment in 1840 – at the end of this year we shall have no better right to that name (Russell & Co) than Coolidge & if we leave him out he may come out & insist on getting under way in that name *leaving us out* in which case we shall probably agree to give up that firm on both sides & do business under others – I anticipate trouble with C if he comes out & he will no doubt divert some business from us – but we must take our chance & get along as well as we can –

23 February – Saturday

– We have nothing new today except the loss of a Brig at Mazatlan[117] on the coast of Mexico belonging in part to J P Sturgis & the same that Tom Sturgis went in – the Captain perished & was the only man drowned out of the crews of 9 vessels totally wrecked – we hear of the Capture of Vera Cruz & the death of Santa Anna[118] – here all is quiet & I am impatiently awaiting your letters per

---

117 Mazatlan, located at the mouth of the Mazatlan River, is a seaport in Mexico at the entrance to the Gulf of California. It was and still is a place of considerable foreign and domestic commerce.

118 This information was false. In 1838 when the French attacked Vera Cruz, Santa Anna took command of the defending troops and beat back the foreigners. Santa Anna went on to be president of Mexico and fought the United States when war broke out in 1846. He did not die until 1875.

Morrison & *Panama* both which ships are in

26 February –

Am still without my letters although Russell Sturgis & Mr Innes have got theirs per ship *Morrison*...the way our letters are delivered is this ship arrives & the Captain has orders to send up only the owners letters that the said owners may avail of any good news that their ship may bring to purchase goods more favorably than if every body had letters to same effect this is all fair enough – the Capt goes to Canton some 80 or 100 miles from the ship & under the best circumstances the letters cannot be got up under three of four days & are often detained a week or more on board the ship below – in the case of *Panama* which sailed 28 October we had only one letter from her owners saying that there had been a considerable rise in Teas within a few days & ordering purchases –Mr Green our honourable premier was brought up with the owners of that ship & he favors them in every way he can & although the market is in a state to make it impossible to avail of the news he has had the letters unnecessarily detained & I am very savage in consequence – I think it would be well for you to tell George or whoever informs you of opportunities to write just one line by every direct ship leaving *it open & putting it under cover to the consignor of the ship here* saying – only – that all the family are well – this would relieve me of some anxiety & it is very annoying to know that one has letters close by & cannot get them or even know whether his wife & child is alive or not – We are leading very inactive lives lately – but little to do & the weather has been damp & cold preventing us

Chests of tea are loaded into a lighter in this painting by Tingqua. The "French Folly Fort" on the river at Canton is shown in the background.

from going on the river...the monotony of a Canton life is such that one actually craves work & time flies much more rapidly & pleasantly when we are very busy – In about three weeks more you will hear of my safe arrival here & perhaps sooner & I calculate on my letters being more & more interesting (Your letters I mean) our boy will be making daily progress & you will have an inexhaustible fund of material to write about from home alone – I hope however you will not confine yourself to him alone but tell me all the news as well as the gossip & do not forget to name the Sturgis family who seldom write much themselves– I shall not resume goose quil until I get my letters per *Morrison* & *Panama* – mean time with much love to...Sally & Bob –...

Wednesday 27 February –

Went to sail last evening as usual & returned just after sun set – in landing we were confounded to learn that a chinese implicated in some way with opium trade had been executed in the public square in front of our factories – When this was attempted on the 12 Dec last you will recollect the residents interfered & succeeded in having the execution carried into effect in the usual place – a mob ensued & we (that is those who were in Canton) were driven into our homes – the Chamber of commerce issued a remonstrance to the Government to which the Gov replied that they would carry any future execution into effect and that they would send a sufficient force to protect the mandate of the law – this was looked upon as a mere threat by most people – I thought they would watch a good opportunity & carry their threat into effect & accordingly – at 5 1/2 oclock yesterday an hour when most of the foreigners are walking over the river or sailing or pulling their boats a guard of one or two hundred soldiers arrived in the square with several officers of note & in ten minutes the poor urchin was executed & removed – every one was quiet & shocked in the greatest degree & a good deal of excitement prevailed but as the residents could do no more than talk they did not interfere – a parting of the English was holden last night & they agreed not to hoist the British flag again – this morning our Consul Mr Snow called a meeting of the Americans & I was nominated secretary & we voted that the American flag shall not be hoisted until Mr Snow should receive orders from his Government to hoist it – the fact is within the last two years the Opium trade has been made a regular smuggling transaction carried on in spite of law & reason by a parcel of reckless individuals – formerly the trade was considered legalized by the connivance of the mandarins & local authorities – the Government having determined to suppress the trade have pursued various severe measures against it & among others have taken the lives of several poor people while those high in rank who have connived at it even unto the Vice Roy – his sons are allowed to go free – there is little doubt but the Gov are determined to suppress the trade & we as a house have written to our constituents to say we can receive no more of the drug – when the dreadful effects are brought before our very eyes we cannot compromise ourselves by dealing in it & thus perishes one of our most important sources of business – the Gov have no doubt a right to execute their criminals where they please & all we can do is to express our indignation quietly in a dignified manner – We have no fear that they will attempt the insult again as they have now carried out their threat – old Houqua who has not been well for some days came out yesterday & tried to soothe the irritated residents & to explain that the Gov had ordered it & it could not be helped but he fainted & was carried home almost insensible – I fear these troubles will kill him – he is the go between from the Gov to the foreigners & he has to bear the brunt of all the difficulties between them – but to more agreeable subjects – when I got home with my nerves somewhat shaken I found your two sheets per *Morrison* No 10 – beginning 3 Oct ending 12 – the only unwelcome piece of news being the death of little Gordie Holland which came directly home to me having received a kind letter from him [the child's father] dated 5 Sept in which he thinks of his boy & ours in fine health – I shall write to him in mean time tell him & Susan that they have my deepest sympathy – Your No 2 & 4 are still on the way as well as 6.7.8.9 – I expect to get No 11 per *Panama* not yet up from below – in No 10 you merely allude to Gordies death & to having received my journal per *Chariot* but do not say when...it wont do for me to undertake to recapitulate all your information – it is enough to say I have read over & over the eight clearly written pages & every word is interesting & your account of our dear Boy fills me with joy & gratitude – You do not say a word of your health so I conclude you are either perfectly well or so much of an invalid as not to mention the subject as none of my other letters give me any cause of anxiety in this subject I conclude you are well...I have a long letter from John 10 Sept giving an account of a jaunt to Naushon & lamenting my coming as a great deprivation & saying he would willingly have given up all luxuries to have kept me &c&c – I hope he will never feel whatever is my fate that he decided it – I aim to be free of a load of debt & obligation – He says my affairs are turning out worse than we expected & I have no doubt but I was a beggar when I left he says "if you are not likely to bound well in China do not stay an hour but come home & I will give you capital enough to get on keeping only enough to exist on & if you succeed you can repay me if not I shall have enough left" –

he has done all I could have asked or expected...I sat up late last night reading papers &c & must say good night & God protect thee & thine –

March 1 –

The letter bag of the *Panama* is at last up but as the letters are not yet distributed I have only taken one directed to me namely your No 11 dated from 14 – 19 October – the ship sailed on the 28th so I hope I have something more under cover – I notice that you had called on the Dr for Bob on account of his teeth but I am not at all anxious about him – his constitution is good & he must get along well – I notice that he has been much admired & would give a great deal to see him – I hope before many months to have his portrait – I thank you for naming your Mother & Sally in your last which you had before neglected if Sally dont write to me I will *cut* her dead – in the course of two or three weeks more you will get my *Mary Chilton* letters & the Chinese dress in which our boy will look very funny...I was out yesterday in my boat & again to day with fresh breezes – Flora generally accompanies me on all excursions either to sail or to walk – she has but little ambition however & I am almost disgusted with her filthiness – I have half a mind to send her home for a pet – she may as well have the mange there as here – my sheet is out & I will say good night & God bless you –

Sunday March 3

Since my last date I have your No 12 beginning 20 Octo ending 24th – this was directed in Georges hand writing & consequently was not taken out of the letter bag so remember not to put your letters under cover except in your own hand writing simply directed to me & marked private should Bryant & Sturgis, Bacon or any of your friends have a ship coming enclose your letters to them with a request to forward with the ships dispatches to me on arrival & do not refer to business even if you should *accidently* know any thing about it...the expression in your letters fills me with the first *pang* I have had since my arrival here in regard to your acting up to your principles – you say "were it not for *you* I think I should long to sleep the sleep that knows no waking" – you say you must bear up & I beg you to put on good courage & take the ills of life as I do them & bear up against them – do not give way to fancies, act up to what you know is right & remember if you get into a morbid state it will be very hard to get out of it again but I hope your depression was but momentary & for your Mothers sake as well as mine bear up – remember not only my happiness but my success in my undertaking depends on the spirit with which I work if I have good accounts of you *I will be happy* in spite of absence – but why should I use these arguments when they are *copies of your own*...I got nothing from Mother or Emma by the *Panama* – John says the former is in better spirits – & Margaret in better health & he reports you looking very well & your own assertion that you are or was better than you had been gives me relief – John says he gets into Town at 10 & leaves at 2 & has hardly a moments time to see you or any one in Town – I think he will get tired of a country life soon though he dont say so...I often leave my business to go to my letters to you & make such time as I can get & having only a business atmosphere about me I should not be surprised to find myself quoting prices of Teas to you...You had been to Watertown & was well–received by Mr Cushing – I write to him occasionally & I know he will do all he can for me without saying much about it – I shall send his boys some toys bye & bye...– R Sturgis leaves us soon & goes to Macao & Manila he will be a loss to me as well as to our general society tomorrow we collect a few friends by Delanos invitation to give him a farewell dinner – he reports "Tell Rose I am much obliged for her friendly interest"...he says you must write him a line by vessel going to Manila & he will pay you in forwarding your letters to me – so pray do so & tell him anything that may interest him particularly he tells me the news of Caroline Bartletts death – which you have not mentioned –

good night –

Thursday 7 March –

Nothing new – all is quiet here – We are dispatching the *London* to New York & are consequently pretty busy I shall forward by her all the sheets since the *Trenton* & *Gopler* sailed – although she is a slow ship I shall cut out of the book the same to send by the next dispatch & I now desire as all cases where you get duplicates –that you will send back the old paper copies by Boston vessels that I may have my files complete & know to what you refer when you scold me – I have just been to ask Houqua if he had my commands –he was out – he has not been well for some days & has lately fatigued himself very much in committing to the ground his Father who died 35 years ago – it is the custom in many cases to keep the bodies of the parents until a lucky spot is found to bury them in – it is said Houqua has kept a man at pay learned in such things & he has been searching the neighborhood these twenty years to find good earth & at last has hit on the place – the chinese pay great reverence to their parents & this is a remarkable instance of it – It has never occurred to me till Russell Sturgis suggested it that you would be alarmed at the late events & the newspaper comments therein – the fact is there is not the least danger of personal safety here the chinese policy invariably tends to embarrass trade & if this wont do they stop it & if they were to punish us they do it through the Hong Merchants by preventing them or forbidding them to trade with us – if we undertake to rival the law forcibly we must expect to reap the consequences –I care not if they execute one every day in front of the factories so long as they remove the corpse when it is done –for I should take my boat & go on the river & smoke my cigar till it was over – I came here to make money not to interfere with the laws & shall mind my own business until I am ready to pack up & go home – I have written to every body I believe that I am in correspondence with – I send you the last No of the Chinese repository & the late papers – if you dont read the papers give them to George for the Editor of the Atlas who sends me papers occasionally & if you read them give them to him when done with –dined yesterday with Russell Sturgis at Delano's & shall dine again at club to day if we get through our work to enable me to do this I must cut short my _ of private yarns & say with much love to you & Mother & Sarah & any quantity of the same to Bob – adieu & may all the good angels preserve you –

Every affectionately Yr RBF...

I shall send your new pelisse silk per *Niantic* to go in three weeks & will be home in a week after this being a faster ship & perhaps before her –

EXPLANATION OF OPIUM

Canton 10 March 1839
Sunday

Dearest Rose –

Since the *London* sailed we have been quite busy with several arrivals from India and several dispatches, wrote enough yesterday to give me a head ache but am quite well again to day – The Imperial Commissioner who is sent here to put an end to the Opium Trade & the export of bullion moved yesterday & we shall soon know the fate of the Opium business & as this has been a very important branch of business I will tell you something about it that you may speak learnedly – The import of Opium has gradually increased under the connisance of the local authorities until the quantity has amounted to near 50,000 Chests worth nearly 15 millions of dollars– it has been in general use & although contrary to Law the trade has been carried on with greater facility than any other branch of business here & it has generally sold readily for cash down – fifteen millions of dollars is a great deal of money & all at once the Gov determine to cut off this trade which has been demoralizing the minds, destroying the bodies, & draining the country of money – the trade has been carried on by the most respectable merchants here & the great & honorable East India Company who have been Lords of the East has been the cultivator of the drug in India consequently there has been no moral feeling of indignation connected with the business & if any thing were wanting to give it respectability in your eyes I would mention that I made my first fortune by the same – Two years ago the earnest attention of the Government was drawn to its deleterious effects – & they have gone on from one step to another until the sales are entirely cut off & this vast amount of property is laying in our stationary ships at Lintin unsalable – the owners of it are in England, India & here & the agents for the sale of it here who have advanced large sums of money on it in India before they heard of the entire annihilation of the trade must be sufferers to a large extent –

I will tell you what I mean by an advance on Opium – A speculator in India has ten thousand dollars *more or less* he wishes to buy forty or fifty thousand dollars worth of Opium to send to Mr Smith in China for sale with this ten thousand Dollars so he applies to Mr Smiths friend or agent in India who allows him to draw a bill on Mr S requesting him to pay forty thousand dollars to a third party – this bill sells for cash which is given with the ten thousand dollars

On the previous pages are opium smokers at Canton, depicted in an engraving based on a painting by Thomas Allom. The engraving above shows opium chests being unloaded from a vessel.

to pay for the fifty thousand dollars worth of Opium, the Opium is sent to Mr Smiths consignment & the person who bought the bill also sends it to his friend here for collection, when it [is] due here say 30 or 60 days after the arrival of the Opium Mr Smith must pay it – this would all be very well if the Opium was saleable but being unsaleable where will he get the money – the Opium has been received for the security of the bill drawn against it – the object being to the man who consigned it to Mr S –to get a profit on it & Mr Smiths object being to get a Commission on it & perhaps a freight of so much per chest for his ship that happened to be looking for freight – Therefore Smith to procure consignments owns a vessel ready to bring on Opium at $16 per chest & agrees through his friends to be drawn upon for half or two thirds its value & he pays the bill if he has capital on hand or if he sells Opium – the person who buys the bill may be & generally is an indifferent person who gives cash for it & expects to get his money in China & he has bought this bill rather than carry hard money with him which would be expensive on account of the bulk & risk, when his bill gets to Canton he presents it to Mr Smith & demands payment – Smith says I can't pay, there is no sale for Opium & you must protest the bill & look to the person who drew the bill for payment with damages but what can he expect of the drawer of the bill or man who had but $10 thousand dollars – so Smith fails & the poor victim can get no redress except to take the Opium which is not half the money his bill cost him – now most of the English however here have received Opium & advanced large sums in India for its purchases as I have described & they must lose heavily or break in toto unless this Imperial Commissioner slacks the reins & allows the trade to go on & on this point hangs the fate of half the Commission agents here – Our Mr Green in contemplation of leaving here before this about a year ago wrote to Indian friends ordering them not to advance a dollar on Opium & thus we by the greatest good fortune almost alone & cannot be affected by the unfortunate state of things – the English houses here have bought largely on their own accounts & we fear a crash among them – we do not own a catty[119] of Opium though we hold a good deal on consignment on which we have made no advances – Our house never was in so safe a position & although the cutting off of the Opium trade is a serious thing even to every person who sends here to buy Teas & Silks yet we shall suffer least of any – How does it effect the Tea & Silk men – ! I will tell you –

Mr B wishes to send a ship to China from Boston – he goes to Mr Ward & asks for a letter of credit which is neither more nor less than a letter authorizing R&Co in China to draw on Barings for a certain sum to pay for the cargo of the ship – this letter comes to us & we want to use it so we draw a bill which is a piece of paper requesting Messrs B&B & Co London to pay so many pounds to Mr so or so – now to get the money for this bill is the rub to enable us to buy Tea & Silk – we offer it to your friend Mr Smith or any body else & he says he dont want to pay – he cannot sell Opium & therefore has no money – The people who sell opium often buy large sums of these bills – but the Opium trade being cut off there is no money & the bills are unsalable except at a very losing rate to Mr B – who sent it here to buy his Tea with – thus does the Opium Trade affect every one trading here & us too for if we cannot sell B's bill in Barings we cannot get money to buy Tea & so we do not get our Commissions – you will ask why does not B send you money to buy Tea instead of Bills – I reply because in ordinary times the bills are saleable at a good rate – the seller getting here a dollar for every sum representing a dollar in London on the face of his Bill & when this can be done it would be folly to send dollars because they cost a premium at home & must be Insured at a premium & if the ship is lost the funds dont get to China – I have now endeavored to explain to you not exactly as I would to a merchant how the houses are situated here – & some of the risks even of Commission business –

Mar 11 Monday

...to day have been quite busy loading the *Francis Stanton* & *Vancouver* – Russell Sturgis has left us for Macao where he will stay a few weeks with his children & then...to Manila he...went away in rather high spirits – he has been in country 5–6 years – has lost his wife & gained only gray hairs – when I look at his situation I am satisfied with my lot – also lost a Mr Lindsey who is a very gentlemanly member of our Club & are about to lose Mr Inglis also one of our best men – they have gone home with very different prospects owing to the bad turn things have taken in the Opium trade –...the Commissioner has called upon [the Hong Merchants] to produce two of the opium brokers whom they never saw perhaps & in default they are threatened with heavy fines – Houqua it is said is called upon to go to Macao with the Commissioner to look into the Opium trade... – he is in great distress & says he wished he was dead – he is near 70 years old & complains that he has not half the peace that the meanest "cooly" or laborer enjoys – I sincerely pity him & hope he will survive the trouble –

119 A catty is an Asian unit of weight — about 1-$^{1}/_{3}$ pounds.

COMMISSIONER LIN DEMANDS ALL OPIUM

As Commissioner Lin fulfills his obligations to the Emperor and begins to destroy the opium trade and the chests of opium on hand, RBF assures Rose that he is in no danger, and that Lin's severe measures may be more apparent than real. RBF and his colleagues, meanwhile, are restricted to the neighborhood of their factories, and the British abandon Canton. This leaves RBF and his colleagues an opportunity to profit from trade the British firms might have had.

On page 106 is Commissioner Lin, one of the Chinese Emperor's most reliable officials, sent to Canton in 1839 to destroy the opium trade. This drawing, made by an anonymous Chinese artist, appeared in Doings in China *by Lt. Alexander Murray, published in London in 1843.*

15 March

Four whole days since I have put pen to paper except in that way of trade in which I have been pretty deeply engaged – We are loading three ships & I can only make you understand how much engaged I have been by telling you I have not been out in my boat for several days –

...Our friend Houqua is quite bright again – he seems to rally with every new trouble & like double refined young Hysson [120] is every time better after coming out of the fire – the Imperial Commissioner is going on very quietly looking into the Opium trade & although determined to put it down he is not taking violent measures – he kills no body but has merely deprived all the petty Government offices of their badges of distinction, he no doubt finds the evil too deeply rooted in trouble to hang all the guilty for if he did there would be few local officials left...I think of you many times during the day & every night I pray for you & our dear Boy – good night

19 March –

The *Omega* goes to day & I write in some haste having a good deal to attend to – No arrivals from the U States & I am getting quite impatient for further accounts of you it will soon be five months since I had any thing from you last dates being 24 October or thereabouts & there are missing several of your letters which must be on the way up here...– *evening* –

... have been quite busy all day writing except two hours this afternoon we went up to the hills & had a game of ball – it is capital exercise & makes a little variety after sailing, pulling &c such exercise is indispensable here – [121]

The Imperial Commissioner has come out with a proclamation, demanding that all the Opium ships shall give up their drug to be destroyed publicly & ordering foreigners to give bonds that they will never bring it again to China – we cannot of course consent to give away the property of our customers but we shall send all the Opium away to other Ports – I have no doubt when it is out of the way the regular trade will go on more smoothly –

Just think how soon one year will be past – I have been working too hard to day to write any more at this late hour & must save my eyes...Just think how soon one year will be past – I find time goes pretty swiftly here & while the Commissions come in as rapidly all must go well –

Good night & God bless thee

Canton 20 March 1839

This afternoon I received *three* of your interesting letters – #4–6–7 – only 8–9 missing...– just as I was finishing your letters I received one from Russell Sturgis at Macao enclosing a letter from Charles Greene to him dated 28 Octo which came to Manila per *Nantasket*, in this letter he said a good deal about you & our boy of a gratifying nature & so Russell sent it to me, among other things he said you "looked prettier than he had ever seen you look before" & that you had just returned from a ride to Copleys new purchase & that he had dined with you the day before, & so I have by a round about way three days later accounts from you than I had before – The a/c C W Greene gives of little Russell Sturgis is very gratifying – Greene talks about your "Noble husband" what think you of that? I was much amused at receiving to day a letter from *your* friend John Tyler

[120] Hyson (RBF's Hysson) is a kind of Chinese green tea from the early crop.

[121] RBF and his colleagues may have been playing rounders, town ball, or some other variant of New England bat-and-ball games that were ancestors of baseball as we know it.

sending me some papers & saying that he hoped the good news he sent me about trade & the papers would prove an apology for the liberty he took with me –...Yours of the 11 of Sept gives me the same good accounts of our boy & you cannot write too much on the subject which can never tire me – Sept 15 – had not yet got my *Chariot* letters –...in this letter you give me an account of your economy – which I see you exercise in the quality of your paper which is the best English – a *little* better than *this* – You are right in living genteelly & may expect some friends bye and bye to see you from me – I notice what you say about Temple Place & Johns being slow – He is rather slow *but sure* – I am deeply indebted to him so pray do all you can to keep on good terms with Sarah cold & heartless as she is, you were a little *warm* when you wrote about her – but it is pardonable in one so feeling as you have always been towards Sarah –

We are quite busy trying to get the *Vancouver*, *Niantic* & *Fr Stanton* off before the trade is stopped but I doubt if we shall succeed as the Imperial Commissioner has demanded such terms in regard to the Opium trade as cannot be complied with by the consignees of the drug –...I wish you could look in upon us say eight *grave* if not *grey* merchants playing ball every afternoon – we enjoy it very much – far more than writing as I am at the desk – it is hardly fair to write to you at the long end of a busy day so I will close & bid you good night – it is near 12 oclock

Monday 25 March 1839

Dear Rose –

On the 21 while dining at the club a summons came to meet at the Chamber of Commerce where the Hong Merchants, Houqua & others were requested also to come & tell their story which was that they had orders from the high officer whom I have alluded to & who is called the *Yumchi* to produce the Opium to be publicly burned on pain of *losing their heads*, the foreign community were so much deceived by this real or imaginary danger to their friends the Hong Merchants –that they agreed to give up 1036 chests of Opium (which had cost some half a million of dollars) under protest of compulsion to be burned – at 2 AM we separated – next day we learned – that the Yumchi would not hear to any thing short of *all the Opium* being delivered up, that the Hong Merchants were at the Consoo a public Council house, Houqua & Mingqua with *chains round their necks* & that they were to be executed unless Mr Dent[122] one of the most respectable merchants was given up to be examined in the City – This intelligence of course filled us with consternation – the residents met at the Chamber of Commerce & there I had the infinite mortification of seeing my old friend [Houqua] deprived of his official button & with an iron chain about his neck – he was calm & dignified enough – but very much degraded of course – instead of a heavy iron chain however I found that it consisted only of a mark of disgrace being a light iron chain loose over the shoulders like a necklace or rosary – he stated that the Yumchi wished to see Mr Dent to inquire about the Opium trade & that he would be perfectly safe & he asked if the chamber did not think he ought to go to which it replied that it had no power or right to give any answer –but that every man there would give his opinion if necessary – finding the Merchants as a "chamber of commerce" were incompetent to decide on such a subject – the Hong Merchants went to Dents house where he was kept by his friends & negotiation upon negotiation was had – officers of high rank came

---

[122] Dent was one of the oldest foreign residents in Canton. His firm handled more opium than any other except Jardine, Matheson & Company.

out of the City & begged Dent to go – they said the Yumchi *must see Mr Dent that day or the Hong Merchants would be executed,* much excitement prevailed & the community as one man declared *Mr Dent should not go into the city voluntarily without the guaranty of safe conduct under the Imperial Seal from the hands of the Yumchi alone* – if they must have him they must come & *take him by force* or rather by *compulsion* it not being the *intention of* Dent to resist by force of arms, but merely to insist on being carried out of his house by order of the Yumchi – about 3 oclock afternoon the third officer under the Vice Roy came in person to Dents house & endeavored by offering his own & the Vice Roys safe conduct to get him to go – but his friends declined firmly as above – the officer alluded to declared he would not leave Dents house until he went with him – by this time the panic had begun to subside– we had plainly seen that the merchants though they demanded 1000 chests of Opium to be given up as the price of their heads – had not given all up and still had their heads on – then we were told that unless Mr Dent went into the city the high officer alluded to would not leave his home & yet he went in 15 minutes to the Council house – here Mr Inglis (Dents partner) was told that the officers in waiting in the city would like to see him & hear why Dent would not go – so Mr Inglis & three others went & were curtly interrogated by several high officers & in two hours sent back with a promise that Inglis should induce Dent to meet one of them at 10 oclock yesterday morning – we were a little anxious lest they should detain Inglis until Dent was given up – but Mr Inglis & his friends were so thoroughly convinced that they intended no harm to Mr Dent that it was made a matter of favour as to who should accompany him & I was promised that I should go – but after Inglis got home say 10 oclock at night he remembered that the day he had named for Dent to see the officer was Sunday & so it was determined to put them off till to day – & the best proof in the world that the Hong Merchants had been playing upon our feelings was that the authorities admitted an excuse of Sunday & agreed to wait till to day – I have no doubt that the Hong Merchants were required to produce Dent & to guard against his escape – one or two hundred men were posted at & around his house – these men were unarmed at first and were all men in the employ of the Hong Merchants thus matters stood, all day Sunday up to 5 1/2 oclock PM when we were as usual quietly walking in front of the factories, though all communication with the ships at Whampoa was cut off & the river guarded by war boats – we were really prisoners –

ELLIOT'S ARRIVAL

well I was quietly walking with Mr Green & Wetmore when a tremendous *hubbub* began & it was evident that a boat or boats were endeavouring to find their way up to our assistance – In a moment all the before apparently idle men in the square ran to the edge of the river & returned with their war caps & spears & presented at once an efficient body of police belonging to our friends the Hong Merchants ready to keep order & protect us as well as to prevent Dent's leaving here for whom they were responsible to the Yumchi – In a moment a boat was seen pulling & sailing as fast as possible, pursued by four china mandarin boats, *who were taking especial good care to keep behind,* in the stern of the boat stood Capt Elliot (a captain in the navy) & her Britannic Majesties chief Superintendent or agent in China – he pulled into the foot of the Companies garden & jumped ashore, ordered the British flag to be hoisted & directly went & brought Mr Dent to the Companies Hall under his own custody, read a very *pretty* circular to the residents all of whom had simultaneously assembled the moment it was known who was coming – told them he would protect them, demand passports for all British subjects to leave Canton in ten days if not granted he should surrender himself a prisoner to the Chinese Govt – requested the cooperation of the Americans & asked them to be equally assured of his protection – he had come up above Whampoa in the Camp cutter a boat as large as the *Sylph* & when he could come no further in her he got into the jolly boat of the *Larne* sloop of war (which was laying at Macao) & pulled up as I have stated in defiance of *hundreds* of armed men – he was in full uniform & they dared not arrest him – he thought we were in a state of alarm on account of the Hong Merchants or Mr Dent & being filled with all the fire & enthusiasm of a naval officer of high courage he did the thing in a gallant style – before he had been in the Hall five minutes – every man in the square except the police were dispersed – showing conclusively that the Government holds the Hong Merchants responsible for all riots & disturbances – one *very serious* feature at this crisis occurred – every servant & cook & Comprador was ordered away & we were left to cook our own supplies if we wanted any – the square was guarded all night by our friends the Hong coolies with lanterns & the exit by way of the river entirely cut off by a double line of boats moored side by side in a half moon shape, the horns resting on the extremities of our limits, all the avenues to or from the streets were also shut – but what makes this whole farce supremely ludicrous was the fact of men being sent in with loads of provisions wood coal &c – In Lord Napier's [123] time 1834 – there was no communication with Whampoa for three weeks & after taking away the servants as now & putting him under guard & sending him down to Macao in a China boat, the English had to give up all the points – they had tried to gain & resumed their trade as before – And it will be so now I think, they will continue this system of plaguing us & annoying the Hong Merchants until we send away or give up the Opium – You would have been much amused to have seen me making fire, splitting wood & boiling the Tea Kettle this morning – I went into Delanos 1/2 past 7 & there found him, Low [124], King & one or two more boiling the Eggs – cooking potatoes, rice, ham &c in the very *worst* style – The only good things we could get for breakfast were the Tea & Eggs & bread – for dinner we are better provided having a sailor boy & a lascar [125] to help us – our poor cows have had to be sent away as we could not well act servants & grooms –...

---

[123] Lord Napier was the British Superintendent of Trade before Elliot. In 1834 at the age of forty-eight he arrived in China. He had gone from Macao to Canton without the proper permission from the Viceroy. The Chinese were so outraged by his behavior that they withdrew all Chinese servants from the British factory, supplying the British became an offense punishable by death, and all British trade was stopped. Lord Napier in response ordered two British frigates from Macao to Canton, and a guard of marines was sent to the British factory. The Chinese were outraged that the English had broken the laws of the Empire by bringing foreign troops into the foreign settlement and threatened to attack them. For two months the situation remained in this critical state until Lord Napier, because of serious illness, left Canton with a convoy of eight armed boats. The Chinese proceeded to harass and delay the group as they came down the river. The trade was reestablished, but poor Lord Napier, whose illness had gone untreated for so long, died.

[124] Abiel Abbot Low was born in Salem, Massachusetts, one of a family of twelve children. He received a grade-school education and then became a clerk in the house of Joseph Howard & Co., which engaged in trade with South America. He moved with his family to Brooklyn, New York, and there his father founded a firm to import drugs and India wares. Young Low worked for his father's company for several years, and in 1833 sailed to Canton and became a clerk at Russell & Co. He soon learned the routines of the China trade, and by 1837 was admitted to the firm.

[125] A lascar is an East Indian army servant, also an East Indian sailor.

PRISONERS IN CANTON

WEDNESDAY
27 MARCH –

Things are in a fair way of being amicably settled – The Chief Superintendent of British trade (Capt Elliot) has this morning issued in peremptory order for all Opium belonging to British Subjects to be given up to him, saying that he had received a *direct demand* from the Yumchi or Imperial Commissioner to give it up to the Chinese Government – the holders of the Opium are therefore prepared to give it up to day – Elliot assures the Agents that his Gov will pay for the same & he will undoubtedly make his present high position a good excuse to demand that the general trade disconnected with Opium, shall go on again under better auspices – I consider all the difficulties as in a fair way of being got over in a few days –

Since my last date the guard over here has been kept up strictly, about four hundred armed men with lanterns have been stationed in the square – the river completely barricaded – a thousand vague reports flying about – but no fear entertained of safety – The guard being placed over us not only to prevent any foreigner leaving Canton or any coming up to Canton but to prevent all disorder from the populace who have been excluded from the square entirely – Canton has never been so quiet & as we have no servants or coolies with us – our houses have been perfectly quiet – I went down to Houquas house about 10 oclock night before last to see what was doing for Elliot had kept all his proceedings to himself – I found the old Gent almost exhausted & the very picture of despair, he had hardy slept for a week, his feet & legs much swollen, his house filled with soldiers, horses &c – at that time Elliot had done nothing but demand his passports & Houqua was afraid that he would act rashly & get into further trouble – I told the old Gent I had been acting cook & chambermaid – he said he would send us in cooked food & accordingly some of his men who had guarded our doors smuggled in Tongue, Capons, Hams &c & he sent us a cook – so that we have only had to set our own table, wait upon ourselves, make our beds &c – one of our Parsee friends has been very kind in sending us an abundance of cooked food it being their custom to retain their own native servants – so that instead of being short of provisions we have had a table groaning with solids & are more likely to suffer from repletion than starvation – there is of course no business doing & we got a good deal of exercise in carrying water, making up our beds &c &c – As I am the only tenant of Mr Sturgis house with Mr Snow I trim the lamps, empty the cuspidor, &c fill the pitchers – sweep out the verandah &c&c – but he gets his principal meals with us at Russell & Co – Houqua told me the other night to give myself no uneasiness on account of safety, around the Americans to keep aloof from the general question & to keep at home & he would see us protected even if a riot should take place from the imprudence of any of the English men – I am well known to all his men & should fear nothing under any emergency – Had a game of whist last night at Delano's & through the whole we have been quite easy after we were satisfied that the Hong Merchants were not in danger – The weather has been delightful & the moon at full so that the array in front & the whole scene of Elliots landing has had a sort of dramatic effect –if we had any thing to do in the way of business we should miss our servants much more than we now do –

The only thing that troubles me is that a ship (the *Omega*) having sailed just as we were getting into trouble & carrying a vast mass of exaggerated reports will frighten people at home who are not acquainted with the Chinese character – I was entirely persuaded from what Houqua stated to me that there was not the least personal danger in going into the City with Mr Dent & I volunteered to go –but Green applied for the same *privilege* – but as matters have taken a new turn & Dent is not required to go I am disappointed –the Yumchi had even appointed a Europe cook & sent for Europe wines to treat us with kindness had we gone – one of our community – Mr C W King[126] has *always been* a great opposer of Opium trade & he has to day received a "chop" from the *Commissioner direct* approving of his conduct –

THURSDAY MARCH 28 –

All quiet last night – the Hong Merchants entirely relieved of their anxiety – the whole matter now rests with the Chief Superintendent of British trade & the Yumchi – Yesterday the former demanded & obtained about *20000* Twenty Thousand Chests of Opium value *Ten Million dollars* which he will give up as the British Governments property to the Yumchi – We have given up over 1400 chests to the British Agent which of course belongs to British subjects – We get on very well as to provender – yesterday Mr Delano & I made two Tureens full of the mess I have before described to you consisting of Foul, Pork bread &c – It was quite amusing to see the different foraging parties going about yesterday – some shouldering a leg of mutton, others a piece of Beef & another with a pail of water who had never been used to helping himself before – Although they take away our servants & forbid anyone bringing us supplies they have not yet prevented us from buying food out of doors & if they do we have salt meat and bread for a month within – I went to the Hongs last evening & was invited to partake so that we are in little or no danger of starving – The people at Macao & Whampoa must be very anxious as they know nothing of what's going on – This immensely important step of giving up the Opium I think must involve China in a war with England – the only good effect of which will be to send me home – I wont stay here to be uncomfortable & if I cannot get a living here quietly I must cut & run – Thank Heaven we are all well & merry as crickets –

FRIDAY 29 MARCH 1839

Still grounded as before – this morning 10 oclock a great cackling of geese & grunting of pigs caused me to look out & there I saw about a dozen sheep, as many large baskets of geese, ditto of small roasting pigs, & loads of hams – which it is said are sent to relieve the *hunger of the barbarians* – in consequence of their submission to the Yumchi – all this mess of stock was put into a yard & is at the disposal of whoever comes to go & help himself, but as we have no servants & only one cooly & a cooks boy we cannot avail of the bounty to a large extent – Yesterday Mr Delano made two rice puddings *by book* which were excellent & we are eating double our usual allowance – I suppose we shall require a week more of negotiation & imprisonment before all matters are arranged to deliver up the opium – Elliot will then ask foreigners to leave the place & close all their accounts preparatory to a blockade – but it is in vain to speculate on the future –

---

[126] King was head of Olyphant & Co., the only American house that felt opium was morally wrong and refused to participate in the use of the drug for trade. Olyphant & Co.'s quarters in Canton were called Zion's Corner because of their friendliness to missionaries and their righteous attitude toward the houses that were active in the opium trade.

30th March –
still grounded as before though our cook & one cooly are allowed to wait on us – after the supply of livestock yesterday to the English there also came 6 bags of rice, 16 Hams, 16 Geese, 4 pigs, 40 fouls, & 2 sheep for the *famishing* Americans – Mr Snow the Consul told the Linguist that bought them that these things were no use to a man who had no servants or means of cooking them – the Linguist left them & went his way & I succeeded in distributing them to the other resident Americans – last evening all our sailboats & pulling boats were rudely taken from their homes where they hung & dragged over the rough stones into the square in front & there they lay – this measure was ordered so as effectually to cut off all escape, they have also unshipped the rudders of all the large schooners or sail boats on the river – these paltry measures are resorted to on purpose to bring Elliot to more degrading concessions – he declares he will not give up the order for the Opium until they release us from bondage & send away the guard – I fear however the Chinese will hurry Elliot into thin measures – when Lord Napier came here & had 2 British Frigates at Whampoa (which had forced their way past the Forts & demolished them with the loss of many lives) to protect him – he was compelled to go to Macao in a China boat with gongs beating & he died shortly after (Sept 1834) of fatigue & anxiety – John was here at the time yet I cannot read a line he wrote at the time, the danger was then thought to be much greater than it has been on this occasion as the Frigates actually forced the Bocca Tigris forts [127] –

It is cool enough for fires to day and luckily we have a cooly to make them – but the novelty is over & as we have no business to do time drags heavily – had whist last night – Old Houqua gets hardly any rest he was in here at *12 last night* from the Consul house to request our interview *at 6* this morning – I have not been better since my arrival in China than I am now – The excitement & fatigue of the first two or three days has entirely subsided – it may be several weeks before we are allowed to dispatch our ships...–The *Nantasket* to 1 November is in but no letters up yet & cannot have till our prison gates are opened –

Sunday 31 March
Yesterday & today we were entirely cut off from all communication with the back streets where we had sent out foraging parties to buy eggs, fish, &c – the reason of this appears to be the fear of our getting any accounts to Whampoa or Macao of the state of things here through the shop men or any stray servants, Aho sent word to me that he could get my clothes washed if I wished but I have an ample supply for two months & I hope Elliot will hold out so long –If I were in his place I would not give an order for a chest of Opium until I should be guaranteed liberty before the order was given – The Hong Merchants sent their Lingos to ask what stores we required & each one gave a list & this morning we have a full supply – but are threatened with the removal of the two coolies or porters who now help us keep tolerably clean & help cook, set table &c – Whist last night at Delanos – but time begins to hang heavy & I am heartily tired of this state of durance vile – I shall go to church to day & pray for a blessing on you & *confusion* to all the China Gov – What a petty mean & despicable people they are, here

---

127 The Boca Tigre or Bogue was 20 miles north of Lintin. Here the Pearl River narrowed to less than a mile providing a natural protection against foreign ships passing up the river to Canton. Five large forts stood in various directions, and gave an impregnable look to the Boca. However, this was not the case. The cannons of the forts were not on carriages, but fixed in place, so they could only hit a ship if it was directly in front of them.

are about 200 English & Americans in Canton hemmed in by some thousand men & yet they dare not trust Elliot at liberty until they get the Opium & at the same time they ask him to guaranty that his Government will not resent the insults heaped upon him – I hope the day is not far distant when they will be drubbed into the list of civilized nations & were it not for you I would volunteer under *any flag* to help do it –

Monday 1 April 1839

Last evening our two coolies & our cow-keeper were ordered away & this morning we had to get our own breakfasts – We are organized as follows –

Green – sweeps out parlour & makes the Tea
Forbes – cleans the glass & silver
Low – sets the Table – Delano head cook
King second cook – Spooner cooks mate –
Hunter – trims the lamps & lights them &c
Gilman – Looks out for Beer, wine, cheese & begs, borrows, buys or steals small grub such as Eggs, bread &c
Miranda & Silva (two Portuguese clerks) wash dishes, clear away table, clean knives –
in addition to these duties every one must of course take care of his room –

Went to Church yesterday & heard a good sermon from Mr Parker – I have forgotten to say that on the 30th the hospital over which this Gentleman has presided exclusively for the benefit of the chinese – has been shut up – The Linguists come in with supplies daily & even offer to have our clothes washed for us – but I am for shutting out all chinamen & depending solely on ourselves – We have not yet heard of the *Omegas* sailing for Macao – rather a queer coincidence that the last ship sailed before the stoppage of trade should be called the *Omega*...

Tuesday April 2

Nothing important transpired – Whist last night at Hathaways & Tea a sailor boy tending table – All servants & coolies were yesterday warned not to Enter the factories – but the Hong Merchants send us by the Linguists all we want except attendance – One of these came up yesterday from Macao & reports the death of Mr Turner one of our most worthy merchants, he caught a bad cold on his way to Macao where he had a family & died on the 28th much lamented, his wife came out here from England about the same time I arrived – she lost two grown up daughters in England before embarking & has two or three children left with her at Macao –

Last night all the streets except one leading from the square were built up at the ends opening into it with brick & mortar – this is merely one of the measures of annoyance which this miserable & despicable people use to intimidate Elliot...

I am perfectly willing to have this state of thing last a month rather than yield – Some people suppose the Yumchi is afraid of receiving such an amount of property, say 10 million dollars from the Queen's agent & that he had referred the matter to Pekin – others say he is venal & is only awaiting a good opportunity to make a fortune out of the Opium – time will show – I am quite well & lay the table beautifully –

GOOD AND OBEDIENT BARBARIANS

Thursday 4 April 1839

Dearest Wife

Yesterday it was suddenly arranged that Mr Johnston the 2d Superintendent should go to Macao accompanied by two Hong Merchants & some of the local Mandarin to receive the first installment of Opium say *5000* five thousand Chests – when rec we are to have our servants & coolies back, when the 2d parcel of *5000* Chests is received we are to have the guards removed, when *5000* more are received we are to be allowed to go up & down the river & have trade renewed & when the balance to make up the *20000* is rec[eived] the Yumchi is to petition the Emperor to give us the name of good & obedient barbarians!!!!! I suppose it will take some two or three weeks to get through with this matter & in mean time we must keep quiet & pocket the insult –

I dispatched several sheets of journal to Manila yesterday by Mr Johnston & hope it will arrive before this...I also wrote you a small letter which I hope may be smuggled away safe & get to you by some round about way – dismiss all apprehension & believe me when I tell you we are perfectly safe & well –

April 6

Nothing new among the diplomatists – the weather dark – rainy to day with thunder & lightning –...I am in hopes to get my *Naples* & *Nantasket* letters soon – the former left about 27 Sept – the latter 1 Nov from Boston direct – The Imperial Commissioner is quite intoxicated with his success & it is said intends to send a high officer to Cap Elliot with compliments – I hope Elliot will kick him out of his house if he comes – It is now pretty evident that a distrust of China will keep people from sending their property here – the crop of Tea gone is very short & I hope to get some chance of making some money yet before the year is out – The face of things is much changed by this Opium question & the result will be disastrous to some of our English friends – even if the Queen pays for it – it will be a long time first – If I could have been sure of Houquas business if I had not joined the house I might have done something beside Commission business – this year –

Monday April 8 –

went to church & heard a good sermon from Mr Abiel yesterday – no diplomatic business done yet – expecting momentarily to hear of the first delivery of Opium – We get along perfectly well with our provender which is sent to us ready cooked & we shall be quite disappointed if no body is hung drawn or quartered – The opinion seems to gain ground that the high Commissioner will squeeze his own subjects to pay for the robbery of the Opium – getting letters ready for the India ships – adieu

Tuesday 9

Yesterday PM it was determined that Mr Snow, the American Consul, Mr Van Barel, the Dutch Consul, Mr Wetmore Chairman of the Chamber of Commerce, Mr Teanur interpreter to the same, Mr King the only Godly man in China, & Delano & my self should go in company with the Hong Merchants to the Council Hall or Consoo House at the head of China street to hear what the head judge & three other officers had to say – We accordingly went at about 9 oclock, it being arranged before hand that we should sit if they did & stand if they did & that we should not be subjected to any degrading obeisance –We were ushered after waiting half an hour in an anti–room into the presence of these great rascals – seated on a sort of elevated divan covered with a scarlet cloth richly embroidered – as we entered each one was introduced by name by a Linguist & each made his bow – as he would to any gentleman at home, we then took seats – They began by complimenting Mr King (who has never dealt in Opium) asked him as a good man to set a good example to the rest of the foreigners by signing a most outrageous bond to give up to execution any foreigner bringing Opium – He referred them to Mr Snow the Consul – Nearly two hours elapsed in demanding Snow & Van Barel to give the bonds on behalf of their countrymen – they declined, finally we were told we might go home but that he (the head man) should come again to Consoo at 10 this morning to receive the bonds & that he *must have them today* – The Consuls have replied that they are willing to obey all reasonable laws, but that they cannot give bonds implicating the life of any country man that they have no power to do so – if it is *exacted* they must leave the country with their property – The Consuls have refused to go to Consoo with a *verbal* promise to give the bond, the Hong Merchants are afraid to carry the *written* promise & I am to go with the interpreter & deliver it – at 2 to day – The misery of communicating with these rascals is that you cannot have access to them except through Chinese Linguist – & these abject slaves are afraid to give your precise & manly replies but misinterpret & corrupt your meaning into a degrading answer – The matter of the bonds in the form proposed cannot be given & if exacted must compel us to go away & stay a while till they are brought to reason – I should be very glad to spend the next three months at Manila & am ready to go –

10 PM – At 7 oclock I went to the Consoo house alone to deliver Mr Snows reply or rather "petition" as all such papers are called – I was ushered into a separate room where I found some of the Hong Merchants – Houqua presented Snows paper & while I was in waiting I saw it brought out & copied after which I was called before the same officers before whom I went last night & having made my bow as I would to any Christian I was asked to be seated – they then asked me why Wetmore, Snow, & others did not come – I replied that I was merely Mr Snows messenger & could make no answers – They then gave me back Mr Ss paper saying it could not be received that I must tell Mr S – he must sign the bond – I replied that I could carry no verbal message to Mr S – that I was merely requested to hand in the paper & if it did not suit I would take it back & I was accordingly, graciously permitted to make my bow & go home, of course under a suitable escort – We hear no positive news from below though it is reported that some ships have come in – getting very impatient to receive my private letters per *Nantasket* which are still laying on board the *Lintin* – good night dearest –

Thursday 11 April –

Nothing new, grounded as before – had a pleasant whist party at Mr Snows last night – We hear the Opium is being delivered & hope in a day or two to get back our cooks, servants &c – The English begin to talk as if they should leave Canton – they consider their national dignity hurt – but the fact is they have a large stock of Tea in England & expect the Queen to pay for their Opium & if they leave it will be a gain to the bulk of them, now our case is very different, we as Americans have no interest in the Opium except as agents for a very small proportion of that which has been given up, & we have no stock of Tea at home & many ships on the way – personally I say – can any sacrifice I may be called upon to make here of comfort or convenience compare with the sacrifice of leaving my wife & child & family – I made this sacrifice to procure some money & I will not rashly leave the country – I will stay here & make money until I conceive my personal safety is compromised – then I will leave & hang about the skirts of China until matters get quiet again – I cannot go away & leave other peoples property unprotected

Friday 12 April – 10 PM –

...Letters were received from Macao to day & among others had a line from R Sturgis wherein he says he has written to you fearing I might not have had a chance, but I suppose you will get some of my letters quite as soon – it was very kind of him however – I have been amusing myself to day writing a play entitled "the Yumchi or the Imperial robbery" – giving a strictly true account of the late proceedings – You must now be in possession of my letters per *Albion* & *M Chilton* and are no doubt as happy as you have been during my absence – This unforseen & unprecedented state of things here may interfere seriously with my gains, but I am determined it shall not keep me an hour away from you longer than I bargained for at starting – The sacrifice is too hard to prolong my exile & I sometimes secretly wish we might be absolutely driven away from China so that I might make an honourable retreat...–

The gentlemen who are here have wives at Macao are getting impatient & I really feel quite glad that you are not there – what a stew you would have been in –

April 14 Sunday Evening

...little to do but Grumble – To day we hear of the arrival of the *Rambler* to the 15 November direct from Boston & I am anxiously waiting letters from you –

During this period of inaction I *think* a great deal too much & I find my mind constantly wandering to you & your forlorn state – I sometimes think the ship I have taken was not justified by any state of affairs, that it was a cruel sacrifice – then a pain comes to me & the reflection that I could only have remained at home in a state of dependence, (wrote independence but crossed out in) that I must have incurred obligations which I could never cancel – by coming here I have done all I could do to retrieve my fortunes & procure an independence – The whole course of affairs is changed by this new revolution and the results yet involved in mystery & uncertainty & it is useless to speculate on the result – thank God I am quite well & be the end what it may my position is as good as any mans here –

The Yumchi & other high officers of the Government have gone to the mouth of the River to inspect the delivery of the Opium but owing to bad weather it has gone on very slowly & I fear we may be detained here yet some 10 days before we are allowed our liberty – We are promised our servants & Compradors to day but we learn that the Government requires of them certain bonds which make them nothing more nor less than spies upon all our acts – I doubt if they will be willing to come back to us – I staid at home to day reading & did not go to meeting as I should have done –

Wednesday 17 April –

...still this state of suspense is very tedious, we hear from Houqua who has just been in that nearly five thousand chests are delivered – I have been reading novels & playing whist half my time but it hangs heavily –I do not write pages to you because I should only grumble, grumble & make you think I am very unhappy – this is not the case, I have during this *scrape* never felt any thing like the uneasiness of leaving home in the morning owing money beforenoon & not knowing where to get it – Whenever I am inclined to murmur at my present lot I look back to 1837 – during which my only comfort was in disburthening my troubles to you – I have now come a great distance & made a great sacrifice to get a Competency & *I must have it* –

FRIDAY 19TH –

Yesterday we got back our cooks & coolies, the latter are *porters*, chamber maids &c – but our servants being required to give bonds are afraid to return – Half the Opium must be delivered by this time, when this is ascertained the communication is to be opened which I shall be very glad of...indeed Russell & Co have not had a line from any quarter for nearly four weeks & we will be overwhelmed with work in a day or two – Russell Sturgis has written a line or two to Delano which was smuggled up at a cost of $8 or 10 – among other things he says there is a Higginson in the *Rambler* who saw you very well & the Boy on the 17 Nov – this is good news & I wait more patiently your letters –

I have been looking over a book called "China Opened" during my *experience* of *China Shut* up – it is by a Mr Gutslaff[128] (merry bowels) & I recommend you to *borrow* it of Mr Cushing – it gives a good account of China as does "Davis history of China" which I will send you – They are by no means so barbarious a nation as you would suppose from their late acts, & this is a good reason why they should be punished for their incivility – I think England will drop the Opium question entirely & will merely send a force here with a suitable agent or Ambassador who will say to the Emperor – We have helped you put down the illegal trade now we want some guaranty that your local officers will not on every slight pretext stop the general trade for the offenses of people beyond the control as well of your own laws as of the Laws of British merchants residing in Canton, we want a regular & well understood system of duties on imports, we require to understand how far we are to be held responsible – then knowing the Laws if we break them we insist on the *guilty only* being punished – If the Emperor says in reply "I have allowed you barbarians compassionality to come here and buy Tea & Rhubarb without which you must surely die, why come ye here whiningly asking further bounty – begone if ye break the laws ye shall be punished & I will make & mind the laws when I please" then John Bull will say "d__n your Tea & Rhubarb pay us for the Opium you have robbed with interest" & if the Emperor wont pay John Bull will blockade his Ports & bully him into compliance –This will be war – But – before any extreme measures can be resorted to – Elliot must wait the settling the present delivery through the midwife Mr Johnston, this will take three weeks then it will require four months to get the dispatcher before his Government, then three or four more to discuss the matter in parliament, then two more to fit out the necessary forces, then four more to get them here in making at least eleven months before it can be

[128] The Reverend Doctor Charles Gutzlaff was a Prussian medical missionary who spoke and wrote Cantonese fluently, and had also mastered local dialects of Chinese. He lived in Macao and toured the mainland and along the coast, distributing translations of the Bible and various ointments and pills to the villagers. In 1832 he was hired by Jardine to sail up and down the China coast in the *Sylph* acting as interpreter in the sale of smuggled opium. His conscience questioned this activity, but he rationalized that the greater the trade, the more opportunities he would have to convert Chinese to Protestantism. He trusted that later, when the natives had been won, the opium would be substituted by more desirable Western products. His first goal was to save these poor heathens by introducing them to his Christian God, who he believed would save them in the end.

at all necessary to leave Canton – I am so well satisfied with the imbecility of the Chinese Govt that any demonstration of war will make them as civil as whipt curs – The sooner the demonstration comes, the better, for it will diminish the confidence in English houses & prove a benefit to us – however speculation is useless & we can only wait patiently & decide what is best when the time for action comes –

Monday 22 April –

I had hoped before this time to have received your letters from below but we are still waiting, not having yet heard of the delivery of more than 8500 chests on Friday out of the 20000 I fear we must be several weeks more in limbo –...The High Commissioner is still at the Bocca Tigris or mouth of the River – It is said he has demanded the Surrender of the Macao Forts & that the Governor has provisioned them & determined not to give them up...

Wednesday 24 April

No letters up yet – The Commissioner still requiring an odious bond & making various other excuses to prevent our getting our letters up – our guards remain as before – Time drags on heavily & reading, whist, playing ball & walking in our prison yard are the only occupations – Now & then a smuggled letter gets up from Macao folded up about the size of a dose of jalap – My health is perfectly good, I can truly say I have not been so well for any similar period since I left Boston in the *Lintin* in 1830 – there will be a great interval between the arrival of the *Omega* in the US & the arrival of my present sheets & during that time I fear you will get uneasy for her owners will make the state of things as black as possible here to effect the market –

Friday 26 April –

No letters or boats up yet & our guards are still at their posts – Thus do the Chinese Mandarins keep their faith, more than three quarters of the Opium must be delivered by this time yet we have not our liberty – as promised

Time moves very slowly – our principle amusement after dinner is to witness the gambols of the sailors who are accidentally up here, they play Ball, Blind Mans Buff, Leap Frog &c – I am getting very cross & if our letters dont come to day I shall go mad – It is impossible to fix ones attention to study at such a time & I have almost exhausted my store of light reading – I wish I could have a sight at Bob – he would not be *in the way* just now!

Saturday 27 April – Ditto – ditto – do –

I might get over the day in this summary manner & I have nothing to record save a fall of 20 degrees in the thermometer from 86 to 66 – it is now raining like a young flood –...It is more tedious than being at sea & quite as bad as being within sight of home with a foggy calm day & a contrary current – dreamed last night of seeing the Milton folks & being scolded by Mary & Franny[129] for not writing to them! I retorted that as they had not written to me I would not have written a line if I had been away five hundred years – I have as yet only received letters from Mother & Emma & shall only write to the rest when they commence a correspondence –

I am doubly anxious to have the trade opened – firstly to get my letters, secondly to forward letters to you, & last not least to get rid of Green, mind this

[129] Mary, RBF's younger sister by ten years, was married to the Reverend Francis Cunningham.

is confidential – do not even name what I say to John – That individuals character is so entirely opposite to my sense of what a liberal & high minded merchant ought to be that I could not get along with him a year if my fortune depended on it & I fear a regular blow up with him if he stays much longer –He is *crabbed*, ill natured, grasping, vain, & very ugly & having no *power* to control the expression of his features & *no wish* to conciliate – he makes himself disgusting to every one about him –He is a good merchant, very industrious, & very quick but is so fully aware of all this & pays so little attention to the opinions & so little regard for the feelings of his associates that I can only wish he may get away before I quarrel with him

Monday Night 29 April –

cold rainy weather –...Yesterday we heard of the arrival of a vessel from Bombay & to day we have overland extracts to the 7th December from New York – by way of England, Red Sea, Bombay & Sincapore –...The US frigate *Columbia*[130] Commodore Geo C Reed is announced at Macao & I hope he will kick up a row with the Yumchi – it is too bad to be penned up here like a parcel of slaves –

I have been at work at my account books all day to day & it makes me feel sick to remember those last days at home...however I hope to get oceans of letters from you in a few days & then I shall be quite happy again – it is now 37 days since we were made prisoners – What are we but prisoners here at any time – we can sail & walk little to be sure – but social intercourse with the people is out of the question & the city is a "terra incognita"–

kiss Bob Good Night

Friday May 3

Still prisoners & no letter received – We hear the *John Adams* sloop of War is in & that the Commodore Reed will not take any measures of retaliation until he has consulted with us here – This is all very well & his presence, with that of the *Larne* belonging to Queen Victoria will keep the Yumchi from doing any further mischief – When I put my head on my lonely pillow at night & pray for you I think of a great many things I want to say about my state of mind, my prospects, feelings, hopes & fears – but when I get down at my desk I say – What's the use of dwelling on these things – better to put aside all melancholy feelings & look forward to a reunion...I think of our Boy every day & of the pleasure he will soon take running about on the common or on the side walk of Beacon Street –

Saturday May 4 –

No release yet but we hear to day that our order has arrived to open the trade tomorrow – that is passage boats are allowed to go down & any person may leave Canton excepting 16 of the oldest residents who have been engaged in Opium business – of these there is only one American named [Green – Head of R&Co] & they are to be allowed to go about their business when the whole of the Opium is delivered – I suppose there is now a chance of our getting our letters in a day or two more & I shall wait quietly till I get mine

---

130 The *Columbia* and *John Adams*, both American naval vessels, arrived in the midst of the imprisonment at Canton. Although this was a comfort to the Americans, Commodore Reed had agreed with the consul that the bond required by the Chinese not be signed; so, as soon as the trade reopened, the squadron left the Pearl River despite frantic protests from the mercantile community.

Sunday May 5 –
...The guards are nearly all gone & the river is clear but only two boats are to be allowed to go to Macao tomorrow – in the meantime cargo is to be allowed to go off & the communication is to be opened with our ships – I have just written to young Wainwright...a midshipman on board the *John Adams* & to Revere offering them the civilities of Canton also to Commander Reed & Capt Wyman – I have today packed up your piece of Mandarin silk & two pieces of grass cloth enough to make gowns & frocks for the whole family for ten years – the finest piece cost *$16* or nearly 33 cents pr yard – the other $10 or 21 cts if you dont want it all you can no doubt sell a piece of it!!!

Canton May 7th 1839
My dearest Rose
As the *Vancouver* sails tomorrow direct for Boston I will keep my journal for her & having much to do this morning preparing the *Niantic*s dispatches I can only write a very short a/c of events –...I have sent John a sort of journal which he will send you to read if you wish –...Green embarks...this month & we shall not be much troubled with business during the hot months & I shall go to Macao bye & bye –...The interests of all tend to a state of quietude – unless England takes measure to retaliate on the Chinese all will go on quietly & if they do make trouble we must leave Canton for a time until the squall passes over – I shall in the least prospect of danger go to Macao or Manila & you may depend on this, that I care vastly more for home & for you than for anything under Heaven & I would not put your peace at risk or my own health or safety for all the money in the world – Still I have come here to effect an object & I must accomplish it if I can, with a thousand kisses to Bob & love to your Mother & Sally – am ever devotedly thine – RBF

RESPONSE TO ROSE'S LETTERS

Canton May 11, 1839
My dear Rose
I was made inexpressibly happy to day by the receipt of your No 8, 14, 15, 16 up to the 15 Nov – the missing numbers being 5, 9, 13 I believe but then I have some without any numbers & dare say I have received all you have written for you female women are rather careless about matters of business – I will begin with your No 8 of Sep 16 & ending 27th Sept –...you...tell me in this letter that you have only visited church but once ! I say nothing!!!

... 18 Sept – when you & Mary Ann Chandler (you say) drank my health as did Lucy & Esther[131] I dare say you were all dr – – k & thats the reason your eyes were wet...Sept 27 – Here comes your first lines after getting my letters from Sea...I am rejoiced that you were satisfied with my letters for though I can realize you might find much in them to like I feared after they have gone that I had not said enough (you dont say a word of the snuff boxes I sent) – Heard had called to see you...

November 1 – which could not begin more satisfactorily than by telling me how well & healthy our boy was – you cannot write too much on this subject...John

[131] Esther was the Forbes' cook and Lucy was Bob's nurse.

been at the Hunt [in Naushon] has not written me about it – indeed he has had so much to attend to that living in the country as he does I cannot see where he gets time to do half his business – he says he wants me daily & Councils my return directly unless I am established here to my mind –

November 2.. study to bring [Bob] up hearty – no child compares with him –..."often think how you ramble on to me" do you – if you didn't so ramble I wouldn't answer them – you say your life is without incidents – what is mine – get up in the mornings, bathe, breakfast, compting room, dinner, walk, tea, write, go to bed after a walk, no sailing now, not allowed any exit from the square, same faces every day, why woman your life's a perfect wilderness of incidents compared to mine, if it had not been for the Yumchi I should have died of ennui before now –

Nov 7 Mother spent the night – good –I have a letter from her dated in Sept after getting my sea letters...[her] letter is taken up with the *beauty* & intelligence of Bennet – she is afraid he will be made too much an idol of & I fear the same –

...I have an excellent letter from [Joe Lyman] dated 15 Nov –... he says you are *thin* but well, cheerful & good humored & study the happiness of all around you as much as ever... he also says that John is more malleable & everyday like – You had also received a visit from Dr Robbins & he gave you reason to feel well about my prospects – such intelligence coming as it did from Bryant & Sturgis is worth something – I rejoice to hear that your finances flourish & that your health is improving

I have had many misgivings about your health my dear & when after all your assurances that you were well, you tell me (or rather Joe tells me) you are still thin I must have fallen short of the true estimate of trouble you have gone through – but I am certain you will keep up your exercise & spirits for my sake –

Nov 9 – you have been having Clark to take Bobs face [a portrait of Bob is being painted] & I look forward with much pleasure to receiving it per next ship –...the Col has concluded to keep his old woman (do you mean by this that he had any idea of parting with his wife?) or have you told me in one of your *missives* that you had a prospect of pawning off your old nurse upon the Col – she was too good looking!! I suppose & Mrs Col would not have her – respecting the weaning do just as you please & dont wait to consult me...– you want to see the history of a lost portrait do you – I fear it was poor rubbish – I find I am dreadfully careless in my writing & do not punctuate & divide my sentences right –I am reforming however & write more carefully except to you who would overlook *any thing* in me – you allude to the scrimmage between you & Sarah – you know my opinion therefore I say nothing, only beg you for my sake to bear with her –...

Nov 11 Had a pleasant call from John – been to church all day...Boy has six teeth & not much trouble in getting them –...

November 15 announcing the birth of Johns daughters[132] – I suppose this catastrophe of twins is to make up for time lost in China[133] – John wrote me a

---

[132] John Murray Forbes and his wife produced tiny twins, Ellen and Alice, who weighed seven and a quarter pounds together.

[133] In February, 1834, John Murray Forbes, at the age of twenty-one, married Sarah Hathaway after a short courtship. Following a honeymoon less than a month long, John left his new bride to sail again to China, where he spent three years pursuing his fortune as a partner of Russell & Co.

line just after the event, & not having anything more from him though the vessel was detained to the 18th – I am a little anxious to hear that all was well – but then you did not write anything after the 15th – glad to hear you dined with THP [Thomas Handasyd Perkins] – I think he likes you & so does his wife –... good night & heaven bless thee –

Sunday 12 May

I wrote you a sheet full last night & am sorry to say I have written to day about half a quil to various people & my eyes are not very clear – I cannot therefore run over what I have scrawled nor add much to it to night – I have read over your letters again & am well pleased...dined to day with Hathaway & drank health to the Mrs Forbes's – I went yesterday to call on Dr Parker & met Capt Elliot – I told the latter I had news of twins from John whom he knew – the Dr not understanding exactly began to congratulate *me* when I put on a long face & said – Dr I have been here over seven months & was four in coming!!!! Elliot roared & like to have burst –he then told me it reminded him of a remark made by John with the same sort of face – when he (Elliot) was recommending John to marry a young spinster then at Macao – says John very gravely "There is a law against bigamy in the US" – Elliot was not aware that he had committed matrimony at that time – I have some business at Macao & am off in the morning – we are not very busy here & I can well be spared – The fact is I want to see the frigate *Columbia*, the *Rose* & Mr Sturgis &c –...I shall write you more fully on the way down & being quite tired now say goodnight & God bless thee...I have good letters from Mr Cushing...

RBF RELEASED FROM CANTON

Boat Union near the Bocca Tigris

14 May

Dear Rose,

We left Canton at 3 PM yesterday – got organized at 6 & as it was necessary to wait till 2 AM for the tide to float us off...We have seven passengers in this boat & a large quantity of baggage like a moving to Nahant – plenty of spiders, cockroaches & mosquitoes – I brought my mosquito curtain luckily & six nails in my pocket & therefore bid them defiance – My companions are Bradford supercargo of the *Gilpin* & his friend – two English Captains & two Portuguese – We are now awaiting the turn of the tide to pass the Tigers mouth – or "Bocca Tigris" the entrance to the River – The Yumchi is within a few miles of us – waiting completion of the delivery of Opium & he is getting impatient to receive the last chest when this is done I trust he will go home to Pekin & let us go on with our trade quietly – but I am not sure that he will – The Superintendent of the British Trade has ordered all her Majesty's subjects to prepare to leave Canton & has forbidden their bringing in any more British Property except at their own risk – I hardly think the Americans will leave Canton but I think it would be good policy to go away for a few months to Macao after which I think the trade would be allowed to go on unembarrassed – I do not mean the Opium Trade, that is done with in Canton & will only be carried on near the skirts of the Empire by the smugglers – All the houses of Canton have given up the agency of Opium have received no less than four letters from C W Greene lately which is very good of him –

Wednesday 15 May –
On board the old Lintin –

Here am I now dearest on board my old *prison*[134] in Macao roads – At about 2 oclock yesterday we passed the Forts at the Bocca Tigris which seemed in full preparation to sink & destroy all "barbarians" who might think of passing without permission – "The Chinese are a very peculiar people" this remark is applied to all their overt acts & furnishes every one with a ready excuse for anything they may have done or may premeditate – & when I saw the contrivances for shutting up the "Tigers mouth" or Bocca Tigris as the entrance to the river is called I involuntarily made the same remark – The water at this point is very deep say more than an hundred feet yet they have contrived to anchor (with chains) a great many large rafts of timber within thirty feet of each other all the way across the river which at this point is as broad as the common opposite Temple Place, these rafts are put there for the purpose of supporting near the surface of the water an immense chain running all the way across the river & so fixed to windlasses that it can be *slacked down* (loosened) at pleasure to allow any ship to pass or to be tightened to prevent the passage of any intruder there is one gap left in it where boats are allowed to pass – then they anchor & are examined these measures have all been taken since the late troubles began – The river at the point in question is strongly fortified by batteries filled with cannons & the place in good hands with proper guns could be made impregnable, yet I should like no better fun than to spike every gun with two hundred men – We have had constant rain all day to day & a great part of yesterday & I assure you I am glad to get on board the old ship out of the crowded *Union* where we were staved seven *strong* – without servants & only one small boy as a general steward & cook & to give you an idea of his capacity or invention need only say that he washed his plates in the wash basin & wiped them on a towel I had used to wipe my face & hands on & he had the foods of the table half cooked in two hours after they were alive and kicking – but what is all this to a sailor – I cared nothing about it & if we had had good weather I should have enjoyed the sail – I shall go on Shore in the morning & see Mr Sturgis but as the Commodore is expected down momentarily I shall close this to night –...I kept up a *devil* of a thinking last night as I lay awake about you my dear & tussled & turned every act of my late life...Keep up a good heart then, one year and one third of my time is over & I will not stay beyond the time if I return a beggar – The late events have cut off much of our earning this year, that is we have not been able to load half the ships that have come & those we have loaded are not filled with very valuable cargoes – Private not withstanding this the Commission paid in amount to over Thirty thousand dollars since the first of January a quarter of which is mine & if the trade goes on without any more interruptions we shall pocket full half what the house did last year at any rate we are doing better than our neighbors & have a staunch friend in Houqua –I deal with you in full confidence that you will not talk to any one about business matters *particularly John* – say in general terms that I am doing "as well as could be expected" –...I wrote also to Sim Forbes, John, Mother & Emma – I have neither received from or sent a line to Mary, Fan, or Margaret & had nothing from the late ships from Emma – I suppose she was hurt that I did not write to her from sea – cant help it...– I now dearest must go to my roost & pray for you – when I put my head on my pillow my mind is filled with a thousand tender recollections & a thousand things occur to me that I ought to say – I think I have written coldly & that you will be disappointed in my letters – "but what is the use of sighing when time is on the wing" fal– lal– de bal– lat – fal lul di da –

[134] Old prison refers to the *Lintin* and time spent on board during his previous trip.

18 May 1839
Macao
Dear Rose –
...I landed in the morning of the 16th & took up quarters at Hathaways house which Mrs Howland has just vacated in favour of said Gentleman & Mr Hunter – Dined with Uncle Jimmy & Russell & spent the day there – Yesterday ditto in company with Commodore Read [135], a fine old Gentleman of 50 *odd*, he knew my Father & my Uncles & myself too – have promised to take him on board of your namesake & take a sail among the islands for a couple of days – expect a pleasant time –

The *20286* chests of Opium are nearly delivered & we expect all our difficulties will be at an end in the course of a week – when the Englishmen are leaving Canton we shall have the field to ourselves...Capt Wallis whom I knew in 1832 here did not know me I had grown so *young* & the ladies tell me I look much better than I did in Dec – It is dinner time & I must close with Love to Bob & Sarah & your Ma – ever RBF

Macao 23 May 1839
Dearest Wife
On the 20th I got under way in the *Rose* with Commander Reed & 10 of his men & a young midshipman as "aid" & went over to Hong Kong Capsing Moon & all about the little Bays & harbours – got back on the 21 in the evening after a *very good* time except the last day it rained *all the time* & I got a soaking for we happened to get into a narrow place during a thunder squall & I did not like to stay below to look on – the cruise has done me no harm except a little healthy sun burnt look – I am as light & merry as a cricket & if I could only have a climate like this I should get fat into obesity –

I returned on the evening of the 21 & as we could not get on shore very early we went on board of the Frigate *Columbia* – & then I *hung myself* up in the Commodores Cot & had a good night & wishing to see the ship & the sloop of war *John Adams* & young Revere, Wainwright & others that I had not before I allowed the Com to go on shore without me & remained to dine visited every part of the ship & thought I should like to command them – found one Lieutenant whom I met in the Pacific in *1826* – I had some chat with him – married man with one boy – looking forward to the Supreme felicity of getting $10,000 (Ten thousand dollars) after a course of years to stay on shore upon! – he had no letters later than *July* & I had almost a mind to read him some of yours – poor fellow he said he had "not been happy an hour since he left home" – that he was living quietly in the enjoyment of all that man could require except money, when the order came to prepare to go on a three year cruise – how much worse a situation than ours my dear – The Commodore too is the Lord & (ought to be) the Master of a dashing wife whom he bade adieu to with great regret – he is 55 or more she *30 odd* so I presume the sacrifice is less to her than if they had children & were of same age – he appears to be a very gentlemanly man though I should judge some thing of a Tarter on board ship –

It is rather singular that I should have been consulted by S C Phillips [136] member of Congress from Mass about the objects to which this very squadron

[135] George Campbell Read (1787-1862) served as Captain of both *Constitution* and *Constellation* during his career. From April to August of 1838 he was in Chinese waters in command of a small squadron of ships.

[136] Stephen Clarendon Philips (1801-57), a Whig from Salem, Massachusetts, was a member of Congress from 1834 to 1838 and an antislavery activist.

should be devoted – when he (Com[modore] Reed) told me how little power he had to act & finding his opinion & mine agreeing I *hauled out* the copy of said letter & found that we agreed as to the right course – but our Government know & care little about China & he is sent to sea with orders to go here & there & come home again without going into any detail of the objects to which the squadron should devote itself – on my way on shore yesterday I called on board the *Nantasket* to see Eckly but he had come on shore & I did not find him till morning though he sent me yesterday your No 13 up to 29 Octo & an envelop covering a "watch guard"[137] which Russell Sturgis offered me 50 cents for last night & as that would furnish you with a dinner I was almost tempted to sell it! but I did not – I also received your introduction to Eckly with one from his Daddy & Mr I A Lowell – I am pleased with the youth & remember having seen him before – he is disgusted with the life of a sailor & I shall take him into our house when his ship goes into the river & if I find him handy I *may* keep him but this of course will depend much on his turn for business, for it would be only a waste of time to have him here unless he can be profitably employed for himself as well as us – he looks very well but has been eating fruits & was a little inclined to diarrhea – I made him poke out his tongue which being a little white I *immediately* called on Dr Anderson & carried him to see him – I suppose he wants a little medicine & that he will do very well – I am going to Canton in the morning as I hear Green is off in the *Panama* in a few days & I must see him off – so I have requested the Capt of the *Nantasket* to let Eckly stay on shore a few days & keep him well under the Doctors eye – I shall also ask R Sturgis to have an eye to him – your letter of introduction was of more avail to him than a letter of credit from Baring would have been & as I like the youths looks I think I shall do him no harm –I asked him why he did not eat the crab apples[138] & if he were well I should still tell him to do so – but as I have been civilly treated by Mrs Pearce when I dine to day I shall send them to her –dont tell Esther I have not eaten them all myself – Mrs P goes home shortly in the *Horatio* & I wish you to call on her & she will give you a good account of me – she is a Salem Lady & quite passable, if *Mrs* Howland goes to Boston pray call on her also – I have received a newspaper from Boston dated 15th Dec a month after your last letters...

I am glad you have got into the way of going again to Church...You tell me in this letter more of your health & I am rejoiced to find how much better you must be to be willing to allude to what you were – that word "emaciated" filled me with horror – I had often feared you were depressed, unhappy, desolate, but I hardly realized I fear how much so you were – But I trust it is over & that you are now really & truly looking *forward* – I must finish this sheet as my dinner hour approaches...

Love to all & many kisses to *Bob* –

THE ENGLISH DEPART FROM CANTON

Canton May 25, 1839

Dear Rose –... Left Macao at 1 oclock yesterday & landed here at 9 AM to day after a pleasant passage with only one companion –Yesterday Capt Elliot & ten

137 A watch guard was a small pouch, sometimes leather and sometimes of cloth needlework, used to protect a pocket watch.

138 A box of crabapples was sent to RBF on this ship with Eckley by the Forbes' cook Esther. RBF frequently mis-spells Eckley as Eckly.

proscribed Gent left here & on the departure the communication with the Hongs was thrown open & we were allowed to go into the back streets & the people were allowed to come in the square, they were very civil – The new wall & fence surrounding the greater part of the square is nearly down & I think will be a great advantage to us –...

Sunday 26 May –
I have been to church & heard a sermon from Doctor Parker delivered to a congregation of 10 people myself included – There are very few English remaining in Canton & in 10 days there will not probably be one – They are very annoyed...because the Americans will not go away – We shall remain here and take care of our business...I dare say [the English] will be coming back again if they do not we shall have a good deal more business – It will be the endeavour of all who are inimical to the interests of Americans to represent the state of things here a great deal more than it is & the newspapers will make the most of this crisis to frighten old women – I am assured by Houqua that all the Local Government is waiting for is the departure of the Commissioner when the trade will be returned to its former footing as far as we are inclined to have it – I have made arrangements to hire a house at Macao for Russell & Co & if there is the least necessity for a retreat there we shall of course go at once – but I do not apprehend that it will be necessary for us to go – I find my ten days absence has been of great service to me & this is the only way I am made aware that I was not perfectly strong before – but a trip to Macao or any where else has exactly the same effect on me as a trip to Naushon used to have – one gets fresh air & becomes invigorated & when one gets back here everybody looks sober & seems to wonder why you are in such good spirits – I shall make these short excursions whenever I can & put health down first, money second – One third of my time will be up on the 10 June, think it has passed very quick & I am always in good Spirits & better than usual at home – adieu for to day

Monday 27 May –
The *Carrington* gets away this afternoon & as I have a good many business letters to attend to I will only say I am quite well – Had a pleasant little dinner yesterday at Delanos – Our Mr Green goes on Thursday in the *Panama* & I shall give him a letter to you,...I would give a great deal for his mercantile capacity – He is much annoyed at being expelled the county & obliged to give a bond never to return although he wished to embark in March he does not like to be turned out – He has the recommendation of a fortune not less than Three hundred thousand dollars mostly acquired in Canton, he has resided here about 5 years – pretty good pay is it not? Yet I would not agree to stay five years for that sum – I am daily expecting the miniature of our dear Boy & hope you will continue to write in detail, your letters can never tire me –I hope to hear you are running about gay as usual I am much more afraid of your keeping too much aloof from society than mixing too much in it –...Love to Sarah & Rose – ever thine – Benjamin –

Canton May 29 1839
My dear Rose –
...no arrivals, no news – One of the Opium Ships on the Queens birth day the 24th & the day I left Macao, amused herself by firing into a war Junk, it seems the Capt being pot–valiant wished to try the effect of his long brass gun & accordingly he fired several shots at the fellow who bore up & took protection

under the Town of Macao – No body was hurt & we hear the matter is hushed up by the Owner of the ship paying a couple of thousand dollars to the Capt of the Junk – This place is nearly clear of English & in a week there will be neither ships nor men of that nation here – We Yankees having the fear of the Yumchi before us & the interests of our constituents & last not least ourselves at heart intend to remain here & do all the business – I expect to have my hands full all summer, its an ill wind that blows nobody any good...

I shall send you per *Panama* two boxes of sugar candy sugar but dont think I shall continue to do so for it costs delivered at home full 16 cents per lb & calculating the value of money here it stands a full 19 cents, so you had better buy loaf sugar at home – you see I am calculating close – I am glad to inform you that Dr Parker declares he will remain in Canton as long as any body does, the Chinese Government have shut up his Hospital & he has nothing now to do but take care of our souls & bodies – At present we stand much more in need of the butcher than the Dr yet it is well to have him at hand for Dr Cox has deserted to Macao in conformity with the orders of Capt Elliot –

We have new to our address the *Lintin, Porcia, Paris, Nantasket, Cashmere, Panama, Edmonton* & are expecting more – We are cutting out our neighbors & rivals Wetmore & Co who have only had three ships since I arrived while we have dispatched 8 or 10 – All goes on well & our prospects are extremely good –...a plague on these mosquitos – good night

May 31

...I *am convinced* that you are reasonably & rationally happy & that you do not wish to fill me with pain & uneasiness by constantly introducing the subject of your lonely condition as Sarah used to do to John – She was very differently situated, she married young & knew John must go away yet she must have said a good deal in her letters to make him unhappy while here – on the other hand you imagined we were settled for life, stern fortune has torn us asunder, yet you make the best of it & look *forward* without murmuring – this is worthy of you – Were you to write to me despondingly constantly picturing your forlorn condition I should be very miserable & might relinquish all my – hopes of fortune and Competency & go home to sacrifice those hopes I am well aware what you feel, what you suffer, but it does not come home to me as it would were you always talking about it – I am sure when we are reunited, two years hence we shall not repine – I shall as you say succeed & acquire an independence – while if I had staid at home I should have sunk under the load or become a melancholy & morose old man at 35 – Now I feel I have done right, I have made a great sacrifice to be sure but it is for the purpose of accomplishing great ends – besides which I think it is well on some accounts that we are asunder – I feel that your health will be benefitted thereby – I beg you to take a great deal of exercise & keep up my old acquaintances it is very important to me as you say that I find you younger on my return & not a moping desponding care worn body – Respecting our noble boy I cannot inculcate too strongly the necessity of cultivating a good *digestion*, it is in sane to talk of his moral nature if his digestion be not good he will be unhappy – keep from him all sweets, comfits & pastry & give him good plain food & exercise & fresh air – & dont make a monkey of him teaching him tricks – make a man of him –& if you punish him severely let it be whenever he is *afraid* of anything – Flora has gone to Macao for her health being too fat & lazy here, she will have sea bathing & fresh air and will get good exercise –

I was quite amused with Sturgis' children at Macao – they are nice children

– but they did not take a great fancy to me – When I was to take leave of Sturgis I asked him to send for Lucy & John – he did so & told Lucy that I had a little Boy at home & that she would see him & Aunt Rose & that she must recollect me & tell Aunt R about me – she seemed to understand what he meant – Then he tried to tell Johnny the same, he looked quite sober for a moment, I gave him a kiss & told him to carry it to my little Boy at home – I was quite affected & Johnny looked sober, but got off my knee stuck his thumbs into his side pockets & went swinging away as unconcerned as possible – I suppose he will forget his Father in a week after he sails – What are we but children on a little larger scale & how happy for us it is that grief & its consequences must give way to time – I am surprised every day to find myself so happy –

June 1 –

Raining like great guns – Green is off directly – We had a party of twelve yesterday to dine him off & had quite a lively party – drank toasts &c – I had rather a restless night in consequence (of course) of a mosquito or ten having got into my curtain – Among other things I had a dream – methinks I was at TH Perkins Jrs & asked where you lived – I then went in search of you going down Park St met Mary Appleton & Miss Austin – They told me you were very well & spoke of the beauty of our Son – soon after I met your mother in great spirits & joined her to go home to you – we had not got far when (confound the luck) my boy entered my room "seven oclock Sir" so I did not see you – I was very angry at being awakened – as you may suppose – I dont dream except after too much eating & drinking, or mosquitos –

I have packed up a copper vase of olden times & directed it to you per *Panama* & the Comprador brought me a Tad of dried fruit which I have told William to seize upon for his children –

My time draws to a close dearest & I feel that I am parting from you once more, one year out of three will be gone in 10 days & it has gone quick – bear up then & continue to act up to your principles...– Adieu dearest –

Monday 3 June –

My dear Rose –

Yesterday I closed my journal sheets & dispatched them by our Mr Green who took passage in the *Panama* – he left here during a hard rain & old Houqua notwithstanding went to the point ungainly called "Jackass Point"[139] & saw him off – I felt really sad at seeing him depart yet abstractedly considered it is a great relief to me to have him go – it throws more responsibility on me[140] & on the rest of us – Green was a thorough man, but arbitrary & uncompromising & I really felt very little like acting or advising while he was here, now I feel a weight & responsibility upon me that will make me feel of more consequence – You are aware that I have always had a responsible post from boyhood & you may imagine that it did not suit me very well to have Mr Green doing every thing even to the opening of letters before me – We received Mr Edward King into our house on the 1st as a partner, he has been about four years – in Canton – Notwithstanding all I have said of Green I parted from him with a pang that almost ensnared me – the idea of his going home direct to see you – & of his success &c came over me & I sighed for the day when I should be saying adieu

[139] Jackass Point was a small piece of land that jutted into the river in front of the factories; it was a convenient landing for small boats.

[140] When Green left, RBF took his place as head of Russell & Co. in Canton.

to Canton forever – I had a very kind note from Green this morning &...I hope he will get a wife that can rule him – he has about half a million of dollars which I dare say will make him perfectly lovely in New York – Flora has gone to Macao for air & exercise –

THURSDAY 4 JUNE 11 PM

This has been a very hot day & not much to do except to keep cool & drive away the mosquitos – I have read over all your letters & cut out all the leaves out of an old book except about an inch – to this remaining part I have pasted your letters according to date & it makes a valuable volume...– I shall read over my letters to you & see what effect a life of business has had –...indeed I have written volumes to you & John & probably never wrote so much in a year as I have during the last 8 months here – It is really perilous to write as much as I do, sometimes my head swims & I am obliged to go & walk it off I conclude I have written less satisfactorily but then this is natural enough –... I generally write to you late in the evening after a busy day – this is not fair yet I have no other time so easily at my disposal –...The seizure of the Opium has deprived us of some $25000 say twenty five thousand dollars of Commissions that would have been earned and if it had been sold in the ordinary way – but we have earned over fifty–thousand besides this since January 1st & are likely to do much better when the trade goes on uninterruptedly – good night –

THURSDAY 6 JUNE –

Nothing new here or from you dearest – I have been very much occupied to day & it is late at even – I think of going to Lintin early in the morning to charter a ship for a friend of ours & to forward some important letters therefore I will close this sheet for the *Horatio* for fear it might miss her, I shall only be gone three or four days –...believe me ever thine most Truly RBF

JUNE 7

As I have not gone to Lintin I continue to write – I am in great spirits to day at a new consignment, the *Splendid* from New York to the 18 February – more than three months after your latest date –she brings no letters! The Captain who contracts the ship & her owners have always before done business with Wetmore & Co *our rivals* & it is peculiarly gratifying to get these consignments –(is it not human nature?) – We have a late ship from England also with prospects of several ships – & we are more likely to have too much to do than too little this summer, we have engaged a Mr Spooner in addition to our other clerks & young Eckley came up to day & is at his desk where I introduced him five minutes after he arrived...he is a little delicate & I doubt if it will be good for him to stay – the mosquitos are "a eatin me up" – I have bought a clay Cooly for Bob to go per *Horatio* –

good night dearest love to Maa & Sally &c

SCHOONER SYLPH – 8 JUNE 5 PM NEAR SECOND BAR

pitching about more or less – left Canton at 11 AM – I am going down as I have before stated on business & it is under these circumstances that business is a pleasure – I intend to return in a few days & hope to get letters before I go up –...My companions are Mr Gilman our clerk & Mr Clarke, a missionary from the Sandwich Islands – It has been raining most all day but we have fine weather below decks & not crowded – I shall write more poetically when we get to our anchor bye & bye – I will cut off here for the present –

9th June morning –

just outside the Bocca Tigres & bobbing up & down in a head sea, I suppose you are Bob–ing too – pretty good? I was up & down all night writing, getting up anchor, anchoring &c &c very well notwithstanding –...I have asked Mr Hathaway to go & see you & I beg you will call on Mrs Capt Howland if she gets home safe & *he* has promised to get John to introduce him if his wife should not be in Boston with him – They will tell you I am well – I expect to work hard all summer & to get a little *wilted* & require a run to Macao occasionally but the winter will set me all up again – I am determined not to work myself to death & with this vein I shall get Delano into harness as soon as I can after he gets his two vessels away...

June 12 Macao –

I landed on the 10th at 9 AM & it has rained almost ever since & I have been very busy running round with a multiplicity of business – I am staying at Mr Hunters & I have not even had time to call on Mrs Howland & Mrs Pierce – The *Horatio* is expected down daily, say any moment & while I am occasionally casting my eye Northward for her I am doing the same to the South hoping for an arrival from home – my dates are 7 months – I will add a line when the *Horatio* heaves in sight, if she does so before I embark for Canton tomorrow

June 13

My dear Rose –

The *Horatio* is here only waiting to embark Mrs Howland, Mrs Pierce, Miss P – Miss Sturgis & Mr Sturgis Jr [Russell's children]...and Mr Hathaway...if she remains over night & if I do not go up this afternoon to Canton I will write again but the press of business letters &c prevents my enlarging now – much love to your Mother, Sarah & Bob & remember me to Mary Motley & her Lord, Copley & Lizzy & *Bob* last not least Yrs in *haste* as usual RBF

Canton 16 June 1839

My dear Rose –

Behold me back in Canton – I arrived here yesterday morning...all things very quiet here, no confinement in the factories except by flood, went to make calls yesterday in a small boat – I have at last got permanently located in my own room which during my absence has been painted up & made quite *homey* & comfortable –The wall is our favorite green, a large curtain bed big enough for two, a square cushioned couch covered with chintz, a writing table, with the madonna hung up over it & the child & mother below, a large wash stand, book case, wardrobe &c – this room opens into a veranda paved with marble, whenever I have my bathing tub & all things are quite "come il faut" I am not writing these just now but I intend to do so though there is one serious inconvenience in so doing & that is I am away from the desk & have only one of these pens to write with – I dare say I should write you better letters & say more heart breaking things there in the solitude of my cell, but this is not good for me – better I should snatch a moment now & then from my labors & write you merely of facts – feelings are hardly safe always to record –

Monday 17 June –

No news from home yet – we have one letter from John via England overland to 21 November – wherein he says tell RBF all his friends are well – You have no idea how dull Canton is, there are only about 20 foreigners here & but little trade going on – We are the only people who have ships at Whampoa – As soon as trade begins we shall be very busy & time will go more rapidly – the Thermometer stands at 85 to 90 & it is too hot to think much & I get clear of as much labour as I can & put it off on my partners – I am quite well though I feel that the heat pulls down the flesh & strength & the want of our boating & walking, playing ball &c is severely felt – I look forward to spending a month at Macao before October, after that we have fine weather – Flora is still at Macao & *doing as well as could be expected under the circumstances* – I am getting very impatient to hear from you my letters being about 7 months old, when they begin to come in again they will come as before all in a lump – A plague on these mosquitos & with love to all good night –

Wednesday 19 June –
On the way to Macao in the eternal everlasting "*Union*," going down to settle some business of importance & coming up again directly –I was made inexpressibly happy yesterday by receiving your letters making up the numbers from No 16 – No 20 & I laughed & cried over them – I had invited the Rev Dr Parker, Rev Dr Taylor of the frigate & two or three more to dine & I had not time to read my letters till dinner was over, I merely looked at the last date (Jany 7th) & found *all was well* got through dinner which singularly enough was on the birth day of Dr P & one of the company & also the anniversary of the battle of Waterloo & the launching of the *Lintin* – I then retired to my chamber & gave myself up to the hungry luxury of *devouring* your letters –...I will now take them up as they were written & review the feelings & emotions they gave being to

REVIEWING ROSE'S LETTERS

November 18 No 17 Sunday !...Your account of the aggregate weight of John's daughters is truly ridiculous 7 1/4 lbs together, this is what my friend Clarke (of the British factory) would call "enormously small" & John writes me that at the date of his letter they were gaining a pound a week & weighed 7 1/4 & 9 1/4 & were 9 weeks old, at this rate they could not have weighed *any thing* at the birth – how exceedingly convenient it must be to *have* such children – John says one is a screamer but both are doing pretty well but he says "your boy is bright & intelligent & what is more wonderful is like you & very handsome" & he says in another letter that mine is worth a bushel of *his* or *hisen* – I am glad they are pretty

You give a good account of your health & of our dear Boys – but it is fearful to think what hangs on the life of that being, I feel that you & I & fortune would sink & that poverty & even disgrace & loss of reputation, chains & slavery, Yumchi's annually & all the ends that flesh is heir to would not be half so dreadful as his loss – No it cannot be that God will take him away – I will not believe it –

November 20 "on the 19th you dined with Copley & had a nice little party" this gives me *almost* as much Satisfaction as if I had been there & I hope you will continue to cultivate those true hearted friends –...

the late ship brings a large amount of property consigned jointly to me (as RBF) & the supercargo – the Commissions to amount to $7 or 8 thousand to be divided between us – but I *declined*, the principal, & interest too in the long run of Russell & Co being never to divide the *loaf* with any one – I told the supercargo we had a hot summer before us & plenty of work & could not afford to work for half price –

I think he will have to pay a full Commission & I am determined not to take the extra care & responsibility without it, if Delano chooses to *cut under* he may have the job – if we relax in one case we should have to in another & the only plan is to be independent –... We have a prospect of as much business as we can do well at full Commissions & we are determined not to be overworked – I merely mention this to show you that we think little of a sum that would induce Dumaresq to go a whole voyage – when my own fortune is secured I shall do what I can for D_ if I have a chance –...I have written to Sarah to day – her letter is full of good feeling & affection & I think she is really attached to us –

Nov 25 – a very cold day – I did not feel it – you went to church & *Bennet* went to walk, I see you have given up the *Bob* – Louisa [Dumaresque] & Margaretta dined with you on the 24th – glad of it & that you had a nice time – & then you revert to the good old days of Naushon & my return &c – then come some of your good geniuses & you say our trials are for our good, this may all be very true, but I think we are good enough not to deserve to go though them again of the sake merely of improvement ! hey !!

Let bye gones be bye gones, & look ahead & aloft –...

28 Nov – call from Mrs Crowningsheild – I dare say she went to see whether your Boy was all he is cracked up to be –...You seem to be getting a very good opinion of yourself & I am glad of it as it shews a clear conscience –

Nov 29 Thanksgiving day – Aunt James [Perkins] likes Bennets picture – you don't say what your Ma & Sally think of it – Lizzy Green & Mary Motley dont like it – sorry – I shall if it is handsome –...

Dec 2 – Joseph had been with you three weeks this is pleasant –... I am alive am I "in the hearts of all" – this *is* a comfort – "Mr & Mrs Coolidge *not* going to Canton" – true I dare say...

Sunday again – Mr Greenwood preaching on the duties of hope & cheerfulness – I am truly glad to believe that you really do bear up like a man & R Sturgis has often told me (as you say that you would be surprised at the gradual "victory of hope over despair" constant activity is the true thing & this I practice – On the 8th you had a congenial party & it went off well – I should have liked to have been there – it gives me dearest sincere pleasure to see you are getting again at your old tricks – you say here that Bennett with the aid of one finger can walk across the room – huzza.

4 PM We have dined & had a nap – We are Wetmores Son & myself – we are now through the Bogue & are going along merrily & I resume your letters –

You say Bennet struck you!!!!!!!! & that he is like both of us – I never struck my mother did you? Why did you not flog him well –I fear he will get the upper hand of you – Emma is getting *very* fond of him – likes the picture –

Dec 13 letter – you have had the mark[141] removed have you – I had entirely forgot it – he is no longer a re*mark* able boy – it must have been rather tough for you to have it done after all – I am glad it is well over –

Dec 16 Last night you had a regular frolic – you are getting on & I expect to hear of a Ball & supper soon – quite a nice little party pon my words, wish I could have been there –...

141 Bob apparently had a small birthmark on his face which was removed.

Dec 23 Boy 14 months old – fine accounts still of the Boy – true we were in danger of taking the goods of this life as a matter of course –...

Dec 27 – you say that you shall feel better now that you have got through Christmas, why you tell me along back that you were doing well before – I begin to doubt if you have been excessively happy – I am glad you have had a good *cry* – I also had one at your description of the Christmas meeting – I am very susceptible to flattery & your notice of my being missed really made me feel badly...now I come to that part of your letter about Wetmore's wife – I would show it to him if I thought he had any soul – he is asleep by me – he has not minced much feeling for his loss & he is constantly bound up in business – Stanton Parker dead – Ah me – we are more lucky than we are willing to admit –...I had a large order for the Commissioners wife – silks, lace, ware, toys, china &c&c – I recommended him to let me reduce it for said I all these things will cost money– say $450 – so he wrote me a kind letter & requested me to do as I please – I'll cut down the dashing wifes order I will !! She shant spend her husbands hard earnings so –

MY DEAR ROSE –
Canton 25 June 1839
I got up here yesterday at 10 oclock after a very pleasant passage & found all friends well – I called last night on Parker to get his written opinion on my old complaint which I asked him to give me to satisfy you that what I say of my health is true – I had so much confidence in Parker & knew he had leisure to attend to me & I therefore intended if any course of diet or medicine was necessary to take his advice – therefore I gave him a history of my old enemy & now give you his answer – I also sent him Dr Jacksons letter to read –

My dear Mr Forbes –
The full & distinct account you have given me of your health for the last *15* years, has received repeated & careful perusal &...– my full belief is that you have no organic disease of liver, spleen – or kidney or intestine, that your *nervous* system has been tried & is easily excited at the present time & that your slight gastric disturbances depend chiefly on this, the connection between the nerves of the stomach & the brain being very intimate – In the case of your health let me repeat – that the 4 simple directions of Dr J_ cannot be dispensed with, while I add –

1st Endeavour to meet the responsible & exciting occurrences of a mercantile life as *philosophically* as possible or rather to use the expression & excellent advice of Dr J to Mrs F – "Trust in God" for he will keep in perfect peace all who repose in him –

2nd When these attacks of gastric uneasiness recur an occasional use of Calomel, or blue pill will do good –

3rd When the soreness in left side is unusually great *rub* the part with lineament –

I will only add that subsequent development of symptoms may modify my views of your care, but at present I do not perceive any thing that need give you the least alarm & with all due precaution on your part & with the blessing of God may your health be preserved, the object of your exile secured & the utmost of your hopes of domestic enjoyment be realized on earth, & every desire be satisfied hereafter, Yours most sincerely

Peter Parker

Looking serene and very wise in a portrait attributed to George Chinnery is Houqua, the principal Hong Merchant of Canton. On the following two pages is a corner of Houqua's garden, as painted by Tingqua.

I have thus given you my dear wife what I am sure will relieve you, it has given me immense relief for I began to imagine I required medicine, I was getting Hip'd – In conversing with R Sturgis at Macao he told me he had the same sort of business & want of proper action of the Stomack for a year or two after he arrived here, he imagined he was sick & already began to think of the probable fate of his destitute children, he consulted Coolidge or Parker & was laughed at & is now more hearty than he was at home –

JUNE 28 –

I have been quite busy these three days in attending to some of the officers of the men of war that are up here, among them are two midshipmen only 14 years of age – one is Son of Bernard Henry Esq & the other is a young Read, they are fine boys – I took them to day to see Houqua & he was quite pleased & invited them to go to his house at Hunan [142] tomorrow – I had applied in the morning for permission to go with some of the elder officers but he discouraged me, perhaps he wishes these youths to be seen by the Mrs Houquas –They dine with me tomorrow, they are diminutive for their years & one of them looks so much like that young scape grace Scarborough that I took him for him, the other (Henry) is a very handsome Boy –...– The *Osage* brought bad news to three of the officers of the *John Adams*, one lost wife & child, one his Father & Captain Wyman a Brother – so you see my dear Rosy we are not the most unfortunate people in the world – Since the Doctors letter I have given up cigars, fruit after dinner & all wine & I am now as well as can be, quite in good spirits & I hope with due care to overcome my old enemy yet –

We have to day finally settled the matter of securing our Ships & have reduced the bond demanded to a very moderate certificate amounting to little or nothing more than a bare assertion that the ships have no Opium & that the Captains being aware of new & severe laws will not violate them – We must have letters ere long from you of a much later date & I am anxiously expecting the portrait & your letters after hearing of my arrival at Anjier...

SUNDAY 30TH JUNE –

a fine day, read prayers at home & went to church at ll oclock heard Dr Parker – Lieutenant Magruder first of the *Columbia* & two others dined with us quietly on a fine boiled leg of mutton – yesterday I went over to Hunan with the two young midshipmen & walked all over Houquas place where I had never been before – it is in a state of dilapidation, one of his Brothers occupies it, there was a good many women peeping out to get a look at the boys & I sent them to see them, they returned with no very flattering accounts of their beauty, after seeing all that was to be seen at Houquas we visited the Temple & saw the priests at worship, chanting much after the manner of the Roman catholics – The officers leave us tomorrow for the ship –... We shall begin to be quite busy in a day or two for we have three ships at Whampoa & three outside –...I find I have written you whims of nonsense – say full a page & a half a day – I have from you 20 letters averaging three pages is 60 pages in 6 1/2 month – say 1/3d of a page per day – you will have a great deal to make up to be square & when you consider that I write as much to John in the way of gossip & business together & as much more to other private friends to say nothing of business letters, you will naturally conclude you are very remiss or *I* am very good – I suppose I average 10 pages a day besides vast quantities of talk & a good deal of figuring

142 Honam (RBF's Hunan) was an island six miles long, directly across the river from the factories.

"American Merchants Buying Tea" is the title of this painting by Tingqua, one of a series of paintings of tea cultivation and tea trade done by the Chinese artist.

– All this is good for me it keeps down thoughts of home & I seldom take up the thread of home recollections – till I retire to my room where I am now writing to you for the first time, it being Sunday – I do not like to write in the compting room as that would look too much like business – I have begun to read prayers every morning in my own room & think I feel the benefit already, our Heavenly Father cannot but listen to the sincere prayers of his creatures, & I feel that it is not a mere form with me: I think adversity has had a good effect on both of us & I hope when I get home to find you calculating on your daily devotions as upon your daily bread – I find myself cheerful & satisfied with myself after such exercise –I hope you will cultivate a devotional spirit in our Son...– Our commercial year expires to day the chances of making a fortune at one single dash this year are very good & if I were not in a house pledged against speculation I would attempt it, but we cannot trade beyond a Commission agency & we must see others lose or win as the case may be, & pocket our slow but sure gains –...I have had no time to read lately – Perhaps one reason I am more happy lately is the fact of being at the helm here – I consult daily with Houqua about the general trade & am in his confidence – He is a grand old fellow to us & I wish we were sure of his life for twenty years – Good night & love to all & remember you are never too name Houqua to any one –

July 5th –

...*I have been enormously* busy & have hardly left my desk till 11 PM any night – Yesterday I had the pleasure to hear from the capt of the *Oneida* that the *portrait* of Bob was aboard the ship & I saw the Bill of Lading of the same, $4 1/2 for freight – why you ought to have made it come freight free, I thought it was a Miniature but suppose from the Bill of Landing that it is full length – I hope to get it up in a few days as also my letters per *Oneida* which must be five or six weeks later than any I have from you, We have accounts from the US to 6 March by way of England...I have no cause of complaint for you have been exceedingly good in writing & have sent me letters several times when I got nothing from John – Remember this is your first duty & I hope also your greatest pleasure...

July 6

...I was agreeably surprised yesterday to get a long letter of two sheets from you my dear, dated from Sept 27 to Octo 2 – No 9 – I had entirely forgotten of late that No 9 was missing though I have no doubt noticed it at an earlier period – But I got several interesting items in this letter which were necessary to make the chain complete –...I will not now particularly review your letters but wait till I get those per *Oneida* & then I will have a good "sit down"–

Sunday July 7 –

Nine years since I left Boston on the *Lintin* – yet I find myself as well as I was then though more grey, you will not be surprised if you hear that I am more grey, or that my hair had turned *black*, Macassar[143] is not far off & I may try its "incomparable virtues" – We have had a busy day about 10 AM the Imperial Commissioner, the Vice Roy & other high officers came out of the city to take a Survey of the square & see that their orders in relation to the enclosure, the removal of the terraces from the Tops of houses & other things were obeyed – quite a posse of soldiers, lictors & executioners & a mass of ragged & dirty servants came out, all the Linguists others not on duty as guards prostrated themselves – as these fellows passed, his highness went into the Hall of her Majesties Superintendent & from there took a survey of the square &c & in about an hour went off again & we went to church & had a good sermon fr Dr Parker – after which I returned home & read over old letters from you & mine to you & I do not see that you have any cause for complaint as to quantity –... I had made up my mind some days ago that Eckley would not do for us – he has never been put to hard work...he dont write correctly & it is as much work to go over & correct his copies as it would be to write the letters, & I have no time to devote to his instruction – the fact is we want clerks who have some experience & not Raw hands especially Gentlemens Sons who have not the motive for constant exertion – he is very amiable youth & I did not know exactly how I should tell him he would not do – so I wrote a letter to his Father & gave it him to copy – I have not held out to him any promise that David would be retained & I thought it best to be explicit – he has said nothing but I can see he is dispirited about it – I have put the matter principally in the score of health & hard work, telling his Father I did not think the present position of his Son was good for such a body & this is true for if I were to put him to his work as I must if he were to be a permanent clerk he would not stand it & I dare say that having him up here at all may make dissatisfaction – but I cant help this & I shall deal quite plainly with Mr Lowell (his guardian) when he is ready to go – It has been a hot day – as I have nothing new from you I will say good night –

---

[143] Macassar refers to an oil used as a hair dressing for men, originally imported from Macassar, a seaport on the southwest coast of Celebes, Indonesia.

BUSINESS AND BUSINESS ASSOCIATES

This is Saturday night – weather looks a little typhonish – I get on remarkably well with my partners & Low is very active & shrewd & King is indefatigable – either of them does double the work that I do – I do most of the talking & a good deal of correspondence –The mill works well & the Commissioner account is incredible fast in short all I want is to see you once more & to clasp that dear Boy in my arms –

Wed Aug 2nd 1839
...Aho has a son a month old or less – send him some little stockings, mittens &c, also some for my Boy whose wife is able to bear him a child – unless he lies for the sake of getting rid of going to Macao with me on the 10th – when these China men want to go home very much they generally say their father or mother is just dead & this boy having buried both several times has perhaps *got up* a new excuse –

Mar 15 Interesting about war with England – that's no go – I have never feared it a moment –

three more double teeth that makes 32 & 16 single – begin to talk I suppose he will be able to read this by the time I get home

9 oclock good night

Thurs 8th
I left off late last night & having a headache I took two of the blue pills & am well this AM –

Mar 23rd – letter from *Mary Chilton* – Boy walking on his own for first time in open air did he walk on his hands before? another double tooth makes 33 – "wild with spirits" – I don't think ardent spirits are good for such young children –

I am glad you had a talk with Russell Sturgis – If he finds I am going up he will help no doubt – John says he seemed much pleased at my good fortune – but he did not write to me – Our boating is all done for & I feel the deprivation very much

Mar 21 – Bob 17 months old – that was the day we were effectively shut up here – time has passed very quickly – I send you the Repository for May which has an excellent leading article of Opium from the point of the poppy king of Olyphant house – if you read the late China papers you will see some articles signed by our house & will readily recognize me therein "I did not come here for my health; neither to effect a reform, moral or political, but to get the needful where with all to be useful & happy at home & I shall stay as long as I can carry on my business in safety & I consider myself as safe in China as in any place of the world" – Send you 2 caps & covers I sent them long ago, you unreasonable woman & I dare say your next order will be for 2 or 3 pieces of silk – one Blue like your old pelisse, hey? & some to squander away – 2 cups & saucers– why you will ruin me – What piece of furniture did you sell to pay for Bob's picture?

Mar 27 – a nice long letter from Joe – I bet I have a longer – now comes your plan of C lodgings which I approve of entirely & I have fancied all your arrangements – just what things you took out – here & how much you are enjoying the June air – are there any slaughter houses near? I doubt much however if you are enjoying much of any thing just now as you must be getting accounts of our Opium battles & our imprisonment which time I look back to as the most amusing of all my China days – I see you are looking forward to laying up money during summer for timber wood, doctors – both no doubt will have been necessary – for you cannot expect our dear boy to escape measles, whooping cough & a thousand ills which young juvenile flesh is heir to – I should not be surprised to hear at any moment he was sick & should not be alarmed –

Mar 28 – Fast day – that was the day we gave up 20,000 chests of Opium – see if your imagination doesnt carry you too far in praise of my character, pray do not be carried away by ideal images of my perfection for you know I am sometimes crabbed & unjust –

I rejoice to find that you are running about again among our friends –

Mar 29 just opened the things per *M Chilton* – George Winslow been to see you – glad of it – it seems you were much pleased to have George talk of me – No doubt he soon found out your weak side –

...Made up your first dress in 15 months & cost 1/2 dollar a yard, as you are only a yard & 1/2 high – I suppose with trimming it cost $1 – You say I must be prudent & economical – I have no time for prudence or economy on small things – our family consist of *myself*– Low, King, Spooner, Gilman & two Portuguese lads – each has a servant – we have two cooks, a cowsman, two English cows, a Comprador – man to go to market, four coolies or porter making 25 souls – including the 2 cows – our family expenses are about $8000 per annum – besides each ones private expenses which are light $1000 each

July 12

Quite a long time since I took pen in hand, & I can hardly realize that I have not done so since the 7th – on the 10th received your letters per *Oneida* No 24 beginning 31 January & ending 5 Feb these letters gave me very great pleasure & have been read over & over again & I will now take them up according to their dates & see what I have to say in reply – The first shows some anxiety about the state of things here – how entirely unnecessary this was when you take into view the late events & these do not require any fretting – I see you had made a cozy visit to Mr Cushing dined & got home *at 1 AM* Pretty doings!...You give me some a/c of Papantes[144] assemblies & your chill waltzing story is exultantly good – Mrs Cabot is quite the go I see –...I see you have many invitations & that you have not been to the balls, this is all well enough, I never liked large rants, but I hope you will go frequently into small family circles & keep up our acquaintances –...You give me such accounts of the beauty & intelligence of our dear Boy that it makes me almost home sick, & I should not believe one half of it if the facts were not confirmed by all who write to me – You tell me of Marshall Springs death, which I have noticed before– You tell me of Margaretta & the plan for Dumaresq to go to Lowell, it wont do, he is on his way out here with his wife – I am very glad you did not send the picture by Osgood for he may not be here this month, I am expecting it most impatiently from the ship which still remains outside – I must have it tomorrow I think – Let me again remind you that you

144 Papanti's was for many years Boston's most fashionable dancing school, conducted first by Lorenzo Papanti and afterwards by his son Augustus. Besides classes they held assemblies several times a year.

must use good black ink, your letters are scarcely legible & my eyes are hardly able to make them out, particularly the first day of reading!...I am rejoiced that you take exercise & run about, I get as much as I want this warm weather, but have sent to Manila for a horse & intend if possible to go to Macao for a month before November & enjoy riding about – I wish I had the old judge here – You ask me to keep up a good heart if things don't turn out quite so bright as I expect, *here* all goes on profitably – but my letters from John with accounts show that my old affairs were much worse than I expected, & I cannot expect under the best circumstances, to be more than square with the world at the end of this year, but my only creditors will be Mr Cushing & John & they are willing to wait – It is rather hard to feel that I am working up hill with a burthen on my back, but I am not in the least dispirited & if I were I would not make it apparent for were my real situation known here or at home, it would have a bad effect, next year I should feel that all I get is clear gain if the Chinese do not drive us away from Canton we must do well– *very well*–...John has advanced for me *$60000* sixty thousand dollars full half of which my old affairs can not return to him – I must inevitably have failed with out him – I am glad however that I did not – You say in the end..."Your journals are precious indeed"– this is the only intimation in any of the letters received that lead me in the smallest degree to believe you had got my second journal from Anjer – Johns letters to the 21 February do not say a word about anything but having received generally my long letters & as neither of you refer to my patient nor to Flora I think you could not have received my Anjer letters...I am quite happy & satisfied with what I am about & the worse things turn out at home, the more reason for coming here –

...It must now be near midnight & I have written to day about 20 Pages – so I must not write much more –...I cant make out what the thingumabobs are that you sent me with mottos on them, I sent one to Dr Parker for a mark for his Bible, with "Deeds not words" on it & told him it applied admirably to him – Good night

PORTRAIT OF SON BOB ARRIVES

Sunday Evening–

Yesterday the ship having my picture on board arrived at Whampoa & this morning I hired a China boat after a good deal of negotiating, as these privileges have of late been cut off, & at *1/2 past 5* this morning I started for Whampoa, got alongside the *Nantasket* & sent for the box to the *Splendid* – I was at first view disappointed, it did not look exactly as I expected & he must have changed a great deal– but the more I looked at it the better I liked it– The boatman after seeing it said it could not go up in his boat, I told him I should in that case have to go up in a ships boat & he would lose his fare– this made him relent & at 11 oclock we left Whampoa to return– I had invited three Gentlemen to dine, but owing to a head wind & unfavorable tide– I did not get up till 1/2 past 3– I left the box on board the ship & gazed at the face most of the way up– Delano & Low were with me, they both thought it handsome– I finally cut out a hole in the new paper & covered up the body & as a head & liked it much better, it grows familiar to me every minute & the more I look at it the better I like it– the Gents who dined with me thought it looked like me particularly the upper part–[145]

145 This picture was painted by Alvin Clark (1804-87), who set up a Boston studio in 1835 and painted many portraits.

Portrait of Son Bob Arrives

After dinner I took it up into my chamber where I am now sitting, writing on my table covered with your red breakfast cloth, I took it out of the frame & put it into the frame of the Madonna that is– behind the glass so as just to cover the body leaving the head & bust & it is a great improvement– It seemed lost in that enormous frame which has cost me $5 for freight– You must send me another done on a piece of canvas 18 inches square & carefully packed that I may see how he improves & I shall immediately have a miniature in ivory done for you, it will only cost 6-8 dollars– I think it will be well spent– I have got Master Bob before me in such a position that my lamp shines brightly on him & every now & then as I turn my eyes up to him as to my guardian angel I think I see a new expression & I almost imagine a smile, it don't look half so stiff to me as it did at first, beside, the drapery & *hands* are badly done, they look unfinished, or rather fin-ished– for the paws are more like turtles fins or "flippers" than hands– it is a fine head, the head is a little large in proportion to the body– but then the body is turned side ways– it is very valuable to me– Of course I did not go to church to day & I shall read the service before I go to bed– I feel that I have done a good days work– You will recollect that in making my criticism on the portrait I do it upon my own opinion & having had nothing from John or Emma on the subject I think I am unprejudiced– I shall look at it all the leisure time I have– I have cut out some scraps from newspapers which I enclose– In looking over Johns letters to day again I see he says you have given him the history of the Pirate & the Lost Portrait to read so you must have received my Anjer letters, or some of them, If I remember right I put up the Romances under one cover & my journal under another & marked them to go by different vessels, & I have just found Dumaresqs letter in which he says "I shall hand your package to Mrs F–" Dr Parker just came in as I finished the last sentence & he is delighted with our boy, but he prefers the whole– he says if the body is covered up it looks 4 mos older– I had a long talk with the Dr & am glad always to commune with good men– He cautions us not to make an idol of that Boy but to hold him in trust– I read to him some of your remarks on this subject & he thinks no doubt that you are a very good girl– If the Doctor was married I should open my heart a great deal more to him & as it is I find a good deal of sympathy in him– I have eaten no fruit except before dinner, & I have been better for it & smoked no cigars & drank no wine this month & I have had little or none of that soreness in my stomach & have been regular in all respects– I am not so heavy by 10 lbs as I was in winter, but that is the natural consequence of the warm weather, I take but one nap all night long that is from 11 or 12 to 6– get up, shave, bathe, dress, read prayers & breakfast– My life is a satisfactory one, I feel that I hold a very responsible place, I feel my importance now that Green is gone & I have nothing unpleasant to look forward to except Coolidges coming, unless the John Bulls should make a row here now & if they do we must go to Macao till the breeze blows over– Russell & Co have hired a house there to retreat to at $850 per annum– a large double house, half of which can be let for $500– Our business is going on well & we have nothing to ask for– I received a friendly letter from Mr Bates–[146] the head man of Messrs Barings house, in which he acknowledges my letter to the house announcing my arrangements here– he is also friendly to Coolidge & has evidently been waiting to see what I was about before he compromised himself– In a letter to R&Co he excuses the

[146] Joshua Bates was an expatriate Bostonian who had married into the Sturgis family. He was an able banker who was selected to handle the accounts of Bryant Sturgis & Co. and Perkins & Co. in 1820. He took over the accounts of Russell & Co. when that house was formed.

house for holding on to certain goods, by saying "It was decidedly less profitable to offer my merchandise for sale in 1837" in replying to this letter I might have said "I am aware of that & regret you did not act upon that opinion with my goods" meaning R B Forbes's which you will recollect were cruelly sacrificed by Barings in a time of panic– I must not write any more by this uncertain light my eyes are tired– I dont think you will have any cause to complain of my not writing enough– If you were to have your choice my dear would you rather I should stay here my full time & return to you to live in Boston or would you that I should return a year sooner & fix myself with Cary [147] in New York, think well of this, if I should go to live in N York it would be for years– If I return to you in three years from the 10th of June 1838– I cannot expect to return rich, but may get 40-50000 nett– If I find that my affairs are likely to result even worse than I have stated to you...I may *order* you to come *out* & calculate to stay a year or two longer than I now contemplate– the thing I have determined on & that is not to be separated from you more than the time I have promised to you– Good night & God bless you–

Folks what live in glass houses should not throw stones– this very quaint adage is intended to apply to the very pale & emaciated appearance of this letter, the fact is that I am getting short of this black paper[148] which is an invaluable thing to you for I should not write half I do if I had not this writing apparatus– This is the 16 July– We have dispatched the *Nantasket* but are to send a boat after her in the morning with more letters– I have already put Bob into the hands of a painter & he is going for to make a miniature, say the bust & head which I shall send you per *Rambler*...– It has been darned hot here– but I am so well that I have been at work all day & am none the worse for it– besides which have dined heartily– drank three glasses of Beer– but thats a long time ago– it is now near Midnight & I shall close this pretty soon– I put into it a letter from Hunter which will give you some insight into his character– He is an open hearted clever fellow– appears to take my schooling in the right spirit–

He speaks of Flora who is likely to add to her responsibilities in a few weeks or days– you must give a great deal of love to your good mother & my black Sally, for whom I have a very great regard which I am sorry to think is not duly returned– What do they really think of me– I have just had to do a very hard thing namely to refuse to help Mr Sturgis with an endorsement without positive security– He was good to me as a youth & I would willingly stay in China a year longer to make him easy in his circumstances, *but* while I owe JPC [John Perkins Cushing] I must not be to liberal– Good bye dearest perhaps I shall write more tomorrow– & perhaps not– rather more perhaps than not, Yrs ever affectionately Benjamin Backstay....

Canton July 25, 1839

Dear Rose–

...I am writing this to go per *Rambler* or *Splendid*– I keep the long letters for the best ships & you will get most per *Nantasket*– We have had no arrivals from any quarter of late...– it is a singular fact that the most important of your letters, namely those acknowledging mine have been the last to come to hand– What a

---

147 Thomas Graves Cary was married to Mary Ann Cushing, a daughter of T. H. Perkins. He became a partner of Sam Cabot and T. H. Perkins in the firm T.H. Perkins & Sons in 1832. Prior to that he had had a career in New York City.

148 Black paper refers to the carbon paper Forbes used to make duplicate copies of his journals and all other correspondence.

comment too on domestic & wifely affection & Brotherly love, is the fact that I have letters in my desk that have been there ten days or more, dated in Phila 9 March, by way of England & India & in reply to mine of 20 October dated here!...After the *Splendid* is off in ten days I shall make a short visit to Macao before that time I must have my *Canton Packet* letters & later ones too– I shall write to you by way of Mazatlan in a day or two– The miniature of Bob gets on very slow & will not be done for a week, it will go per *Splendid* & I think will be with you before this....Tell me when you receive my letters– It is too hot to write any more, good night–

27 July

...Therm at 95– but I have not had much to do & have kept pretty cool– A friend of mine has one of those South American hammocks which I get into occasionally & find it a great comfort....

I have given old Capt Bensen a letter of introduction, he is a nice sober sided old man whose wife has six children & he has promised to go & see you– he is a clever old man,... unlettered but honest & he has taken quite an interest in my Boy & wanted very much to take the copy home, but it will not be done for a week– This is Saturday night & the weather looks a little Typhonish– I do not mean to go to Macao until there has been a gale after which we shall have good weather– I shall send you two little feather fans by the *Porcia* or *Splendid*, I feel that every ship ought to take some memento some little token so I have put up two pieces of the narrow ribbon to tie up letters with–

The Summer is passing away fast & I look forward to October with much pleasure, this warm weather pulls one down very fast, I get so little exercise that I cannot eat largely– yet I am quite well & as we never expose ourselves to the sun & wear very light clothes we do not suffer from the heat as you do at home– the Punkah a large swinging fan over the table is a great luxury–

I get on remarkably well with my partners, Low is very active & shrewd & King indefatigable, either of them does double the work that I do– I do most of the talking & a good deal of the correspondence– The mill works well & the Commission account is increasing fast– in short all I want is to see you once more & to clasp that dear Boy in my arms– But it wont do to think of this– it is too far a head yet– down down into your dungeon my thought of home avaunt ye! Flora was safely delivered of 6 pups on the 23rd & is doing well at Macao–

I must now close this letter & go to business–

Give much love to your Mother & Sally & an hundred kisses to our dear Boy– I suppose he can talk as fast as any body now– adieu dearest Yrs ever RBF

Sabina Canton July 29, 1839

Dear Rose–

I have lately written you a good deal....Yesterday I received some letters from Manila & Singapore & among them was one from you 30 January...you had just been to Mr Cushings & he had received my Anjer letters, yet *you* dont say a word of mine– I suppose you had exhausted all you had to say in some of the above or that you had not yet got my best letters...nothing from John later than yours– You see the necessity of being prolix & of devoting a page to me daily, this cannot take up much time & when two ships are going do not fear repetition....I enclose a note rec from W Hunter– two pups are since dead & four living– I shall send one home if I can get a good opportunity– The weather has been very hot for a week until today it is cold & rainy...business with us is brisk, the English are all at Macao & very angry because we dont bite our own noses off as they are doing– We have just got an English Ship to our consignment & expect several more besides one or two Dutch ones & a Dane– We have but little leisure to think of time & hardly any to write–

I am quite well, though lighter by several pounds than in the spring not much pain in the side & very little soreness in the chest, I eat heartily drink my Beer regularly & sleep well, have given up cigars, fruit after dinner– Ain't you quite ashamed of yourself when you pore over the endless sheet I have written & reflect that as yet I have only...75 pages of writing or about 1/3 of a page per day– I dont say this because I think you neglect me but because I wish to get more– Low received yesterday 5 sheets from his sister in London, she must have very little to do or a good deal to say– Now don't be angry dear, nor sorry either for you have been very good & I feel that you have not wished to recapitulate all your feelings & make me unhappy– I went to church yesterday in the rain, Dr Parker & myself sat half an hour & looked at each other when we agreed that, one man was not a fair subject to preach to, so we went home– The rain abated & 7 people assembled to hear a sermon from the text "set thy affections on things above"– Love to all & Good Bye RBF

Sabina
Canton August 1, 1839

Dear Rose–

...Our boys miniature came home to day– it is a very good painting but at least 18 months older than the other & that must have looked older than the original– I have sent it back to have it altered & I fear the man will have to make another– The *Splendid* to sail in a week will take this one if it will do at all– The frock I have had made blue, with a red belt & it sets it off– The *Sabina* has been detained for her "Grand Chop" (Port clearance) which gives me this opportunity to write a line after all the business letters are done with– We are getting very impatient to hear from the US & know the result of the border troubles–[149] Without letters from you my life here would be intolerable, we go from the desk to the table & from the desk to bed– I have not even taken a walk through the suburbs for a month nearly–

Love to Mother & Sally– tell the latter if she dont write to me I wont send her a kiss nor give her one when I return!!

Ever thine RBF

Canton 3 August 1839

My dear Rose....I resume my journal having little to say....my latest dates from you are Feb 11th– almost 6 months! I have put off writing lately hoping daily & hourly to see some one coming into the Hong with a large bundle of late news....The miniature of Bob is hardly worth sending , it fails just as much in depicting the life & animation in the large picture....I shall send it to you with this under care of Capt Lund of the *Splendid*, which I hope will get home on the 10th December– Mind you let me know if I am correct & I also send you per *Splendid* four little feather fans, which cost 75 cts or a dollar each (very

---

[149] On 12 February 1839, the Aroostook "War" began with the seizure of Rufus McIntire, a land agent sent to the Aroostook region, between New Brunswick, Canada, and Maine, to expel Canadian lumberjacks who had entered the disputed area. After McIntire's arrest, Maine and New Brunswick both called out their militias, $10 million in war funds was appropriated by Congress, and the conscription of 50,000 men was authorized. However, war was averted when General Winfield Scott arranged a truce, and the issue was settled in 1842 by the Webster–Ashburton Treaty.

extravagant) pray give one to Lizzy Greene, 1 to Mary Motley & one to Sally & keep the other yourself– with common handles they are very cheap– I am not in the way of making presents & I expect you will think I am a very shabby fellow for not sending you some gew-gaws– no– I think you have become a more sensible woman than that– We have heard of Green's passing Anjer in 36 days which is very good for the time of the year– I am going to Macao on the 10 instant to stay a week– Am going down inside with Mr Lyce of Wetmore & Co house– Flora was well last account– Love to Bob & all hands & good night

Sunday 4 August–

Here am I sitting in my chamber writing on your old red breakfast cloth, Bob is near me & "ever & anon" (Shakespeare) I look at him & he at me– We interchange nods & smiles, the more I look at the picture the better I like it– I think the head very well done....It is a great comfort to me....We are still without any news from home & I am getting very impatient–

Wednesday August 7, 1839–

Yesterday about 11 AM a most lovely looking youth came in with several large bundles of letters, I grappled with them forthwith, with a palpitating heart– I tore off the envelopes one after the other & at last hit upon one marked private in Georges hand, off with the cover, it was from you, another package from C W Greene with a parcel– I have already requested you & John & Turnbul never to enclose your letters for several reasons which will be obvious to all business men...– all came from Java here in the "*Morea*" together & I will now take them up & review them beginning with a scolding– No 29,30 are so *pale* that my eyes can hardly read them & I have also discovered from the different sizes & brands of paper that you buy by the quire– this is enormous! You should buy by the ream & buy good paper it is very bad economy writing on bad paper– I cannot tell you how my nerves were upset at getting so many letters from you & John & others public & private– I just glanced over your envelopes to see that you & the Boy were well & put them aside for my closet– I always cry with joy when I get your letters & I feast upon them & am so angry when I turn over & find the sheet is finished & quite frantic when I get to the end of the budget, nothing you say can be uninteresting to me & I "*sort of*" feel half angry that you dont take up my letters & allude to every thing– this I know would not be possible & would deprive you of much time to write– but the object is to keep on reading something from you– I have long letters from Mr Cabot, J Lyman, Hooper & others– all satisfactory– so much for preface & now I will take up your letters & run through them, noticing the most prominent parts– No 29 Feb 17-24– Capital idea that of putting a mark under the date, it enables me to see the days & is quite mercantile– Dumaresq just got home & as you say Margaretta must be very happy– Whitney been to see you– Drank Tea with Martha Amory & she gave me the sketch of a Deer– I think it beautiful though there is a defect in the tail– I shall have a copy made on paper & send it to her in return or to you & you can give her one of the Fans from me with my love– 22 July referring to one of two visits from Capt Dumaresq and to what he said of my letter at Anjer in which I alluded to your coming out with him– I will now deal plainly & candidly about that matter....*I will not be separated from you more than the three years stipulated, if I cannot go* and take something handsome you must *come* & I should hope that Dumaresq with his new ship might be coming out about the right time on her second voyage– If you come you must of course bring your Mother & Sarah for it would be cruel to separate them & you & as you would be much alone at

Macao I could not do without them– Then comes the long voyage, the idea of dragging a lady at your mothers time of life to sea & for four long weary months & Sally too who is always sea sick– all this would be cruel– every thing seems to work against your coming & nothing but a failure of my plans can induce me to have you run the risk & even then had not I better go home & try my luck in January I shall decide & you will then have a whole season before you to prepare & get here in October– I think the chances are as 8 to 10 that I shall do all I expected & get home within my time & I think you had better make your mind perfectly easy on the score of coming out– enough on this head....

March 2– My first letters from Canton via St Helena– this must have been a great time for you– you would like to have Flora's picture if it were not for the extravagance of it– you little thought it was so near at hand– It is quite wonderful how I have hit just what you wanted & the covered cups too– quite as singular as the death of the two Presidents on the 4 July,[150] or that Houquas three correspondents in the US are *John* M Forbes, *John* C Green, *John* P Cushing, now if John C G – & John P C would only have twins it would be very singular indeed & to add to the novelty of the case they might all be called Houqua–...a call from Aunt Tom [Thomas H. Perkins' wife] & Seaman & lots of others to congratulate you on my arrival....I shall now expect to go right to the traces as a domestic economist when I return & if I dare so much as lift a cigar I shall expect you to run & seize it & say "let that alone, *you* can't afford to smoke"

March 3 glad the dates come so thick together– you ask me if I have the same feeling about you as you have about me– you say "you dare not bring me too vividly before you" I do little else when I have leisure– I recall you not as we parted, nor as we lived that last year, but as you describe yourself now, playing with Bob, or enjoying the society of our friends– You say Ben sometimes looks like me, several people have seen that in the picture, *Aho* went up into my room to see it, he said directly that the mouth & chin were yours, the upper part mine– I showed him your miniature & he said if I had not told him that was you he should not have known it, Why said he "that looks like a woman of 50– Mrs Forbes can't be over *28, very* little said I with a *pecu Liar* screw of the mouth– You have been giving me an account of a tooth a day for at least two months & I suppose by this time he must have an hundred– Bigelow says I did right with Forbes, so does Sam Cabot Jr....[151]

No 31 Mch 5– I am glad I *aint* at sea to night for it is blowing a gale of wind– visit from the cousins of Forbes & to his mother– great a/c of the Boys *monkey tricks*, I dare say I should teach him two to your one but I dont approve of it nevertheless– dont for Gods sake & his own bring him up to depend on excitement, he will naturally have enough of that sort of temperament– Aho has a son a month old or less– send him some little stockings, mittens &c also some for my boy whose wife is about to bear him a child, unless he lies for the sake of getting rid of going to Macao with me on the 10th– When these China men want to go home very much they generally say their Father or Mother is just dead & this boy having buried both several times has perhaps *got up* this new excuse–

---

[150] John Adams, the second President, and Thomas Jefferson, the third President of the United States, both died on the same day, 4 July 1826.

[151] Dr. Bigelow and Cabot have confirmed RBF's care of his patient Forbes during the voyage out to Canton.

Your a/c of the fancy Ball is excellent, but I can't quite make out whether you went as a loafer or a guest– Anna Robbins &c Mother and old Dr Holbrook called– dinning with Copley– G Perkins drunk tea..(Bob)...begins to talk– I suppose he will be able to read by the time I get home– 11 oclock good night–

THURSDAY 8 MCH

I left off late last night & having a head ache I took two of the blue pills– am well this morning– I resume my letter– [152]

March 23– letters per *Mary Chilton* – I am much pleased at having sent Flora, I wonder how you will like my own miniature– Boy "*walking on his feet*" for the first time in the open air– did he walk on his head before?" another double tooth makes 33– "wild with spirits" I dont think ardent spirits are good for such young children– Thanks for the interest you took in the boat race–...John says he seemed much pleased at my good fortune– but he did not write to me– Our boating is all done for & I feel the deprivation very much

March 24– Bennet 17 mo old– that was the day we were effectually shut up here...– I send you the Repository for May which has an excellent leading article about Opium from the pen of that puppy King of Olyphant house– if you read the late Canton papers you will see some articles signed by our house & will readily recognize me therein– I did not come here for my health, neither to effect a reform, moral or political, but to get the needful where with all to be useful & happy at home & I shall stay on long as I can carry on my business– in safety– & I consider myself as safe in Canton as in any part of the world– Send you *two* caps & covers, I sent them long ago, you unreasonable woman & I dare say your next order will be for two or three pieces of silk...some Tea to squander away– two cups & saucers– why you will ruin me– What piece of furniture did you sell to pay for Bobs picture–

March 27...A nice long letter from Joe– I'll bet I have a longer & now comes your plan of country lodging which I approve of entirely & I have fancied all your arrangements– just what things you took out there & how much you are enjoying the June air– are there any slaughter houses near?– I doubt much however if you are enjoying much of any thing just now as you must be getting accounts of our Opium troubles & our imprisonment– which time I look back to as the most amusing of all my Canton days– I see you are looking forward to laying up money during summer for winters wood & Doctor– both no doubt will have been necessary for you cannot expect our dear Boy to escape Measles, Whooping cough, & a thousand ills which juvenile flesh is heir to– I should not be surprised at any moment to hear he was sick & should not be alarmed

March 28 Fast day– that was the day we gave up the 20,000 chests of Opium– here comes a description of your lodgings....

I am rejoiced to find you are running about again among our friends– Why dont Mary Motely write to me & Sally & your Mamy & Aunt Nancy [153] March 29–

---

[152] RBF here repeats letters to Rose that comment on her letters to him. These appear in slightly different form beginning on page 142. These are similar letters apparently sent by different vessels, or both overland and by sea.

[153] Aunt Nancy is most likely Nancy Cushing Higginson (1782-47), the sister of J.P. Cushing.

just opened the things per *M Chilton* – I should much have liked to have seen Bob in the dress...– I think the head of Flora was capital– Sally writes a PS to your budjet...she says the miniature of you was better than the other I thought so too– you dont say if Child looked like Bob– George Winslow [154] been to see you– glad of it– it seems you were much pleased to have George talk of me– No doubt he soon found out your weak side– You say Lizzy expects to be confined the last of this month say in March, you dont mention its having happened on the 4 of April– Crofts have a son & lost their fortune so far they resemble us & having the same happen at the Morlands is a coincidence– lucky fellow to have a fortune to lose....

No 34– Mch 29– George Winslow & Manton to dine that was right & so you made Bob cut monkey shines for their amusement– made up your first dress in 15 months & cost half a dollar a yard,? on you one only a yard & a half high I suppose with trimmings it cost $1– you say I must be prudent & economical– I have no time for prudence or economy in small things– Our family consists of *myself*, Low, King, Spooner, Gilman & two Portuguese lads– each has a servant– we have two cooks, a cowman, two English cows, a Compradore & man to go to market, 4 coolies or porters– making 25 souls including the two cows– our family expenses are about $8000 per annum– besides each ones private expenses which are light– perhaps $1000 each– What follows is a secret– Since January our gains by Commissions are nearly $90000 say Ninety thousand dollars– my share of this is $18000 & I see no good reason to doubt that we shall make up our earnings to $130 thousand before the year expires– & in the next year my share will be more– I think my net gains this year will be $25 thousand after paying all expenses at home & here– this sum will pay all my debts & leave me square with the world so that my next year will be all clear gain–...I do no more than get home free of debt I shall be quite happy–

30 March Easter Sunday that was the day that we had our live stock sent us– You made a mistake for the 31st was Sunday here– What a goose you are to be worrying yourself about English war– I dare say at this moment you are in a quandary about me– but I have no doubt my account of the proceedings will make you laugh more than cry

April 1st– That was the day we organized our establishment– the Boy had been to Gibbons the grocers & came back "full of spirits" is that the way you bring up my Son, I thought grocers were forbidden to sell a less quantity than 15 gallons–...

I have before me my Canton Journal corresponding with your dates you must have read or are now reading that with intense interest do you mark my letters, *when received* so as to compare notes– So Esther is going to marry a watchmaker, I suppose they will "go upon tick" when short of cash, but then will not be short for "time is money"– She certainly ought to have her own property settled on her, or her children if she have any, but my advice will be too late– I shall send her something bye & bye– as a wedding present....My imagination places me in your pleasant summer abode– I am sorry it is so far from Mother– I have not a line from mother, Emma, or anybody but John...I trust Mother is

[154] George Winslow had traveled over to China with RBF on the *Mary Chilton* and returned home to Boston. RBF asked him to pay a call to Rose.

not hurt at any thing I have done or left undone– I asked Emma not to show her my letter– indeed I doubt if it had arrived then & now I come to your last No 35– you ask me if your letters convince me that you are cheerful & tolerably resigned– I say Yes– at the same time it would be a great pleasure to me to get a line from Sally or your Ma– just to say that you are much better & that what you write *is true*– I mean about yourself–...What you say about your health before I left only confirms me in the opinion that I did right to come away– What you say of Bob's health & constitution is very encouraging– but you must remember that all this is mortal & that sickness & even death cannot be kept at arms length– I cannot believe that I am so good as to deserve the chastening which the death of that child would involve, but I know it is within the bounds of possibility that he should die & I am always expecting some alley to your good accounts– if anything should happen to him– I should not stay here one hour– I could not leave you there alone– & if you survived such a calamity I should never leave you again– but away with such intruding thoughts– I think I know exactly how he looks– his visionary form & expression flashes across me occasionally...– the trade is at an end and a man who now encourages the Opium trade in any way is looked upon with different eyes from what he was formerly...– I will have Bennets portrait varnished– it goes to Macao with me the day after tomorrow to see Flora & J P Sturgis & the puppies– If one looks like Flora I will send it home–

April 3– That was the day...[Captain] Drew called to see you, I have a letter written that very night after he left you in which he refers to you as my "very agreeable lady"– he also speaks of being disappointed at not seeing the Boy asleep–...He is a much better fellow than he looks to be– & as he evidently has great respect for me, you should have for him– but he is just the man that fiery salamander sister of yours would like to get hold of by the back of his head & then wipe (blow) his nasal organ with a tremendously energetic pinch– I have now got through your letters...– the curl– is safely deposited in a Black Box on the table to my chamber...– I have now given you a good deal more of my time than I can well afford & shall take up & reply to Johns letters which are very good– he seems to think I have done exceedingly well & that I shall have no trouble with Coolidge– it is quite uncertain (to us) whether he is coming or not– I have a friendly letter from him– disclaiming any unfriendly feeling– also letters from Joshua Bates of a friendly tendency– both however point to a desire to maintain a connection which will *not* probably be agreeable to me as regards to Coolidge but *will* be as regards Barings– *we* have sent Barings large consignments & that will keep them firm & Houqua who makes them through us (mind this is a secret) is staunch as steel– adieu

Canton
August 9, 1839
Dear Rose,
...I am well & shall tomorrow be on my way to Macao wind & weather permitting– I give the miniature in charge of Capt Lund a very nice old Gent & a note of introduction– He is married on Cape Cod & will perhaps call on his way through Boston– He said the package would be a sufficient introduction but I prefer giving him a line –...I am ever Yrs Truly & devotedly RBF Senior...

A VISIT TO MACAO

As the conflict intensifies, the British leave Macao and take to their ships anchored at Hong Kong. RBF travels to Macao and Hong Kong and pursues business with both British and American ships. He also awaits the arrival of a possible Russell & Co. rival, Joseph Coolidge. In the midst of his hurry and worry over business, British warships fire on a fleet of junks downriver from Canton.

On page 154 is the Pria Grandé at Macao as painted by a Chinese artist about 1840.

Fast boat on the way to Macao 10 August

My dear Rose...I will now describe a "fast boat" such as we go to Macao in– They are called "fast boat" because they are so very slow in their motions & apt to stick fast whenever a good excuse happens for a little delay– It is the only lawful mode in which foreigners are allowed to go to & from Macao with their own cooks, servants, furniture &c & it is the most luxurious mode of travelling in the Empire & perhaps in the world– The boat we are in is some 50 feet Long, having a house in the middle 12 feet wide &15 feet long, with a pantry abaft & abaft that the cooking place, we have at least a dozen stout men, two masts and sails, plenty of long bamboos with which the boat is pushed along in the shoal creeks & winding inner passages, of which there are many branches, in the middle of the house a room above described is a round table upon which your devoted Lord & *master* is now scribbling– Bob's picture stands near me & my constant companion the old Iron box with my papers also– The advantages of going inside are first greater safety, second greater comfort, third better opportunity of carrying down traps and lastly it gives you an opportunity of seeing a good deal of the country & there is a great deal of beautiful scenery, though the country is mostly flat, rice fields– We have ample room to spread our beds & hang up our mosquito curtains, but the mosquitos are not abundant– My companion is Mr Lyce (one of Wetmore & Co) a very clean young man lately admitted a partner in that house– I have been reading over your late letters & I find I have been pretty good in replying to them, though I have just discovered that I write very carelessly & can hardly make sense of half I scratch down– This is a most lovely day & the relief of getting away from the desk is very great– I do not find in your late letters that you allude to my history of a lost portrait, or my piratical sketch– I suppose you were obliged to give them some passing notice per *C Packet* or *Aurelius*– I hope in my next letters to get some good account of Lizzy Greene & her expected heir & to receive some further letters from cousin Joe, Hillard & others– I have nothing yet from Copley– & mother & Emma have quite given me up– we shall get to Macao tomorrow where I shall expect to see Osgood– The ships of war sailed on the 6th, on the 7th we had a gale from the East– I hope they suffered no damage– I am now thinking about you at Watertown enjoying the pure air of summer in the country & my letters dated in March & April– these will be peculiarly gratifying !! We shall have no vessel for home until the *Robert Fulton*, unless we get the "*Apthorp*" away before her– this last is a vessel which we have chartered– I shall see Flora tomorrow & deliver your messages to her, & make a selection from one of the pups– Good bye for today I am determined not to write any thing during my present cruise– Love to all

Macao 12 August 1839

Here I am ensconced in Mr Hunters house for today, Flora laying as usual under the table, Bob standing up on the mantle piece– I arrived here at 1/2 past 2 yesterday just in time for dinner– Flora jumped up on the couch where Bob was first deposited & licked the face just as if it had been a living child & then kissed me– There are four pups– one of them looks very much like the Mother & that one shall be sent to you bye & bye– No *Canton Packet* or other arrival from the United States, but a Bark is in the road that looks a little like *Salem*– it may be a new arrival– I received on arrival here a long letter from Green at Anjer & one from Capt Elliot of a friendly & confidential character– The sound of the surf under my windows reminds me of Nahant, the position being much the same– the air is delightful here & I anticipate a very pleasant visit– The late gale was not very severe & I hear of no serious damage– I can not help feeling a little dull though the long years have elapsed since that fatal gale– ten years ago to day or yesterday perhaps, the remains of that Brother were deposited in their present home– That he died when we were just *beginning* to feel like Brothers, has always been a source of great uneasiness to me– His situation here bore such a strong contrast to mine (as I was then labouring hard while he was living in luxury) that we had never come together as Brothers should do until within a year or two of his death & then only at long intervals– however I have nothing to reproach myself with– It was a dreadful loss to our family & one that can never be forgotten–

Tuesday 13 August

Fine weather– busy most all day running around in the Sun making business calls– Yesterday sent Bob round to Chinneries Studio with note–

For Mr Chinnery with the Compliments of the author–

about 10 oclock I went round & made a call on him & after a considerable desultory conversation asked him to show me what he was about, we walked through his rooms after a little while said he (puffing out his large cheeks) "a very singular little incident happened to me this morning– look here sir I've received a present most singularly little incident– pon my word (reading my note very slowly) – 'For Mr Chinnery with compliments of the author!!' very odd isn't it! Pon my word see I was not aware that any of our Canton artists could paint as well as that!– however I dont think much of it– "

Said I– I think the head is very good a very pretty child!–

–Oh– child's well enough, but the execution my dear Sir– quite below mediocrity–

He dwelt very much on the last word & I called his attention to other paintings & soon bade him Good Morning– now if I did not think practical jokes bad generally I would get some one to say it came from them & was the work of Sully– he would then say it was capital– very good &c– I shall not do this but tell him the fact– the *Splendid* passed out yesterday afternoon without stopping

14 August–

wrote to Chinnery yesterday to say that I never encouraged practical jokes, therefore I must inform him that the portrait sent him was that of a young Gent professing to be my Son, that it was the work of a very promising young artist who had as yet *performed* but little– He replied that the moment he saw it, it struck him as the work of a *young* practitioner who had studied Alexanders style & that he by great study & much thought would improve– that it was not destitute of merit & that he should take special care of it on a/c of its being my son– I have made no calls as yet except business calls– to day I must go & see some of the ladies & babies– of which latter I fell in with a lot on the Campo which latter means the Camp or open country where we walk every day– they look pale & *milk & watery* & must be very different articles from Bob–

I tried to charter a horse yesterday but could not find one & went on my own trotters a walk of several miles & wished you were with me– Last night I took possession of my own castle which is an immense house with 8 or 10 large rooms in it, verandahs, porches, outhouses, bathing rooms, I had sent down only furniture for two rooms & the house looked naked & desolate, however I had an excellent night & awoke to a pleasant sunrise & a cool bath & am just now writing myself into a good appetite for breakfast– I made use of Alex Selkirks soliloquy when I got up this morning–

"I am Monarch of all I survey–
My right there are none to dispute–
from the kitchen all round to the sea
I am lord" &c&c

I have agreed to eat with Hunter & otherwise occupy my own house, this latter was hired at a time when we expected to be driven away from Canton for the use of R&Co– I do not see any reason to expect that we shall occupy it for a long time to come if ever– No *Canton Packet*[155] yet– Letters from Manila per *Aurelius* to the end of Jany have come to hand– I mean letters which went to Manila in that vessel– I have only one from John & think mine must be coming by some other route– These letters are the first written after you received my Anjer letters & when I get yours they will be very interesting– do you keep any record of what vessel your letters come in– it would be well to say when you write– my last No __ went per ship __ then I shall be able to trace their flight– I had a call from Dr Cox the day before yesterday– he recommended a dose of Calomel & Rhubarb which I agreed to take on going to bed being a little headachy– but I forgot it & eat my breakfast & dinner as usual yesterday– at 7 oclock I had another call from Cox and the following dialogue took place–

Cox– Well how are you today ?
Forbes– pretty well Dr but hungry
Cox– any — today —?
Forbes– Oh yes Dr very good –
Cox– Let me see your Tongue –(so I poked it out)

much better today– you dont want *any more* medicine, Ill send you some bitters–!!

& so I am quite well– the dose of Calomel & Rhubarb being snugly deposited in my waistcoat pocket–

Flora is quite well & the pups also

THE ENGLISH PREPARE TO LEAVE MACAO

Aug 14, 1839 Macao

My dear Rose

I am writing one of my random shots by the way of Sandwich Islands & Mexico or perhaps home from the first in some whaler– Just as I had finished my daily Journal this morning I got your letters per *Aurelius* Nos 21.22.23 with a letter from Mother– these were in acknowledgement of my Anjer letters– the budget is now complete up to No 18 of April 4 except 26 & 27 which I have been looking for a long time per *Canton Packet* –

I find that when your letters are want in any particular point the desired news comes in the next letter– I asked you lately why Mary Benjamin did not write & lo a letter comes for me & she endorses all you say about our boy & about yourself– I am much obliged to her & have told her so & this very day in

[155] The *Canton Packet was* a 350-ton ship built in Swansea by Mason Barney in 1836. It was owned jointly by Thwing, Perkins, and RBF. It was named after the ship that first took RBF as a cabin boy to China.

a stupid letter– She differs from all other Mothers in not lavishing praises on her own child– I shall not undertake to review your letters by candle light for the paleness of the Ink prevents my reading them except by day light & you seem to be quite satisfied with my journal & I can conceive of it being a great relief to you– I have certainly written enough in quantity to satisfy any reasonable woman as to the quality I hardly think the letters should bear criticism– I left Canton on the 9th & arrived here with Bob on the 11th shall return in ten days or a fortnight– I am quite well & shall be kicking if that *Canton Packet* dont come along soon– The *Splendid* left a few days since with a good lot of letters & Bobs miniature– Since I left Canton we learn that the Chinese Imperial *Robber* is coming to Macao in person to demand an Englishman to be given up to Suffer death for a murder lately committed at Hong Kong, it is said 800 to 1000 soldiers accompany him & that he is determined to carry out his measures– To day Capt Elliot & a jury of the English Merchants have returned from trying the supposed murderers– Three men are to go home in Irons & to be put in jail at hard labor 6 months in England– 2 for 3 months– but no proof could be brought against any one as the murderer– The Chinese we hear have ordered the Provisions to be cut off from the English, but the Portuguese & Americans are to be supplied as usual– I think it quite likely all the English here will have to embark for Hong Kong– The Americans will keep entirely aloof from the quarrel & I do not anticipate any trouble to our business– Our latest accounts are to 5 April per *Navigator* & *United States*, the letters of these ships came to us by another vessel from Singapore– This is such a very out of the way route that I must not write a long yarn, if John dont hear from me by this route tell him the news & add that Exchange is 4/10-4/11– Freight up river $4 per bale per cotton & say that I have just written to him via Bombay– Let me know when you get this– Bob is well & Flora & 4 pups ditto– Love to all– Yrs ever RB–

August 16

On the 14 I wrote you a letter to go in duplicate to Bombay & overland, & the original to the Sandwich Islands to take its chance for a whaler or an overland conveyance through Mexico– tell me which gets home first– on the 14– just after I had finished my usual journal in came your *Aurelius* letters to 27 January say 21.22.23.& so the numbers are complete to 35 excepting 26 & 27– I find it is no use to scold about your letters for just as I begin to do so, I get letters filling up the gaps– I received a very good letter from Mary Motley in which she praises our boy beyond every thing & she also says something about you which pleases me– Her own account of her child is not very encouraging as to beauty but she tells me he is very good– I hope you will in duce her to continue writing– I have told her that if Lathrop [Mary's husband] is jealous of our correspondence he must take it up himself– I now take up your letters per *Aurelius* & review them noticing the most interesting parts–

Jan 8 No 21– you say you have sent off another sheet for the *Osage* to be sure that I get the last *accts* by her!! she did not sail till 20 February & has been here near two months– I *say nothing*– I am rejoiced to see you had then begun to feel better in health & spirit– Bob's first *pantaloons* hahahaha!

Then you give me an account of your paying up all your bills monthly– this is *capital*– certainly *capital* saved– You tell me you had given up the idea of having Esthers Nephew – that was well too–

You tell me you give John two shillings a week to split wood & shovel snow– Why he tells me he gets into Town late & goes out early & I do not see how he can find time to do that for you![156]

January 11– Been dining at T Perkins to meet Dr Coolidge, glad of it, he is a plain, clever man & has done our family good service– Mrs & the Dr Kirkland been to make you a visit–

Jany 13– Quite an interval– Two excellent sermons from Mr Greenwood– visit to Susan Hillard– want me to express my sympathy to him, this I have done but on looking over my letter I have found I only give my love to Susan, I have sent her a message however by M Motley– to whose letter I have replied– Capt lost his fortune & obliged to leave the Morlands–

Jany 17– large gap– acknowledging my first Anjer letter of 13 Sept How funny that this short letter should have arrived first– you tell me Mrs Cabot intends to write me if only a PS– hope she will & when she does, I shall write her a letter– Your account of your dinner at T R Curtis is very funny– especially the "fine=luck" story– Capt Ritchie who lives with us in Canton & with whom James Amory went as passage was asking me if Miss Greene was pretty I told him I thought she would be if it were not for a cast in her eyes, a sort of cross eyed look– The point of this is in the fact that Ritchie is very cross eyed– Bobs party must have been very entertaining– I wish I could have him here to play with–

No 22 Jany 25– Quite an extensive vent– This letter acknowledges my Anjer letters received by you on the 23 Jany– It gives me infinite satisfaction to learn that my letters satisfy you for I always had a sort of feeling that your lively imagination would have led you to expect far more interesting details than I have the power of getting up– This is contagious! & when I am travelling or residing among witty people, I can do my share, but here the mind is constantly fixed on business subjects & there are no wits here abouts– Here you notice the History of a lost portrait & the Escape, I don't see that you have yet spoken of the piratical Schooner we really saw– I have your Brother Tom's letter of April 1838– 16 mos old– nothing yet from him in answer to my Anjer letters, indeed there have been no opportunities– I hoped to hear from him soon & to get the long expected good accounts– If your mother was so much gratified by my letter why did not the dear little woman say so herself–

Jany 26 You tell me you don't dream of me– I do not remember to have dreamed of you or the Boy more than two or three times since I left home–

Here you speak of Sarah Forbes & the family not sending the young man any token– I say nothing– You are afraid that your letters wont satisfy me you say– They can never satisfy me for I am insatiable– I take them up when first received & read them very deliberately & turn over deliberately when for fear there should be a blank leaf– I am quite mad when you get through– All you say is interesting but there is not enough of it– yet I fear if I insist on you writing every day– you will think it a task–

Every little incident that turns up with you must interest me– I am afraid my

[156] John was a handyman who took on occasional odd jobs for Mrs. Forbes. RBF is pretending here that he thinks his brother John is shoveling the snow.

letters will not interest you as they ought to do– for I am sensible that they are very dull since my arrival here, compared to yours–

Jany 27 No 23 Been to Church to hear little Whitney– gives an a/c of Goddards failure & Stanton Parkers death– I can hardly conceive that he should have died so poor– His wife will ill bear up under such reverses for I am under the impression that she is weak & likes show– Boardman with great eccentricity is very generous & highly honourable as a Merchant– Your account of the Catholic converts Mrs Griswold & Mrs Lyman astonishes me– I thought they were both gay & giddy– You ask how I should like to see *you* prostrated among the Sons & daughters of Erin– for prostrated, put prostituted & then you can imagine how I should be pleased!–

Your account of our dear Boys good health is a source of unspeakable pleasure to me– he must be as near perfect as can be– I fear you indulge him too much & that his natural self will grow upon him– however you cannot spoil him very bad before I get home– Ah– that word– home! What a dreary road I must traverse before I can expect to see it– I am made uneasy just now by reflecting that you are in receipt of my letters in March & April giving an account of the Opium crisis– It will be a long time before the thing is settled so far as concerns the English & Chinese– We are daily expecting the Commissioner here– reports say he comes to demand an Englishman to be given up for the Chinese murdered at Hong Kong by a party of English sailors some time since– These men have been tried & five of them sentenced to be sent home to England in Irons & imprisoned 6 months– But the murderer has escaped punishment for want of proof– There is no doubt but that the Commissioner is coming not only to demand the punishment of this man, but to look into the Opium trade which is going on in this vicinity quite briskly on a small scale– None of the regular Canton Merchants are participating in this, but it is done by the Captains & the Parsees who have before been acting as agents– The authorities have issued a chop *here* forbidding any provisions to be sent to the Compradors of English homes & it is daily expected that all the Chinese Servants in the pay of the English will have to leave– The Portuguese & the Americans are not involved & it is looked upon as a good joke rather than as a case of starvation, the supplies of Rice & Salted Provisions is immense & we are ready to stand a long siege– You must know that this place though professing to be Portuguese is really so much under the contract of the Chinese that they can hardly say their sails are their own– The Portuguese occupy it & have done so for many years on suffrage the Chinese collect duties here & there are 20000 Chinese inhabitants to 4000 Portuguese– the place is strongly fortified & might be well defended but there are only two or three hundred soldiers & the English rather than cause any injury or even alarm the Portuguese will vacate the place & go on board of their ships at Hong Kong– Mrs Elliot & some other ladies embark to night & others are preparing to do so–

August 17–
I was interrupted while writing yesterday by a Captain with a cargo from Java consigned to us & was obliged to make myself busy with him–

A meeting of the British Merchants was held yesterday to decide upon the course necessary to be pursued in the coming visit of Mr Lin the Imperial Commissioner– I believe it was voted the English proscribed individuals who had been expelled from Canton, should embark directly for the Ships & that the balance of the British Community should be ready to go at a moments warning– Some of the Chinese Servants have left & it is thought all will go– The American Compradors have painted on their doors in Chinese their names & country &c – on ours for instance is written– "This is a branch of the American factory in the Swedish Hong No 2 Canton"

The uneasiness of the English is to me quite amusing– never felt more secure in my life– This morning I had a delightful ride just before sunrise on a spirited little pony, I enjoyed it very much & I must have a horse– the health of body & mind requires it– A very good horse may be bought here for $70 & they require no shoeing– They must eat however & this costs $10 per month with a man to take care of the animal– The day before yesterday dined with Uncle James with Hunter & Delano & then dined here with Hunter yesterday– I dine always with H– sleep & breakfast at home– I must get you a view of Macao & show you where my house is– I have told you already that it is an immense place– on the beach being a complete double house, two entrances, two kitchens &c

No 1

I shall now begin & number *each sheet* so that you can tell when any are missing– To continue the description of my house– It occupies 60 or 70 feet on the water & has eight large rooms on the upper floor– Two back verandas & a terrace in front & rear– The rooms are very large & all have venetians to the windows– there are a few flowering Trees in the rear, bathing room, offices & places for servants on the ground floor– Our furniture thus far consists of two small bedsteads, six chairs, two couches, two small & 1 large table– but then we have fresh air & room in abundance & we have a sort of look as if we were just packed up ready for a start–

My own opinion is that the Commissioner comes here to get up a secret negotiation with Capt Elliot to try to get him to open the British Trade but it is now too late, Elliot has referred the matter to his Government & he must wait the result– The Chinese are very friendly towards the Americans & it must be our policy to keep upon good terms with them– We are daily getting English business & have now two English ships & one cargo in an English Ship at Hong Kong– the Americans are reaping a rich harvest out of the English & I hope their ships will be kept out of Port a good while– It is quite time we had letters into May from you & after having heard of our December riot– I dare say you will be kept in a stew, but I have no great Sympathy with your weakness on that score– We are perfectly safe here– more so than in your *mob* country–

WEDNESDAY 21 AUGUST

Just returned from a cruise in the *Rose* to Hong Kong with Delano, had a good sail though rather hot at times & dined yesterday with Captain Gilman on board the *Edmonton*– Captain McDougal consigned to us– he has his wife with him & 2 fine children, one boy 3 years old & the other a girl just 17 months– just the age that Bob was when your last letters were written– this child has fine large black eyes & long dark lids & is as hearty as possible– I was quite pleased to see the little thing & compare notes– it understands all that is said to it, but does not speak English–

A large chop boat has come down for Mr Snow & Mr Delano but as my name is not in the permit I shall wait a few days longer, indeed I wish to be here when the *C Packet* & *Navigator* arrive–

Many of the English are leaving to go aboard of the ships at Hong Kong– the Commissioner finding that the Portuguese slaves & others in the employ of the natives of Macao, were assisting the English has issued a chop stating that the supplies of the Portuguese shall be cut off unless they drive the English away– so rather than trouble these people Elliot advises all to embark, the Americans are also threatened with the removal of their servants & provisions because they are said to entertain the English– at the same time that these measures are taking, the Chinese tell the English that their ships must either go into the River or return to their country– all this system of annoyance is an old custom with the Chinese–

They think if they continue this system of annoyance that Elliot will give up a man– but he has positive orders from his Government never to give up a man on any account– I dont know where all this is to end– Mrs Mclane embarked today in charge of Dr Anderson expecting momentarily to be confined– Mrs Page was confined three days since– I am glad you are not here for you would probably be in some such scrape–

Friday 23 August–

Fine weather still & nothing new– the little bay in front presents a very pretty scene– there are 15 schooners & sloops & a dozen large ships– boats anchored there, ready to embark– the rest of the English upon the least appearance of an attempt to disturb them further, all their provisions & conveniences say washing &c are cut off & most of the ladies have already embarked, some of the common establishments remain, but are in readiness for a sudden escape– Elliot very properly refuses to recognize any command from the Commissioner & he will insist on all his country men going away the moment the Portuguese suffer any annoyance on his a/c–

We have our servants & get along without the least trouble–

I take my ride on a beautiful little Arab pony which I should buy, it belongs to an Englishman & as his groom is not allowed to stay with him he must sell his horse– took tea last night with Uncle Jimmy, his house is very pleasantly situated & bears ample evidence from its neatness that some firm administration is at the helm– the house is large & a porch in front with columns overlooking the Bay, a pretty garden with flowering trees, shrubs & vegetables occupy part of the ground & while I sit in the door way *smoking my cigar* (which is always a sign of good health with me) & looking up at the splendid moon I could not help saying, well if Rose were here & my Boy I should be content never again to see home, here might I rest for life & be happy, the situation may justly compare with Nahant or the Morlands though the beauty is a different kind, Mr Sturgis says if you choose to live quietly you need not spend more than $4000 per year & can live respectably for $3000– I told him if it were not for the cruelty of dragging your mother so far & leaving my own never to see her more I would go home, bring you out & plant myself for life at Macao, it is indeed a pleasant place, Mr S has a small garden & terrace commanding a beautiful view of the sea & situated a mile from his house on a high point of land, he goes there everyday after dinner & sits & smokes till after sunset– if he can enjoy this daily walk for so many years it must be pleasant– However against these pleasant things is the present disturbed state of affairs & I am thankful you are not here, for if you had no other annoyances than the pain of seeing whole families, before comfortably located in spacious houses now fleeing as it were from Macao to go on board of small cramped up ships, that of itself would make you unhappy– I do not myself think there is the least danger even to the English but it is unfair for the comfort of a few foreigners that the whole population of Macao should suffer annoyance– therefore they embark– Elliot has been watched & dogged from place to place & he thinks the Commissioner would not hesitate to seize him if he could get a chance– It is very unfortunate for this great rascal that he did not rest content with the suppression of the Opium trade, that was a good cause, but now to make such a row to carry out the bloody laws of China which demand life for life is a great mistake & his late conduct will attract the attention of England more than the other trouble– I suppose the Commissioner has been censored for going so far in the matter of the Opium & that he now is trying to make it out to the Emperor that the Stoppage of British trade is the natural consequence of a refusal to give up a man for the murdered chinese– The sailors have been regularly tried, five sentenced to jail for 6 months at home, but the one man that was indicted for the murder was acquitted for want of proof– The Chinese were invited to the trial but declined going or sending any witnesses– What more could Elliot do & what more can he now do than to refuse to sacrifice a man to have the trade go on– In the mean time British property is going up daily in American vessels to Whampoa & the Americans are reaping the profit– I should not be surprised if my warmest expectations respecting our years work should be realized– No arrivals yet from any quarter, we *must* have letters soon from you to May–

Saturday 24 August–

Nothing new to day– the dose of Calomel & Julep which I put in my pocket to take on the way down, still reposes in anxious expectation of my calling it into operation– but it wont do– I ride every afternoon & yesterday went to the extreme limit of Macao to see if there was any movements of a hostile character, but I found all quiet & it is reported that the Commissioner finding it impossible to open a negotiation with Elliot is on his way back to Canton– God speed him–

I called yesterday on Mrs King– she is a pretty little woman, fond of chat, but rather reserved– I asked to see the Boy– 17 months old– she said it was asleep– I told her that was the general excuse when ladies did not want to exhibit their children– that my wife was so proud of her Boy that she lost no opportunity to exhibit him sleeping or waking– You know I have had a good deal of sparring with King both in the prints & in Private, nothing like a quarrel, but from my first arrival he has lost no chance of calling up the Opium question & alluding to my former life at Lintin, but lately he has shown signs of relenting & as I am never backward in making friends even of those I respect but little I called on Him–

Mrs King says it costs them $3000 a year to live in their quiet way– I also called on Mrs Page who says she is a niece of Sir Charles Forbes[157] – I did not see her as she was confined only a week since–

Bob is at Mr Sturgis on a visit & behaves wonderfully– he *is* the best & most quiet child I ever saw– give him a kitten or a blue ribbon to play with & he will sit quietly for a whole day– Flora in good condition– the four pups are growing daily– one of them is just like Flora only a Gentleman & that one shall be sent to you per first good chance– Mr Sturgis likes the picture better each day– he has a fine head of Gustus Perkins which I brought out in the *Lintin* in 1830– he says he shall give it to Dumaresq– No arrival yet– I have been here 11 days & I secretly hope to remain 11 more– this depends on arrivals– I am at least 6 lbs heavier than I was on arrival & feel stronger & stronger every day– indeed I have no recollection of being better than I am now within ten years–

[157] Sir Charles Forbes apparently took great delight in the fact that he was related by blood to RBF. He lived in London and was head of Forbes, Forbes, and Co.

Tuesday 27 August–

Fine weather & a beautiful roaring surf under my windows– Yesterday the Bay presented a gay appearance, Brigs, Schooner, Sloops, & ships, boats of all sizes going to & fro, the "praya" which means beach crowded with Trunks, boxes, bags, parsees, moors, caffres, china men, Capts, Mates, Supercargoes, all busily embarking for the British fleet, at this moment not an Englishman remains at Macao, except old Mr Beels & he having once been Prussian Consul claims the protection of that Power & remains quietly at home–

This general evacuation is in consequence of the Portuguese being much annoyed by the Commissioner who is still in the neighborhood– he ordered the Governor of Macao, upon pain of having all his provisions cut off to expel the English & this Gent having little power & not a great deal of will, desired the English to go & they fearing greater annoyances to the Portuguese accordingly embarked– They went with very bad grace & evidently much annoyed to think the Yankees are quietly remaining & doing business here as well as at Canton– the field seems to be left entirely to us & I hope we shall be able to keep clear of the quarrel– Macao from being quite a gay place has suddenly become desolate, the British & Americans have seldom mixed with the Portuguese & there is consequently very little regret by the latter that the former have been obliged to flee– The English have no great reason to fear any thing more than having their provisions cut off, but the Portuguese if they are not pretty civil will have to give up Macao & then they have no place to go to– No arrivals yet– a Bark came in this morning & I almost imagined her to be the *Canton Packet*, when she hoisted the English ensign– her letters are now very old & I am hourly expecting further accounts to May–

You have never been in a Catholic Town have you?– the bells are going all day & half the night– ding dong– ding dong– this is a great annoyance– Get away Flora, want water? Well roll over then, there that's a good dog– go lay down– & accordingly she goes & lays under the couch– Took Tea last night with Mr Sturgis & Bob–

Macao 29 August

Yesterday I closed several sheets & gave them in charge of a friend going to Hong Kong where the *Robert Fulton* is expected to stop on the way out– but I continue writing by her hoping that some opportunity will occur to forward the balance of my budjet– Yesterday I took Hunters sail boat & went over to the Taypa (a port two miles from here) there I found many of the English Gent– still waiting a fair wind, I fell in with Matheson[158] the head of the principal British House & he volunteered to send goods up to us, which he has never done before– So if the whole Trade is not stopped I shall have my hands full– We have thick rainy weather to day & no arrivals– nothing politically new– the Commissioner promises to visit Macao to be sure that all the English are away & he has issued a chop commending the Portuguese for expelling them hence– I think a day of retribution must come upon this people ere long– The late acts of the Commissioner strengthen Elliots position very much– Did not get my ride yesterday on a/c of the rain & do not expect to to day– I am spying in the offing customarily to see if no ship is coming– Macao is getting rather dull & I think I shall avail of the first good opportunity to go to Hong Kong– & there take ship for Canton– Flora sends her love– the puppies are growing daily– I want some

---

[158] James Matheson, son of a Scottish baronet, began his career at Canton in 1819. In 1832 at the age of 32 he entered into a partnership with William Jardine to form Jardine, Matheson & Co.

new letters from you very much– it seems as if all the ships had sunk– We have accounts from England to 11 May– revolution in France & change of Ministry in England are the only items of consequence–

August 30–
A British frigate arrived yesterday[159] & will be very welcome to the John Bulls– Hope she wont blockade the Port–

I hope to go to Hong Kong in a day or two– Meantime an opportunity offers & I close what I have written–

Love to all– thine ever RBF

LIVING ON BOARD SHIPS OFF HONG KONG

2 Sept 1839
I came over here in the morning of day before yesterday, slept or rather *stood* on board the *Canton Packet* which vessel arrived three days since– Unfortunately all the letters for me are sent over to Macao & I have dispatched the *Rose* for them– I had a good deal to say to Capt Osgood & slept but little– yesterday morning I took up my quarters here, all the English being here it is almost as necessary to have one of the houses here as to have one any where else– There are sixty or seventy vessels laying in this beautiful Bay & they present a beautiful appearance– Capt Gilman is on board of this vessel & as I said in a former letter Mrs McDougal & two very fine Children, one a boy of 3 full of the devil, the other a very fine girl of 18 months with splendid black eyes & long lashes– I asked Osgood this morning how our boy compared with her, he says our boy was taller & of course broader in the Chest than the girl & more intelligent– I should be quite satisfied to hear him as good looking as this girl– Yesterday afternoon a large parcel of ladies & Gent landed & took a stroll over the hills– There are nearly twenty five ladies in the fleet– a British frigate guards the entrance of the Bay & all the ships are well armed & ready to repel any enemy–

Sept 5
On the 3rd the *Rose* returned with a whole bag of letters & it took me from 7 PM to midnight merely to open them & glance over their contents– since then I have been *very* busy answering them & attending to many things– in fact my presence is indispensable & I find it no sinecure to be here, all the English are here but I have as yet made only business calls– I got not a line per *Canton Packet* from any one except Thwing & Perkins, No 26 & 27 are still missing– The weather has been very hot & I have exposed myself a good deal but am gaining flesh & health every day & I consider the summer now nearly over– Osgood says that too great a disparity in ages is bad, that his wife is a little younger than himself "which is proper" but that when there is so great a difference as between you & I it is not so well– I asked him what he thought your age was he said 25 or 26!!! & I 45-48!!!!!– What a nice man you will think him when you see him again, that opinion did more to confirm me in the beliefs that you are brisk & well– than all your assertions to that effect– Yesterday we had a little variety in

[159] The H.M.S. *Volage*, a twenty-eight-gun frigate under the command of Captain Smith, sailed to Hong Kong from India in response to Elliot's request for protection.

an action between Capt Elliots Cutter mounting four guns, the Brig *Pearl* with as many more, a boat well armed from the frigate, and four men of war junks mounting each six guns– for your information, four times 6 are 24–!!!! Hearing the firing I took a small fast pulling gig & went round a point of land with my long spy glass to see the fun, while many ships sent their armed boats, & the frigate got underway to protect them, it was quite a farce– I kept a mile off not intending to mix up in the quarrel– The Chinese fired bravely & it is reported to day that several are killed & a Mandarin among them– Capt Elliot had a small ball pass through his hat, & Capt Douglas of the Cambridge one through his arm, one sailor shot through the jaw & one in the leg, all doing well to day including the hat– The cause of the action was as follows– The Capt– (Smith) of the "*Volage*" & Elliot went to a bay quite near here to demand provisions which have been cut off by the vigilance of the Mandarins, they sent five different petitions to the junks asking for supplies & gave the Chinese half an hour to decide whether they would allow provisions to come off or not, they still refused & then Elliot & Smith according to promise opened fire upon them– The junks retreated but fired bravely & what is wonderful they were left in quiet possession of the field at dusk & the boats returned to their ships with orders to appear again this morning at day light to burn, sink & destroy, but after sleeping on the matter Elliot concluded that he had done enough "fool pigeon" & came home, frigate, boats & all, quite crestfallen–[160] Having gone as far as they did, they should have sunk the junks & silenced the Fort on Shore– Provisions have been much more plenty to day– I dare say the matter will be hushed up– good night, I am tired, sleepy & almost blind with writing & pulling about in the Sun, I have been on board of 17 vessels today on particular business & that's enough for tonight– Bob is at Macao with Mr Sturgis–

Sept 11–

Six days since I wrote last, I have been much taken up with writing lots of letters transhipping cargo &c & it has been quite hot so that I have economized my time & patience–

I am getting quite fond of little Anne McDougal just 18 months old & she is also fond of me– but she wakes up in the night & cries sometime like a new one– the boy 3 years is spoiled by too much indulgence– To day Elliot & the Captain of the frigate have given notice that the Port of Canton will be blockaded in six days from to day & any vessel not getting in within that time, is not to have egress! I instantly protested against this but made all exertions to get the *Rose*, *Lintin*, and *Apthorp* into the River & shall succeed– I am quite tired with a hard days work & must close my journal & say– God bless you & the boy & good night–

Sept 13, 1839

We are much relieved to day to hear that the boats crew supposed to be missing have arrived safely, having got drifted away & finally gone to Macao roads & there got on board ship– the frigate & several small craft have gone to Macao to demand of the Governor if he intends to be friendly to the Chinese or to the English, if to the former then John Bull will be down upon them & take possession

---

[160] This sea fight became known as the Battle of Cowloon and is generally dated the beginning of the first Anglo–Chinese War. It is interesting to note that Reverend Gutzlaff approached three Chinese ships asking for food and water in his perfect Chinese over a period of six hours. Each boat refused him, so finally an English boat was sent to get provisions from a shore village. As the goods were being loaded on board, the Chinese police stopped the transaction. Elliot was furious and lost his temper when the boat returned empty. At that point he gave the order to open fire.

of the place the moment they get a sufficient force, if they are to be friendly to the English then they are to protect them as they are bound to do– the Captains of the English ships are protesting against Elliot as well as the Americans–

I regret that the Port could not be kept open a little longer for we are doing a splendid business– We shall get the old *Lintin* into Port & can get all our property away from Canton in her so that in any case the trade being stopped cannot subject us to any direct loss– I am quite as well satisfied to be outside the Bogue as in– Little Anne McDougal is getting so fond of me that she wont leave me, the poor thing has a bad cold & some fever– she is a sweet child, plump & fat & has large blue eyes & long lashes– I fancy she looks like our Boy something– but I suppose it is all fancy– certainly in– fancy– the boy got a flogging & deserved it–

Sept 18

This is a great day– Nature should be gratified for the birth of one clever fellow– I mention no names– but Capt McDougal hearing me say that this was to be my birth day, has invited– Mr Wetmore, Rawls, Ritchie, & two or three more to dine– it is a beautiful day & last night a blanket was acceptable– you have no idea how busy we have been loading the *Lintin* so as to get inside before the blockade should take place– On the 16th Capt Elliot returned from Macao with the frigate & soon after issued a notice saying, as the missing boat supposed to have been captured by the Mandarins had come to land all safe & as negotiations effecting the trade had been opened with the Government, he should not blockade the Port until further notice, we Yankees were of course much rejoiced, but all the English are extremely angry to see such sudden measures taken & at once abandoned, I applaud Elliot for having fallen into a great error, he was bound to retrace his steps at once, which he has done– I worked hard most all day on the 16th, actually doing mates duty on board the *Lintin* to get her away before 10 oclock on the 17th– & on the arrival of Elliot I addressed him a letter to ask at what hour the time (six days) expired– but as he had just issued his notice withdrawing the blockade, there was no occasion to have him reply & so I sent for my letter back again– The *Lintin* notwithstanding sailed at 10 yesterday morning with a handsome freight & she will clear $8000 by her last trip & nearly double by the present & all in less than three months! Thats what I call a living profit, provisions are now plenty & the Chinese have been frightened by the battle of Cowloon [see letter of September 5] & are very anxious to see the trade go on but Elliot will never allow British ships to go into Port without some arrangement through his Government with the Chinese– I shall remain here until we get ships from home & am very anxious to have letters for I have nothing since the 4 April– 5 1/2 months ago– a very rare thing at this season of the year– I have said very little to you about Coolidge of late– He wrote me on the 5 April from England that he should be here on the 1 Octo with Mrs C & *perhaps* Mr Heard– He will be quite confounded to hear of the present state of things & should leave his wife at Batavia till his plans are settled– What I most fear is that the English trade with Canton will go on as heretofore & that the Americans shall not maintain the great advantages we have lately acquired– If the British Trade is suspended for 6 months & the Port not blockaded we shall do a splendid business– My heart yearns to hear from you– as for seeing you I put aside all thoughts of that for the present– my time is nearly half up– think of that & think of my accomplishing all & more than I expected! My little friend Anne has been quite unwell & when she cries at night I cannot help feeling anxious to know whether our blessed boy has any cause for crying– It has been most lucky that I was here to take the responsibility of arrangements in these variable times– if the blockade had taken place we should have lost a great deal by not having any one here– I am hourly looking out for a ship coming in– the *R Fulton* does not go for several days– I have given old Mr Rawls a letter to you– he promises to call & see you– he is a good natured old Gent– rather fond of Ben!

Sept 20–

Had our dinner on the 18th– went off well– Our beautiful weather continues & it is perfect– No arrivals yet & nothing exciting, the hurry of loading the *Lintin* & other ships for Whampoa being over– I have a little leisure to think of home & to write more letters for the *Fulton*– I left Canton, as I have probably told you to be gone ten days & I have exceeded that time by a month– I brought out a small supply of clothes & as the communication with Macao is very uncertain I am oblidged to *shift* as well as I can– Some days ago Hunter who is very selfish in small things, took care to remark that he would not lend a shirt to any man– That very day his clothes came from Macao but mine did not & I had on my last under garments– so I privately abstracted three of those necessary garments from his bundle & have been wearing them ever since– To day I have the last & dont know what I shall do for another– Hope however to get an arrival from Macao today– The navigator whose letters come here per *Morea* two months ago has not arrived yet– what a blessing she sent them up– Mrs McDougal gave me on the 18th a silk purse which will cost me $20– for I have ordered 2 *silver* mugs for the children– but then just think of the annoyance of having to keep me & all my hats & Mr Hunter, to be sure the ship is consigned to us, but then we have no right to intrude on the Captain but it was a matter of absolute necessity like that of Mr C W King's working all day Sunday to get his ship into Port– Oh the wicked witch– $5 a bale of Cotton I find will make a Saint break the Sabbath–

Good bye for today– Love to Bob

23 [Octo written but then crossed out] September–

I wish it was October for then I would be a month nearer to home– We have nothing interesting since my last– no arrivals– & I am getting quite impatient to hear from you– Capt Elliot has gone over to Macao to demand to the Commissioner that the English be allowed to go to Macao to reside as usual– I do not think he will succeed yet I hope he will for the sake of the ladies who are shut up here on board ship– I am quite at home here & being pretty fully occupied I have no time to grumble, the contrast between my situation, making money rapidly, & the situation of the English who are losing it as rapidly, leaves no room for discontent– I get letters every few days from Mr Sturgis & Mr Delano is now here making us a visit of a few days–

The *Fulton* sails in the morning & I find myself with little to add & if no ship comes in during the night, nothing new to reply to– The June overland mail is close at hand & I must very soon have some direct to the middle of June– The weather has been superlatively fine for two weeks & no symptoms of a change though it is just at Equinox–

My little friend Anne McDougal has quite recovered & came to me in preference to her Father, pray send some of those little socks , I dare say there may be more of the race, therefore the size is immaterial– I wrote you also to send something of the kind to Aho for his Boy–

Give my best love to your Mama & Sally & kiss Bob a million times– I have some long business letters to write & must finish– Thine ever RBF

Ship *Edmonton*
per *Cynthia*
Hong Kong Sept 30, 1839 3 AM
My dearest wife–
My last date per *Fulton* of the 23 left here on the 25: on the 23 I imprudently came down into a lower cabin & slept in a draft, or rather I went to bed in a proper place but the ship swung round & the winds coming in upon me I got up with a severe cold & symptoms of fever, I immediately took the advice of Anderson, as well as his physics & have been at it ever since till yesterday, my fever which had hardly got ground entirely left me & my skin was in good order, but a diet of pills & sassafras for 6 days has pulled me down to a degree– I have been up every day dressed & receiving business calls & letters & writing so you may readily imagine I have not been very ill, but I have been very uncomfortable, though in excellent quarters with Captain Gilman, Mr Delano, & Hunter for nurses, the two last daring to laugh at me when I cursed– On the 25th the *Lion* arrived from Providence without a letter, direct– the day after the *Levant* (my old ship) direct from Phila– I have given the supercargo a sample of your hand writing & he declares no such letters are in the bag, & he sent some to open & examine which I did without finding any from you, I was obliged to return them without examination further than unsealing, to make up for all this my dear, I got per *Albion*– also arrived your very welcome letters 36-38 from 6 April to 18th & by way of Sincapore the continuation of your journal to May day No 41– these 2 budgets are decidedly, all in all, the most satisfactory letters I have yet received for they give a little history of each day & bear evidence of your being in a proper frame of mind & good state of body & although you say you do not repeat, I see you give duplicate accounts of the Boy– I have one letter per *Levant* from Mother of 20 May & one from Mr Cushing who both spoke of you as well a few days before & I am therefore quite easy & think some letters per *Levant* will yet turn up, Mr Cushing & Mother praise the Boy as much as you do besides these arrivals, the *Valparaiso* is in consigned to our friend Ritchie & through him to us in 99 days from Phila or to nearly the middle of June, I fear you must have missed her by having moved out of Town– Ritchie has examined his letters & declares there are none for me in your hand– he tells me of several late vessels on the way, the *Trenton, Tenobia,* & *Eben Preble* & I suppose Coolidge must be in one of them, these three are likely to come to us & I wait here for further operations–

I suppose you want to know by this time why I am up at 3 oclock, why the fact is I have been laying abed so much these last five days that I got tired of it & as my mind was wide awake my body would not sleep & so I thought I would just get up & spin a little– although Mr Hunter & Delano left me for Macao two days ago, I have made arrangements to load the *Valparaiso* up the river to our consignment– we buy her cargo so that it is equal to a real consignment out & out except that we cannot have the pleasure of all the letters– well patience is the word– it is a comfort to know that there are accounts of you a month & a half later at hand– Among the important good items is the Engagement of Mary Magee, the birth of a daughter to Tim Motley, your visit with Bob to Mr Cushing &c &c– but alas on the other side of the Picture I have, the death of Copleys daughter which I can truly sympathize with him & her for the death of J L Gardners little girl, & Curtis & that Mr Lawrence at Lowell, what a chapter of ills– I shall take up your letters when I have more strength & wit in me than I have now & give them the regular review– your joke about a third wife for cousin Russell is so good that I shall put it to your credit in private a/c & retail it as my own property– pretty good too of Monroe & Sally– "didn't know her Father was well off"

Sally has become quite impious–

I am getting quite tired of this life on ship board for these children are spoiled by having native nurses always running after them and they roar when they want a thing till they get it, & when they get it they roar again for pleasure, so that between pleasure & pain they roar all the time– However the MacDougals are very attentive to all my wants & I ought to bear patiently with their little infirmities– There is so much important matter to attend to here that I must wait a week or two longer– I assure you I have been quite sick & had to work too much & I have wished many a time that I had my heated pate in your lap with a little cool Cologne blown upon by that little mouth of yours & with Bob to say "Poor Papa"– however I am gaining now very rapidly & shall be more prudent– most of my illness was caused by living too freely and getting my stomack out of order without any exercise of consequence– I wrote you very fully per *Rob Fulton*, but the *Oneida* I fear passed out without taking any letters from here– You have been most good in writing & I have often got letters from you when I had none from John & my general business correspondents– I have now tired myself a little & will go to bed & try to dream of home– Good night–

OCT 1 1839

Yesterday it blew a gale of wind all day, The long expected *Navigator* arrived– have not seen the Capt yet– all the letters were long since received– I am still quite weak having taken not but sago & broth in small parcels– My attendant or chief nurse is a curious specimen– he resembles an arrang-autang– is short & black with sharp little eyes & peaked features & a nose that looks like a Parrots Bill & a long black strait beard– he is a native of India but of what part I dont know & answers to the name of Major, I believe he accordingly received this appellation from being seen with a sword in his hand at Mr Hunter's door at Macao– he was long in the employ of Captain Macondray as a boatman– he is servile in the extreme & delights in doing all sorts of tender things for me such as tucking me up, & then he generally comes in when I have just dined & cleans away my eating tools & he wonders,"What for Master, no eat? Master no eat, Master no get well"– he entails about as strongly with the dear little nurse I should have at home, as my present apartments do with your snug rooms– however I am getting on as fast as I can considering that I am still taking medicine daily– my tongue is still coated & the Doctor keeps at me– I shall go to Macao soon & recruit there– I have been reading Clay's Speech & am in the midst of Channing's reply–they are both very forcible papers, but I go along with Clay– the Dr is too visionary– he expects too much–

I received per *Levant*– half a dozen beautiful lambs wool frocks which are excellent & a Seasonable supply of boots & shoes– I had on my last *borrowed* flannel jacket– you will recall I left Canton for a few weeks & have been away nearly two months–

2 OCT–

Had a good night & am quite well– my tongue all cleared off & my appetite good & in a day or two more "Richard will be himself again"–

The *Trenton* arrived last night from New York June 11th, I was just eating my biscuit this morning when in came Mr Hallet much to my surprise, it is only a week ago or less that we heard of his arrival home– he has gone for my letters & I now expect to be over run with them for as she is the latest every body will

Here is Hong Kong as depicted by Tingqua, circa 1845–1847. British ships and the buildings of such firms as Jardine, Matheson and Dent & Co. are already a presence only a few years after the Treaty of Nanking in 1843, which made the port a British Crown Colony.

be dreadful glad to hand over in hopes of a reciprocation– but that wont do– I shall have lots to do & hope Mr Hunter will come over to my relief soon– But I am so impatient to get your latest letters that I cannot finish this page so adieu–

Octo 3–

quite well today, yesterday I got your 49.50.51.52 per *Trenton*– & was much pleased at the Continued good accounts of our great Boy who I see has a new name Bimbo, I had the real misfortune this morning to drop some hot wax in sealing a letter directly onto my little finger nail & if when you are writing you will examine you will find the weight of the burthen comes upon this small member & my friends will be deprived of much valuable correspondence– All my letters from home are encouraging & the only thing in the way of peace & quietness is Mr Coolidge– he writes to *me* per *Trenton* to say that he embarks in a fortnight in the *Eben Preble* & that if on his arrival in Canton the house shall not think it for their interest to make such propositions to him as he can accept, he shall establish himself separately in connection with Mr A Heard & another, with the distinct assurance of the business & influence of Messrs Barings & of

the confidence & good will of some of the principal merchants of the community, but he adds "deprecating such a result however & reserving more particular information until we meet–" John writes me– that the people are surprised at Mr Coolidge bruiting about the probability of a rupture & that I need not fear for Appleton, Bryant, & Sturgis & Co, Peabody, J L Gardner, Goodhue & Co, Neal & Co & other staunch friends & I know enough of Barings to feel sure that they will stick to us while we send them good consignments, when they influence 1 lb to us we give them directly ten pounds & *I* have the control over all this– Delano is worth six of Coolidge & I shall stick to him even if I have to send for you & spend five years here, he & Mr C would never get along together & I feel that harmony is out of the question while J C [Joseph Coolidge] is in the concern if the young members are sincere & true to me & to our arrangement with Delano we need not care for anything but the absurdity of setting up another house of Russell & Co which would be folly– for we who are now on the ground hold the books & papers & are bound to liquidate the old concerns– I judge from a passage in your letters that Mary Magee has been playing false to the old man Phillips, who is his rival– old

Lyman as you say lived just long enough to put me on his list, peace to his ashes, they are but few, I shall take up your letters & review them when more at leisure– This will be sent to Lintin by a fast boat to meet the *Oneida* & I shall write you more fully– per *Apthorp* & other ships going soon– Elliot is trying to make some negotiation to open trade I *fear* he may succeed– at present we Yankees are doing all the business & that I like– I think I shall wait Coolidges arrival here– but am not certain– perhaps I shall go to Macao for a week–

Give yourself no uneasiness about my health– I am quite well again– & shall be all the better like a ship newly rigged for this little bout– Continue to write just as you now do– You will see that there are several letters missing– I have none whatever from you per *Levant*– which is very odd– I know you wrote & they must have gone West in somebodies Carpet bag–

Give much love to your mother & Sarah who could not say less to me if I were a dog– I am really angry that Sarah with all her vivacity & talent should not have written me a line– your mother I know never writes– what can Sarah suppose but that I make up my mind she hates me & merely tolerates me because I am your husband– I am seriously offended that I have not one kind message from either & think it entirely undeserved & gratuitous– I cant make out what Mrs Bacons measure for the foot means, for it is a foot long– Ever Thine truly– RBF

Edmonton

4 Octo 1839

Dear Rose

I have just written you per *Oneida* & have acknowledged your letters from 6 April– No 36-41 on the 30th April & No 49 to 52 inclusive from May 22 to May 29– & I will now read them over & if there is any thing in particular to reply to I will do it now while I have a little time–

You express a fear that I shall miss Russell Sturgis & I do really miss him, for he was the only one that I could talk to of home who could sympathize with me in the least– the rumour of war that you worried yourself about did not cause a passing notice here from any one and had not the slightest effect on business here–

I have read Dr Channings pamphlet & Clays speech & I go entirely with Clay, though the Dr wrote well he is an hundred years in advance–

You had been to ride with Martha Amory & passed the Morlands– I have the same feeling about it that you have, namely that we did live a happy summer there & there our boy was born & I cannot but feel that I shall once more live there–

You talk of having Bennet taken again & I have already written to you to that effect– Your interview with Mr Tucker was very funny– but he dont trade this way so you need not think you have gained any thing for me on the coms line– April 10 you got my *Albion* letters– your joke about a third wife for RS is very good– What you tell me of Ben Greene surprises me & I regret it much because he has not means of getting a living for himself in the world–

April 11– Lizzy Greenes' daughter born but I have the account of the poor things death both from you & Copley– he did not appear to think much about it– & Maria Motley has another child!– you "never can hear of the birth of daughter without a pang" pray cure yourself of such strange phantasies– Why there are born daily a million of daughters in the land & there is no reason you should have as many pangs– George Dexter twins! I am sorry that you dont go to the family circle in Temple place– Why should not my son have quick perceptions? I am sorry for Mrs Curtis bereavement– You cannot bore me with the little every day details– it is just what I want– You did say something in one of your letters about not sending a present to Sarah, but I heeded it not– though I sent no present I am saving money & sent presents to no one– It is a waste of money– Speaking of the past I have no time to look back & my thoughts & time are so taken up with business & great responsibilities that I feel that half the time I am writing even to you my thoughts are wandering away from what I am about & I find myself writing such flat & unprofitable things I am quite interested in your account of the Nurse & the young Oliver Twist– which book I read lately for the first time– Then comes your account of the attempt at weaning– Then comes Mary Magees engagement– & the breaking off– I have no account of the latter part– but Mr T G Cary gave me to understand it was off– Dr Jackson says I must give up smoking does he– well I have not smoked for a couple of weeks– Can you realize that the letters you acknowledge left here only 8 months ago.

Your account of Aunt Barbara's lodgings & Mrs Kirkland's ridicule of them & every thing else is very amusing– Ned Perkins supposed to be attentive to Emily Warren why not when Sarah (whom you dont name) is a Mama– I am very sorry to hear of John L Gardners loss– You have been very particular about dating & numbering while I have not kept it up for a month– I see you have the margin as I desired– indeed you are quite a good woman– I have no account from you of the breaking off of M Magees match & presume it must have been on account of Joe Lymans arrival– I am rejoiced to find my letters satisfy you so well & I assure you yours are just the thing– The picture of Flora seems to have been a good hit– Grand fair at Fannuel Hall, Josiah Sturgis manager–

April 26– Mr Cushing sent for Bennet– this is really gratifying to me– I must here tell you of an act of uncalled for generosity– which I suppose John must have told you ere this– You must know that Mr Cushing sent to China & recommended a cargo of Teas to be sent to himself & for a/c of Houqua & himself, they were bought, but before I left home Mr Cushing offered Bryant Sturgis & Co half of his half interest, they accepted and consequently the Teas went into their hands for sale– Then as Mr Cushing originally intended that I should have the selling of the whole parcel, & although I was absent from home when they arrived he told John when the prospect was good for a profit of $30,000 that he should give it to me & although the outcome is only about $12000 gain he still gives it to me– is not this an overwhelming act of generosity– It is now late & I must say good night & resume my goose quil in the morning– I have written to Mr Cushing & tried to say what was right & proper but the fear of saying too much has prevented me perhaps from saying enough–

Sunday 6 Octo–

A year yesterday since I arrived here & when I review the good fortune that has attended me & the good prospects before me I have not a word to say except in gratitude to a kind Providence– The *Oneida* has just come in here to finish some business & will sail tomorrow– The *Cynthia* is also here but as she goes to Manila & Java I do not write by her, but as I fell in with a very honest "niggar" on board of her & an old friend of mine I have engaged him to take charge of the puppy which Mr Hunter brought over yesterday & deliver the same to you, you will pay him $4 if he does so & although I have told him he will get nothing if the dog dies (of which I think there is a great chance) but you may give Sambo (don't know his real name) $1– for the note addressed to Madam RBF which goes with the dog– I think he will take good care of him– I do not go on with my review of your letters because it will be tiresome to you and takes up time– all the accounts of Bob are good & I am grateful for it– I have later letters than yours because you were out of Town, I have one from Sarah John in which she speaks of the miniature of myself, she ridicules it very much & says it is 50 years too old–

We like to have had a tragedy today– Mrs MacDougal has an old negro servant woman who has shown symptoms of derangement for several days & to day she ran on deck & down the ships accommodation ladder & plunged overboard, but there were men at hand & they pulled her out– she says she is in a family way, but not having used the means to become so declares the devil is in her– poor old thing– she is now watched– the other nurse is sick & the children cry half the time & I can't stand it any longer– so I am going up tomorrow in the *Navigator*– I have quite recovered from my bilious attack & am better than I was before it– You dont say a word about my miniature so I suppose you must have received it in the intermediate letters not yet received– Coolidge dont come yet & I have a sort of feeling as if he would not come– You need be under no concern about me, even if I give Coolidge terms to keep peace I shall still do extremely well & if we lose any thing by letting him go, it will be made up for by the business Delano will bring to us– Henry Sturgis I hear is going home to return again– It is very odd that I dont get a line from you either by the *Levant* or the *Valparaiso*– I must now go at my business letters, Sunday though it be– There is no rest for the sole of a coms merchants foot I find– Love to Bob & all the family & believe me dearest ever thine– Truly & faithfully RBF

Oneida
Hong Kong
Oct 9 1839
My dear Rose,

I thought I had done with the *Oneida*, when this morning your long letters 42 up to 47 came to hand, the first dated May day– the last May 18– 6 sheets– I had intended to go to Macao at 2 oclock but the reading of these letters which came per *Levant* & have been sleeping in the supercargo deck a week have spoiled my forenoon for business & so I must defer my departure for Macao– I wanted to go there to see Houqua & learn from him what is going on of a political nature–

The letters just received are extremely acceptable as they fill up the gap between those received per *Albion* & *Trenton*–

I note that Mary Magee has been changing her mind and it is not to be supposed that at their time of life love should be the predominating feeling I cannot forgive her, she should have made up her mind when he proposed– she is a fool not to marry him or was a fool to accept him– one or the other that's certain–

I have a long letter from T G Cary Jr & Ed Gardner which I shall duly reply to per this vessel–

I received a paper box with a dozen fine nicely done up handkerchiefs, well marked, a week ago & they pleased me almost as much as letters, but I was much disappointed not to get any thing from you, but to day the letters were found– You tell me of a great many things that require notice but I cannot here lay myself out to reply so fully as I shall when I get to Canton in the quiet & solitude of my chamber– These brats of McDougals cry or hallo continually & the necessary work on board ship is not calculated to call up "white-mountain talk"–

I am not at all surprised at your remarks about my miniature, Sarah Forbes said it was horrible– I dare say as it was packed quite fresh that the colouring changed & I was aware that the expression was bad, Greene did not like it, then I dare say I have grown old– my hair is much greyer than it was– but my health is good– you must calculate on my growing six years older (in the three) than I was when I left you– for I have much to think of, business transactions of much importance & thinking certainly is bad for me– never mind the heart is still young– We have had two Balls on board the *Hercules* & the *Charles Forbes,* the first ship I have since bought, the second is an old East Indiaman named after the former Governor of Bombay who was a great uncle of my Fathers– I did not go to either party– The evening of the last day before yesterday while the dance was going on, it began to blow a gale of wind & all day yesterday it blew so violently that nothing could be done, Mr Hunters boat with two men in it was driven away before the blast without our being able to render them any help, & I fear they are lost for a Chinese boat dispatched this morning to search for them has returned & heard nothing of them– Many China boats were lost & I expect to hear of disasters on the Coast, hope Coolidge & family are safe– In my last budjet per this ship, I gave you a copy of what I said to Mr Cushing about the present of $10,000– This would be a fortune for many men– poor old Mr Snow the Consul says he only wants that sum & I hope by having finished the means by the purchase of the *Hercules* on his a/c with our money to make that sum for him, charity begins at home however & by purchasing this ship we get the consignment of her Cargo which enables us to earn some 2 or 3 thousand dollars– I have written another letter to Coolidge & told him I should have had no objections to making a settlement with him had he not have first opposed my views in every respect– I do not tell him our arrangement with him is impossible but I suggest to him the great probability that we can not pull together– I am positively engaged to Delano & I do not think there is the least chance of my doing any thing with C– but I must quarrel– you can understand that I have the full contract over Houqua & he made it a matter of stipulation that if we wanted his business we must put C– one side– I am not at all afraid of losing any thing by cutting him– the business that Delano will bring to us is more than equal to any thing C can take away– the only awkward thing will be that C & Heard may come here & set up for Russell this would be the height of folly– if they would only hoist the flag of C & Heard– I would give them a bonus for I am certain that our firm of Russell & Co or Mr Delano & I as Forbes, Delano & Co would carry much more weight– Our prospect for this year is as brilliant as can be & I have little or no doubt but our commissions will be Two hundred thousand dollars for the year my share of which will be near Forty one thousand dollars– so dont be uneasy about the "Kail pot" [161] another year here & one or two at home with a reduced share will make me a rich man again– when I get back to Canton I shall take up all your letters & write you more fully– but now my hand is full of proclamations & I must cut off my yarn– Give my best love to your mother & Sarah & a kiss to Bimbo & believe me ever thine most Affectionately RBF

Bark *Trenton* off Lintin
Octo 17, 1839
Dear Wife–
My last per *Oneida* was dated on the 9th & I believe I have never passed so long a time without writing to you– I make no excuses for I have been so continually engaged night & day that I have never had a moments time even for you & I

[161] Kail or kale was a slang term for money.

have felt that I should not be doing my duty to you unless I put aside my pen the moment I could do so & go to rest– yesterday a vessel arrived from Manila & brought me your No 48 which I believe fills up the gap– I have acknowledged per *Oneida* all up to 52 except the last which begins May 12– I have abused you in former letters for not mentioning Sarah Cleveland– in the last you give me an account of her & the child & I find I cannot scold you to day, but that on the morrow there comes some new letter with the desired information– Mary Magee is a fool– Phillips an Insurance to be disappointed! why she is mad!!

I am glad to hear the Hillards are doing well enough to offer Eight hundred & fifty dollars for a house was this for *one* year or two– but you are such a worriment at figures that I place no reliance on you– for instance you tell me that P C Brooks has bought the Webster house for "thirty seven dollars"– now I cant believe this especially as you go onto say that the Perkins house in Temple Place is to let & cant be had for under "seven thousand"–

Your mother & Sally send much love & this makes up a little for their former neglect–

I have now said enough about your present letter & shall not look over your large & late budjets until I get back to Canton where I am now bound– but will tell you something of myself– I did not go to Canton in the *Navigator* because I could not get ready & I did not go to Macao because I heard Houqua (whom I wished to see) was at the Bogue– Indeed I have left many things undone & if I had not absolutely torn myself away from Hong Kong I should have had more instead of less to do– I have only had my foot on shore twice since the 5 of September & then only to bathe on the beach– You can imagine how much I have had to do when I tell you that we have four English ships at Hong Kong to our consignment & Eight Americans there & at Whampoa besides one Hamburg Brig & to day as we were sailing away from Hong Kong I saw a vessel that looked very much like a consignment, so I jumped into a China boat & boarded her & found her to be the Swedish ship *Hilda* from Java consigned to us, making *14* vessels, those figures stand fourteen– Wetmore & Co have two & one of those is their own vessel! So we are not much in arrears of our neighbors & rivals– On the 14 Inst Capt Elliot gave notice that he had completed arrangements to open the British Trade which you will remember has been only carried on through American ships for several months– his plan is to deliver cargoes at the Bogue to Chinese, paying the usual Port Charges & receiving produce in return, but he strictly enjoins all British Subjects not to go into the river within the power of the Chinese– I do not think the English Merchants will avail of the permission temporarily to trade upon this footing & I think most of them will prefer to sell through us– besides these reasons–

I think the arrangements will be set at naught by the folly of the skipper of the *Thos Coutts* a large Indiaman with over an hundred men, the Captain having contract over the ship & having agreed in India to deliver his Cargo at *Whampoa* on arrival applies for a pilot (with a perfect understanding of all Elliots prohibitory injunctions) & goes to Whampoa where he now is with his ship– others will follow & thus it will be clearly shown to the High Commissioner that Elliot has no power over his Countrymen & is not worth treating with–

I regret the ship the *Coutts* has taken on many accounts, firstly because it is much more for our interest (R&Co) that the English should remain outside, secondly because any attempts to get a fair commercial treaty out of the Chinese will be of no avail while ships, *British* ships– go to Whampoa– thirdly because I have a sincere regard for Elliot & it must be excessively annoying to find that he really has no power over his Country men–

Coolidge does not yet make his appearance & I *fear he may never come*– My partners are getting quite anxious to see me back to Canton & I go willingly as I have had a fatiguing campaign outside– all the British Merchants are still at Hong Kong & quite tired of their residence there– Bob is still at Macao & I have ordered him sent up per first good opportunity– I am quite tired of the McDougal children, the Boy– three years old is the most complete Cad– that ever was & the little girl though interesting, "*screeches*" (Webster) half the night with sheer passion– I hope you will bring our Boy up to behave like a man for the sake of being one & not because his mouth is stopped with a sugar plumb or a play thing every time he cries– Children should be taught to value indulgences from the scarcity of them– presents continually given to children must have a tendency to pall their appetites and render them dissatisfied if some new thing is not continually put before them– but enough of this– the "Major" my black valet has been sick & I have had the pleasure of attending on him & you never saw such a grateful creature–

Mr Hunters boat, for which I entertained great fears, kept before the gale, though only a small open boat 26 feet long (those figures are for *26*) & actually arrived safe at Macao, a distance of more than 40 miles in a rough sea, this speaks well for the boat & the men too– I must now close this letter & write to John & Green– this is intended for the *Apthorp* but I may miss her in the River & if you get nothing from me by her you will know why– I have given the puppy in charge of the steward of the *Cynthia*–

I am now laying at anchor near Lintin the sight of that island awakens some pleasing as well as melancholy associations– it was just in this very spot where my Brother Tom bade adieu for the last time & it was near here that I spent some eighteen months so profitably during my last visit to China– perhaps Providence took away my fortune because I made it in Opium– What I make this time will be free from that stain– Love to Bob & good night– Thine ever truly RBF

Bark *Trenton* in the mouth of the River
19 OCTO 1839
Dear Rose–
I have amused myself to day in making a copy of a letter I wrote to Mr Cabot & I consider that I am showing great trust in your discretion in sending you the same for perusal that you may understand the subject & then seal & send the letter to John– I would send you copies of my letters left at Hong Kong to meet C– I feel however that I write a great deal more than is good for me & the glare of the sun on the water has made my eyes quite weak– Last year we had it cold before this but to day & yesterday it was as hot as summer, we have cool nights however & that is a great comfort– I hope the Bark that passed us in the night was not the *Apthorp* – she was too far off to send letters to– I must now wind up my days work & say God Bless thee– love to Bimbo & all the family– Ever thine faithfully RBF

BACK AT CANTON

CANTON 24 OCTO 1839
My dear Rose–
I have written you several long letters recently while on my way up in the *Trenton* from Hong Kong, I arrived here on the 21 the letters attended to went per *Apthorp*, but it is quite likely that this will get to you before her– I have received all your letters up to No 52 –& also an old one without numbers which was dated

in January & was handed me by Copley Greenes Boy– Ayow with a letter from him of similar date–

You need not be told that this is the second birth day of our dear Boy & I have no doubt that you drank Papas health as we all drank his at table to day, this did not help my digestion much for I had taken a dose of Salts in the morning– after an absence of more than two months you may be sure I found plenty to do on arrival here– Indeed I have no time except to sleep & shall be glad when the work is over– We had on 22nd–14 vessels to our consignment–8 American, 4 English, 11 Bremen, & 1 Swede & the extensive correspondence necessary to keep all their owners, Captains, & Agents informed of their movements hardly leaves time for private letters– Yet I feel I have done my full share of these– If any of my friends complain that they do not hear form me often enough– tell them I sit neglecting even you so as not to fatigue myself too much– I feel that the intense thought necessary to carry out all the plans intrusted to us, often makes my head snap & I feel that a new grey hair springs up on such occasions– health good– weight 145– shall get up 10 lbs before January– The weather has lately been oppressively hot & the Therm to day was at 86–

The *Lehigh* is in from Philadelphia to 10 July– more than a month later than your letters & the *Eben Preble* having sailed on the 29 June must be in or very near at hand– No letters are yet received by the *Lehigh*– Our friend Mr Ritchie who puts his business into our hands was made very happy when the *Valparaiso* arrived at hearing that his wife had a son & was quite well & could not come out for the present– & the day before yesterday he heard of her arrival from Phila in the *Lehigh* at Macao, he started instantly & has the offer of my house (as has Coolidge)– When Dr Parker told Ritchie of his good fortune he pulled out his gold watch & gave it to the Dr saying "Dr if you dont take that, I will never speak to you again"– He must feel quite happy–

I to day committed the extravagance on a/c of Russell & Co of sending Mrs McDougal a shawl costing $30 & a piece of silk at $16– they were kind & attentive to me & I could not get McDougal to receive any compensation for lodging us– I who sent the Children a silver Cup a piece & have engaged one for Bob– being his birth day present– I also bought you a splendid Green & White Shawl cost $30 worth $50 with you– which you will no doubt want by the time you get it for I dare say you are getting *shabby*– I have great hopes of getting my letters per *Lehigh* & *E Preble* in a few days & shall hear by the former if Coolidge really embarked in the latter– The trade (British Trade) is very unsettled & it is quite uncertain whether the negotiations between Capt Elliot & the Commissioner will amount to any thing– One British Ship has in defiance of Capt Elliots repeated injunctions come up river & is now at Whampoa– she is not yet secured & if some of the Capts English friends do not come up here to take care of her business we may have to do it for her– Another Ship the *Royal Saxon* Capt Tain is coming up– she comes to us & I should not be at all surprised if more were to come in– Capt Osgood sailed without my seeing him again– I must look up some token to send to Esther, perhaps a dinner or tea set– with much love to Bob & the rest good night–

Sunday 27 October 1839

Dear Rose–

Here I am scribbling in my own chamber waiting for Church time, I have not heard a sermon for a long time & shall be quite glad to get one of Parkers best to day– We do not yet get our letters per *Lehigh*, since my last date we hear of the arrival of the *Tenobia*, but are not yet in possession of our letters & are not sure that she is to us consigned, she belongs to D P Parker & is a fine large ship– I hear nothing yet of the *E Preble* & fear she may have put in somewhere on account of Mrs Coolidge health– Yesterday I employed myself in copying into one of these books all the correspondence *with* & *relating to* Coolidge, I find from the letters received by Delano & myself from parties in New York, that C created quite a sensation among them, but Delano says he has only told us half of the story & that he shall give such explanations to his friends as will put the matter right– he & I are sworn to stand by each other, I have told him all along that "I want but little here below," but want that little quick, that I *must have* a good share next year & retain a small share for a two years term after– then I will do all I can to promote his interest– If we do as well in 1840 as in 1839 I shall be quite independent & quite ready to go home within the time *perfectly satisfied* & longer I will not stay, satisfied or not, I think it quite probable that I shall say to Coolidge when he comes, you may take care of the business of Barings as they are so fond of you & we will take care of the rest– but as to his coming here to contract our general business I wont consent to it– Houqua came up yesterday from the consultation at Macao & *derangements* are concluded on to open the British trade upon terms more disgraceful & absurd, considering all they have said, than you can imagine– I have already told you that Elliot was in treaty with the Commissioner, he has now concluded to allow British ships to come up as far as Chuenpee[162], under the guns of the Forts six at a time & discharge their cargoes, two cargo boats a day to each ship– this will require at least four months to discharge all the fleet & whose turn is to come first? After the cargoes are declared to be all out the ships are to be searched & if one single Catty of Opium is found on board, the ship is to be condemned & the guilty man owning the Opium is to be given up!!!– After the ships are duly searched they are to be allowed to go to Whampoa 24 to 30 miles above the place of discharge & to take in the produce of the Celestial empire without giving any bond for having been proven empty & consequently free of Opium outside it is not necessary to give any bond–

All ships willing to come under a bond much more severe than the American Bond may come directly up to Whampoa & trade like the Americans–

Now I should like to know the difference between the assail to the Chinese Law outside the Bogue or inside the Bogue– British agents must be within the power of the Chinese, they must come to Canton to negotiate their Bills & make their purchases & sales & I cannot see for the life of me why they dont come to Whampoa at once– The trade is in a most uncertain & unsatisfactory position & we are fortunate in being only agents & having nothing but the interests of Constituents at stake– By the time the English get fairly at work upon this new system of derangements– the British Government may send an Agent here & cancel all Elliots doings & perhaps make a row with China–

I had a long talk with Houqua about Coolidge, he says it is of no consequence whether he establishes a house or not separate from us & he advises us to treat him civilly until the first day of January & then say– adieu– good bye– god bless you &c– I suppose it will be but right as he is an older man & an older member of the house than myself to let him take the head of the Table, this would be no more than common courtesy, but Delano says, treat him like a guest merely, he cannot well be here till 10th November & cannot therefore if he would, assume the lead for it will take him till January to get to

---

[162] Chuenpee was the name given to one of the Chinese forts that guarded the Bogue–the narrow portion of the Pearl River below Canton.

work– My feelings to Coolidge are by no means rancorous, but he certainly is not entitled to any consideration from me– He was so puffed up by Bates that he really imagined that he was the only man in R&Co & then he quotes "my character as a Merchant"– I feel that the sort of life I lead at home gave rise to the belief usually that I was rather a gay fellow, or sporting man, & I now feel that all the enjoyments of boats, Nahant house &c are turning out bitter seeds– to me– I certainly felt independent & acted so & I never thought that I should so soon become a sort of public servant– I am sure that was C & I put into the seals he would be found much less practical as a merchant, as a man of letters & accomplishments I yield readily to him– I am surprised to find here that he is considered very mean & penurious & that his character for indecision is notorious– my late campaign at Hong Kong has fully convinced my partners that I can *act* when necessary–

It is now Church time & I will only say for fear I forget it that in selecting some shawls for a large order I saw one which particularly struck my fancy– It is white ground with heavy Brown embroidery, shaded from a very dark to a very light colour– I ordered a heavy fringe put to it & shall send it to you that you may choose for yourself between the Green & White & this, one must be sold, the Brown & White at $60– the other at $50–

Sunday evening–

A remarkably dull sermon from Dr Parker, a visit to Houqua & the Hongs generally & then dinner– invited John Cunningham, son of John C deceased & John Codman Jr, son of Rev John Codman– Dorchester to dine, the latter promised to go to see the Milton folks & the former, a very nice young man promised to call on you, they are joint supercargoes of the *Morea* & will sail in a day or two for New York– They will tell you that Russell & Co are the legitimate people & say a great many good things about me which you will not believe– I am getting quite short of this black paper which is invaluable to me– I expect a supply however from *London* & when I get it I shall write a good deal more– it is necessary to economize now– I have requested Mr Sturgis to send Bob up per first good opportunity– though your account of him gives me a very different impression of his appearance from what the picture does– I also want to see Flora very much poor old thing, like her master she is getting quite grey– but never mind the application of a little Macassar will make me quite young again– The time is coming round when the Tea Cumshas [gratuities] come in, when I shall send you a supply– & an adventure for Bob

Good Night

October 30th–

Quite well– No letters up from the *Lehigh* or *Tenobia* which I am anxiously expecting– Since my last date we hear that the negotiations between Elliot & the Commissioner are at an end– The Chinese seeing one ship (English) at Whampoa are unwilling to believe that all cannot come up & they demand that they give the same bond which the ship at Whampoa gives & she having given it they also demand that the Americans do the same, this we will not do until obliged to & I am to day preparing a remonstrance to the Great Man declining to sign any new Bonds– The effect of the English not coming in will be to put gold into our pockets & therefore I am glad of it & I hope they never will come until they can trade upon better terms than they can at present– Whatever they gain politically we must also reap the benefit of– The multiplicity of letters to write & the limited time must be my excuse dearest for writing you such meagre letters– But I must economize not only my body but my eyes which are rather weak with night work– The heart is strong however & always devotedly thine– Love to all & good bye for to day– RBF

Per *Morea* & when she's gone she will be no & more & here

CANTON 1 NOVEMBER 1839

Dear Rose

You are so slow at taking a joke that I am obliged to underline my puns–

To day I finished my business letter per *Talbot*, you will get a couple of sheets by her, which is a small quantity for me– but I have really been so much taken up with business letters & arrangements that I have had but little time to devote to pleasure– I have been in a fever too to get the *Tenobia* & *Lehigh* letters which are not yet up & we dont know when they will be– No *Eben Preble* heard of yet– I have given Mr Cunningham 2nd supercargo of the *Morea* a letter of introduction to you, I know but little of him but what I do know is good– & he will tell you that he met me at Macao, Hong Kong & here & that he's left me very well, if not excessively corpulent–

I write but little by this opportunity because the ship always makes a long passage & the *Talbot* & other ships to follow will give you more full accounts of me– A week since we thought the British trade was opened but the Commissioner has backed out & all is afloat again– This is well for the Yankees & if they keep the Port open we must do exceedingly well–

I have been making up the a/c which I named to you to what amount Mr Cushing *gave me* & I find it must be at least *$20000, those figures stand for twenty thousand – that with the 30 or 40 that I shall get out of the house this year will make me quite rich – But I am tired & must say – Good Night*

SUNDAY 3RD NOVEMBER 1839

MRS RBF

My dear Rose

My last was a short letter of the 1st Instant per *Morea*, & a few days earlier per *Talbot*– I have as yet nothing more from you since the *Trenton*, but am daily expecting the letters per *Lehigh* & *Tenobia*– which ships have been in some days– the first two weeks & brings dates to 10th July– We have to day various rumors that Elliot has given up his power to the men of War & that they are coming to Whampoa to take the *Thomas Coutts* out of the River (the English ship that came in against Elliots orders) & then to declare a blockade– The blockade part is much more probable than the rest, let them do what they please it will result well to the Yankees– Our dear old ship *Lintin* is now nearby ready to come up the third time & will make a grand thing of it if a blockade is put on– in short we are doing "as well as could be expected under the circumstances" which quotation is from the mouth of a certain old Gentleman about his wife who was always expecting an heir but never had one– Heard a tolerable sermon to day from Dr Parker, & dined with Delano & two or three strangers, dont feel any the worse for it– & Our hurry will be over shortly & I shall begin to write you more fully– I always think of you on Sunday more than any other days– when I put my head on my pillow I think of a thousand things to say which I dare say are best omitted– Love to Bob & Good Night

THE BRITISH MAN THEIR CANNONS

Wednesday 6th November–

On Sunday between 12 & 1 oclock we distinctly heard a cannon sounding & I told every body that it certainly came from British Guns– but as the Bocca Tigris Forts are 31 or 32 miles in a strait line I was laughed at– I thought it so serious a matter that I took considerable pains to find the Captain of the *ThomasCoutts* & recommend him to get on board of his ship at Whampoa as fast as possible– He accordingly went–

On Monday morning a Boat came up from the Ship *Morea*, which vessel at the very hour named above was passing the Bocca Tigris & saw an engagement between the Frigate *Volage* & the Sloop of war *Hyacinth*[163] against a fleet of war junks, some 40 in number– Yesterday I went to Whampoa & met the Supercargo of the Swedish Ship *Hilda* consigned us & he gave us an account of the battle which he also witnessed– three junks were sunk & one blown up in a very short time & probably some two or three hundred men drowned & killed– We know no further particulars, but we suppose that Capt Elliot went to the vicinity of the Forts & made a demand of the Commissioner (who is near the Bogue) whether he really intended to drive the British ships away or whether he intended to allow British subjects to reside at Macao– the Commissioner probably told him in reply– I will not only drive the Merchant ships away from Hong Kong, but I will send my Admiral to drive you away with your two vessels– he probably attempted to do this & has met his deserved punishment–

one report says that the Frigates fired first– I do not think it a matter of much importance who fired first– It is always admitted among civilized nations as proper, that where one power makes preparations to attack another, the latter has just right to spoil the preparations & take care of duty– The Supercargo of the *Hilda* says the British poured in their fire from both sides & in 20 minutes not a flag was flying on board the junks– It must have been cruel work– but the Chinese deserve punishment & must have it & if John Bull does not do it effectually now, he never will have so good a chance again– The Captain of the *Coutts* was in Town again yesterday & does not seem to have any apprehensions for his safety– indeed he has a safe conduct from the Government– These are exciting times and we Yankees will take advantage of them– I am expecting daily to hear of a blockade– We have a letter to day from Hong Kong to the 3d– all was quiet there– an American Ship going in perhaps this was Coolidge– I have a long letter from Heard, extremely friendly, he speaks of having called several times & not been admitted– I hope if he is in Boston that you will explain to him that you were really out– I doubt if he comes out when he hears of the state of things in March, which we then thought unfavourable, but which has since proved a benefit to us– I have lots to say on business & cannot write any more for this ship– Love to all & good bye– Thine ever RBF

Saturday night

Canton November 9, 1839

My dear little wife–

My last date was per *Providence* on the 6th Instant– I then gave you some account of a battle fought last *Sunday* at the Bogue & I now enclose Hunters letter giving a description of it which pray read & send to John– The latter part of said letter

[163] The *Hyacinth* was an eighteen-gun warship which followed the *Volage* to Hong Kong, but arrived after the Battle of Cowloon.

referring to certain figures will be understood when I tell you that I wrote to Hunter that we should charge him $5500 for not securing us the consignment of Mr Parkers ship *Tenobia* which arrived at Hong Kong after I left–

You will I dare say recollect Ashew who lived with Copley he came here this evening & told me that he was at the Bogue & saw the battle, that out of 70 men (those figures stand for 70) in the junk that blew up only six returned & he states that near two hundred men were killed– We hear that the Commissioner is much alarmed & is trying already to conciliate, two days since he sent word to Houqua to request him to assure Capt Warner of the '*Thomas Coutts*' an English ship & the only one at Whampoa, that he need be under no apprehension, that the fighting was his affair & Elliots should not compromise any innocent men– he also directed Houqua to say to the foreigners that he (the Commissioner) should not molest the ships at Hong Kong, nor punish the English any more at present!!!!– 200 men killed against one man slightly wounded !!!!– I have always contended that the Chinese would never get into the list of civilized nations until fairly flogged into the list & I am really of opinion that negotiations are of little avail compared to bullying– It was a cruel business however & Capt Smith *will have a great deal to answer for, both to his government & to that God above all governments who will finally judge him.*

Our good ship *Lintin* is on her way up the third time with another fine freight– If I had originally retained my interest in her & just sucked my paws without doing any other business I should now have been worth at least three hundred thousand dollars– which sum she has earned since she was built– but should I have been any happier or any more respected than I shall now be when I get safe home with my $500000– I will now put aside my goose quill until I get some further letters from you which I must have in a few days 13th Nov– received letter No 53 of June 6 before you started out of Town– I have long letters from John to July per *Lehigh* delivered after 22-23 days! Mr Coolidge coming with wife letters expected– I am very sorry to hear that you were so long without letters from him (Tom) this *must be* a source of great grief to your Mother & I feel that every letter you get from me must give her a pang– You tell me that Mrs Cushing is again in a certain predicament & I hope with you, that it is a daughter–

I have received a very good letter from John C Lee he as well as yourself gives me a famous a/c of the young Gent– Cannot you have him betrothed to *Miss Cushing* & have 50 or 100,000 put in trust for him at once– John has been hard at work for me counteracting the influence of Coolidge in New York & elsewhere & he has given me copies of his (John's) letters to Joshua Bates & The Words which are exactly to the point– if all that John says is true, the man has done himself more harm than good–

The year is nearly expired & I shall not give him the head of the Table unless he comes soon– John says all the principal merchants formerly friendly to the house, continue so to me & that those who are not so well known to me, sworn Brothers, we must come outright– but it will be disagreeable to me to be harsh to Coolidge & if he does not put on any airs & will be content to make propositions *to us* all will be amicably settled, quarrel I wont under any circumstances– I shall send you herewith a couple of Repositories, a piece of grass cloth cost 50 cts a yard here– Two embroidered shawls, the one embroidered in Brown is my fancy & perhaps a piece of Rich Silk for some of your rich friends to buy at $2 a yard– I enclose herein a note from Mrs McDougal whose guest I was so long on board the *Edmonton*, she writes a pretty hand– I have got entirely over my cold & am in good spirits– good night & love to all friends & Bob

Sunday Evening 17 Nov 1839

Dearest wife–

Another Sunday has come round & I am a week older– a week nearer home– I am playing nurse to night– Yesterday our Mr King went to Whampoa with Low & Delano & pulled an oar all the way in a hot sun, then took more dinner than was good for him & got a violent cold & has a good deal of fever– I have just had Parker to see him & have par boiled him & he is better, Mr King keeps our books & could not be well spared at this moment so I must get him well as fast as possible– That old pain in the bread bucket is almost gone & I have now mostly to complain occasionally of a heavy bilious feeling from want of exercise & fresh air– called on Houqua after Church– I am on very confidential terms with the old Gentleman & this gives me an immense advantage– We get any political news stirring before other people & gain other solid advantages from our intimate connection with him– Barings & Coolidge know this & will act warily– *Eben Preble* letters from June 6-July 3– does not come– we hear she was to go to Batavia & there I dare say Coolidge will exercise his skill in putting in a full cargo of Rice & other useless stuff– I have had two Boxes of preserves put up for you & your friends & have told John that I send Sarah a piece of silk– I shall leave you to choose the rich figured claret silk if you like it better than the piece flowered which is narrow – The piece I intend for you is rich & chaste– the other is rich & beautiful for a dashing cloak but not so handsome for you as the plain figured one– I must bid you good night & attend to my patient

Friday 22 Nov–

If any one had told me that I had not put pen to paper on your a/c since Sunday I should have said they lied– we have had a busy week of it– Mr King not being very well & Mr Hunter away we have been hard at it till 11-12 every night– I stand it remarkably well though I must confess that I shall be extremely glad when the *Navigator, Trenton, Wilhelm Lording* get away– they will go on Sunday & I shall give Capt Bridges who is a very respectable fat old Gentleman a letter to you– I have to day bought two caps one is for Mrs Bacon with my compliments– besides the ships named going away, we have the *Valparaiso* just starting, *the Lerna* & *Lintin* discharging & a new ship of Daniel P Parkers, the *Tenobia* consigned to us by the supercargo– then we have the *Hilda* (Swede), the *Baring*, & *Royal Saxon* outside– rendering it necessary to write a bushel of letters per day & it is now 11 PM & I will not do you the injustice to write much more– I have sealed & directed to you a letter of Russell Sturgis for your amusement & edification– don't undertake to read it aloud & when read burn it–

All is quiet here & two more American ships have been made by purchase of British vessels–

I shall close this letter to night & mark it up for *Trenton* having already closed one for the __ lest I should forget I mention that I send per *Trenton* to Cary a box marked JSCG containing cuspidors for Copley to whom give my perpetual regards & to Lizzy– all is quiet here– I am expecting Flora & Bob & Coolidge every day– What a fool the latter was to go to Batavia, perhaps he will hear such accounts from here as will induce him to leave his wife in that place– The evacuation of Macao by all the British makes it a dull place for ladies– Houqua gave me an order yesterday to John & to Barings & Forbes, Forbes & Co to send back all his funds & property to me, this will convince them that I *am* somebody & Mr C is *nobody*– If any of our friends complain of my not writing to them tell them I have hardly time to sleep five hours a night– Thank God I am well & King is about again–

Hunter daily expected up– give my love to your mother & to Sally & a hundred kisses for the dear boy– A vessel arrived a few days since from the coast of South America with dates to August but I get nothing from Thomas– I hope he is doing well again–

thine ever Truly RBF

CANTON NOVEMBER 24, 1839

Dear Rose–

I finished my Navigator letters at 1 oclock this morning & I laid abed till 9 & took my breakfast alone– I went to bed as tired as two dogs & expected to get up with a head ache but I find myself quite smart to day & successfully entertained 16 people at dinner in addition to our own family– no I mean in*cluding* it– we yesterday got rid of two Captains, one supercargo & one "interloper" a Russian Gent introduced to us by some of our English friends, Mr Inglis also departed– he is Brother to the Inglises that are keeping school on Staten Island– I gave Capt Bridges a letter to you, he appears to be a clever old Gent– We have got the consignment after all of Mr Parkers big ship the *Tenobia*– & Capt Kinsman who is an intimate friend of Whitneys has told me of the alterations in his house, he says the home has cost Whitney a great deal more than he can afford to pay away– All our affairs go on well, though I think it is almost time to hear some news from England about the Opium surrender–

will the British Government take the matter up seriously or not? I think there is a great chance that the British Trade now carried on by the Americans will be at an end before long– I am now disposed to keep snug & reduce our business while the British are, at the wrong moment disposed to go ahead– I had an agreeable surprise this morning– I had locked my door to keep the boy who comes in the morning to bring me water &c from waking me up too early & because the door was locked it seemed to me that they were determined to get in– I got up at last & opened the door & there stood Bobs picture which a friend had brought up from Macao– fresh varnished & he now stands in his old place–

I expect Flora up in a day or two with Hunter & her pups– I shall almost be reconciled to the arrival of Mr Coolidge because he will bring me your letters– The *Asia* must be along soon with letters to latter part of July & the *Lotos* that left about the same time as the *Lehigh* must also bring me something– It is fortunate that I have such constant occupation for I have no time to be discontented & unhappy– The Capt of the *Lehigh* was second mate of a ship at Whampoa when I was also second mate of the *Leonard* 17 years ago & we were also school mates at Milton Academy– He is a married man & poor into the bargain– is looking forward to $1500 a year as the acme of human felicity!! Is it all luck? all good fortune I say to myself many times a day– or have I any positive talent– or what is it– I tried last night at midnight to write Mr William Sturgis a sober letter but for the life of me I could not get my mind down to any thing but fun & I have been in good spirits all day– I have been very extravagant in my presents by this ship, let me see

1 Piece of claret coloured silk more than enough for a gown, pellisse or cloak	28
1 Piece of dove colour or light satin fig silk	25
1 Piece of superfine grass cloth Brown 40 yds	20
1 Brown embroidered Crape shawl	33
1 Green & White do-do-do[164]	30
1 Piece white lining Pangu (good to dye)	00
1 Piece of silk figured in colours for Sarah John	30
one hundred sixty-six dollars	166

[164] This is RBF's abbreviation for "ditto".

Why I am a ruined man & clean daft– remember these things will keep– I have forgotten Esthers Tea Set– but will get it bye & bye– measure the silks before cutting them– the cloth may make two pelisses[165] or gowns...

You have got back to Town long before this & I have some hopes that Esther has got divorced by this time & that Lucys Father is dead & so that you are all snug again– should not much wonder if Coolidge left his wife in Java & comes here on a reconnoitering visit only– If he is not a fool he will turn back– You have had old Greene with you for some time– what did you think of him– I find we get along without him much better than we expected though *he was* a good worker–

The weather has been unnaturally hot for several days & I am momentarily expecting a great change for the better– I fear you will be much dissatisfied when you get my late letters, for I have really had no time & to day I could not get to Church– I have been writing all day–

remember me to your Ma & Sally & tell them for not writing to me "I have little or no respect for them" & last not least to Bob give a great many kisses– I dare say the poor fellow has the whooping cough or something by this time

Canton Sunday Evening December 1, 1839

My dear Rose–

I wrote you last per *Albion* on the 29 Nov & now continue my budjet by the *Osage* which will probably be home first– We have had more leisure the last few days & have had a little rest from our hard labours– The *Preble* does not come yet & the only important news is an Edict issued by the Chinese authorities prohibiting, after the 6th Inst, all transhipment from the English to American vessels & all changing of vessels from the British to the American flag– This will interfere seriously with our business for a time & God knows how long, but I cannot bring myself to think seriously of the matter & I am inclined to believe that an accommodation will take place before we feel the effect much & if the trade is called off it will bring about a change for the better very soon– & should the trade be suspended in part, we shall still go on with our regular American business disconnected from the English outside trade, perhaps the English will all go to Manila & we shall then have to go over there for cargos with our ships– But enough of trade– my last dates from you are nearly 6 months old say June 6th & we ought soon to get letters to August– Perhaps you would like to know just how I am situated at this moment – my table is covered with your scarlet cloth & before me against the wall stands my guardian Angel Bob & against him stands the pretty sketch of a bounding Deer sent me by Mrs Amory– on my left is a black lacquered box containing my bible & prayer Book– on one side my bed & couch & on the other my toilet table, over which hangs the Madonna– I have my room carpeted & it is altogether comfortable– the walls are our favourite green– Flora & Mr Hunter came up yesterday & she was particularly glad to see me after a separation of more than two months– You can only partly imagine what a great comfort my Bob's picture is to me, dressing & undressing I always watch him as though I could hold communion with him & the face grows on me every day– I think the head is well done & every body says it is a noble looking creature– It is a weary thought to look forward to that distant day of meeting & there is many a thorny path to tread before that happy day, however 18 months are gone– which is half my time, & I already begin to look forward to this time next year as our era of delight– In fourteen months from to day I shall probably be on my way home & when you get this, you will only

165 A pelisse was a long cloak or outer coat often lined or trimmed with fur.

have to think of me in Canton ten months more– To look back it seems like a dream & my time since my arrival has been so profitably & so fully occupied that it seems as nothing & if I continue to get good letters from you & Bob I shall not pine– My sacrifice has been attended with single success & my health is better than when I arrived– in short I am quite well & have entirely given up the idea that my complaints are any thing more than nervous & rheumatic–

A few days ago there arrived here the crew & several passengers of the Spanish Brig *Cassador* – who had been conducted overland from a distant part of the coast where they were wrecked last October, they had journeyed forty four days under guard, supplied occasionally with food & clothes by the Mandarins & robbed of them directly after by the people– Among them was a young man named Barrette, this fellow was clerk on board the *Lintin* a year ago, another was a Mr De Souza of Macao, who lives next door to my house, & is well off, they were bound to Manila– All shipwrecked people are kept as it were prisoners until they are fully examined by the Magistrates & in the mean time are kept in the Consoo House where I visited them on Friday, they were poorly clad & very much begrimed with dirt & I hardy know them– I had the satisfaction of sending them beds & edibles & all that they required– I wish the crew of the *Sunda* were as well off, this vessel was lost near the same time & place as the other– She had on board a Mr & Mrs Macpherson & an infant born on the passage & I am quite grieved when I think of the fatigue & anxiety this poor woman must undergo before she gets safe– Immediately on hearing of the loss a vessel with money & all other necessaries was sent to seek after the sufferers & the only fear is that the Chinese in their mistaken humanity may have started to bring them by land before the vessel gets there– I am somewhat fearful that another source of trouble may arise, these People being English & knowing that the Chinese & their country men are almost at war, may call themselves Americans & when the cheat is found out (as it must be eventually) it might cause delay in procuring their safety, but then an overland journey of forty days without proper conveniences is no joke– If they are brought here I shall try to be useful to them– Heard a good sermon from Dr Parker to day– the next ship will probably be the *Levant* in three weeks before which time I hope to have done with Coolidge– I feel daily more assured of my right course & reflection only brings the conclusion before arrived at, that *I* have not done Mr C any injustice– I have just received a present of seven Boxes of fine Tea from Houqua which I will send home per first ship– I *think I* shall send a box to the Colonel & one to Mr Greenwood & some to Hillard & some to you (more than you want) to distribute– However don't lead any body astray until the ship is ready for I may get stingy & order it all turned into *cash*

Good night dearest....it wont do to dwell on home too much, for it spoils ones digestion–

RBF DEALS WITH COOLIDGE'S ARRIVAL

Canton December 3 1839
Mrs Rose G Forbes
Dear Rose–
The *Osage* does not yet make her exit & I have an opportunity of writing another short letter– This morning the intelligence of Coolidges safe arrival came– he landed at Macao on the 28th Octo & I have received from him a letter after he got my countless epistles & I send you enclosed a copy of it– nothing can be

more pliant & supple & I dare say the unwelcome truths which I have told him have had the effect to convince him that your husband is not the insignificant man that he thought him to be before his arrival & when he (JC) Narcissus like was contemplating his own image in the water– I do not learn which if any of the children are with the C's– The enclosed letter will not tend to mollify one as to the value of Mr Coolidge though it may lead to a compromise– if as I feared he had assumed a grandiloquent tone I should have been as stiff as Lucifer but as he seems to be quite manageable I shall meet him civilly– When you write you must give me your candid opinion & tell me when I have been too hard or too soft– I do not think I have done Mr Coolidge any *injustice* & I shall not certainly be doing myself & Delano *justice* if I make a bargain with Mr Coolidge & give him a share worth staying here for– I hope to send him back again with a nominal interest for a short period– None of the letters of the *Preble* or the *Asia* (which last put her letters on board of the former at Java) are yet here– I am looking impatiently for these as they must be very full & my last from you is to June 6 nearly 6 months– We got letters to day to 15 July from *London*– if you had written to me care of Barings on the 1 of July I should have had your letters– write once in a while by that route– the *Argyle* is also in from the West Coast of America & I hope when her letters are delivered to get something from Tom Smith– Mrs Coolidge has gone to live for the present with Mrs King– We have nothing politically now here & the monitoring of Canton is quite *ridiculous* as the fellow observed when he found his house & family burned to ashes!

Canton 12 Dec 1839

My dear Rose–

Just think of my having neglected you since the 3rd Instant, neglected did I say– no I deny the imputation– I have thought of you more than usual, but I have been much taken up with Coolidge & with my other business– Coolidge landed on the 6 after dinner, hearing he was close at hand I went to meet him & we met as Gentlemen should meet– one hour or two before he came I received a second letter from him dated below say Dec 3– much to the same purport as the first– it did not appear to me to call for the suppression of my letter of the 4th so I sent it to him to his room– In the evening we had a short interview in which I reiterated what I had said about explaining in writing– next day we had a three hour sitting which I have fully detailed to John & which he will read to you, the substance of it was– first I told him to say nothing about Green that I must not repeat to him if I pleased– He then gave me a history of his life from the time of his coming from Europe to the US, resented Greens conduct & spoke of him in no measured terms & he expressed his distaste to John very plainly– He was very smooth & Gentlemanly & kept his temper as I did mine, after he had got through I took up all my letters to him & others relating to him & read them to him & particularly those relating to his waiting for us to propose to him– I told him plainly & honestly that his reputation as a business man was not good though I had the greatest reliance in his integrity & honor but that I should be unwilling to connect myself with him without Delano on any terms that I did not wish to say any harsh things but that I must speak plainly, he took all I said very well & we shook hands with the understanding that if he had any thing to say of the future it must be in writing & that all which had been said was merely to clear up any personal ill feeling, there were some little things that were explained mutually to our satisfaction, but on the whole our interview very directly covered a good deal of ground but did not bring on the point– We had several conversations afterwards, the last yesterday– the purport of which are embodied in my letter of this date which John will show you (Dec 12th) I also refer you John's letter to me of to day which John has a copy of– there is certainly a Gentleman–

The day before yesterday I invited him to call at all the Hongs with me which he did & I also invited nearly all Canton to meet him here yesterday to dine– we sat down 26 people at 4 oclock I was the oldest man *except three or four* Mr Coolidge as my guest sat on my right & Dr Parker on my left– the first night I also treated Mr Coolidge as our guest, but the next morning in consideration of his being my elder & an older partner of the house I gave him to understand when he was about sitting down at the side of the Table, that the head belonged to him– well to the dinner– We had an excellent one & after the cloth was removed I gave "The health & prosperity of Mr C our guest Pro Tem"– He thanked us & sat down– next Parker made a speech too long for the occasion & gave Mr & Mrs Coolidge– Mr C returned thanks neatly & gave "Mrs R B Forbes & Son" this was loudly cheered, as were the others, just as we were finishing cheering somebody cried out "once more for the Boy"– then they cheered again– I told the Company that I had no idea of sitting down while they Rose to cheer my wife & child but that I would join in the libation & thank them afterwards– I returned thanks & told them if you were here you would thank them with the corner of your handkerchief– Then we toasted Wetmore, Green, Gordon, John, Olyphant, Dr Parker, Mr Archer, Mr Cushing & Sam Russell & Houqua– I returned thanks for John P Cushing, & Houqua– For the first I said "If John were here he would twist up his mouth & say nothing & I could do no more"– For Mr Cushing I said I had the honour of being his nearest of Kin in China– at least to speak of & so I thanked them"– For Houqua I said," I may claim to be his oldest friend here, I thank you for your kindness in his name & hope I may enjoy his friendship for an hundred years to come"– When Green's health was drunk I told Low as he held his power of Attorney he must return thanks, the toasts were fairly showered down with hardly a breathing space, we broke up early say 9 oclock & I was snug in bed by 11 & having stuck to toast water mostly I am pretty well to day– the dinner went off remarkably well, I assure you & all hands agreed that they had seldom had passed a more pleasant evening– I sat down tired & half sick but my spirits Rose & I left off quite well & happy & *said* as usual a great many good things, & *eat* some too all of the first are forgotten, the latter still stick by me!

I must confess I was a little nervous & somewhat thrown off my balance when Coolidge arrived, but this was partly owing to my being a little fatigued with work & to my getting so many letters from you and others– I received letters from Mr Appleton, R G Shaw, Mr Ward & Mr W Sturgis,[165] the three first are anxious to see the breach healed, Appleton only has any business here & he is too much aware of my influence here to divert all his business from us to Heard & Coolidge– one great reason for fighting shy of Coolidge is that Green will certainly oppose us if we take him in & his friendship is worth having & again the prospect of a more serious rupture would be much more likely if he were in the house than out of it & if we quarrelled after signing articles the scandal would be much greater & the injury would be in the long run greater– It is very

[165] William Sturgis (1782-1863) began his career as a sailor at age 15 and was captain of the ship *Caroline* at 19. He engaged in fur trading with the Indians of the Pacific Northwest, in the course of which he learned their language. As a Boston merchant he was in partnership with John Bryant for 53 years in the firm of Bryant Sturgis & Co. He also served as a member of the U.S. House of Representatives in 1814.

disagreeable to me to have this discussion on hand in addition to my other cares but I must go through with it calmly & coolly– I wish at the same time that I had you here to consult with for you are clear decided on points bearing merely in general rights– Coolidge says if he had known how well the House has been doing he would not have come out– I think the prospect of an accommodation very remote– Low goes home in February with an hundred thousand dollars he is a mere child yet in years, though he has excellent business capacity & an excellent moral character– I think I shall send Flora home with him as she gets too fat & lazy here– I received an immense quantity of letters per *E Preble* & John in particular has worked like a Beaver in my cause– I do not think the effect of Coolidge & Heard forming a house here can be at all serving & it will be of little consequence to me, for they cannot under any circumstances get well under sail for a year or two & then I shall have made my competency– I must do the justice to say that he behaves like a Gentleman in all particulars & I shall regret that he should be entirely disappointed– He desires me whatever may be the results of our negotiations, to go & see Mrs Coolidge & keep up my acquaintances to which I reply that as I should be the loser in any other case I should be a fool to forego the advantages of an acquaintance so agreeable to me– Mr Coolidge urges me to send for you– I tell him this is quite impossible– I cannot conceive why Mrs Coolidge did not bring some of her children– I consider the chances of C's remaining here six months, as very doubtful indeed– He talks of a connection with Mr Maclane, an Englishman, besides Heard– I dont think this would be for his good–

I have said enough about Mr Coolidge for tonight & as it is nearly eleven & I am really tired I shall only enumerate the letters I have received & make a few general notes leading to a future day the pleasure of going over all– 54-61 beginning 10 – July 6– They are full & satisfactory in all particulars & the illness of Ben Bo from eating green peas half boiled was a just punishment & I am always prepared to hear of his being sick–

Delano has just come in & I must say good night & God Bless thee–

Sunday 15 Dec–

Since the 12 I have had several letters from Mr Coolidge & have replied to them, he has made his proposition & it has been rejected, among other modest things he wished to quit us provided at the end of our proposed Copartnership we would give him 50,000 fifty thousand dollars– I had a good mind to say yes & then make a house for *10 years*– We have issued our orders for our new circular & we are maturing our articles of copartnership & I consider all negotiations are at an end & I am fully persuaded that this is for the best– I shall request John to show you all the letters that have passed between us & also those written to Mr Ward, Appleton, Cushing, & Shaw, all of which I think are good & he will also show you the letters of those gentlemen to me, copies of which I have sent to John also– I cannot yet take up your letters....My time is so fully occupied that I have little leisure on my hands– I have not yet told you that the survivors of the crew of the *Sunda* fifteen in number arrived here ten days since, that ill fated vessel was wrecked about the middle of October on the Island of Hainan,[166] all the passengers perished including Mrs Macpherson & a poor little infant born on the way at Anjer– the Captain, Doctor & officers escaped & were brought up here after a journey of 26 days by the chinese Mandarins & they were treated

166 Hainan (lat.19 N, long.110 E) is a large island belonging to China that separates the Gulf of Tonkin from the China Sea. It is separated from the mainland by Hainan Strait.

with the greatest kindness by these people, not long before them there arrived the crew of a "Spanish Brig" lost about the same time– I visited them at the Consoo House where they were lodged by the Government– supplied them with necessaries: clothes, food &c my old wadded coat alas! has gone, my hunting coat, my fur cap, in short I am destitute & have been compelled to get me a new wadded bed quilt, a new dressing gown & a new cap– The Captain of the *Sunda* is a tall good looking man & able one would think to bear any thing but when he related to me the horrible scene, his heart failed him, he had been compelled to leave the cabin into which the sea had broken & while on deck holding the babe in his arms, a sea came & took it from the one hand while he tried to save the Mother, she was cast half dead among the broken spars, her husband tried to aid her, a second wave came & took them both away– but I will not tell the tale lest it make a coward of thee–

The ship had on a cargo worth over a million of dollars– I have talked with Houqua about my arrangement with Coolidge & he approves of all I have done, he says if Mr Coolidge had established himself in Co with Heard under their own names he would have helped them if they required it–

I do not think the establishment of Mr Coolidge & Heard here will do us much harm in a functionary point of view for a year nearly & then I shall have got what I can for a competency– this is barring accidents– remember I do not calculate surely on any thing till I get it home safe– I must now say good night & God Bless the Boy

Dec 18 On the way to Tonkoo[167] in the ship Hilda–

The day before I left Canton Mr Coolidge announced his intention of abandoning the name of Russell & Co & of coming out under that of Heard Coolidge & Co or some other– he asked me again if there was no possibility of him making terms with us– I told him that so far as I was concerned I should be willing to give him a small share to go to England for two years, but that I feared that the minds of our partners were made up & that I should be sorry to subject him to the mortification of a dismissal & therefore thought it best as we had paid our circular to the press, not to agitate the matter again!– I think there is still 5 chances in 10 that he dont stay at all, he will have to receive 120 thousand dollars from the House & has had already 80 thousand out of it & if he were to invest this & send it home he would do well and be rich & he is a fool to stay– However let him go in his own gait– we are on palpably good terms & he talks of going with my house for the present– I must now to my business letters– I send this to Java as there is no ship going hence for the US soon– adieu– ever thine RBF

Tonkoo Bay 21 Dec 1839

I have been here two days & having had the arrival of *Asia, Lotos, T Perkins, Sunda, Sumarang* besides the dispatch of the *Alexander Baring* & the *Hilda*– you may easily imagine that I have little or no time to write to so small a personage as yourself– In short my long letters to John & to you per *Baring* to St Helena[168] leave me nothing to say & I merely write to tell you so & that I am going to Macao in the *Asia* this evening & shall stay with Mr Sturgis, & go up in an inside passage boat–

---

[167] Tonkoo is a tiny island located about five miles south of Lintin in the Pearl River estuary between Macao and Hong Kong.

[168] St. Helena is an island of 47 square miles, a British possession in the South Atlantic Ocean. It is 1200 miles west of the nearest African coast. Before the Suez Canal it was of great importance to ships because of its excellent harbors and as a place of supply for provisions and water. Napoleon lived in exile here and died at the island in 1821.

I shall be glad to meet Mrs Coolidge & shall also have the pleasure of seeing Mrs Ritchie & her children, for the youngest I have a cup which I intended to have sent home per *Trenton* for Mrs Bacon, shall replace it per *Levant*–

This letter is a mere chance shot & I do not write to John so if he has nothing you will please tell him that a new edict lately published entirely cuts off all communication with British vessels– This is a serious thing for the Americans, but is just what might have been expected months ago–

God Bless thee & good bye Fr RBF

A SHORT VISIT TO MACAO

Macao Christmas day

My dear Rosy–

My last was from Tonkoo Bay 21 Inst per *Baring* to St Helena, it is quite uncertain when & how this may go but as I am going up to Canton in the morning with Coolidge I must leave a small letter for you to be cast upon the waters & take its chance of being wafted to you– I came over here in the *Asia* on the 22d– have twice seen Mrs Coolidge & have received a letter from her in reply to mine in which I asked her to give me a true a/c of you & the Boy, my first interview with her was in presence of Mrs King & my last was this morning, nothing has passed in relation to Mr C & his affairs since I have been here, I have told you per *Baring* & per *Hilda,* the latter to Java that we have agreed to maintain the ground taken 14 months ago & paddle our canoe apart from Mr C– who I believe is still determined to stay in China & most likely make a fool of himself, still I think there is an even chance of his not remaining– he will have at least one hundred & twenty thousand dollars to receive from the house– besides what he has already received which is nearly ninety more & he is a fool to stay here under these circumstances– I want much to tell Mrs Coolidge this but I am afraid I cannot say so in flattering terms– I dare say she like yourself is weak enough to think well of her husband– I have had the most delicious weather ever since I left Canton & the air of Macao with the murmuring of the waves in the back make me feel how completely happy I should be with you here– However the more I think of the uncertain position of the China trade the more glad I am that you have stayed at home & I have given you no encouragement to come here– I have been to see Mrs Ritchie who is a plain good humored personage who says yes Sir & no Sir– has probably been educated a little distance inland, she has a young sister– with her a tall & rather pretty girl with parting lips & black eyes, & two sweet little daughters one 6 & the other 4 years of age & an infant 7 mo old, just such a fellow as Bob was when I left home, fat & hearty only he has light blue eyes & light hair– I think it rather made me feel strange to see the children & I have not called again– Mrs Ritchie invited me to dine tomorrow at 6 PM & I declined on the plea of going up, then she changed the day & asked me to come to day, I then had to come out plump & plain with the truth that I did not want to dine out especially at a female dinner party with Mr & Mrs King & the Coolidges, in short I have been so hard worked lately that I am quite satisfied to lay idle half the day at Mr Sturgis & read a book & let society & business go to the dogs, it is a great bore to be asked to *dine* with a Lady when husband is away & I must be considered a great *Bear* for declining an invitation to a meeting evidently got up for myself, however I cannot help it & if I had gone I should no doubt have enjoyed it– I have sent the baby a Chinese Cap & so made peace with him at least & I shall call &

sweeten up the Mother tomorrow– I take my ride every afternoon & mostly alone for Mr Sturgis dont ride– I think I am happier in Canton at work than here, for when I get here & am at leisure for a moment I feel that I am alone while on the other hand at Canton I have no time to think of that– I will send you Mrs Cs letter per *Levant*– she looks thin & old & parched up & is a distinct fool to separate herself from her children for ambition's sake–

Mrs Coolidge desired me the first time I wrote to you to give her best regards to you, which I accordingly do– I am anxiously looking for late accounts from England as well as the U S, we ought by rights to have letters to the 2d of September very soon– I received a letter from Tonkoo this morning stating that an American vessel was there in sight, I dare say this is the *Ann McKim*[169] from the West Coast of America–

About that flannel gown, I beg you will send me per first opportunity a garment made by a tailor of stout *shrunk* flannel, much like my calico dressing gown, or like a short frock coat with side flap pockets, a sort of shooting coat, loose & easy– to be the length of a frock coat– I can afford this easily as Mr Sturgis had just given me a splendid pelt cloth pea jacket, (wilten carpets)– besides which I have given to the poor & consequently lent to the Lord, my old molded dressing gown & my pea coat or Brown shooting jacket– There comes dinner I must be off– clear the table cries Uncle Jimmy– Good day & a merry Christmas which I dare say you are teaching Bob to say at this moment

Love to Bob & your Ma & believe me thine ever RBF

COOLIDGE BEGINS HEARD & CO.

Canton 3d January 1840

My dearest, bestest, & littlest wife–

My last was dated in Macao on Christmas day, on the 26th I left there in company with Mr Coolidge for Canton by inside passage boat & we got up safe & sound on the 28 after a pleasant trip– I dined with Mrs Coolidge & Uncle James at her house, the day I left & saw enough of C in his preparations to start & in his management of every day matter on the way to satisfy me that he is very inexperienced in the ways of this world, he is as mean as dirt in small matters & I dare say in large too, we said not a word of business & as he was waiting at the last moment for his circular I think he expected me to the last to make some proposition to him– I came up to my room to night early 1/2 past *eleven*! so as to write to you, I have not been in bed before one of late & having got some cold & cough it keeps me awake till 2 or 3 generally, however I am well otherwise & shall get over it in a day or two– on the morning of the first of January Mr Coolidge was missing & it then occurred to me that he would not stay with us any more, so I wrote him a kind note to say that I did not expect him to cut quite so early & asked him *particularly* to dine with us that day & *generally* to make our house his home until he got established in his own house, he declined on the ground of being too much engaged in preparing his house– I had a few friends to dine & a quiet game of whist in the evening– Drank only the usual toast of,

169 *Ann McKim* was a 493-ton clipper and was the first full–rigged ship to be built along the lines of the fast little Baltimore schooners from which the name "clipper" was derived. She was a remarkably handsome vessel, with her bottom sheathed in specially imported red copper, and her deck and interior furnishings of mahogany. She mounted twelve brass guns and carried three skysail yards and royal studding sails. Although she proved to be unusually fast, her carrying capacity was small, and therefore no other ships were constructed like her.

"absent friends"– Coolidge has issued his "chop" under the style of Augustine Heard & Co & we have duly congratulated him on his happy prospects– on the 2d I thought I would call on him, I found him in a small sixteen foot room with a poor fire, a straw hat on to keep him warm– trunks & boxes & china were scattered round & every thing in disorder, no carpet, & he pointed out to me the place where he had slept on the floor & caught cold– the painters & cleaners were in the house & every thing appeared cold & comfortless, now mind you he had been sleeping at No 4 our Hong & had a good room & a warm compting room all to himself & this move of his was all for effect, intended to go home, he no doubt expects some day to be the greatest man in Canton & then to look back in his imposing way & say "the first night of my commercial career in Canton under my present firm, was spent on the floor, without a bedstead or a friend to cheer me, my wife absent, my children away, & myself turned out of the house I had long occupied & by my clerks!!!!"– I told him plainly that his conduct in thus leaving us & putting himself out would be a reflection on us, did not any one knowing the circumstances of the case be inclined rather to think him crazy– I told him it was perfectly absurd, we then had a talk on business settlements & finally got back to his objections to me & I explained to him in good English the contradictions in his saying he should have pursued a different course had he known my influence & in the same letter stating that, he was so well aware that I could command a place in my house that he thought he was doing me no injury by dissenting & he undertook to explain this & got deeper than ever into the mire for he said he supposed that I should not succeed if I stand here alone or in Company with Wetmore & here came out the clever fool– I can't express to you how glad I am that we made no terms with him– I regret exceedingly that Heard is coming out for I think instead of adding to the little he has he will lose it – Coolidge let out accidentally, that Mr Heard would not come out until he should hear from him– for he said, "when you write to Heard pray tell him that your wife did not purposely deny herself to him"–

A great many *funny* things have happened this last year, the last scene in the chapter of events is the seizure of Capt Gribble by Mandarins, he was going back from the ship *Royal Saxon* to Tonkoo & was in a chinese fast boat which is illegal, they being ordered not to aid & abet the English, he was pursued by a Mandarin boat & captured & brought to Canton, this Gent arrived only ten days since in the *Thames*– he has a wife, sister, & children on board that ship, he was missed & the alarm being given– there were two or three expeditions fitted out in pursuit without success– The frigate also went to the Bogue to inquire why he was captured & detained, I received a petition from Mr Hughes, Gribbles partner, to the Vice Roy and Commissioner & I received a favourable reply– Yesterday morning Gribble came to Canton & after an examination before the Vice Roy he was allowed to come out of the City to the Consoo House, where he now is, he was six days after capture in coming to Canton, & was carried in a sedan all the way, he had on some of his Company uniform & was he thinks taken for Elliot or Smith going to stop the "*Royal Saxon*" from coming into port– I have sent him all my bedding & my new wrapper, & my best pants & am almost ruined thereby to say nothing of a fine large blanket bought only three days ago! Oh dear! I have sent several dispatches to his wife at Tonkoo & I do not consider him in the slightest danger, he is a stout man & cares little about it, Dr Parker got access to him to day on the plea of his being sick & says he is quite well– There is that everlasting midnight bell striking & reminding me that I must look up to Bob's picture & give him a kiss for good night– Our gross commissions for 1839 are 230 thousand dollars– say *two* hundred thousand nett & my share is over 43 thousand, which with what Mr Cushing gave me & my share of the *Canton Packet* & other small good things must make my *earning* (provided we make no losses) since I left you about *sixty five* thousand– pretty well say you– were I not bound in honour to Houqua I would cut & run now & my share this year is half as much again & more & at the end of it– I am OPH...Good night or good morning rather–

CANTON 12 JANY 1840

My dear Rose–

The *Levant*s Captain started an hour ago & I now undertake a short letter merely to say that I have been very remiss in writing of late, but this you must attribute to the right cause, a real want of time, I have been fully engaged from 9 AM to 1 AM– at my desk or in running back & forth to & from Houquas & the place of Gribbles confinement– besides which I have had a cold & cough which is now wearing off & it has kept me out of sorts & I did not feel like writing to you– To say one has no time to write to my wife is to deny ones sanity, I must keep my Book in the compting room and write a little daily– I have just finished a letter to mother & one to Green, but I have not written a line hardly to John– Coolidge sent me a present of a box of cigars yesterday– I have not been near him for a week but shall call to day– He is a fool to stay here– We have no accounts from home for six months, though our letters from England are to 12 Aug & there are letters at Macao to 15 Sept– but none are received here– from all I hear from England I am expecting bad commercial news from America– Hoping before next Sunday to hear from you– I send a kiss to Bob & Love to your mother & Sally & remain Thine ever RBF

RBF DEALS WITH A RAT

CANTON JANUARY 14, 1840

My dear Rose

On the 12 I closed my short & shabby letters per *Levant* & I have nothing to say in my defense save that I was daily too much fagged with work to write any thing after my work was over– I have not been in my bed till 12 or 1 oclock since I came up from Macao & I wonder that I am not sick– I did get a bad cold ten days ago & had a cough, but thanks to Parker I am now well again & not a bit the worse for dining Gribble & a few friends to day, he was yesterday liberated on parole & to day he came out unconditionally free & is staying with us– He is ordered to leave however in a few days, he is a fine manly fellow & having been a ship master found in me a congenial spirit (why that's praising myself aint it)– I dine with him at Coolidges tomorrow, though I have not been in C's house for a week– I had a funny time last night– after writing to my constituents till 1 AM I went up to my chamber & after a customary survey of Bob & a prayer for you & him I soon lost myself in the arms of Murphy– but had not long been dreaming of Hyson, Young Hyson, Souchong &c when my pet Rat made a rattling among my soap boxes & woke me, Oh you rascal says I, aint you contented to eat up all my meal & my soap but you must make a noise about it & wake me up?– He made no reply but kept on & I soon dropped asleep again, & had just got into the middle of my nap when I was again awakened by the rascal running up & down my bed curtains & shaking the rings, Oh-Ho says I are ye there– he made no reply but whisked his tail about & again capered up

& down the curtains, till at last I got angry & threw my hand at him & nocked him off on to the floor & went asleep expecting no further annoyance– but in an hour after I was again awakened & lo my Gentleman not content with caricoling up and down *outside* the curtain had got inside & was enjoying himself– you see the misery of not having a Mother to tuck me up, having a wife would have been of no use because she would naturally, like the rat, have preferred the inside of the bed & could not have tucked us up– but to my Rat– I found where he came in & shut up the place & now says I– Mister Rat your time has come, make your peace, bid adieu to soap & meal & prepare for that end to which Rats as well as men must all arrive, tis true you & I have long occupied the same chamber & I have set up in my bed many times watching your innocent gambols, but to come naturally within my bed & awake me thrice in one short night deserves death! He whisked his tale & mournfully squeaked & with a desperate jump round and round me, seated in the middle of the bed he tried to escape, having none but my natural weapons I struck at him & nocked him this way & that in the soft bed to no purpose, at last after a fight of a minute I gave him a smart slap & stunned him & then opening the curtain & seizing my slipper I gave him his quietus & for fear he should come to life put him into a certain small vessel which for some purpose unknown usually stands under my bed– I then turned over & went to sleep & had no further trouble– this is literally true *tail and all* he was half a yard long– poor creature he never harmed me & would probably have snuggled quietly at my feet if I had not been so cruel– We are still without dates later than July 10th, but we hear of dates at Macao, from England to the 15 September & shall thereby get something from you (that is from the US) – I despair of your ever writing me overland–

I hear Russell Sturgis has a touch of the "Varioloid"[170] not at all severe however–

15 January–

nothing very new to day, but hearing that Elliot intended to day to establish a strict blockade of the Port today, I hurried Gribble off & hope he has overtaken the "*Margaret*" which was to have sailed this morning, if he makes his appearance I trust Elliot will not put the blockade into effect– dined with Coolidge to day– Dr Parker & Mr Moses– there, Gribble was to have been–

Tis now half past 11 & I am determined to go to bed early– so Good Night– no rats last night– Love to Bob–

17 January–

no news from home yet, letters received from England to the 16 Sept– same symptoms of hard times at home– it is now 1/4 before the witching hour & I have merely to record the date & say good night & alls well, I have entirely got over my cold & cough & am very hearty– I shall probably close & send this shabby sheet to Helena per "*Thomas Coutts*"– This morning we heard of the *Chesapeake, Lintin, Ann McKim,& Valparaiso* having got into Port again, they have only been gone a short time– so we keep the mill a going– Delano is getting into harness & I shall soon be more at leisure– Love to Bob & Good Night

---

170 Varioloid is a mild form of smallpox in persons who have previously been vaccinated or who have previously had the disease.

SUNDAY
CANTON JANUARY 19, 1840
My dear Rose–
Another Sunday has come round, & tomorrow will be the anniversary of our marriage, a day which I dare say you would readily forget except that it has finally brought happiness with it & we are all in all to each other now & we were then– only the feelings were harrowed up by the ill feelings of those who should have contributed to our happiness– I do not look back to those days, & strange to say I look back to my last year of trouble at home with more pleasure than to any other, because it called out your true character & showed us how much we depended on each other– then the two trials of losing children– which appeared so hard to bear, served to cement our affections– Ah was me– when will that happy day come when I shall clasp thee to my heart once more, & see that dear Boy–

I have hardly time mid the excitement of business to think of you, but when I go to my lonely pillow– tis then I feel that I am making a sacrifice indeed– however, it is one that so far, has led only to good fortune & I think it will follow me– I never allow myself to be unhappy, but I count the days & months– It is now more than nineteen months since I left you & I must leave here in a year to redeem my pledge– Many people would think me a fool to go so soon with my prospects, but I must– We are likely to have the Port closed & a cessation of trade by April or May, then I shall make a trip to Manila & Macao & wait the result of the quarrel– you must not make yourself uneasy about me– I can take care of myself you well know & having lived most of my life amid busy scenes I am by no means nervous about the future– whichever way the cards fall– we have the trumps in our hands & must keep the lead–

GRIBBLE CAPTURED BY CHINESE

An English Gent by the name of Gribble was seized near Tonkoo by the Chinese a few weeks since & not being directly liberated, the English man of war went up to the Bogue (the entrance of the river) & demanded him, but the Chinese were obstinate & refused– unless the frigates should first go away they accordingly put on a blockade of the Port, he was released & we suppose the blockade is now off– the day it took effect four ships came into Port to us & we have now fourteen vessels on our list & are expecting others– I have not had time lately to read a line of anything– I have entirely got over my cold & am as hearty as I have ever been in China or the US for ten years–

I am not very superstitious I mean, but yesterday in wiping my hands roughly I broke my ring & was obliged to part with it for a day to get it mended– I suppose it dont mean any thing–

The *Ann McKim* arrived lately 54 days from the West Coast of America, the Capt has not yet delivered his general letters, but he tells me that Tom has made a grand year of it, I hope this is not mere report & as Flour was very high on the coast I think it must be true– God grant it may be for your mother would then be much easier in her mind & I should expect to find her younger than when I left–

Love to Bob & all the family & Good Night

The new year holidays are approaching & we are driving on as fast as possible to get the *Tenobia* & *Eben Preble* away– We have shipped off to day ten thousand chests of tea to different ships & more than twenty thousand packages, we have 14 ships on our list & seven of them are loading so I have no time to write to wives & sweethearts–

Mr Low, a very useful member of our hong embarks in the *Tenobia* & will call on you, he will bring home more than One hundred thousand dollars & a good name– he is a very smart, shrewd little fellow & will make his way– he has not been used much to society being only 25 or 26 years old & has been here six years– Delano works capitally & I am comparatively at ease–

Love to all you family & Good Night

Saturday-Night– 25 Jany–

No letters from home yet & nothing very interesting, except that Capt Tom (one of our consignments) is very ill & I must go to Whampoa tomorrow & see him,

One of Tingqua's paintings of tea, its cultivation, curing, trade, and shipping, is shown here, with peasants planting tea seedlings.

he has a wife with him only 23 or 24 years of age, he is over 50– his wife came to Whampoa when the ship ran away from Elliot & came in without his permission– I have had another long letter from Coolidge to day in which he attempts to make some excuses for his letters to R&Co from London, or rather he calls his letters an "explanation" but he persists in saying that his letters are not unfriendly & that his quotations of my letters to Barings & Forbes are not unfair– I wrote him at some length & told him that I had expected in justice to himself a candid explanation but if he is satisfied with what he considers an explanation I have nothing further to say– I will send you or John copies of the letters bye and bye– Good Night

29 Jany– 1840

If I wait two minutes longer I shall have to go into the 30th for it is within that of midnight– We have just closed our *Tenobia* dispatches & am pretty well fagged out, more especially as we had a dinner party for Low, day before yesterday & a supper party at Mr Nyes last night– Whiskey, punch &c &c– At our dinner– your health & *the Boys* were proposed & I was cheered to suffocation– I went up stairs– brought Bob down to answer for himself, he attracted great attention & was much admired– every body said he looked like me– killed another rat in my room last night which makes four within a month– indeed I do not consider my days work up till Flora & I have killed one– I did not ask Coolidge to dine with us– I have given Kingman a letter to you, he is a neighbor of John Lees & knows him well– there goes 12 oclock so I will seal up this miserable letter and write you more per *Lehigh– Eben Preble*, both will be home before this I think– Your crapes will probably go on the *Preble–* in the next ship I will return Bobs adventure– Love to Bob & your mother & African Sall & good morning Ever thine RBF

Canton Jany 30, 1840

Mrs RB Forbes–

Dear Madam!

I have sent to care of Mr John M Forbes, per *Eben Preble* as follows– RBF

No 2– 1 Box Superior Pouching containing about 25 or 28 lbs–
No 4-5-6– 3 small boxes of superior Black tea a perfect nosegay
No 8– One Box fine Pouching about 20 lbs No 10 "Pekoe"
No 12 "Hyson" 15 lbs–
No 14 "Porching" 25 lbs–
No 15 "Porching"
No 16 "Pekoe" 25 lbs–
No 17 very extra Superior– Souchong–
Oosong Souchong about 25 lbs–
No 18– 1 Package Contg– 2 small Boxes each 13 lbs extra superior Souchong Tea
No 19– Package contg 2 do each 7– 13 of same Tea–[171] very fine–
1 Box contg 6 Pieces of Crape–[172]

I leave the disposition of all this Tea to your discretion & have merely to observe that I have sent Tea *direct* to Mrs James Perkins, Col Perkins, T G Cary– Mr F Cary & Sam Cabot– I would suggest that Pekoe & Porching should be mixed half & half & if you give one you should give the other– *but* the quantity in each box excepting the Nos 4, 5, 6 is too extravagant to give away– these are things which must be managed with discretion & judgement, last year I ordered my present Teas sold, then I felt poor – now I am rich I must be liberal– however notwithstanding nevertheless perhaps it will be prudent to realize hard cash for the whole or part of the Tea–![173] Having the matter left to your discretion entirely I have merely to observe that I should like to have you remember Geo

[171] Lapsang Souchong is a black tea with a smoky, full-bodied taste. Pouchong tea is slightly less fermented than oolong tea, which sits for a longer time before it is fired (put through a drying process called "taching"). Hyson, like all green teas, is not allowed to ferment before it is fired. It has leaves that are twisted or curled. Pekoe is a grade of black tea which is allowed to ferment or oxidize before firing, and is made from the leaves around the buds.

[172] Crepe de chine or (as here)Crape is a light, soft silk with a crinkled surface.

[173] RBF is suggesting that Rose sell some of the tea to her acquaintances. He gives her similar instructions when he sends Chinese fabrics.

Hillard– C W Greene for writing to me– my Mother if she has not a supply, Mr Greenwood– say for him one of the small boxes– No 4, 5 or 6 or one of 10– give one of these or part of No 17 to Copley– tell them it must be mixed with other less high flavoured Tea– alone it is too strong–

Then there are those two worthy individuals Doctors Jackson & Bigelow, if you can be sure your Pekoe & Pouching & No 17 is fine– it would be well to make up a mixture say 1-2 lbs to each a 1/3 Pekoe 1/3 pouchong & 1/3 No 17– or 1/4 of one of the 4, 5 or 6– well mixed up & sent with my regards & then if they dont pronounce it good "call me Tea pot"

By devoting a little time carefully to this matter examining the Tea yourself & attending to it– you may give a great deal of satisfaction to my friends– I have not named Caroline Gardiner perhaps you owe her something–

about the Box of Crapes I have written to you per *Tenobia*, but should this ship *Eben Preble* get home first which is likely you will want some description of the crapes so I cut out my page & send it herein– All the numbers of Tea *above* 13– came from Camera & are not probably so good as No 1 to 12 but they *may* be bitter: for Houquas servants cheat him in these matters– I shall also send you two pieces of Mosquito Curtain & and respectfully suggest that you have a curtain made for the Boys crib if not for the large sleeping apparatus– I send no nick nacks because they are in the way–

Dont be in a hurry to give away your Tea– it will be all the better for keeping in a dry place–

A Special edict "Haste"

Low embarked this morning

CHINESE NEW YEAR

CANTON 31 JANUARY 1840

My dear Rose–

tonight we clear the *E Preble* & *five* other ships so that I have literally not a moment to say my soul's my own– I have an order from J L Gardner for various *curious* things & as you are well aware I like to indulge my fancy at other peoples expense– so I have "let him in" for about $160 worth of rare articles– some are exceedingly old & handsome (like me)– going to Macao in day or two to spend the new year & to meet a direct arrival from home &c&c– It is now 6 1/2 months since I have had a line– we received today letters from England to September– up to this time not a line from you overland– nothing politically new & after tomorrow we shall be comparatively at leisure– Flora sends love, her son is a fine puppy & is just recovering from a broken leg–

I shall have time on my way down the River to write to you particularly per *Lehigh* & with large quantities of love to Bob & all other friends I am ever thine– RBF

Princess Louise off the Bogue

FEB 3, 1840

My dear Rose–

Here I am again on my way to the anchorage off Tonkoo in the Prussian Ship *Princess Louise*, I expect to find the *Lehigh* still at Tonkoo & as I have written you very sparingly of late I owe you a letter– My late letters are per *Tenobia* & *E Preble* both of which have gone to sea– I shall remain at Tonkoo to dispatch *Royal Saxon* some three days & then go to Macao– spend three or four days with

Sturgis & then go up again inside– I need not tell you that I have been really too busy to write to any one of late & I have already told you that, we have dispatched seven ships during the last week– I have not been in bed until one or two oclock in the morning & yet I am quite well– the excitement of mind keeps the body up– However I had a most magnificent sleep last night & we are now just through the "Tigris Mouth"– Coolidge is already at Macao– I fully expect to find some late arrival & shall be very angry if my letters have gone up– the Pilot tells us that a ship is in from England– Yesterday I was much amused at a smiling Chinese who came on board, I know him very well but pretended not to & asked him who he was–

"Hoyo– you no save me– my makee before, old smug– you that time makee smug too– old *Lintin* – now my have honest man all same you!– I thought this was pretty good, the truth is that he was a Capt of a smuggling boat in 1830-32 & had like myself left off his evil courses & gone into other business–

It is now nearly seven months since I had a line from you, or rather since your last letters were dated– I am getting very impatient to hear more of the Boy, Mr Ritchie who is my travelling companion has a boy about 9 months old which he thinks beats all the boys in the world–

I shall cultivate his acquaintance this time & be a little less boorish than I was when at Macao last Mr Hunter & Flora have gone down already by the inside passage leaving King & Delano at the Oars–

The Chinese are buying foreign ships to make men of war of, We have sold them one for $25000 profit (in one month)– They will never be used against the English & if they are they will go to Davy Jone's locker in very short time– The *Lintin* will be perhaps sold, if we can get twice or three times her value–

When you get this letter you will have begun to look forward to my return, let me see you will receive it on the 15th of May & may calculate to see me in a year after, it will soon pass away, just think how short a time since I wrote to you at Hong Kong early in September five months ago–

It seems but a day– In political matters there is little to say– the Commissioner Lin is appointed Governor over Canton & "Tong" the former Governor is going to Lin's former Province to assume its Government– The Emperor is determined that Lin shall finish the work he has begun & the pending difficulties between the English & Chinese will not be settled so easily as was expected– We are quite ignorant as yet what England will do– but I will give you an outline– of what I think they will do & as the time draws nigh I should be able to see how I came out–

PREDICTING THE OUTCOME OF THE CONFLICT

The *Official accounts* of Elliots imprisonment last March will have arrived in England on the 10 October, the previous newspaper accounts will have prepared the public mind for canvasing in the question– A naval force will leave England on the 15th November & arrive here with an agent or Commissioner empowered to act, on the 1 of April, the said agent will be a gentleman of high attainments and one in all probability, *formerly* well acquainted with the Chinese character, but as Mr Lin is a different man from any before brought in contact with the "Honorable Company" he (the agent) will find himself entirely at a loss what to do, his instructions will have permitted to a very different state of things from what exists here at this moment & he will have to await further orders– If he comes here to negotiate with the Chinese upon strait forward & honourable principles, he will be floored– & after long delay the trade will be allowed to go on after the old fashion– the Chinese will have the best of it– If Lin agrees to allow British ships to come into Port, it will only be on condition that the British Government submit to his Laws & prohibit the growth of Opium in their dominions– If contrary to my expectations some hot-headed old Admiral comes here with full powers, he will blow up the Bogue Forts & go to Whampoa & demand to see Lin with full honours– this being refused he will burn Canton & lay waste the Sea Coast & finally go to Pekin & make his own terms–

after all Elliots mad freaks I think if he had power he would, under present circumstances, make the best terms– He is full of spirit & is better acquainted with this question than any one else & none but a mad-cap will do the necessary punishment– I hear that the Chinese are again ordering the English away from Macao, stopping provision &c

Here comes the steward to set the Table
so good bye RBF

Ship *Delhi* off the Bogue
bound to Whampoa 10 February 1840
My dear Rose
I wrote you a short letter from Tonkoo, a day or two since, & sent original to Manila & Duplicate to Sincapore– I had the good fortune on my arrival at Tonkoo in the *Princess Louise* to find this ship & the *London* arrived from the US– by these two ships I got your 67-76 from August 13 to Sept 25– No 68 & 74 are still on the way, one probably per *Surat* & the other by some other ship– I will now take up these interesting letters & make note of such parts as are particularly *worthy* of reply– Yours of *Aug 13– No 67–*

Acknowledges my *Omega* letters– I dont wonder at you feeling anxious about me for the newspaper accounts of the events of last March were blue enough– thanks to Bacon for writing to you– Tom Perkins house burned, Bennet got another tooth! You had told me before of at least 30–

No 69 Aug 17- 18 Heard from Cary of the sale of Tea & intended to appropriate the proceeds to sending me a flannel gown– couldnt make a better use of the money "Charity ought oftener to begin at home"– I am quite amused at the idea of your giving so much of your mind to economy, it is laudable & necessary– the contrast however between your views & mine in this day of success is great– I am sending you some valuable crapes to the tune of over $100 & you are talking about saving up the proceeds of two pence worth of Tea for a rainy day– However I beg you will persevere for I am sure I shall never make an economist without your aid– Never heard of the Vicar of Wakefields quince before– however when I get home I shall give up trade & go to school with my Son & get an education, read good books, & forsake salt water– George Dexters twins– Mrs Cushing going to be in the straw in the Autumn– Lizzy Greene, Tom Dwight– Susan Jackson– Charles Jackson, Miss Dwight, Mary Magee, Margarettas Diary, haven't seen it– his Phantom ship is a poor thing just reading it– Martha Amory sends a message to *Albion*– might as well look for a needle in a hay stack, haven't seen the ugly brute for a year– very *Green* to trust him with money– Tell Copley I tried to get Low to take home a good boy for him, but couldn't find one– it is a great responsibility & I dont think I shall be able to do any thing about one– "Bennet a perfect chatter box" What else could you expect of Rose Smiths son– Hope you will teach him to say Father & Mother & not Paa & Maa I detest those expressions & Papa & Mama are still worse to my ears– Your account of his running after the little Davis & throwing a kiss to Dr Jack*son* very amusing– Heards pictures in Mrs Boydens parlour if B should die– Heard might slip in for the widow– hey!...August 18 "glorious day" walked to Church &c sat with Jackson, walked home with the Lees, found Tom Dwight & Copley– mother & Cushing been to call with all the children– I should like to have seen this meeting & the group of Children with the old folks– I have not a line from mother & Emma has never written me a line since my candid letter to her– very funny that Bob will not play with little boys– he takes after his Father in that respect– I always to the present day associated more with my elders than my juniors– Sally is really "a sneak" not to write to me & you can tell her that I shall punish her by not kissing her when I return– however I shall be so old that she will consider that a mercy– I have written to Russell Sturgis & thanked him in your name for writing to you– Why don't you sometimes name his sisters & Grandma– devil take Dalton–

No 71 Aug 26 Your anxiety about me was just what I expected of *you*, but not what I should expect from any other sensible woman– the idea of our "suffering for want of food" is truly amusing– we suffered a great deal more from eating too much & if you had said a great deal more about the want of our usual boat sailing I should have considered you quite in the right– Aunt Nancy, Newport, cold water even referred to guests– Ackermans Goethe revived by Motley– Boy been to pass a day with Copley & Lizzy, Fanny Brooks & husband, who are they? dry ditch not a running stream– wonderful precocity– Sarah & Cleveland been to see you– break down &c– horse bare backed & not Cleveland! Mr Kurner & Miss Cochrane– Hypersion– Fanny Appleton– Rev Jim & Leman both had Sons John's dead– Dont wonder Mr Cushing ridiculed your fears– visit from Mrs Cary & Sally, "William Gardner on the Sear's side" shouldn't have known any thing about what you meant if C had not told me "a heart Searing affair"– Sorry to hear so poor an a/c of the Tom's– Your account of Margaret & Fannys life at Nantasket shows an abomination of intellect if your a/c is true– poor things– Note what you say about Mr Walkers sermon– the "law of *compensation*" is what we are most desirous of seeing carried out here in reference to the delivery of Opium to the Chinese– Never make any excuses about writing on trifles– every thing is interesting & appreciated–

August 30– Northerly storm– hypersion– Longfellow, Fanny Appleton "Look not mournfully into the past it comes not back again, hereby improve the *present*, It is thine, Go forth to meet the shadowy future &c &c" this is exactly what I have been at– Young S , Elliot, Sam Sturgis & Millicent Deblois– Sam ain't flirting with the girl is he?" Little Tom gone to Coolidge, silver plate to Mrs Wells "chop basin & all, Copley & Dwight– Autumnal tints, "outlived French war, English war, Yumachi war" pretty good *Sept 3* Letter from Charles Greene, I had one too to 31 August a day or two since from Batavia by a ship which brought none from you, uncle Sam very ill & well again, Lizzy, Copley, Dwight took Tea– I shall begin to think Dwight is after your Sally– Mr Sullivan dead– made Gardners head–

Sept 9 Charles Greene– *Surat* 7 sent No 7 by her– you are very good about the numbers & the margins– George Trumbull– sorry he has left John–

Went to Boston with Bob– dined on Soda biscuit– don't tell me whether he is weaned yet– dont wonder the fellow prefers "Beef Take" to Irish milk– Joe came to see you & don't look well– tell him not to mind the pain in Chest– I have had it more or less these ten years– Mary Watson– twin dead– Esther Allen – Barnstable Anniversary– verses not so bad– Bob such a rogue–

No 75 Sept 12– Grant Western arrived– How is Mrs Chapman– Return of the Greenes– slept with Lizzy– wouldn't mind it myself!!! Heard, Gray, Mrs Sutton, R C Hooper– *Loafer* is *the* word for Dutton– Tea at Jackens– Beaver Brook farmer–

Sept 13 You feel quite bright do you glad of it– "Opium question settled" why taint settled yet & won't be for a year! poor old Houqua & the Chain, all this was got up by himself the old rogue to create a feeling of sympathy– four miles walk to see the Greene's– I am very much gratified at the attention of your friends, all on my a/c I suppose !!!! Paris dress for Bennet– Russell Sturgis & Sarah Greene– twont do– George going to the west– sorry because he will be a loss to me– as well as to you– have written to him– *No 76 18 Sept* my birthday– I was at Hong Kong that day on board the *Edmonton*– I also hate anniversaries which tell me I am getting very old– I fully appreciate all your feelings on these occasions & I hardly allow myself to think of home– I rivet my mind to business as much as possible– Mr Ritchie is with me & he says that his wife observed that Mr Forbes appeared to be a very nice *old Gentleman*!! Went to see the Greenes & fell envious did you– oh for shame *I envy no man here*! Why because I am at the Top of the ladder in Canton & it is a great deal more reasonable that I should excite envy– I told you that Coolidge expected Appleton's business– well the fine ship the *Delhi*– comes to R&Co direct without a word about Coolidge & I have a copy of a letter to John from Bates which is very satisfactory– our list of about 14 ships keeps full– for since the *Tenobia* & *E Preble* sailed, we have the *London*, *Delhi* & *Robert Bourne*, the latter comes to Delano– (all the same as us)

Sept 24 Just got my long journal of 2 April– "*Loss of golden prospects* " that dont go down after what I have just said– Put a wing on the plain house– not I– I must live snug in Town & lodge in the Country & save some of my income annually for the children– child I meant to say– I thought you would laugh at my a/c of our "imprisonment"

Do pray learn to dismiss all these silly girlish feelings about perennial safety, you have a great deal more to fear from my indigestion than from the Yumchi– I have now a bit of dyspepsia from eating two pounds of hot bread for breakfast & half a pound of butter– The Colonel drove over to see you– He gives me an account of his visit & writes 3 pages of friendly matter stressing that he really entertains a kindly feeling for us both– Heard called again & did not see you– 14 weeks absent– I had the pleasure of forwarding to Mrs Coolidge her private letters per *Delhi*–

Sept 27– John sends for letters– your mother had the Cholera! glad she is quite well again– love to her & black [crossed out black] Sally– Margaretta not in liberation to go by water, but to *travail*– well, such things will happen in the best regulated families– shall be *very* glad to see Dumaresq– you tell me to write you initially about my concerns for that is all which keeps you alive– you have been telling me all along that you are in perfect health– I will now put down my pen till after dinner

BACK IN CANTON

Still exceptionally busy transacting business with ships from several nations, RBF travels to Macao and to Hong Kong, and falls from his horse in a freak accident at Macao. As both the opium conflict and RBF's business successes escalate, he begins to think of returning to Boston. He is now assured of the "competency" he came to Canton to earn. He sails for home early in July.

On page 208, in an engraving made from a drawing by Thomas Allom, is the "Yellow Pagoda Fort" on the Pearl River approaching Canton.

Canton 11 February–

I was too lazy to write you any more yesterday– We arrived at Whampoa early this morning got our breakfasts & arrived in Town at 11 am very glad to get *home* again– I dare say Mr Ritchie did not thank me for calling at Macao for him– but how did I get to Macao– I will tell you– After spending a few days at Tonkoo & attending to the business of several ships I embarked in the *Union* & ran over to Macao Roads, there I found the *Delhi* with her pilot on board & as it was a dirty rainy day I concluded not to land but sent the boat for Ritchie & started during the night for Whampoa– The fact is I hate to go to Macao for a single day or so, one does not get comfortably fixed in ones house under three days & I thought I could not spare time to remain a week– So I have got back to Canton without having had my foot in shore since leaving here– I am quite well & find all strait– I have not yet received my general letters per *London* & *Delhi,* only yours & Johns & one from the Colonel which I will send you bye & bye– I have already told you how *enormously* lucky I am & that I am almost a rich man again– if I had not good confidence in your discretion I should never name these things, so mind you "keep dark," remember rich men pay all sorts of taxes we wont be rich before the world–

I can tell you a secret– will you keep it? Our commissions in January amounted to 25,000 this means twenty five thousand dollars & our profit in the ship *Landrone* sold to the Chinese

for a man of War as much more — 25,000

& probable profit on sale of the *Lintin* — 20,000

Commissions in February– say_ — 10,000

80,000 making *eighty thousand dollars in two months!!!!!*

My share of which will be Thirty-thousand– hey! Ain't that earning the root of all evil– cannot expect that to last long, but shall be very much disappointed if I dont make a clean 60 thousand in 1840 & then I am off for home– home sweet home–

I hope I shall not be spoiled by all this success but grateful to a kind Providence for watching over me & over you– I have read your late letters over and over again & every little incident relating to the Boy fills me with hope and pleasure & the attention of our friends is a source of great happiness to me– I feel that I am not "out of sight out of mind," I think as a matter of business you are much better off where you are for I have no doubt that some of our friends keep up their recollections of me through you– I forgot to say that I had a long letter from Sarah John Forbes– she does not give a particularly brilliant a/c of her twins– but rather an amusing one of Dr John Jennison who it seems had got home and been robbed– you don't mention him so I suppose you had not seen him– I should have had a letter from Joe Lyman– but had not– good night

Sunday 16 Feby 1840

I have already written to you advising receipt of 67-75– to day finding the Supercargo of the *London* impatient to get his letters, I offered to give him his letters per *Delhi* if he would give me all mine & R&Cos per his ship, he agreed & I got your 68 & your 62-67 making all your letters up to 76 inclusive complete except 74 which I shall probably get per *Surat* from Manila or by some other indirect route– I have read over these letters with great interest & shall now (it being a *quiet* Sunday) take up all your said letters & run over them noting any remarkable incidents– beginning with

No 62– July 12– Gives an a/c of your hot weather, thunder storms &c I am delighted to hear such excellent a/cs of your quarters & thank Heaven you were all so well– You tell me of the Greenes & Timmons &c– B D Greene not yet arrived– I am glad of it–John has told me all about Nashaun & Nantasket– hope Johns children will not live to drag out a miserable existence as cripples–

"July 16" Just received my letters to the 7th of March– I have not the letters by me which you say made you feel so melancholy– but one thing I am sure of, namely, that with all my imprudence, want of exercise &c I am better off than I was when I left you *in health*, I read all your good advice on the score of diet &c & shall be prudent when it is necessary, a fig for Dr Jackson & his diet– I will tell you what I had for dinner to day– Chowder, Roast Mutton, Curry, sponge cake, cheese, beer, claret, oranges & cigars and here I am writing away with Bob looking at me, as well as can be– You say you feel so unhappy about me, that you would come out at once without leave & in opposition to every body did you not fear that you might by doing so keep me here too long– I have always *feared* that when you heard of the opium troubles that you might get into Dumaresq's ship with him & come out & I am glad his wife is in a proper state to stay at home– It is too true, if you were here I should want to stay two or three years longer– I am sure that I should not succeed at home & as I am in a fair way of getting my competency by the end of this year I shall not think of leaving– it is no fake pride that keeps me here, I charted for a three years cruise & it would not be doing justice to my friend Houqua nor to others who have confided business to me to leave before next March twelve months, thirteen thousand miles is too far to come for nothing– I must effect my object–

Don't make yourself uneasy about me– every one who comes here will give you good accounts of me & dont make an idol of that Boy– he is only given to you in trust & he may be taken away– I am fully prepared at all times to hear of his being ill, temporarily– Dont spoil him by indulgence or flattery– but make him hardy & manly– All the difficulty which you allude to in 63 about who shall have the title of Russell & Co is over & Coolidge has not had a thing to do since he started– all has been done just right– very good joke yours about the "*stones* throw"– Glad the silk for your pelisse came in time "Bennet just came in with his blanket full of acorns" Flora & puppy– she has one now called "Lin" after the Commissioner & is likely to have more in six weeks– she is quite of a literary turn–

July 18– Going to send me an acorn– where is it?

July 19– "our intense day" Copley– Sarah, Cleveland & Ned "Sarah expanded into a sort of vazee [*sic*] of her Grandma"– Ned furcal [*sic*] & jaunty and I dare say a rake by this time–

You tell me of Mother, Fanny & Margaret [RBF's sisters]– so does John– I received nothing from Mother per *Delhi* or *London*, & since I left home not a scratch from Fanny, Mary or Margaret, & nothing from Emma since my letter to her– Miss Cochrane engaged to Skinner, you have already told me of her marriage presents– Mrs John Hillard been to Pine Bank– Lows sister– Eliza Nivison reclining on a sofa making a shirt! pity– she would not make a *shift* for herself & children– Glad you have heard such good news of Thomas it is confirmed by what I hear from the Coast per "*Venice*" to RB– arrived yesterday– Then you give me an a/c of Sally & the Boy attracting so much attention– It makes me feel homesick to read these sorts of things & my eyes fill with cobwebs – however it is a pleasurable pain–

64 Here you give me an a/c of what the little child said at school when asked

what sort of beings angels were & replied that they were like little Bennet Forbes– I almost begin to *fear* that he will grow up handsome which would be a decided disadvantage to him– you say you are sorry you sent the picture– *I am not*– it is a quiet comfort to me, I shall expect another by May– If you should or should not have sent it– you may indulge your fancy by having a simple head by Sully if you please & keep it till I return–

"July 22"– Dined with Copley– Pat Grant engaged to Miss Bryant– "Abigail" for the name of a pullet– We certainly will go & visit your late location & Dr Jackens place when we meet– it is a weary long way ahead yet, but my courage don't fail me yet– "July 25" a visit from George– Mrs Eden– Pearson– Boydens– Heard sailed "neglected say you" he thinks you have neglected him–

Then you tell me all about the Sears affair which explains what you said in subsequent letters already replied to–

July 30th Had passed a day with Ben at the Greenes– your account of his odd sayings amuses me– his idea that the Cows– were misplaced– judging as he probably did from the position of his nurses– was quite natural–

No 65 called at the Colonels & Ian Sully & Aunt– you dont tell me how you go about the country, I suppose in a cart– You seem to have been particularly unfortunate in your calls that day & deserve all the inhospitality for not demanding (as I should have done) all you required– Susan Stackpole also showed the "cold shoulder"– You dont say a word in your letters about Mary Motely– where is she? The Perkins cottage, William Appleton's Nahant house– long visit from Mr Cushing, Rob & Tommy– Mrs Cushing unwell but promises to be better in Nov! Why she is a regular breeder–

August 4– Lawyer Livermore & the engagement of Lizzy Hubbard to a young clergy man without any settled curacy– a cure– I see for his heart ache in matrimony– *Omega* letters received– I have been fully aware all along that you would get into a precious stew about your dear old gray husbands imprisonment– the times were black enough then but they have kept on improving & we have done better in consequence of the Opium seizure instead of worse– Old Houqua is quite well & would no doubt be much pleased at your sympathy, if he knew what it meant– Visit from Aunt Jim, Sarah, & Baby– very funny that you poor devil should make such amends for her inhospitality– more particulars of the Sears affair– Joe Lyman been to see you & I dare say the reason he looked so much handsomer than usual was because he was attending to your son–

66 Aug 13– George just sent for more letters– Bennet in perfect health & so ends the chapter–

No 68– 14 August– via Batavia– In which you refer to having sent your journal & to your fears for me when you had my *Omega* letters– Bacon was kind to write to you– You told me before of your Mothers *recovery* to her illness– it did not excite my sympathy– Margaretta not likely to be able to go with Dumaresq & Snow Island burnt to the waters edge– all very natural! Mary Magee match on again– I heard this ten days ago per *Delhi*– there must be a resemblance between me & Bimbo or he couldn't be handsome! Your last jeu d'esprit [pun]– was not bad– about the *cast away*

What do you mean by John Bryant having gone too far of late is he an abolitionist–

Aug 15– orders from John to close all your letters– Don't think I can send Copley a chinaman– it is a responsible order to execute & the good boys like our own can get along alone, it is only the vagabonds that go abroad– Glad you give me such good accounts of yourself, I shall see whether all this is true when Dumaresq comes– You tell me to keep up a good heart & not let my business losses worry me– this is pretty good for a man who has made 70,000 dollars in 14 mos & had 20 given him–

I have now given you at short hand the substance of my letters from you & I wish I had any thing interesting to say in return– one day here is much like the last– very little variety except the variety of trade, to day Flora & Lin came up from Macao, with a young Stone & MacRea of Philadelphia, somewhat supercargoes in the Venice– Let me see what ships have we here now to our consignment *Asia, Lotos, Samarang, Delhi, Valparaiso, Ann McKim, Lintin, Chesapeake, London, Lantao, Gertrude, Venice*– there are but seventeen ships at Whampoa (Americans) & we have twelve of them– It seems to be quite within the bounds of human probability that not many more ships can come in soon– if no more comes & we get away all the ships here & sell all the property on hand my share must be nearly as much as it was the whole of last year & I shall have 80 or 90 thousand dollars without the *donation* of Mr Cushing which will clear off all old debts– There is nothing very interesting politically except that the Commissioner is to remain here as "Vice Roy" & the former Vice Roy is to go to Tokien Province– this shows that the Emperor cannot trust anybody else with the Government– I shall send you per first direct ship the last Chinese Repository the article signed CR which means Charles King is a most libelous & atrocious one & I have as one of the vilified Americans written an article of six pages in reply– I will send you a copy of my article with the Repository– he is an errant puppy– What he is after is the Consulship– the Lord deliver us from this– I believe I told you in a former letter that Russell Sturgis has been sick with Varioloid, I intend to be vaccinated again tomorrow– Why did not that lazy fellow Joe Lyman write to me & Copley & Hillard, the two first must have time– John has given me some amusing accounts of his excursions in the Faun & John Bryant writes to me of the boating business– Winchester of Beef & Pak memory carries the day– Coolidge still at Macao– Mrs C not very well– it must be a great sacrifice to her to be there without her children– good night!

Sunday 23 Feby–

Dear Rose–

I am well & have nothing especially new to add to the above– the Bell is just tolling for Church & I have only time to say I close this for a chance Shot & say adios–

Was vaccinated again yesterday– News from England to 24 October– Bank of US in a bad way & a young crisis will probably be the consequence– We shall not be affected by it directly– No arrival since the *Delhi* & *London*– Love to Bob

Canton 27 February 1840

My dear Rose

I dispatched a few days since for want of direct opportunity several sheets of *interesting matter*, & acknowledging all your letters per *London*, *Talina* & *Delhi* to No 79 of Oct & I believe that not one letter is missing of all you have written–

most of your late letters, notwithstanding the bad accounts of China were written in good spirits, only one or two of the last seem to betray any of your anxiety on my account– On the 27 Sept you tell me in your 77 that you received on the 22 my little note taken to Macao by Mr Johnston– you may well say, "what an eventful year the last was" & may add what an eventful year this is likely to be, 1840 will be memorable in the Annals of China, you tell me I did not name Flora or Ben, I must have been badly off to be sure if I did not, but I believe this is a "white one"– You tell me of Howard at Milton & Jamison in Boston & of the state of your place of abode, & of the weaning of Ben– the kindness of Lizzy Greene &c– On the 28 Sept you were evidently defeated, I mean more than usual you say "your hopes are almost as scarce as the withered leaves around you," this is what your Landlord would call, "flying in the face of Providence" why you naughty critter, you are very ungrateful & I am glad you got upon Susan Hammond for the thought of her must have convinced you of the folly of your discontent–

It is curious to see how the world wags– while I was shut up here "starved" on fat Capon & Beer, you were thinking of my good fortune, & while lamenting my hard luck & making yourself unhappy about nothing, I was going the entire figure at Hong Kong, loading ships & sewing the seed which have produced such a rich harvest–When at Tonkoo in Dec– there came in *Asia, Samarang & Lotos,* when I went down again in the early part of this month I met the *London, Delhi & Robert Bourne,* all accidentally, & just as I was about going the other day, I heard of the *Tarquin, William Gray,* all consigned to us, I believe we have 16 vessels on our list now– indeed we have all that are worth having & the *Venice* from the Coast has arrived lately with large funds in specie to us– In short our business is ridiculously large, & I hope I shall not be spoiled by it– I pretend to be quite humble–

But let me skim over your letters again & see if I can find any thing to abuse you for– you ask of me "how I think of Benbo?" I think of him as a solid young gent– with moderately dark & moderately curly hair & a bronzed skin, with laughing eyes like his Daddy & the impudence & wit of his Mama, with I hope less feeling than the latter & more than the former– but I have not time to think of him or you, until I go to my room & take a look at the picture, say a short prayer for you all (not forgetting myself) & very soon get to snoring– You tell me to take care of myself, I do & I weigh more than I did in October– It was about the time you write that I was sick at Hong Kong–

Sept 29– went to Boston & had a fatiguing time, I can't help it– went home tired & found my *Niantic* letters to 7 May– you say when we meet again & your head rests on my shoulder the flood gates will open!I hope you will do all your crying before I get home for you know nothing vexes me more than to see people play the "spirit of the waters"– Green & I parted friends & I think we shall remain friends while apart– I had tact enough not to quarrel with him & thereby with my own "Bread & Butter"– you say– John & I mixed up together would have made a prince of a merchant– he tells me he thinks much better of my talents for general business than of his own– I find I get along well enough in any thing I choose to apply to, but I am naturally indolent, I hate study & I feel that I am indebted for all my prosperity to a sort of general tact about every day matters, I am extremely superficial in most things & I should hate most confoundedly to be left here without Delano–

Oct 1– John C Lee & young H Lee been to see you– I note what you say about a letter which the former said was attributed to me in the papers– John writes me that Joe Lyman had published one of my letters curtailed– I have not seen the paper– you will see me in print again in the Repository for this month, not yet out, in reply to an article by CR who is neither more nor less than C W King– he is a puppy– but I have served him out pretty well–

I have not seen the article in print, but I thought it pretty good when I read it in manuscript– I wrote after two hard days work late at night & it might have been better done at more leisure– tell me exactly how it strikes you– all the things which I hint at, as "malicious" slander in the end of the article King has been doing all his life here–

Parkinson failed, Alford dead, I have also heard with much regret that Thwing & Perkins have failed– Had I been at home I should have failed too– We hear from England to 22 Oct that the Bank of the US had nearly failed & I am looking daily for a second crisis in the US– it never was more clearly illustrated than in my case, that what sometimes appear to be misfortunes turn out to be quite the reverse– Had the Opium trade & the British Trade gone on quietly, Bills of the Bank & others would have come here largely & our name been on them, & the business of the last six months would not have been half as good as it has been– Now we are not likely to be effected by any state of things likely to happen, most of our constituents are moneyed men–

I have a very long & very friendly letter from Mr Sturgis & another from Mr Cabot & everybody seems to have the most complicit faith in R&Co– poor deluded people! Many people are to be disappointed in Teas this year– too many ships here & too much tea going– Love to Bob & it being 1/2 past eleven– Good night– Flora lies by me

Canton 29 February 1840

My dear Rose–

I have written to you very fully of late in reply to your letters per *London*, & *Delhi* to Octo 1 & *Tarquin* Octo 3– all complete up to 79– I heard yesterday of the arrival, at Manila, of the *Surat* from Boston to 24 October, no letters are up yet, though they have come over in the *Orwell*– our agent at Tonkoo Mr Pierce has advised us of the arrival of the *Panama* & *Horatio* at New York, all well & I suppose when the next Post comes up we shall have letters from Green– The news of the troubles of the US Bank in Philadelphia, causing a sensation here, though we were prepared to hear of its failure from the disastrous accounts per "Mor" from England to same date (24 Octo)– The failure of the Bank cannot effect us in any way & dont make yourself uneasy on that score– I write a line merely to say that I am super excellently well & as busy doing a handsome business as you could wish to see me, & am as contented as any decent man ought to be away from his wife, I like the climate & the excitement of *good* business so well, that were you here I should not think of going home until I had half a million & I imagine you almost thinking of a location for the summer, at last accounts you were just moving, or thinking of moving into Town– I think my letters will get home in the *Samarang* before this so I will only say, Love to Bob, & Sally & Mamy Smith & adieu Ever thine RB

Canton 2 March 1840

I have been made very happy to day by the receipt of your letters per *Tonal*, via Manila– Nos 74, 80-83 & two stray sheets of 20 Octo– one from Mount Vernon– You had received all my letters & were quite easy in your mind– but you having become more easy, makes me feel that you had been very miserable and unhappy and Bacon tells me so– I am provoked that you cannot believe that I can take care of myself here, having done so ever since I was thirteen years of age– however I will wait till we meet & then I will scold you in good earnest– Your 74 is of Sept 4 & rather blue, it speaks of R Sturgis letter, & he writes me from Manila to say how much he is obliged to you, he says his letter from you is worth a "Jews eye"– I take dim note of your having lived within the sum named but you dont send me the accounts! I hope for your sake you will not–

Pray don't mess yourself & be too penny wise–

No 80– Octo 4– continuation of journal– Old Joe Lee called to see you, I must write to him ere long– Bob well through his weaning– passed an evening with the H Lees & heard of Thwing & Perkins failure– this does not astonish me–

I have a letter from Hillard describing Motleys Brook, & one from Joe Lyman who I see is established in New York– Went to church & met Heard & had a long talk with him about Coolidge– I don't see why you should have been anxious because Green was not allowed to quit & I suppose you next will be in expression of intense anxiety because he was ordered away, I have already said so much about Coolidge that there is hardly anything left to say– Heards expectations that Coolidge would divert Appleton, Bates, Goodhue, Quinnel are quite erroneous– Goodhue & Quinnel are Delanos firm friends & if D had joined Coolidge they would have got our business– Bates writes to us without reference to C & will not desert people who send him large consignments,– C has no power here & very little elsewhere– Appletons ship just arrived comes to us & the one Coolidge came in did also as well as the *Trenton*, & the only one of C's friends who would stick to him is Shaw and he has no trade here, however his ship *Surat* is probably on her way from Manila with a cargo to us– C is floored completely, not a foot on ground to stand on, after my last letter to him he went to Macao, on his return– I called on him & had a pleasant chat, & shall stop there unless he comes to call on me– he is a gentleman & will always have my respect– The parties that Heard alluded to had only heard half the story– Sturgis is with us heart & hand, he give us bread & bread give us Bates– all this is for your privation besides I am so far ahead that I almost wish the trade should be again stopped as it must soon be, & so give me a good excuse to go to Macao or Manila for a while– I have told you already that I made fifty-thousand last year, besides what Mr Cushing gave me & in the two months of this year *twenty* more & a prospect of at least ten thousand this month– I am now independent & if John dont get crippled in the bad times which I see are rife with you I shall be independent next March & on my way home– Oh for that happy day– *duty* is all that keeps me here *now*– On the 8th you say you received my "*Canada*" letters & on the 11th in No 82 you acknowledge my letter of 18 May– it seems only a few days ago– you say that I write "that the difficulties are almost over"– my dear they are hardly begun & in the next year (say this year) 1840 China has got to be severely punished– the sooner the better I say–

I am delighted to think the Mandarin silk will come just in time– I am glad to hear Sally Clevelands baby is well– give my love to her– you don't say a word about Mary Motley & I suppose you have quarrel'd with her– oh you naughty woman– No 83 is of 12 Octo– still at Waltham– just got my *Panama* letters & are delighted with them & your mother too– your last date is back in Town & I shall now get more Town gossip, though I dont think opportunities will be frequent during the winter– I see the US Bank had slumpt & I have nothing from John later than the Tarquin, he had been to Nashaun & then bounded off to New York to meet Green & has probably written me fully by the *Niantic*, not yet in, Emma & mother both write me that John is oppressed with business cares & I feel that you do not do him half the justice he deserves no one can write more affectionately than he does, he can make more exertions for me than he does– The other story sheet I spoke of, is Charles Greene, he wrote to me enclosing it, I see it is numbered 75 & am sorry that you devote so many letters to your male cousins, what! 75 letters to Charles Greene & only 83 to me !!!

Oh you ungrateful woman– I have now run over your letters hastily & will put them by for a day or two– We have nothing new here except a ridiculous attempt to burn the ships at Tonkoo with fire ships in the night of the 28th ultimo– this is only adding another link to the chain of grievances– all I ask for is that the port may remain open for a month or at most *two*, & then I shall have done all that I consider necessary & what I make afterwards I shall put to the credit of the "luxuries"– Flora is well & getting portly– love to Bob & mother & Black Sally–

March 7, 1840

Dear Rose,

Here it is 5 days since I wrote to you & it dont appear to me to be more than five minutes– you need not think because I have begun to write in this very small hand that I am going to write a great deal only I have got hold of a new pen & am just a trying of it–We have been quite busy these last four or five days, loading half a dozen ships– this goes by the *Samarang* – I have sent the rough draft of my article in reply to Mr King to John requesting him to read & forward to you– I was in hopes the Repository would have come in time to send it by this ship– I send the January number to John & ask him to read & forward to you–[174]

We have nothing new from home, but are looking for the *Niantic*– I think she must have been sent to England instead of direct– I believe I have told you that I received a letter from Hillard, but I will not answer it by this ship– I have requested Mr Cary to receive 16 packages of tea per *Samarang* & send one to Aunt Fanny, appropriate what he wants himself & send the balance to you, through Mr Bacon– I would much like to send Mother a Box & old Dr Holbrook a box of black Tea–

I have written one million & a half of letters to day & shall have to stay at home from Church tomorrow unless I say good night & finish for to day– Aho comes in & out daily & we do a good deal of trade with the Hong to which he is attached as a purser we buy & sell thousands through him & he will one day be a Hong merchant– Houqua sends his love to you, as do the Miss Houqua's– Love to Bob & all hands & believe me– Yrs ever RB

AN ACCIDENT ON HORSEBACK

[There is a gap in the journals here. RBF's autobiography gives an indication of what transpired during this hiatus:]

... I had not been long at Macao, when I was very much debilitated by the bleeding of leech-bites at night. I awoke in the middle of the night, and found myself very dizzy. I rang for my faithful Chinese servant, who found me fainting,

[174] The texts of C.W. King's article in the *Chinese Repository*, and of R.B. Forbes' reply to it, are reprinted at the back of this book.

and sent for the doctor. I had lost more blood than I could well spare, and was left very weak. Before getting over the unfortunate accident, I mounted my Arabian pony one day, to make a call at the missionary hospital of Mr Hobson. When about to leave, I mounted my horse, while a cooly held him by the head: he had a bad habit of starting before I was ready, and the man not being aware of this, let go before I had got my seat. He plunged, and went off at a gallop; and, in whirling round a corner, I was seized with a dizzy turn, and was thrown to the hard ground, lighting on my head and wrist. I was picked up insensible, carried back to the hospital, and there bled! I came to, and was taken home; but by the 1st of July it was evident that I must change the scene at once, or be carried to the cemetery where rested the remains of my lost brother. "

IN CANTON RECOVERING FROM THE ACCIDENT

Canton 10 April 1840

My dear Rose–

I arrived from Macao last evening at 8 oclock & had a very good night rest & singular as it may appear, felt quite glad to get home to my own cozy chamber & home– Bob is quite well & as smiling as usual– Flora gone to Macao with the puppies & the Consul to enjoy the fresh air– I saw Parker last evening & he gave me two pills & a dose of Epsom & to day I have kept quiet in consequence, but I am pretty well, having only a little head ache, arm & hand recovered almost entirely though found that in trying to roll the ball at nine pins my strength in the wrist has not quite returned– saw my friend Houqua this morning & find him quite well, he gave me a hearty welcome & I am persuaded that there is a great deal of friendly feeling in him– he gave me a lecture on horse riding & boat sailing & tells me to take warning by my lucky escape & refrain in future from horses & boats in toto– Every thing is perfectly quiet here & no alarm seems to prevail on the subject of the warlike threats of the John Bulls– very little doubt is entertained by foreigners that we shall have hot times here by June & a blockade– We are closing up our accounts as fast as possible & expect to be in readiness to go to Macao by the middle of May– I find Delano, Hunter & King & indeed all our family quite well & an immense prospect of closing profitably the last three months earnings– I have promised Parker & Houqua to keep quiet & write & think but little for a week or two until my head gets entirely free from pain– so good night & love to Bob

Canton 12 April 1840

Dear Rose–

I wrote to you yesterday & called it the 10th by mistake, it was the 11th & I must have lost a day somewhere– Mr Shaw came to see me to day with a letter from his Father of introduction merely– he gave me an acorn & a message from Bob for which kiss the dear Boy 999 times I will cherish it & if it is not spoiled I will raise an oak from it & carry it home– it is never eaten however & must grow– my head is almost clear again but I am determined not to write much & so adieu–

14 April

If I wait two minutes more it will be the 15th for the hands of the clock are nearly perpendicular– Richard is himself again– to day I have written a great deal, the

London & *Asia* being under dispatch from our house & the *John Gilpin & John N Gopler* from other parties, "uniting their circumstances" as my friend Lin says in his proclamations you may be sure that I am *not exactly idle* particularly as I have been absent nearly a month & the correspondence flags very much in my absence– I came athwart a news paper piece to day which I enclose for you & which is particularly applicable & pays a *very* great compliment to that word which I have joked you so often for emphasizing– I enclose a note from Mrs Coolidge also to show you that we are on good terms– Coolidge came himself to see me the day I got up– he has had Mr Shaws ship *Surat* lately– feels like a hen with one chicken–...Are you aware my duck that letters written next month by you no– that ain't what I meant, are you aware that the letters I am now writing & to write next month cannot be replied to by you, so I shall send my duplicates when two vessels are going together & you need not return them– to keep my promise– I must leave here by Feb next year, only 10 months & I shall be sure not to stay one hour longer– We are now loading– *London, Asia, Tarquin, Delhi, Lantoa, Gertrude, & Venice* & have on hand besides, *Mr Gray, Lintin, Rafaela, Calumet, Rob Bourne, Joe Peabody & Dos Amigos,* & are hourly expecting the *Akbar, Niantic, Panama, Washington, Ann McKim & Valparaiso & Lima* so my honey you see fortune has not entirely left me ashore–...I have ordered the shoes you wanted & I have to day packed up your Bracelets, chains, card case, comb, buckle in three little packages & given them to Capt Cole of the *Asia* to take care of– I have also put up a box containing two lacquered (Red) Japan vases & some little antique nick nacks for you, I think you had better give the vases to Copley– the Japan cigar or lamp lighter *thing* please send to the Colonel with my regards– Good Morning

CANTON 23 APRIL 1840

My dear Rose–

I am getting very negligent again– yet that is not the right word because I think of you morning noon & night– yes– a great deal more than is good for me & if I had any time I should feel homesick always– I believe I have not written to you for five days– Shaw has gone & before leaving I carried him up into my room & shewed him Bob he said a great deal in favor of the Original but not much in favour of the picture, I also shewed him the curl– I went shopping that day to get something in return for Bob's acorn & determined not to spend much money, my determination ended in getting him a mug costing $9– The same day one of my Chinese friends sent me a handsome piece of figure Camblet[175] & asked me if I liked my colour better– but on the principle that beggars should not be choosers I took the piece he sent which I thought quite pretty for a cloak for you & Sally too & I gave it forthwith to Shaw to carry to you–

I have been getting made several pieces of cross bound silk of the Forbes plaid intending to send enough to each of the girls[176] for a cloak being my only present to them & quite undeserved *only though it be* I have been having painted a view of the burial place at Macao for Mother & this I think will gratify her more than any thing else–...We have not a word from the United States since Dumaresq came on the 10th March– he sailed again on the 23 for Manila & is now at Whampoa having been gone only 28 days & returned with a full freight worth 24000–...pretty well for one month– hey–! should he meet with no interruption here by the vexatious delays of the rascally Chinese he will make a

[175] Camblet is a costly fabric of satin weave, made in Asia of camels hair or angora wool.

[176] The girls are RBF's sisters Fanny and Margaret, who are unmarried and live with their mother in Milton.

good thing from here in freights down to Tonkoo...– I only wish he had an interest in the ship as part owner– Tell Margaretta he sailed in company with the *Valparaiso* & got to Manila before her, sailed from Manila a day after her & arrived at Macao a day before her & he had nearly double the cargo to take in that Capt Lockwood of the *Valparaiso* had– Dumaresq is a real trump & I will put him against any thing which can be found– I wish he were ready to go home & I too– he cannot expect to go home before a year from to day– I mean to *get home* before that day– perhaps I shall go with him next winter– We have nothing new from India or England, you can tell old Joe Lee that I sent your namesake [*Rose*] after the *Porcia* & she made the quickest voyage to Batavia & back ever known having overtaken vessels on the way back which she had passed on her way going to Batavia– The British forces are looked for in June by which time I expect to have my domicilium on board the *Akbar* at Whampoa or elsewhere– for I do not intend to stay at Canton long after a force arrives in China– I think John Bull will commence by knocking down the Bogue Forts & then the Chinese will begin to refer him to Pekin & I hope he will go there & let us alone in Canton– however "we shall see what we shall see" before July– I am intensely curious to know how things are turning out– we cannot expect a regular & quiet trade until a year from to day– if it was not for deserting my friends at a pinch I would return home & come out again next year, but then I have promised never to go away again from home, no that's not it– I have promised never to be separated from you again– the mosquitos are getting very saucy & I am determined not to bid you *good morning* at my desk & so I will say God guard you & Bob & all & good night

DEPARTURE PLANS PENDING

keep this strictly to yourself & mother & Sally ...

Canton 27 April 1840

My dearest Rose,

Within a few days past I have determined to inform you of my intention to leave this country in June or July & consequently to be home in Octo or November– I consider this decision as the most important event of my exile & perhaps it may be the most important event in my life (marriage excepted) on this decision hangs my fortune & your happiness, the fortune of our children, independent of fortune my health will undoubtedly be benefitted by the happy change– I came to this decision principally on your account for I am well aware that if you were looking forward to my being here during this *to be* eventful summer, you would be uneasy & unhappy & even before you can assure yourself that I am well & clear of China you will have suffered great uneasiness– My argument for myself is this– I have promised Rose that I will not be separated from her beyond 3 years– to keep my *vow* I must leave here on Feb 1841– the trade is likely to be stopped by the middle of June & when it may be again restored God only knows, if it is opened again by October or November I should only be here two months or a little more, is it worth the sacrifice of the intervening time to have the pleasure of being here for so short a time– The coming six months will be exceedingly interesting & my curiosity would prompt me to remain at Macao & see the operation of things if I were a bachelor– or had I any want of confidence in my Partners I would remain– for important things must transpire & important decisions must be made– I dare say Mr Cushing, Sturgis & perhaps John will say I am a fool to sacrifice the chance of amassing a large fortune by going away too soon– but I am getting on in life– my head is grey & my nerves more or less affected when they ought to be firm– I feel sure that no mans business will suffer by my going except my own, the sacrifice is mine– ambition is put into one sack & you & the Boy in the other, ambition weighs only as a feather compared with home sweet home– therefore I shall go– Delano first introduced the subject & my idea at first was to return directly to the US, bring you out for two years, letting Delano go home for a visit & on his return for me to take my family home again– but considering the probability that various obstacles might occur to your coming, both on your own a/c & my own I thought it would be impolitic to say to Delano– *I will go home & I will return* therefore I said to him– "I came here for a competency & I have already done in *two* years what I expected to do in three, why then should ambition lead me to stay? If I go home in June I will agree if you will stay here two or three years without visiting home, to give up if you say so, all interest at the end of this year, or keep a small share only, just enough to give me an opportunity to act for the house as a partner at home– I will say good bye to China & you may make your arrangements for another partner when you please, I have my interest in your hands & go–"

He assented & I have decided to go–

Yesterday Dumaresq & I had a long talk in my chamber of home & about you & Margaretta, we came to the conclusion that at heart you were much alike– I showed him your miniature & he laughed at it & said he tried to persuade you to sit for another– he told me a great many pleasant things about you all & he said that your house looked neater & prettier than any house he visited in Boston, he says you all have a faculty of making the best of every thing, & that Bob is dressed in exquisite taste– I told him I had made up my mind to go home & how much I regretted that I could not go with him, I should much like to manage this but dont see how I can....I called on Coolidge yesterday & I will bet you a guinea he will back out of Canton after all before the end of October–...

My decision was made before I recovered from my fall at Macao, but now that I am well of that I still think I ought to go– the time will pass impatiently & ages will roll over between now & July

29th April–

nothing from home yet & nothing new– I have lately petitioned the Vice Roy praying that he would expedite our business & let us go away & stating to his Excellency that the English were coming here to blockade the port by the 1 June, he replies that we are all liars & says how is it possible that England can shut *our Ports*, & why do ye Americans talk of being kept out, are ye tributary to England? do ye intend quietly to submit to blockade– I will protect you, the Imperial orders are to cut off only one Nations trade, the English & not any other– I truly do not desire to put obstacles in your way &c &c &c– The chop is considered very satisfactory & very mild & is very friendly to the Americans–...

Give my best love to Bob & Mother & Sally & believe me thine ever Truly– RBF

Canton 2 May, 1840

My dear Rose

I have no letters on hand from you– my last being per *Olean* & as she may still be in the River I write another line to say that I had the pleasure yesterday to receive my *Niantic* letters & among them your 85,86, & 87 besides one of Nov 1 without number– Whew– Should like to receive your letters always *without number*! very good– I will not undertake to look over all you say, but you may be sure I will not overlook it & will write fully per *Delhi*– I have to day applied for permission to go to Macao & shall start in three days by the river passage taking all my duds & mentally taking leave of Canton forever– I have long letters from John describing the hunt &c & one from Greene & another from Mother–

I went to Whampoa yesterday to see the *Akbar* & two or three other fine ships at Whampoa–...

from all Dumaresq tells me I have no doubt you & your Mother will spoil Bob before he has a chance to be flogged by me– Remember that indulgence is what spoiled you! The man is waiting & I must say "Good Night– alls well"

Yrs ever RB

MAY 2, 1840

My dear Rose–

...have just come from church & had a good sermon from Parker who is our only soul & body physician– the subject was the right view of afflictions he said truly that all afflictions were for our good– that we had our blessing only in trust– I am quite of his opinion– I am in my chamber if not surrounded with *riches* certainly with *Bob & Ritchie* the former is in the Madonna frame & looks much better than the full length, the latter is reading what he calls a *devilish good* letter out of the journal of Commerce of New York dated Canton 4 April 1839 & which happen to be an effusion of mine & so I forgive him the interruption– But to the point (not Jackass point) but the point of your letters, they are always pointed hey? Here goes No 85 beginning Octo 18– "Once more back in the old quarters" very funny that you should have got my letter telling you not to consult me about the weaning, just as you were really thinking about it– You say you *Miss* Esther but as she is married I supposed she is not *missed* by any body else, perhaps she is hit– hit or miss may she be happy & her husband be pappy–

She lives in Myrtle Court so I suppose she is ever-green that is, fond of the family– I fear Sarah will be ever Green too– I mean Sarah Green–...you and your sister have been hard at work getting the house in order, I suppose you Rose & she Sally=ed out in quest of help– you say you are "on the look out for servants a thing you always abominate" I suppose you mean servants– so I will send you a master in two months after you get this– Then your account to me for the very long gap without naming Mary Motley...– You had a good deal of talk about me had you? I wish Mary would write to me...–

"Yesterday Bennets in ecstasies at being able to kiss Papa"– this sounds rather artificial– I hope you are not making a monkey, or parrot of him– London dress for Bob– You say "this is the first quiet moment you have had for a week"– I can as truly say (& probably more so) that this is the first Sunday for many weeks that my mind has been easy & my time my own– my determination to go to Macao has raised me up from a state of despondency I mean bilious despondency– not mercantile despondency– the late drive-drive-drive-hurry- hurry-hurry- has been killing to the mind & body & my letters must have been very unsatisfactory– now I am in excellent spirits–

"Sunday 20 October" just received my Vancouver letter & duplicate journal– I got the letter book two months ago *nearly* by Dumaresq, what a triumph over the *Niantic*– she has been cutting far=antics instead of nigh=antics– George Sturgis & Shaw & the *Acorn*– I got the latter long ago & have sent Bob a silver can in exchange– can do! Shaw did not give me the kiss however, perhaps he intended to transfer the right to that pretty sister of his at some future day! Your story about Sam Green & John C Green getting into the same chamber is very funny– puts me in mind of the story of an Irishman & Scotchman went to bed drunk at a tavern, paddy told the people to call him at day light– in the mean time some wag shaved Pat's head like the Tauney's & when he was called he exclaimed "Be the power you have woke up the Scotchman" & went to sleep again after looking in the glass & seeing his bald head– But the bar keeper could never have been so green as to send a Smith to the wrong room– it is customary at hotels of note to number them for they are without number elsewhere–

"21 October" A pleasant visit from John on his way to NY– I have long letters from him about the Hunt & I must write a private letter to Swain & tell him to put the next one off till late so that I may be there–...

No 87 October 26– per *Niantic*– You say you are sorry they are not longer I mean the letters– they were long enough in coming God Knows– Mother had been in & passed a couple of days– Anne Robbins gave Bob a dress– why it appears to me the public clothe him entirely– you must make Anny a present in return– Second birth day over I dont remember what I was last at Ben's birthday but I dare say I noticed it in some way–

I have just turned to my letter dated Oct 24 stating we had paid due honour to Bob's birthday, although I was under the influence of Salts that day (attic salt) & just as I am writing to you to day Mr Nye says he cannot dine here to day with Ritchie because of the same dose –& he will not be Nye-antic to day–...I had begun to wonder why my Clay-Cooly was not acknowledged– but in your No 87 you mention it & not *cooly*! very good hey? you say your Mother thought it the prettiest thing *she ever saw*– why the Silver Coffee Pot was just now the prettiest & you say it is the most Compleat thing *you ever saw*, I suppose you mean steam engines & some few other things excepted– you must leave off my dear always speaking in *hyperbole* (is that spelt right) how can I tell after such extravagant sayings whether Bob himself is the perfect & knowing creature you make him out– I hope you are not disappointing me in telling me too much of his beauty & intelligence–

For instance you say Bennet talks *all the time* about Flora & however I will not quarrel with your long & interesting letter & will spare my rod until I get home– You appear to be quite content with my effusions & say you never had any thing which satisfied you more entirely than my letters! Myself excepted you should have added & then you have misspelled a word you speak of pouring over my pen, is it not poring? You say a good deal about my health & your anxiety about it in the letter under review– As I am deduced to go off in six weeks, two months at farthest, I have no fears about health & at sea free from care & anxiety & other kinds of *Tea* I shall pick up unto obesity– is not that very *pretty*–...I am quite surprised that little Lucy Sturgis remembered the message to you & Bob– Russell Sturgis will be *very* glad to hear from you & will appreciate your kindness to his children, I now come to your *last received* letter of November 1 per *Niantic* you had just got my *Gerard* letter & the Drama which you say is *capital*– I have already said that I thought it very silly– *"John grown fat"* that *is* the most improbable thing of all– no no– that wont do I can believe that there are flying fish in the sea, that Pharaoh's chariot wheel was fished up from the bottom of the Red Sea, but that John has grown fat I will not credit– Mrs Cushing a fourth son! Mary James Amory a *ditto*– Emma Rodman ditto– these things will happen in the best regulated families–

I shall make some speculations on the way home about who will have more when I get there–...near dinner time so I must go down & do the pretty to my guests–

Sunday Evening–

...A new plan has come into my head lately namely to go with Dumaresq to Singapore in a month from to day finish his business there– take ship from there for home– but I am quite undecided about this– all I have fully determined on is to get to Macao this week & then do the needful for R&Co until a good opportunity offers to be off– These are not times to look far ahead & you must not set your mind fully on the day, or the manner of my departure until you hear positively of my embarkation– I shall not come back to China that's pretty certain & shall be off in July at the farthest– My dinner has killed all my wit & I will not bore you with much more to night, it is warm & very mosquito weather–

I shall begin to be very impatient to be off having made up my mind to go–...Bob would send his love if he could speak– Flora is at Macao–

7 May 11 oclock 59 minutes PM

I have just finished my business at Canton...I am off– but as no body suspects that I am going to remain & never return I am not feasted & dont want to be– I cannot put on a sober face at the idea of leaving Canton & since I determined to go I have gained (in a week) 3 1/2 lbs of flesh & am in better spirits than I have been for a long time, I shall write to you on the way down & only leave this in case my letters should miscarry–

I feel some compunctions at going off & leaving my partners here– but my presence is wanted at Macao during the next six weeks– The clock is striking twelve– good morning–

...I have bought & send you per *Delhi* 6 very exquisite fans which will not be wanted till I get home so you will not yet give them away– I send also one box containing–

4 figured crape– 2 ps figured lulustring[177]

4 ps plaid silk– 4 ps plaid Ribbon–

if I forget to say so in my next remember that the plaid is for the Forbes clan– but Mr Cabot is to have his choice of a piece and ribbon to match– RBF love to Bob

RBF LEAVES CANTON FOR MACAO

Chop Boat on the way to Macao
9 May 7 AM &c &c

My dear Rose

I left Canton about 12 oclock yesterday & have had an exceedingly pleasant time thus far, my only companion except my servant...is Mr S W Lewis who is a young man who came here supercargo of the *Levant* from Philadelphia last October– he is one of those who came to China, with the complete letter writer, twelve shirts & collars & as many bosoms, a family hair brush & a good stock of puppyism in general, there is nothing particularly odious in him– but he looks, acts, moves & has his being as if he had just come from behind a counter saying "Nothing else maam!"

Why then do you go with him to Macao, say you– to which I reply– because a large chop boat with luggage for furnishing two homes cost about 100 dollars

177 Lulustring, as written to Rose, or lustring, is a plain stout lustrous silk used for dresses and for ribbon.

RBF Leaves Canton for Macao

& I make him pay one half & endure his company for two days– but so entirely is this wicked world given to outward show that one forgets the inside– This Mr Lewis is & has been exceedingly polite to me & is as attentive to me as if I were his elder by forty years– So let us say no more about it–You must have a short description of my present vehiculum, a chop boat is a large covered concern as big as a barn (or a piece of chalk), it is the same sort of thing that carries cargo to the ships & being fitted up as this is with pictures & especially with Bobs picture, which is near me, with my general room furniture it is as comfortable a way or more comfortable way of travelling than any other I have ever tried, here there is no danger of the boilers bursting & no fear of a sudden contact with a rail road car to the danger of ones bones, the only annoyance is the mosquitos, & these are kept at Bay with curtains, I had my cot slung last night & slept as well as could be for every mile I get further from Canton I feel my barometer rising–...The only persons in my secret are Dr Parker & Delano & these were consequently the only ones that I felt much at parting from & I was obliged to smother that little of feeling for fear of betraying my intended exit to the rest of the people– With the exception of leaving my friends in the impending crisis to take care of themselves I had nothing to feel for– yet it is a melancholy thing (for people of feeling) to leave any place to which one may be attached by association (especially mercantile association) I have all my baggage, goods & chattels with me, I went to see old H & there I had a struggle to keep the show of feeling down, to him I am much indebted & I could not think of seeing him for the last time without a slight gnawing at the heart strings– however there was just enough of feeling shown by both of us to suit the occasion of leaving him in these uncertain times & on the point of the English invasion– he asked me when I expected to get back– this was rather an awkward question, I told him that was very uncertain & that there was a fair chance if the English came to China of my being away a long time– he thinks negotiations may be long pending but he does not think there will be any fighting– I think it likely that the English will bully and bluster a little at first & afterwards make terms with China & carry on the trade pretty much in the old way– If they undertake to lay down the Law for China they will eventually fail & go home like sneaks (tail down)– However it is no use speculating on the future– the delay in demanding apology & indemnity from China looks like preparation for a large expedition for large expeditions move with *little* expedition– I have told you...that I might go to Singapore with Dumaresq, but...I should have to leave China too soon if I went with him– My stay at Macao must be very important to the house as I shall be able to render very valuable services there– Therefore I cannot fix on the day of my departure, perhaps when I am ready to leave I may not have an opportunity to go for want of a ship–...so do not set your heart on any particular day but be assured that I shall not remain a moment after I am of little use here–

FINAL STAY IN MACAO

Macao 10 PM
10 May 1840

...I arrived here at 5 oclock this day excellently well & found Uncle Jimmy in good care– No arrivals from home, but two or three ships in to our consignment– As usual I shall have my hands full– This has been a delightful day & I have not felt so buoyant & happy for a long time–

There will be no English force here for a month or more– I must reserve an

The waterfront at Macao is shown in this engraving made from a Thomas Allom painting, which was made in turn from a sketch on site by Warner Varnhem.

hour for other letters –

Love to Bob & your mother & Sally & good night

Thine ever RB

13 May 1840

My dear Rose

I continue my journal & am now fairly & comfortably located in my own house, that is the house of R&Co– I am dining & living generally at home & we have the most *exemplary* weather imaginable– yesterday I lent my best horse to a friend, I mean the one which threw me & he went perfectly well & I should not hesitate to ride him, however I am riding a sober beast instead– yesterday I went to see some horse racing by the English after which I returned home & dressed & spent the evening with Mrs Ritchie in part & the balance with Mrs C, I saw Mrs Ritchies two little girls & one of them about four & one about five years of age– the baby had gone to bed– they are interesting children– I sent Bobs picture to Mrs Coolidge that she might tell me if Bob looked at all like it when she saw him last, she thinks it looks more as he did when an infant, when she saw him in the latter part of June 1838 shortly after I left– I am taking an occasional blue pill at the suggestion of Anderson but I am getting stout so fast that I shall be quite independent of every body except the Butcher & Baker ere long– The air is very fine & the murmuring of the surf on the beach is pleasing reminding me of Nahant– We have letters from Eng to 4 Jany & if you had written to me on the 15 Dec I should now have your letters– I believe you have not yet written me one letter overland, I suppose you are getting so economical that you think I cannot afford it, I am convinced that there is no cheaper investment than the Postage a/c– I have dined with Flora & Mr Snow once since I came down the former is pretty well rejoicing in her three little daughters I shall keep one of them though they do not *take after* the mother, (except when they are hungry)– As for Mr Snow he is but poorly & I think may not live many years– ill failure seems to dog him & he makes the most of it by constant complaining–

Mrs Coolidge tells me that she does not enjoy very good health, & he looks rather sallow & hollow about the eyes–...I am expecting later news from you by the overland mail of February– or per some direct ship–

19 May–

It seems hardly possible that I have not written to you since the 13 Instant, time goes much faster here than at Canton, let me see what have I done since the 13– dined once with Mr Snow at Mr Sturgis & eat too much dinner, that is really the only remarkable thing that I have accomplished excepting to write a great many remarkably excellent letters to all parts of the world– I have been pretty busy at my correspondence, I have not yet found time to call on his Excellency the Governor & that is a shame– Last night there was a great "flare up" a quadrille party given by a Parsee, I believe Mrs Coolidge went & Mrs Ritchie, I was invited & accepted & went on Sunday evening to Mrs Ritchie & Mrs Cs to offer myself as beau & if I found myself accepted I intended to take a violent purgative at 5 PM & say I could not go, however I was pretty sure that *before Sunday night* the ladies would have completed all their arrangements for *Monday night* & so I thought I should be quite safe in volunteering– fortunately for me all the people had gone to a conventicle at the missionary rooms & I missed the chance of offering myself as "*beau ideal*"– that's pretty good for it was only in an *eye* & *dear* that I intended to play beau– all my *eye* & Elizabeth Martin which being translated means "all in my eye & Betty Martin"– I am going over to the Cap-sing

-moon anchorage to day to meet Capt Dumaresq & two or three more ships which should be there soon on their way to sea– A man going to sea, his wife desires your prayers– a man going to see his wife, desires your prayers–...

2 PM 19 May

I am off at 5 PM for Cap-sing-moon and have not much time to say more–...Uncle James is sitting at my elbow abusing Mrs Coolidge & Mr Ritchie for having gone to a Parsee man's ball or quadrille party last night– which Mr Sturgis calls a Quadroon party–

I hope you will believe me when I tell you I shall get away as early as I can conscientiously that is without deserting my partners, I have come *out here* to Macao on purpose to make you feel easy & you may be sure that I shall make the other *larger step* homeward as soon as I can– still impossible for me to name a day for starting– I think 15 July will be about the mark–

Bob is hanging over me & smiles as if he would say, Father get ready for dinner– so God bless thee & kiss all hands– Thine True-lee RB

ON BOARD SHIPS OFF MACAO

Cap-sing-moon Bay
May 24, 1840

My dear Rose,

...I have been over here living with Gilman very comfortable on board the *Lintin* & daily looking out for the *Akbar, Tarquin* & *Rob Borne* on their way here to be dispatched– the *Tarquin* came to day & I have invited myself to dine on Flour pudding the first good day, we have had very fine weather without a drop of rain since I left Canton & I have enjoyed it much– I go on shore occasionally & walk here & have some practice at pistol shooting &c &c Capt Downies is here in the Brig *Joseph Peabody* consigned to us, he has his wife on board & a son about 7 years of age & an adopted daughter a pretty little girl of 12– they have already robbed me of some Chinese images which I bought for Bob– however there are some left & if no more children come I shall save a pair or two–

Yesterday several more letters came to light per *Niantic* & were sent to me from Canton...You tell me about the blockade rumour, we have had similar rumours ever since Sept & it will take something more than rumour to make us uneasy– You also lead me to hope for a crayon sketch of Bob– Lincoln at $10 the gratification will be extensive– Clarkes painting is really thought very well of & in the small Madonna frame looks much better than it did in the large one– I am really quite amused at your saving up all the spare Tea money to pay Doctors bills– this is quite a comment on the necessary extravagances which I as a member of the respectable house of Russell & Co am *compelled* to commit– *fifty dollars* say you for cutting off that little spot from Bob's head, quite enormous & if I ever send Bigelow a box of Tea may I be called a niggar for life– but I dare say you meant to say that your years Bill was $50 & that you could not recollect anything else that Bigelow had done– I wish I could say I had never spent a dollar carelessly– the fact is that the immense business we have been doing is enough to spoil me *again*– I will not say thousands of dollars have passed through our hands but millions during the last year & a half & I now think an hundred thousand dollars a mere song– All your late letters end in saying "I am going to spend a night at Milton soon" pray did you ever go?– We have had no arrivals from sea since I got outside the river, & only several from Manila & are looking anxiously for the mail of *February* from England, it will be singular if I get nothing from you after *November* when this comes–...There is fine salt water bathing here & one can be carried to the beach in a boat to bathe instead of being oblidged to walk or ride to it as at Macao–

There are two British frigates here, the *Druid* Capt *Lord* John Churchill, & the *Volage* Capt *Smith* & a sloop of war is at Macao– the men of war have appropriated a small green Island half a mile from here where they have landed about 50 head of Cattle to fatten them for ships use– This is Queen Victorias birth day & the vessels of war have dressed out in flags & firing salutes– singularly enough she is 21 years old & the salute usually fired as a national one is 21 guns & the salute for a Sovereign is one gun for every year, more over it is Sunday– I suppose the Queen must be married by this time–

The bells are striking ten oclock & as I have sworn to go to bed regularly at that hour I must say love to Bob & mother & Sally & good night

28 May–

...[they] say the British force will not be here till the middle of July & the longer they are away the longer must my stay be here for my partners must stay in Canton as long as they can & until they come out I must stay here– I was in hopes the force would come by the 10 June & then I should earlier have been on my way– however the longer it stays away, the more gain–

I am in haste & must close with love to Bob & all hands– A ship is in to the 1 January from Phila– The *Adelaide,* but no letters will probably be delivered for three weeks & so I must wait patiently– adieu–

thine RBF

dined to day with Capt Hunt– flower plum pudding –

Boat Paradox– sometimes called the Pair-o-ducks–
May 29, 1840

My dear Sir–

...I devoured yesterday... a catty or two of Plumb-pudding...on board of the *Tarquin* & which did not set particularly light in my stomach, but as I had been particularly invited by Capt Hunt to eat thereof I was bound as a good agent to do full honour to it & I did– This AM hearing the *Lerna* was in & the Swedish Bark *Actif* I have found it necessary to go over to Macao & do the needful for them & here I am on the way...

The Supercargo of the *Adelaide*– tells me there is only one letter in her for me & that he says is a business letter & that I cannot consequently expect to have it– He has promised to give me any there may be for Dumaresq– I hear per *Lerna* that the Capt of the *Porcia* died drunk at Amboyna[178] & that Capt Gilmans brother who was a passenger in her also died at Amboyna– the latter I believe was also fond of drink & I dare say these are both no great loss–...I hear also that the *Rose* after being sold & examined was found rotten– The cockroaches are flying about so in this boat that I must quit & go on deck– good night

Sunday night
31 May 1840

My dear Rose–

It is almost the 1 of June & I am in no condition to write you a long yarn to night for I have had one of those unsatisfactory Sundays of which too many have

[178] Amboyna, now Amboina, (Lat 3.46 S– Lon 127.59 E) is an island in the Malay archipelago thirty miles long and ten miles wide at its broadest part.

transpired during the last six months– Last night came the *Washington* from London with a valuable cargo to our consignment & under charge of a young Wells whose father keeps school at Cambridge– I knew him slightly before & he appears to be a nice young man– He brought a multitude of letters to us & in addition there came to day a quantity from other quarters & among those the overland mail to 4 Feb from London– I learn through Mr Ballister that the *Lexington* steam boat was burned on the 4 Jan on the sound & that nearly all the passengers perished & among them Mr Follin– times I hear were mending–

I received a short letter from Charles Greene to 30 Dec...– to tell me all my folks are well & also the Sturgis clan, he gives me a piece of intelligence which is very afflicting namely that Mr Snow's only daughter, his last hope is dead– The old Gentleman was telling me only a day or two ago that he cared only about making a little money on her a/c he said his son had already become an idiot & now he looked up entirely to this darling daughter for his future comfort– After I read this letter I could not help letting out some very big drops & it destroyed the happiness I had in getting news *of you*...– However I dreaded to meet Mr Snow & if I had met him then I should have betrayed the intelligence by my looks & acts– however I met him this evening, or rather he came in to my house unawares & I did not make him unhappy perhaps I should tell him– but how to break the thing to him I know not– his spirit is so far bowed down that I am really afraid to let him know it– yet it must be known– what shall I do– Mr Sturgis says dont tell him –...

I have been very busy all day– this is really unsatisfactory to me– body & soul & I wish I were off–...We have now outside the River & in seventeen vessels to attend to & two have just gone– The *Akbar, Tarquin, Borne, Peabody, Delhi* & most of the others will be off directly & the grace afforded by the delay of the British forces will make us to clear off most of our business & handsomely too–

We hear that Sir George Stanton[179] is coming out– he was formerly chief of the EIC [East India Company] here & accompanied Macartney to Pekin– his coming (if true) will be decidedly pacific– good night– I am too sleepy to finish the page–

Tuesday June 2, 1840–

I am off on board the *Paradox* bound again to Cap Sing Moon to dispatch Dumaresq & I leave this on board of a ship in the Roads to go to the *Delhi* on her way down– I have only time to say that I am extremely well & with love to Bob remain Thine ever Truly

RB Forbes Esq &c &c &c

Ship *Akbar* 3 June, 1840

My dear Rose,

...Since I came over here last night I have received several letters from Town, Delano wants me to go with Philip (I put that in to save the labour of writing Dumaresq) to Sincapore & return here in any good ship taking the first vessel after my return to go home in– This plan wont suit me for several reasons, firstly I wont go to return, secondly I should have to be too long at sea to go to Singapore return here & then embark for US, thirdly I want to be here when the *bull is opened*, which from our latest accounts will not be till the middle or end of July– I am very angry at this delay on some accounts & particularly because I hoped my Partners would leave Canton in June, however the delay is

179 Sir George Stanton had accompanied Lord Macartney as a page during the English embassy which approached the Emperor Ch'ien Lung in 1795. He had gone again with Lord Amherst in 1818.

worth to me five thousand dollars per month & that you will admit is *good wages*– I cannot honourably retreat before my partners are out of Canton & I am under some compunctions at leaving China without again seeing Houqua–...You will readily see that my delay here is unavoidable & you must not get impatient– Knowing I am outside I know you will be reasonable– I have been a good deal troubled at the death of Mr. Snows daughter which Charles Greene announced to me in a letter of Dec 30–I have not dared to communicate this dreadful intelligence to Mr. S & I fear it will be almost fatal to him in his present shattered condition–...I came across the lines in a paper of Dec which came in the *Adelaide* (no letters yet)– they not only made me think of Mr Snow, but of myself & my Boy– However I do not allow myself to dwell on such things & my time is *almost* too much taken up to sympathize with any one–

put her for his in these lines & they would exactly apply to poor Mr Snow– I trust in God they may never apply to me–

I notice by the December papers that the small pox had been in Boston, indeed it was there when Dumaresq left & he had two or three men down with it on the way out–

I am going over to Macao with him tomorrow & he will sail the next day for Singapore– Give my regards to Margaretta & tell her that her husbands eye is quite well again & he is perfectly well as is all his crew– love to Bob– RB

MACAO 6 JUNE 1840

My dear Rose–

Dumaresq slept with me last night & departed at 3 oclock, got under way with a fair wind at 4 & was out of sight when I got up– I almost wanted to go with him– he is very well...I am glad to be out of Canton– & heartily wish all my friends were–...Coolidge down last night looking so-so–

Lord John Churchill, Commander of the *David* frigate died three days ago of congestion of the brain, dysentery, goat, rheumatism &c &c

Yrs in haste RB

RETURN TO MACAO

MACAO
11 JUNE 1840

My dear Rose–

Yesterday was one of those very busy days of which I have known so many of late– It was post day, the March mail overland arrived, the Calcutta mail ditto & I was obliged to digest all the news & then send the letters to Canton– I had no time consequently to write to you– I did not forget that it was the anniversary of the bitterest day of my life, or at least one of the bitterest– the two or three previous days were equally so– I know that you thought of me more than usual– however I shall never be away from you another anniversary–

The *Alligator* frigate came in two days ago & brings news that one division of the British fleet would come in directly as it was to leave Singapore on the 20 Ultimo–[180] I have recommended my partners to get out of Canton as soon as possible & the sooner they are out the sooner I shall be on my way home, however it is impossible to name a day & you & I must both wait patiently–... I have not yet told Mr Snow of his *fate*– I feel as if I were the executioner & that

[180] Ultimo means in or of the month before the present one, in this case May.

to divulge to him the death of his daughter would be to strike the shock– so I keep out of his way– I have however written him a letter stating that I have heard that his child was very ill, but I shall not present this to him until the *Panama* or some other ship comes & before he gets his letters announcing the fact– Alas poor old man he mourns for the unfortunate business he has been doing little dreaming that a misfortune ten fold heavier is hanging over him–...

The *Ann McKim* is expected down every day on her way home & Hubbell goes home in her, wish I could also– We got yesterday late accounts from Bombay– Mrs Maclean dead– she was a friend of R Sturgis wife & of every one here though a great gossip, Mrs C W King arrived in Bombay & was confined the day after, say the 17th April & was to leave in the steamer with her husband to go *overland on the 25 of same*– that's what I call doing business–

The overland journey now that steam boats & other conveniences are running is considered nothing & if I am detained here longer than I expect I may go that way because I shall then avoid going on the winters coast in a sailing vessel– I hear of an American vessel at Singapore to the 1 Jany but I get no letters– my last from home being per *Akbar* 17 November when there are dates here to the *middle of February three months after*, oh you naughty woman after all my schooling not to send me one overland letter– I have a great mind not to write to you any more but just cut out of my books my last years letters & let them go–...

There is an excellent fellow here named Fox (John knows him) all his packages come to me & often times his pills & draughts– today some news papers came to me from some one with a scrap of paper directed to Tho Fox Esq so I kept the papers to read & sent him some pills which I had by me with the said direction– I have not learned yet whether he has taken any, the explanation will be made after I have got the news– this mistake naturally arises out of the two names both of which Forbes & Fox the Chinese pronounce Fox or Foxe– I am enjoying my rides every day– am up to my ears in letters & that sort of excitable business that I like, there are none of the details of business here to annoy me– the coming month is to be of intense interest– indeed the coming twelve months are to be fraught with interesting matters– I never was so pulled & torn one way & the other– if you were here I should expect to stay & see the fun– but having but little prospect of profit after this month– I must go– I saw an account in an English paper of *150* lives lost per *Lexington*– can it be– but I am running on & consuming too much time– I must go to business –

Bob is hanging over me & I devote a few lines to him

What think you of them–
We may watch with delight the wild blossoms appear,
but the flow'r we've nurtured is ever most dear;
We may pause midst the flocks of the valley or hold,
But we love the pet lamb of our own little fold,
And thou art to me both the lamb & the flower
Still cherished most dearly for each passing hour
That brings me the sweetest enjoyments– I prove
The watching the likeness of him I most love–

SUNDAY 14 JUNE 1840

I dare say you think the foregoing lines are original dont you?

This morning I overslept myself & did not get up till 9 oclock, so I have lost two hours– I found the Capt of the *Calumet* here, he was in sight yesterday & I supposed it was a ship just arrived from sea & was dreaming all night of letters from home heaps upon heaps– As that ship is very slow I sent only one short letter by her direct to Boston, with three boxes of Toys &c

Capt Shreeve fell in love with a pair of the clay images so you will not find more than four in the box instead of six– these are also in two separate boxes in one an old man with clock work in him making him run round that table opening & shutting his eyes & moving his chin & the other is a buffalo who also runs about– you will of course only give Bob one thing at a time as he would get cloyed with so many valuable presents indeed I expect what I send you now to answer for all my future boys & girls– as well as for him– I am spending my Sunday rather unprofitably dont you think– so in writing to you instead of going to Church– Mrs Gribble whom I sometimes visit has a little daughter about four years of age in whom I am getting quite an interest– I have also spent an evening with Mrs Stewart & she is a sort of connection of my kinsman, Sir Charles Forbes of London,– I received letters the other day from Forbes, Forbes & Co London, in one of which they say "Sir Charles sends his regards to his *Kinsman*–" I shall have to go to London cultivate the acquaintance of the old Gent– I am getting very impatient to hear further from you– I have seen the account of the *Lexingtons* loss– it is indeed dreadful–

I see that there were several by name Winslow & the actor Frun as well as Capt Foster of the *Rose*– how hard that he should have fallen a sacrifice after several years absence– however I suppose every one thinks his case the hardest–

It has been raining very hard the last day or two & I have not had my usual rides & walks– but I have had lots of letters to write & I find I have perpetrated about fifteen pages a day ever since I have been away from Canton–

I hope to get at least 15 pages from you before long–

Uncle Jimmy drops in here daily & we walk together– among the many satisfactions of doing a good & great business here has been that of helping him– since I *came into Power* he has been our agent here & it has done him good in several ways he has been fully employed & besides that it has been of service in lining his pocket– I have also contributed to increase the business of my friends at Manila– Russell & Sturgis– As for our friend Joe Coolidge he has been woefully disappointed– you will recollect the great faith he put in Mr Appletons friendship for him, he naturally expected that the *Delhi* was coming to him & when he heard of her arrival he went over to Tonkoo to meet her, but alas he found me there & that he had nothing to do with her & Then he has all along been nursing up the idea that Bates would stick to him & he went so far as to tell his Chinese friends that he was expecting the *Washington*– she came & the supercargo– young F Boot Wells came direct to me, he showed me Bates letters about the voyage in which Bates says *I quote literally* "the best house to aid you in your business is Russell & Co (Forbes)" then he said something about the possibility of his finding another house of R&Co adding that he would want nothing to do with that! This would seem to show that Bates so far from having any very friendly feeling toward Coolidge was offended with him & I dare say that C told Bates some hard *yarns* about his (C's) power in China– I have not seen either C or Mrs C for several days– but I take every occasion to tell people what a nice fellow C is– then C– has told people that the *Falcon* was coming thereby leading them to suppose that she was coming to him– but we have the order for her– She goes to Manila first– In short my dear my triumph has been complete & the trade having kept open so long will make me almost a rich man– I dare say my share this year will be sixty or seventy thousand dollars &

that I cannot be with less when I get home than One hundred thousand & if all turns out well– *more*– How grateful we ought to be– what an immense thing that determination was– to forsake home & make one desperate effort at retrieving my losses– I begin to have a great opinion of my own judgement & think with a year or two more practice here I should consider myself No 1– first chop– mind you dont tell folks either of my fortune or my egotism– if you do the state will tax me for the first & my friends laugh at me for the second– I am writing along without much thought & occasionally going to the window– my spy glass expecting to see the John Bulls coming round "Caboneta" point– The sooner they come the better & the sooner we shall know what is to be the upshot of all these warlike preparations– An attempt was made a few nights since by fire Boats to destroy the shipping at Cap sing moon, but the men of war very quietly towed the rafts on shore & putting out the fires & thanked Lin for a seasonable supply of fire wood– This is the second attempt & I suppose the English cannot consider it in any other light than as a declaration of War & they will I think capture the Bogue Forts & blockade the Port directly– I am quite ashamed to be away from Canton this time & if any reflections are cast on my character for having deserted my friend in Canton I must put the burthen on your shoulders– It is more to make you feel easy than from any fear of consequences by remaining at Canton that I came away– Of course I have been very busy & very usefully busy & I hardly see how we could have done without me here– at the same time it is the duty of the head man to remain at his Post–

Ann McKim

MACAO 20 JUNE 1840

My dear Rose–

...yesterday morning I got up, (I always get up in the morning) & took my spy glass– (I always do so when I wish to look far) & pointing it off to the roads I put my eye to the small end (which is generally the best to look through) & I found that there was a ship at anchor in the Sand Roads which was not there when I went to bed, or if there that (in consequence of the night being darker here than the day) I did not see her– I called up Captain Martin of the *Ann McKim* thru the glass (as most people do to determine their points) & thought my conjectures were right– I shaved (cutting myself in three places, but not dangerously) bathed rubbing myself with the soap box & drying myself with the trousers instead of the towel, got breakfast, breaking the wine glass & swallowing it instead of the Eggs– poured the cream into the sugar & the tea onto the plate– cut up & swallowed the large Rice spoon instead of the sole fish– (t'weren't a sole fish either because there were two)– committed various other blunders such as putting on my under garment wrong side before & my shoes on my hands instead of my feet–

all these pranks in any other country or under any other circumstances would have denoted a nervous & excited imagination– but in this Country every thing is attributed to the Chinese being "a very peculiar people" & the only evidence of an aberration of intellect which I have been about to discover in myself is that I am now writing to you the first letter I have attempted since I finished at one oclock this morning reading– but I am before my story– well– after my breakfast (I was *born* with a silver spoon in my mouth) I saw Capt *Pulaski* Benjamin landing– I had sent that very reputable Cooly Acqui with a note to hand him at landing saying to him– "Mum, not a word to any one if you have seen *the fleet*, don't reply to any quarters", for as I expected Bull, Lycee & others would be on the "qui vive" for news– *Well* he landed & the said Acqui handed him my note, (I was looking at him all the time with my glass) he looked at the superscription & says he, (you know with a good glass you can hear a man speak a 1/4 to 1/2 mile off depending on the wind oh thats from Mr Forbes, is he here, Yes says Bull, whats the news? & then Benjamin crumpling up the note & saying I am going round to see him so its no use to read that, went on & answered all the various questions &c– Curse him! said I through the glass, why don't he read my note–? he came along talking all the while, like a new arrival & when at Lycee's (Wetmores') house he dove in there– Oh he– says I– "are ye there" & putting down my glass– I came to my writing table & began to write *very coolly* saying to myself, Well, old Wetmore (to whom the *Panama* used to come) has got home & he has been tampering with Griswold, Green has deserted us & the *Panama* comes to Wetmore & Co– my heart sunk within me, (it always does sink within me, when I sink myself) & I said– Well, no letters from Rose for three weeks– no use crying for spilt milk & sour milk too, who wants the *Panama*! Haven't we given up receiving any more business– It is too late to do any thing, the fleet will be here in hectic hurry & then what *can* be done with the *Panama*– by the time I had resolved these very sage things in my mind & get perfectly *composed* &c– I heard a lively step on the stair, Flora barked, thats a stranger says I– however for fear that I should betray any anxiety I went on writing– Benjamin appeared followed by a most lively looking lad & the happy bearer of a small bundle addressed to *Russell & Co...*

How are you Capt B– glad to see you (leave you to imagine his final reception) those statesmanic words *Russell & Co* in the writing of the lovely & intelligent merchants *the* Griswolds– brought by the lovely *Panama*, something must be done for her– nothing is impossible, send for a pilot immediately– *she must go in*!!!

chops must be written, exertions made– fine rafts, sunken junks, forts &c are nothing when an object is to be accomplished– but enough– Capt B– gave me only the Owners letters &c first– then I sent him off while reading & ordered the letter Bag on shore– In short I began at noon yesterday, skimmed over all the business letters by 5 PM– then began on your *pile*, which occupied me until 1 AM to day– I got from 95-118 inclusive beginning 18 November (the day after Dumaresq sailed) ending 18 February– making nearly 24 sheets– (flowing sheets) of interesting (& interested) matter, well written with good black Ink & giving me all the necessary details of all & sundry the events of the day– good, bad, horrible, dreadful, indifferent, laughable, lachrymose, bilious, jolly, witty, stupid (crossed out), dull (very few of latter), deaths, marriages, to be marriages, births & *to be* births, of people who were married & others who ought to be &c&c&c In short I got a *pile*, a *heap*, a *surfeit*, a *bellyfull*, a *pair*, or slippers (now on my sir-feet) & a watch fob (now hanging on my bed curtain) I got enough for once & I have only one thing to scold you violently for– namely– you put several letters under cover to me from Margaretta– how *could* you do such a thing– for Dumaresq– how *could* you thus try to *rob* him of his late news– or did you expect dishonestly to *smuggle* his letters to him through me? Why do you know not that the *Panama* might have met him at sea, at Anjer,...at Macao in the River– just imagine Dumaresq just going away for Singapore & meeting the *Panama* in Macao Roads, as he might have done, going on board full of hope & asking for letters from his wife– Benjamin– looks over the Bay & says *I have none*, Dumaresq sees my *pile*, my *budjet*, my *filio*, he feels sure that there are letters enclosed for him– but "Forbes is in Canton– I can't open his wifes letters– Oh no– well– I must go to sea dull & unhappy– the fate of my wife, my other & my to be Lovely is uncertain, I am sure however something wrong has happened or I should have had letters"– that my dear is a highly colured picture, but it might easily have been true– & now once for all

– never put your letters & tell Mrs Dumaresq never to put hers under cover to any one– let her own pretty hand write the superscription, seal the letter with *good wax* & write private on it & put no bodys care on it & it will find its way– you may think I have much leisure to write so much about so small a thing– but remember dearest, that Dumaresqs happiness, the success of the *Acbars* voyage, the fortunes of her Owners & their children, might have been blighted by this one little act of affectionate & inadvertent kindness– but to leave hyperbole & come down to sober truth for which I am so particularly distinguished– I must say in one word– I have never enjoyed a day of more complete happiness (in China) than yesterday– all my letters– were good– the *Lexington* disaster I had heard of before & fully

Macao
Sunday 28 June 1840

My dear Rose–

...I sat me down this morning at 9 oclock to write to you, but just as I began a sail came in sight & since that period various vessels have been arriving & our Boy has presented so lively an appearance that I have been at the spy glass all the morning– Admiral Elliot must be close at hand as the "*Larne*" sloop has hoisted the *white* ensign & saluted it– Sir George Elliot being "*Rear Admiral of the White*" he is uncle or cousin to our Captain Elliot– my mind is now quite at ease, one exception only, Mr Delano is still in Canton, when he gets out we shall all be at leisure to talk over the past & the future– I must have late letters at hand as there is a vessel in direct from Bombay– however I got such a lot by the *Panama* that I am quite patient & do not expect to get much more before I embark– at Anjier– I hope to find some late advices –I would take up your late letters & note all the interesting points in them but that they are so voluminous that it would require a day or two–

I can easily imagine what a quandary you must have been in at Bobs illness– this would not have disturbed my equanimity a moment– children must be sick, & they are liable even to die–...

I have lately received several letters from Bates & they are perfectly satisfactory, he had received some letters of mine on the trade generally & in the conduct of Elliot in particular, he says he does not reply in detail because Lord Ashburton (one of the Barings) wanted them to prepare himself for the approaching Parliamentary debates– on the China question– I did not expect when I went to sea a poor & pennyless Boy that my opinions & letters would be quoted in Parliament– perhaps Lord Ashburton will give out my opinions as his own– however these are very small matters after all– I doubt if I shall ever be a great man myself– I have not seen Mrs Coolidge for a long time & I do not intend to go to see her again unless it be as a matter of favour just as I am off– C has not been near me of late– & I don't intend to give him any reason to suppose that I crave his good will– he has made himself supremely ridiculous in all the transactions he has been engaged in & has acquired the reputation of being excessively mean in matters of trade– In short he is no better fitted to carry on business in Canton than you are–

Sunday evening– Since morning Parker has been here & made known his determination to go home in the *Niantic* with me at which I am very glad–...he tells me his friends are very anxious that he should go home & return– bringing a rib with him–...he is a pleasant companion & there is no objection to having a medical man at hand in case of need–...Since I left off this morning the

Melville 74[181] with Admiral Elliot & the *Blande* 44 with the *Pylades* 20 have anchored in the Roads– they left Singapore on the 18th & the *Blenheim* 74 with several other vessels of war transports &c were then in sight & will not be long in making their appearance– We are mere spectators in all these movements–

I dreamed a dream last night– me thought I was at some foreign Ambassadors & there met with Sally Nauton married to some diplomatist– her face & her manners were quite natural– I merely mention this believing that it will be considered a very strange thing if it should prove true–

Good Night dearest– Love to Bob & all

July 3– 11 PM

much busy as you may suppose preparing to embark in the *Niantic*, Capt Doty in a couple of days & as I dont intend that this shall reach you before her (per *Globe*) I write but sparingly by her– My excellent friend Dr Parker has concluded that in no way can he spend a year so well as in going with me to the land of the Jonathans–if I should want any thing done to soul or body on the way he will do it & therefore give yourself no uneasiness about me on the score of health– the *Niantic* made a long passage out but I think she will do better going home– I suspect the Doctor is going to look for a partner for life & I hope he will find one–I have also made interest & got Capt Jauncey a passage– he has an eye wounded by a gun shot in fighting some Mandarin junks up the Coast, & it is thought Parker can save the eye by taking him with us– so he goes– our accommodations are only so so– but the Capt is an excellent man and he will no doubt give us a welcome so that we shall be as well off as if we were in a palace with an uncompatable Capt– I trust carry this home from the Post Office myself– but as the *Globe* has the start we cant be sure of that–...

Just think of it– leaving China for home, crowned with success– well in health, in a good ship with good company– It keeps me awake to think of– I am so happy–[182]

Thine ever RBF

THE VOYAGE HOME

Sailed July 5, 6 PM Sunday
Private Journal to my wife
Canton– no–
Macao– no –
At Sea– yes– July 6, 1840

My dear Rose–

"There was an old woman, she lived in a Shoe & all she wanted was a place to move about in"– thats classical– aint it– Never was saying more true than that

---

181 The numbers after these warships note the number of cannons on board.

182 Although RBF barely mentions it, Captain Jauncey's encounter with the Chinese is described in detail in Maurice Collis' book, *Foreign Mud* (New York, A.A. Knopf, 1947)'...The *Hellas* (Captain Jauncey) was lying becalmed off the Brothers, islets on the coast at Namoa near Swatow (in late May). Close by were eight junks and three large rowing boats, which Jauncey mistook for traders, until they got out their sweeps and closed in on his schooner. He cleared for action, but the junks came up astern so that his broadside could not bear. When close enough their crews flung oil pots on to his decks, and set him afire, and in the confusion thought to board and overwhelm him. But while some of the *Hellas* crew dealt with the flames, others leaped on to the junks and fought with sword and pistol. For four hours a hand to hand struggle raged...Finally the Chinese jumped overboard and swam for their lives. In the fight Captain Jauncey lost an eye...Twenty five of his crew had nasty wounds.'

comfort is but comparative– like all the goods & evils of life– Well here I am on board the *Niantic* & I may as well go back & tell you how & when I got here & as for the *how*, I came by water– & as to the *when*, I came yesterday– but I must go back a little further– I had but just made up my mind to take the only *spare* birth in the *Niantic*, & a very *spare* one it is– when Dr Parker concluded that he must go & here he is & lucky it is too, for the Captain (Doty) is quite sick, he has been running about in the sun at Macao & is suffering the consequences– he has not been out of bed, except for *necessary* purposes since he left– I dined yesterday with Uncle James alone & kept up my spirits pretty well– he gathered a bundle of flowers & evergreens in his garden & has sent it to you under my charge, he also gave me a splendid female snuff box, inlaid with precious *gems* is not he a precious Jem too?

This is a present to you & you will be delighted–

I got up early yesterday morning & went with Dr Parker to visit the burying place where my Brothers remains lie– I found this a hard task– I gathered some evergreens there too & went home to prepare for my departure– I called on Mr Coolidge the day before– but I was so much occupied that I declined all invitations to feed away from home– When it was found Dr Parker was coming Mr Matheson urged me very strongly to let Capt Jauncy go– this man was badly wounded in the eye by a musket shot [in fighting some Mandarian junks up the Coast] – & it became necessary that he should go to a better climate & under the care of a Physician or lose the eye– so here he is...the ship...[is] crammed full...– however we are settling down into order & in a few days we shall be as well as if we were lodged in a Palace– I got the ship under way & was on deck nearly all last night beating out of the Landrone passage, however the weather is fine & the mates are good men so that there is no necessity in reality for my interference, but as the Capt has given me authority *I act* for amusement– Poor man he has been very sick all day– I will defer any further critiques on our "accommodations" until tomorrow as I am sleepy– Good Night

July 7

Capt D is a *very* sick man & unless there are some very favourable symptoms he stands a poor chance of recovery– nothing that he takes stays down & he is in a state of great exhaustion as well as somewhat inflamed internally– if Dr Parker were not here his case would be desperate– indeed he was so ill all day Sunday before we sailed that the ship would not have put to sea if Dr Parker were not here– I made myself extensively busy all day yesterday in preparing & arranging my "State room" which is about half the size of that on board the *Mary Chilton* say six feet long & 4 wide– herein is my birth or *bunk*, my wash stand & several trunks– Bobs picture hangs at my feet against the bulk head & a small print of Mr Sturgis giving called "poor relations" is by the side of it & the two occupy the whole width of my room– but then I occupy a corner & by hanging a curtain across this space I then have a splendid vestibule or anti-chamber about 3 feet square– to day I have been taking care of Dr Parker & his room– it cannot be said that his room is better than his company, the latter is more extensively useful to his friends, than any space of square feet– the space we inhabit also lodges the Capt (sick) Capt Jauncy (wounded) myself & my Boy & [Flora], the steward & a Chinese servant of the Drs who also is intended to act as Linguist & who throws water to windward– however these are all minor considerations, the wind is light & right ahead– however we contracted for a head monsoon & as we are homeward bound we say nothing– 10 years today since I left Boston in the *Lintin* & only 25 months since I left it in 1838– to be gone 3 years– I have stolen seven months off of my time– Tis too hot to write long yarns especially when I am homeward bound &– many people would say, "Whats the use of writing when you are going yourself" I would answer all such impertinent enquiries by saying because I feel as if I were more directly in Communication with you when I have my pen in hand

Love to Bob & good day–

July 9

All yesterday & to day Capt Doty has been quite ill, requiring Dr Parkers whole care & attention, as well as skill, he remains still in a critical state & I shall not feel perfectly assured that we shall save him until tomorrow–

In addition to him we have two very interesting lads sick with fever & ache whom I have had bought into the after cabin or store room where the Dr & I can attend to their wants– Our second mate is also ill, hardly able to get about– including Capt Doty we have nine sick, the weather so far has been very favourable which is extremely fortunate...– Capt Jauncy is improving & I hope the weather will continue good– so that our hospital may be less well filled– It seems as if Providence watched over me– what should I have done without Dr P– We are getting on as well as could be expected at this season of the year, though the ship is not a clipper– Love to Bob & good night Lat– 18 1/2 N 4 days out

Friday Evening 10 July

Our Captain is somewhat relieved & Dr Parker feels encouraged & thinks his chance of recovery better than it was yesterday– We have given him a warm bath to night & I hope the worst is over– but he is very weak & in some danger yet– Our steward is also "hors de combat" & both mates indisposed...out of 20 nearly one third are ill...Capt J had a shot cut out of his *eyelid* today & made as much fuss about it as if it had been an arm or a leg– for myself I am very well & as I am acting skipper I am in my element–...This morning passed to windward of the ship *Globe* about 6 miles she having left Macao 27 hours before us– this speaks well of the *Niantic* & the valour & discretion of her pro-tem Captain– Good Night

Saturday eve 11 July

...fine pleasant weather...winds...light...only 31 miles on our course & are now 6 days on our way–

Capt Doty brightened up a good deal this morning & I shaved him & cut his hair & he got up twice & went to our small house & Parker felt very much encouraged–...

Sunday Evening 12 July

...only 63 miles & we are much disappointed at getting no regular SW monsoon as we are in an excellent position to make good use of it– being near the Marcelsfield Bank– This evening ends our first week, Capt Doty is evidently improving, though as yet he takes very little nourishment– We had service from Dr Parker at 11 AM & I have been reading Fenelon & other good books– I think we are peculiarly under the protection of divine Providence in having such fine weather & in having Dr Parker to take care of Capt Doty– without the constant care of an experienced physician *he must have died*

Love to Bob & Good Night

Monday Evening–

...only 29 miles...– this evening we go on our course for the first time since we sailed but have a prospect of a squally night & as I am acting skipper it is not very well relished by me– however I am glad to be so usefully employed– Capt Doty appeared much better this morning but I am sorry to say that his symptoms are considered quite doubtful this evening– I fear that I shall have to record his death before many days– this will be a matter of serious import to me but I will not anticipate evil– I am well thank God– Good Night

Tuesday Evening 14 July–

...92 miles...– this afternoon we have had a steering sail set for the first time & have gone for a few hours on our course– This evening the wind is again light, the weather very pleasant– Captain Doty was so far gone this evening that Dr Parker thought proper to speak to him of the future (beyond this work day world) he told him his case was a dangerous one & not without hope– he bore the intelligence well– spoke of a desire to live for his wifes sake &c– I was not present– after this we gave him a warm bath & an anodyne & he was much refreshed & appears stronger– his pulse has come up from 65 to 76– & the Dr feels more hope–...our sick list is reduced to 5 or 6 & we are now doing bravely– good night–

Wednesday 15 July–

...all stud sails out– I hardly expected this morning, that Capt Doty would get through the day– but he has taken his warm bath this evening & brightened up a good deal, & at one time to day he talked about chicken bones– he bears up manfully & has his senses perfectly though he is very weak & my hopes are slender– I have got my turning lathe rigged & the first little box I turned was for Bobs curl–...

HURON

GALES AND SQUALLS

An eventful voyage home begins with heavy weather and a sick captain and crew. RBF takes over command of the vessel temporarily, and Dr. Parker treats the injured and sick – which include a British Captain wounded in the opium wars. At last, after five months at sea, the ship Niantic *sails into New York Harbor.* ▣

Thursday 16 July– 8 PM

...This morning I began to feel anxious about my night rest, the weather began to be squally & the Barometer to fall– I began in time took in Royals & sent yards down & made snug– at noon we were 113 miles from Land & after dinner reefed Top Sails & by 6 PM had no sail set but the close reefed main Top Sail & fore stay sail–...This evening the Barometer is very low & it rains a deluge– we are as snug as we well can be & there is nothing more to be done even if it blows a regular Tyfong– I am under some apprehensions of one & sleep will be a stranger to me to night–...I pray god we may not have the weather worse & that he will forgive me if I have been ungrateful for all the favours received at his hands– I am sure that you are praying for me & I have great confidence that all will go well– if not I shall say– Gods will be done–

Friday 17 July–

It has been blowing a gale at SW to WSW all last night & all to day– we have been without observations for two days & are consequently quite uncertain as to our situation– but for fear of a current setting us shoreward we have been carrying a press of sail– the ship behaves well, we have not had even a spray on board all day– though it has been raining in torrents in hard squalls– Capt Doty is much better & talks of what he shall eat tomorrow– I have had little or no sleep the last two nights & am a little headachy in consequence– This acting Captain involves a deal of anxiety & responsibility– yet without the command I should feel more anxious– We are particularly fortunate in having met this gale where there is plenty of sea room– The ship tumbles about too much to write & I must now express my gratitude to God for all favours & say good night

Saturday 18 July–

All last night it blew a gale of wind with violent squalls but as the ship was quite snug & headed in a course off shore I turned in & slept more than for several nights past & to day I have been quite brisk– Capt Doty sat up to day for the first time & wonderful to relate he is recovering fast– I shall be heartily glad when he is well enough to relieve me from the anxious & arduous situation that I now play– both the mates are sick though both are groping about trying to do their best– three or four of the men are sick also & two of the boys I have had brought aft into the lower cabin so that they can be under the eye of Dr Parker– add to all these annoyances a sick (sea sick) Chinaman, & a very filthy steward & you have the sum total of our situation– if Dr Parker & myself had not been here the mates would have given up in despair–...the gale has abated at last & we are again caricoling on our way– Our crew so short that I cannot venture to carry sail as I would if they were all well– however I shall make the best of it– if any other Port than Manilla were at hand I would put in & wait till we were in a better state to contend with the elements– my seafaring life stands me in good service & I ought to *charge* the owners for my work rather than *pay* a dollar for my passage– Our Barometer got a nock to day & is useless– What a chapter of unpleasant things say you– It is true but I do not quail– every thing now depends on my exertions & here comes a squall, so good night–

Sunday Evening 19 July–

Last night was an awful night, a fresh gale with heavy squalls which kept me up drenched to the skin a considerable part of the night– At 3 AM we had one squall that laid the ship almost on her beam ends, the fore tack gave way & the Jib went into a million pieces (more or less) however I took the speaking trumpet & soon got the ship snug– This forenoon we had some heavy squalls with intervals of fine weather, got the sun & finding our situation ran in for the land & we are now in the Straits of Northumberland having past the dangerous part before dark– I am exceedingly grateful for this & for moderate weather & almost a fair wind, Capt Doty convalescent– crew improving– myself (last not least) well, but almost burned up with the sun & wind & good night

MONDAY 20 JULY

Fine weather & a nice little run all day which have quite cheered us up– Capt Doty took his meals with us to day but he has fatigued himself rather too much to day & I have been obliged to order him into the cabin several times– I shall probably pretend to be angry with him tomorrow & threaten to give up all charge if he does not keep quiet– Our general sick is reduced to one consumptive youth & one old soldier– I am superlatively well & look forward to my dinner with almost the same satisfaction as I eat it–...I must attend to the ship

TUESDAY 21 JULY–

...75 [miles] which is considered fast travelling in these parts– Capt Doty improving, I ordered him to come into his cabin to day & have kept him quiet–...Capt Jauncy suffers a good deal with his broken jaw from which small pieces of bone come out occasionally– Flora is also doing well– being very busy hunting rats– last night we passed within hail of a ship which proved at day light to be the British Ship *Heroine*, she sailed a week before us–

22 JULY

...Capt Doty is going about mending daily but I tell him I *will not* resign the command until my three weeks are up on Sunday– Our crew is nearly well again– We are now sailing along the coast of Mindanao[183] & hope to be in the Straits of Basilian tomorrow night– Capt Jauncy has been suffering very much with his wounded chin & could not join us at table to day–

JULY 23–

...8 oclock PM... Fine weather throughout & moderate wind made decently good progress for a head wind–...I have been turning today and shall make some nine pins for Bob before I get home– as well as some other pretty things– good night

JULY 24–

...smooth sea & pleasant weather wind very light & our progress small– We are not very far from the Straits of Basilian– hope to get through tomorrow– good night

JULY 25 8 PM

Here we are in the middle of the straits of Basilian & almost becalmed– the weather is fine & we hope to get a land wind & get through in the course of the night– I resigned the command this morning & Doty is quite well again which is of course a great relief to me– the contrast between this calm sea & the troubled waters of last Saturday is as great as it is agreeable–

---

[183] Mindanao (Lat 5.32 N– Lon 9.5 W) is the southernmost and second-largest of the Philippine Islands.

Sunday evening July 26–

...clear of the Basilian Straits and in the Celebes Sea...– Had service this morning & a sermon from Dr Parker & prayers & a chapter or a portion of the scripture to all hands assembled in the cabin this evening– I doubt the expediency of daily prayers to all hands but am very happy to have any thing done to please the good DR– All hands but one are pretty well– good night– Love to Bob–

Monday evening–

A *very* moderate day & fine weather, we have more wind to night but it is nearly dead ahead, hope to have it more favourable tomorrow– I have been rather head achy & bilious to day & have been off my feed– a blue pill to night (No2) will set me right–

Tuesday Evening 28 July–

...At 9 this morning a heavy squall rose & as I thought Doty took it (before it came) rather too coolly– I should most certainly have been better prepared for it– it blew a gale for an hour or two & obliged us to let every thing run– the Jib fore sail & main Top sail were all more or less damaged, the two first so badly as to oblige us to change them, I took the helm during the squall & increased my bilious head ache which has lasted me all day & I must take some medicine to night– I have been reading over many of your letters to day with great satisfaction, & occasionally reading some of your sentiments & witticisms to Dr Parker who no doubt thinks that you & the Boy are perfect– how much mistaken a very good man may be on such a subject–! I expect a restless night though the weather is good–...good night

Wednesday evening 29 July–

Fine weather all day & current against us so that I have nothing very good to record of our progress– took pills last night & salts this morning am better to night though painful–...

Thursday 30 July–

...moderate breeze *dead ahead* and pleasant weather– I have been employed in turning an elegant rose wood box for Uncle Jimmy & in mending Dr Parkers lamp which got smashed a day or two since– I am very well to day– we live like fighting cocks– Then to cut a bottle off (for a lamp shade) tie a piece of yarn round the place to be cut off & dip the yarn in spirits of turpentine or alcohol, then light it & when the fire has gone out immerse the hot glass in cold water & it snaps off at the part where the yarn is tied round just as if it were cut off with a knife– this we tried successfully to day–

Saturday 1 August–

...nearly calm & our progress has consequently been very slow–...took to cigars again yesterday after an intermission of a week– this is a sign of good health– I am reading Ferd & Isabella– We are only about 90 miles from the straits of Macassar at the rate we have been going lately we shall be three days getting into them Love to Bob & good night

Sunday evening 2 August–

4 weeks out & shall not be up with Macassar Straits until tomorrow– I consider that we are now 1/5 of our time consumed– this past week has been a very tedious one...wind light– direction...good, the evening is splendid– Doty has

entirely recovered I find him an obliging man & very anxious to please us, indeed he carries this so far that it is almost annoying– he is so anxious to have every thing well cooked & "got up" that he is in a constant "fuze" with the dirty brute of a steward & instead of letting us eat our meals in peace he is giving lessons to the cook & steward in no stinted measure– I stand caterer & we live very well indeed–

I have nearly cured the Capt of licking the nose of the molasses butter boat by simply putting a large spoon into it to dip out with after he has indulged his fancy in that way– But these are annoyances which should be beyond the notice of a good Christian...

Monday Evening Aug 3–

A very small days work to day & an adverse current of 25 miles– the Coast of Celebes in sight this evening & at this moment we have a light fair wind & are setting the steering sails– I fear it may be very transitory– but hope for the best– good night

Sunday Evening 9 August–

Last Sunday I thought before this time, to have been through the Straits of Macassar & near Batavia but we are further from the Land than we were a week ago–...calms all the week almost without intermission, & a constant current against us has rendered negatory all our efforts to get on– my patience is waxing very short, the weather has been fine all the time– I have been at work at my lathe about 4 hours a day & earned an appetite & until last evening have been perfectly well– I had one of my sour stomach & faint turns & took an emetic– I am well this evening only weak– Love to Bob & good night

August 15th Saturday Evening–

...slow progress..not yet...into the Straits of Macassar, we have had a week of head winds & calms with hot weather but no rain & a fine moon– the current has not favoured us a single day– I have been pretty well all the time only my emetic strained me & makes me sore inside & this is aggravated by the calms & other adverse circumstances– Parker has been reviewing his letter of last year about my health & he says, after another examination of me, that I have no organic disease & this is sufficiently proved by my being as well as I was a year ago– The Dr has found out that his Chinese Boy is a thief & a consumer of opium & if an opportunity presents he will be sent back– his ears should be clipped first–

August 20 Tuesday

...creeping along only 25– 40 miles per day & are still almost becalmed– we have accomplished one point however & that is to get into South Latitude– I had another bad day the day before yesterday & am now undergoing a system of diet– the Dr sticks to it that my pains are Rheumatic– I say gout– gout– gout–

Sunday Evening– August 23–

7 weeks– 49 days out & all well–...

60 & more miles to day & that is a great days work for us of late– We are now returning for the Two Brother Islands & have a good night to expect to see them by 2 AM if not sooner & if the Trade continues we ought to be at Anjer in four or five days, say the latter & if I dont get some letters from you as late as April I shall be very much disappointed– We have just got through prayers & Dr

is now amusing himself with his usual cogitations–

Good night & God protect thee & *us*– we want it as much as you do, as our Captain & officers are not *over* vigilant & prudent–

25th

...54 days [out]– I have been turning to day & finished reading Charles the 5th– I cannot but relate a little incident which to day took place– Flora shewed uneasiness all day & yesterday, but devoted herself to Dr Parker– she favoured him & barked as she usually does if wanting water or food– but in general she appeals to me or to my Boy Joe– but on this occasion she insisted on begging of Dr Parker & to such a degree that he was attracted by it & he said to me that she was unwell, that something ailed her– that she was feverish– I felt of her nose & opened her mouth to look at her tongue, when the mystery was solved, by some accident she had got a stick about the size of a crow quill so firmly fixed across her upper jaw & on the roof of her mouth that it could not be removed without the Dr forceps & after considerable force– the ends of the stick were embedded in the skin & the place where the stick lay had become sore, it must have been there some days– the poor thing seemed very grateful when it was removed, though she struggled a good deal from the pain it gave her– I have no hesitation in saying that she had noticed the Dr operating on Capt Jauncys broken jaw...& of course appealed to him–...it shows a degree of sagacity which endears me still more to Flora– dont be jealous– good night

CALLING AT ANJIER

Thursday 27 August– 53 days out–

We shall be at Anjer (probably) tomorrow morning & I therefore close my journal to leave there to be forwarded per first good opportunity– not that I think *it will* get home before me, but that *it may* & it will be a great satisfaction to you to have it if I should miscarry (which God forbid)– since we have got into the Java Sea I find the ship sails better but she is far from being a clipper...– Doty is not a hard driver & the ship rather dull & if Dumaresq were starting with him he would beat him a month, more or less– God bless thee & Bob & all friends & believe me thine ever– RB

Niantic clear of Java Head
September 1, 1840
Dear Rose,

...[At Anjier] we have taken on board an immense supply of all the necessaries of life & shall not be likely to starve on the way although our passage has been long thus far, some have had much longer– the *Calumet* dispatched by us on the 14 June only got clear of Anjer some four or five days since– & I shall I trust get home before my clay coolies– I continue my journal so that if we fall in with any fast ship– she can take you an a/c of our progress –We are all pretty well *Adios*

Monday 14 September–

Since the above we have been doing very well, say our average of 160 to 170 miles per day & we are now within three days sail of the Isle of France, which we shall not probably see– the last two days we have been going famously with almost a gale, Dr Parker makes a very poor sailor he is very timid & very clumsy & knocks about sadly– he *sometimes* quotes, but *never* practices Chesterfield but he has so many redeeming qualities that I forgive him many faults of "*maniere*", his bump of "savoir vivre" is fully developed, but his "savoir faire" is not prominent– if I were Captain & had only Parker with me I would improve by him & make him improve *by me*– Jauncy is quiet– Gentlemanly & has fewer John Bull prejudices than most Englishmen– the Captain is attentive to us & thinks he is very vigilant, but there are many things which escape him which meet my eye– he is however more active & has better judgement than my little snuffling Skipper Drew had & so we get on remarkably well, my Boy Joe is invaluable & is now acting steward, the ships steward being sick– Bob is before me & although he is not the real Bob, nor like him, I enjoy his society vastly more than that of the thousand cockroaches which infest my cabin, but poor things! they are getting benumbed this cool weather & beginning to keep close the point of "poor relations" hangs at one end of my birth & is so good that I propose to illustrate it some day when I am in the scribbling vein– I am building a pilot boat Sch for Bob on which I employ a part of my forenoon when the weather is good & the rest of the day I read, am now reading Spark's American Biography & have just perused the life of Arnold for the third time, the fate of Andre must be familiar to you, it was very cruel, cruel by the laws of war, but just by the same rule– we are now 71 days from China & 14 from Java head & I now calculate on getting to New York in 77 more– they will pass more rapidly than the last as we shall have fewer calms & head winds– good day

Friday Evening 8 Oclock 18 September 1840–

& my birth day– It is now about one oclock with you & I dare say you are thinking about what you shall have for dinner– *perhaps* you are thinking of me– I am sure you will have up a bottle of wine & drink my health at 1/2 past 2– I will wager a guinea that you have not half so good a dinner as we had– Ours consisted of Turtle Soup (real turtle) Turtle Cutlet– Turtle Curry– Sweet potatoes & yams & flapjacks to wind up with & all well cooked– I drank *two glasses* of Port, a thing I have not done for many a day– I have not drunken a dozen glasses in a month & no beer–

Jauncy was to have made a real English plumb pudding but not being very well it is put off till a more convenient Season–

At my suggestion we cleared out all the moveable things from our round house or cabin & exterminated about a million of cockroaches– I have put down my woolen carpet & made my berth very comfortable– but to return to the glorious 18 of Sept– this is the third I have spent afloat since I left home– one in the *Chilton*, one in the *Edmonton* & this one–

I have not remembered one when I had more to be grateful for–...Fortune has attended me & I am grateful–...[we] are a days sail past the Isle of France or Mauritius–[184] We shall probably be round the Cape in 18 more & then every mile tells *strait home* Bob & you & Mother are thinking of me so I will take a walk on deck & think of you– adieu

Tuesday 22 Sept–

...I told my messmates that it was rather apocryphal whether I was born on the 18 or 19 it being very late at night on the 18 & it was supposed that my head might have appeared on the 18 & my feet on the 19– so we celebrated two birth days & drank your health & Bobs– We had Turtle again to day & excellently cooked– I cannot help recapitulating for your edification all the blessing

[184] Mauritius, formerly Ile de France (Lat 20N–Lon 55E), is an island nation occupying 804 square miles in the Indian Ocean.

n the following two pages, in a gouache painting by an unidentified artist, is Anjier Point in Java, one of the landfalls for RBF's Niantic *on the passage from Canton to New York. The vessel called at the nearby port of Anjier for supplies.*

temporal & spiritual which we have within our reach–

First– Clergyman & Physician– of good quality– three Captains, Cook, Steward & two servants–

We have natives of America, England, China, Manila, Sweden, Denmark, Western Islands, Africa, Cat, Dog, Rats, Pigs, Turtle, Capons, Ducks, Hens, Geese, Monkeys, Parrots, Java Sparrows, Mice, Cockroaches, Spiders, Fleas, L__ce &c–

Salt Beef, Pork, Tongues, Ham, Salmon, Soups, Preserves, Anchovies, Buffalo Humps, Navy Bread, Pilot Bread, fine Boat crackers, china sweet Cakes good, Flour, Indian meal, Sage, Arrow Root, Vermicelli, Rice, paddy, Yams, Sweet Potatoes fine, Excellent tea, Coffee, Two kinds of chocolate, Sugar candy, sugar candy sugar, white sugar, Brown Sugar, molasses Lemon syrup, Port, Madeira, Sherry, Claret, Cherry Rum, Beer, Congress water, Soda water just our– Raspberry Syrup, Nectar powders, Sarsaparillas, China water, Anjer water, Salt water, Pickles, Preserved fruits for Tarts, dried Apples, pumpkins, Pine Apples, Coconuts, Bananas just gone, Capers, Mustard, Cheese, good Butter, Sweet Herbs in bottles, spices plenty, Eggs plenty, Brandy, Gin, Cigars three kinds, Books in abundance, in short *every thing* but female society, when I say we have all the things enumerated I mean to say, that they are all good of there kind & that we know how to *use* without abusing them– Tis now nearly prayer time & I must put away my goose quil– We have two ships ahead & shall probably be up with them tomorrow– I think they are the same two Dutchmen whom we saw in *Sunda* Straits...

Monday 28 Sept 1840
Lat 31 S Long 35 1/2 E

Dear Rose,

Yesterday at 11 just as we had finished our "divine service" we came up with & spoke the British Ship *Tamerlaine*, Capt MaKenzie 49 days from Calcutta bound to London, via St Helena, Captain Doty gave me the speaking trumpet & I hailed him "com il faut", I asked him for a news paper & he kindly lowered his boat & sent me one & in return I sent him some china papers– he left the 4 August & consequently could not tell me of the safe arrival of the *Akbar*, as she only left Sincapore on the 24 July & would not be in Calcutta till the 10th to 15th– Soon after we bade him good bye & gained on him a fine breeze sprang up at NE & we went along merrily till 8 oclock when the wind died away partially, in the course of the evening it began to lighten to the SW, which in winter I consider a sure indication of a sudden shift in wind, but as we had experienced several false alarms we did not feel confident of bad weather, the weather had been fine so many days that I fell anxious & went to bed at 10 expecting to be turned out before morning– At 1/2 past 12 I was awakened by a great bustle on deck, I turned out & found the sky as black as ink & the ship aback & the sails flying in great confusion, the Captain evidently alarmed & giving a dozen incoherent & contrary orders all at once– I called Joe & took the helm & got in the Spinnaker & mizzen Top sail & for two or three hours while we were making the ship snug it rained & blew & thundered & lightened in the most awful manner & it seemed almost a miracle that the lightning did not strike us– I never saw it blacker before, no object could be distinguished at a yards distance & the frequent & vivid flashes of lightning seemed only to show objects for an instant to make them more indistinct, I remained on deck steering the ship till all sail was made snug, it was very fortunate for us that the wind did not blow very hard or we should have lost some of our sails– At 4 AM it began to clear away & now 11 AM it is very fine weather with a confused sea & all sail out again–

I put on board the *Tamerlaine* what I had ready of my journal under care of Barings, the idea crossing my mind that an accident (say lightning) might prevent you from ever hearing from me again– & This would probably seem a ridiculous idea to many, but *to us* I think it will not– all ships are liable to disasters & delays as well as to entire annihilation & why should I not take the trouble to commune with you as long as possible–

We are now within five days sail of the Cape of Good Hope, though I should be very glad to compromise for 10 clear of it, we have yet 64 days before December & I flatter myself we shall be home in 60– however I take things very patiently the great secret of which is in keeping constantly employed at something *recreative*, my health is excellent & I flatter myself that I *look* better than I have for years– a good colour clear eyes, & an incipient pair of whiskers help to make up the sum– Bob is reflected in my looking glass at the end of my "state room" so that whichever way I look, I see the little dog– Flora comes in to lick my hand while I am writing & seems grateful as I am to Providence for a happy fine out of our troubled night– had I been in command of the ship I should not have felt half so anxious, because I should have been busily employed & I flatter myself to better purpose than Doty was– he has not *tact* or talent– no system & consequently much time is lost– Love to Bob & good bye for to day–

October the 7th–

Here we are running before a superlatively fine breeze & nearly up with the Cape of Good Hope, that great "big bear", we shall be up with it at 3 or 4 oclock this PM & we have not had a single *gale of wind* & only one or two double reefed breezes...On Monday 5th Inst we fell in with an American ship which I pronounced to be *Calumet* & accordingly about 12 past 9 in the evening she passed across our bow on the opposite tack & proved to be her, we were rather too far from her to leeward to make them hear our name– she left China 20 days before us & left Batavia on the 23 August where she stopped to get water– she will probably be home some ten days after us & she carries some presents for Bob– I have just finished Bobs schooner & a pretty one she is I assure you– The same evening that we spoke the *Calumet*, a fine French Bark passed within hail bound to Mauritius from Bordeaux– we had no time to hear news as he was going rapidly before the wind, it is singular that we should have spoken two ships within half an hour of each other at sea, it was a fine moon light night–

We get on very well as to living & have not as yet quarrelled– Capt Doty is not blessed with a very sweet temper, but he only vents this upon the Cook, steward & chief mate & when the wind is fair he has got fairly awake he is quite tolerable, though he makes *even me* nervous by diving at the food like a vulture & he is not very much encumbered with tact in small matters– however he tries to please & I should be ill natured indeed if I complained–...Parker is full of the *milk* of human kindness though this sometime curdles a little wants skimming & boiling over– he is very much wanting in good manners for a man who has been in Canton 6 years– & had the advantage of good society so long– par example, he eats always with his knife & half the time with the edge, sometimes uses his fingers to blow his nose, gulps at table– he is a great coward & whenever the wind or weather is at all threatening he sleeps but little & asks a thousand silly questions, I feed his fears sometimes for amusement by predicting squalls &c &c– Then he pretends to be very weather wise but he knows nothing about it– These are nearly all the great sins I can bring against him & they are not worth recording except for amusement– We have prayer & a chapter in the Bible every evening when the weather is good, that is, when the Dr calls it good– We are not likely to have any very bad weather until we get on the Coast of America, though we may have some before we get the trade wind–

Doty has not decided whether to touch at Saint Helena but he intends taking an accurate a/c of all our provisions & ascertaining whether it will be necessary to do so– The weather has been & is now very fine, indeed I never saw so little rain before in 94 successive days– All hands are well, love to Bob & adios...

ABOVE THE TROPIC, WEST OF THE MERIDIAN OF GREENWICH

Sunday 18 Octo

in Lat about 22 S– Long 4 West

...131 [daily]...with good weather– We have now accomplished two more of the stages of our voyage...say the Tropic of Capricorn & the Meridian of Greenwich, being now in West Longitude– We have examined our stores, water &c & find enough for 60-70 days on full allowance & therefore we are not to stop at St Helena– I regret this but little & my curiosity would hardly have tempted me to land & visit the Tomb of Napoleon provided my remaining on board would expedite our departure an hour– My cry is home, home, home– we have now 13 days from to day in October & that should be enough to carry us to the next stage (the Equator) then we shall have the whole of November to get home in & if we have an ordinary chance & no interruption on the coast we should be in New York by the 25th or the anniversary of the evacuation of that City by the British & also the more important circumstance of my having entered it on that day from my first attempt at sea in 1818 & also the day on which I again visited it some years after & as I am fond of coincidences I think that will be the day of our arrival, still I shall not be excessively enraged if we do not arrive till the 1st of Dec–

Patience is my motto & I continue to while away my time quickly, if not profitably, I found during the first part of our passage that idleness was luxury, I had been so overworked, that mere in action of mind & body seemed most pleasant– but this soon wore away & as my health improved I found that I must go *to work* & I apportioned my time, working all the forenoon at my lathe & reading & writing in the afternoons, the latter I soon found induced drowsiness & I have during the last month or more worked from 9 AM to 1 PM, dined & sat an hour & then worked again till 1/2 past 5– when the weather admitted, & made two models of vessels & partly rigged them & have turned various useful things for my friends–

We have just got through *service* I suppose it should be called "*divine service*" but I do not think that sitting in a drizzly rain with ones hat off can be divine especially when the subject descanted on was a medical lecture on the structure of man & an attempt to draw a parallel between the wonderful mechanism of that animal & a ship– I suppose the Drs object is to do good, I could tell him that misplaced zeal does no good– "*Jack*" does not like to be kept out of his bed after being up 8 hours of the night to hear a dull sermon in the cold & so it does him no good– ...

be our passage long or short it is very clear that we are heartily tired of each other & of the ship– it requires a very steady fair wind & good weather to elicit smiles & wit– Jauncy is evidently disappointed that we are not going to Helena as he intended to leave us there & await of a ship for home provided one should have appeared– he has been about some dozen years or more & is anxious to get home–

For my part I am as resigned & as contented as any in *practice* tho the Dr *preaches* both every day– I am quite amused at the Drs attempts to draw me into talking on the subject of matrimony– you have been already told that he is *suspected* of going home for the purpose of getting a wife though he does not admit it & puts his departure down entirely to the score of ill health– he evidently wants some one to talk to him on the subject of the unalloyed happiness of the married state &c &c– & this to feed his desire to "commit matrimony"– he wants *insensibly* to be led on to think of it at first & "perpetrate" it afterwards– I *will not* humour him–

I will give you an idea of what I mean by writing out a late conversation in full– in dialogue– The evening was very fine & the wind fair & just after sun set we began to walk the deck by ourselves–

Dr– This is a most lovely evening, don't it carry you home?

I– Yes Dr– but the wind is light, it carries me rather too slowly–

Dr– I have often wished to ask those who know by happy experience, if the reality, the realization of the dreams of that unfortunate class of men called Bachelors, ever come to pass– or rather if the married state brings with it more of the good & less of the evils than they anticipate or the reverse?

I– Why Dr that's rather a hard question; if you ask me, respecting *my* experience I can reply promptly, but if you ask me a general question to be replied to generally, from my own observation, I must hesitate a little–

Dr– I ask the question in a general sense of course–

I– Then I should say that the anticipations of the young & sanguine who only look at the bright side of the picture of matrimony, who never allow the cares of wedded life a single thought & dwell only on the sweets are in general disappointed, but the man who has been buffeted by the world & arrived at years discretion & who has selected an appropriate helpmate & *secured a competency* to make the pot boil is likely to realize more than he anticipated especially if he be blessed with good children–

Dr– Thats just my view of the case & I should think that as many happy connections are made without a very long acquaintance as after it, & that the passion of love is more dangerous to permanent happiness than the *moral sentiments* so called is indispensably necessary–

I– It is a good deal of a lottery after all, when love, whether as a passion or a sentiment is made *the business of life* to make matrimony *the end,* man may be easily deceived for the object is then arrayed in her Sunday garb & the true character does not appear– Where time is abundant it is better to let nature, chance, fate or destiny take its course–

Dr– I don't like to hear you speak of fate or destiny, or chance, nothing happens by chance & man makes his own fate & destiny as he goes along–

I– True Dr– but you know very well what I mean, I mean to say that the right kind of love steals one unconsciously like a thief in the night– it must not be sought as a business– the inoculation must "take" in the natural way– this is fate, destiny, chance–

Dr– Ah– now I see we mean the same thing only we express it differently– But the transient visitor has a poor chance, he comes to day & goes tomorrow, when as the fixed resident has ample time to profit by the advice of friends &

his own experience & is much more likely to stumble on what you call, "fate or destiny" by "chance"?

I– That is partially but not wholly true, for although I am not a believer in love at first sight, I really think that when a man has made up his mind to be married & has the means, he at once becomes susceptible to that fate or chance & it comes upon him suddenly & imperceptibly too–

Dr– It may be so– I think it quite probable it is, indeed I have known some very happy connections where the parties had a very slight knowledge of each other–

Here he cited several instances of missionaries who had married just before dragging some poor victim to Africa or some other savage land & then he added–

Judicious friends are very necessary, particularly where the fancy, the taste is struck & a short acquaintance renders it impossible to become well acquainted with the character of the object– the accomplishments & the exteriour may be seen but the heart, the character is enveloped in impenetrable mystery without *judicious* friends to shew it to one–

I– The great difficulty is in selecting a "judicious" friend, confidence is dangerous, little less so than the risk of choosing at random– we all see objects differently–

Dr– Certainly the selection of the proper person to tell the truth in such an important matter is almost as difficult as the making of the choice unaided by assistance–

and here the Dr related an instance of a friend of his who wrote to him in the highest terms of a lady who had heard him preach & who had expressed the warmest approval of his address &c– but on a casual & accidental acquaintance he found all true as far as related to accomplishments, but for the rest no inducement could have given him the eyes of his friend! Finding the Dr was determined to come to the point I said plainly– But Dr before you have been in Framingham a month you will doubtless see some fair lady of old acquaintance & find out that you have been in Love with her ever since you saw her last!

Dr– Oh no– I fear it will never be *my* happy lot to be married, I must return to my place in China with re-strung nerves & health & I shall never see home again, I look forward to a return to China as my greatest pleasure–

I– But Dr you would be quite unpardonable to return to China, to your sphere of usefulness without a partner & a helpmate to assist & cheer you in your love, & arduous pilgrimage, you could be much more useful & perhaps ladies will be tolerated in Canton & perhaps I will build a second *Akbar* & take Mrs RBF & the little RBF's to China & you will then surely agree to take Mrs Parker– ?

Dr– Ah– that indeed might be a consideration & as you say, if I happened on the right person I could do a great deal more good–

I– Decidedly Dr– get married by all means– but beware of sisters– sisters are dangerous confidants in matters so momentous– Look for a fair lady of nearly your own age, who is accomplished without being a blue stocking, good religious without being a fanatic, good tempered yet spirited enough to have a mind of her own– get these & all the rest will come in due course–

Dr– But I should labour under a disadvantage having been long absent from America I am not known & the Lady would not like to give me encouragement not knowing me, however as my character may be said to be a public one I may not find that an obstacle–

Whew! think I to myself there's modesty for two & I made up my mind as I have before that the Dr means to be married if he can get any decent woman to have him after an acquaintance of a month & here comes dinner & so adios for to day–

Sunday 25 October–

...average of 140 miles per day, I trust however that the new moon which we shall have to day will bring us a fresher trade & that before another one shall have got large enough to do us much service I shall be with you– The idea of being home in 35-40 days is one that I consider almost as a dream; how much I have to be grateful for! if no adverse cloud darkens my commercial prospects & which I have no reason to expect I shall have accomplished a fortune in two & a half years of exile & toil painful toil to be sure, but it is all past– I hope I have a wife & child to meet me at home, to say a thing of a mother & many affectionate friends– I do not allow myself to doubt this of a moment & I am grateful & happy–

Yesterday was Bob's birthday & we celebrated it in due form killing a fat goose & drinking his health (Bob's not the gooses) in a glass of Uncle Jimmy's fine claret sent him by Mr Cushing–

The weather has been, & is, superlatively fine & tho' the suns rays are to day, perfectly vertical, or in other words, the declination of the sun & our Latitude are the same, & this altitude is 90 degrees, a cloth jacket in the day & a blanket at night, are quite comfortable– I have been industriously employed all the week on the Sch "*Lark*" & she begins to assume the appearance of a real live ship, she is a beauty, I thought of making her for little Johnny Cushing but she is so handsome that I think I shall keep her for myself! The one I first made, is thrown quite in the shade, she looks sorry & sad & neglected,

Tho' she's as fit for the peg hand as any that's made,
And her fame shall be protected–
Dr Parker he says that Boys what plays
With ships, will become sailors,
He might as well say, that one of these days
With pin hooks to fish makes whalers–
Love to Sally & Maam Smith–

Sun 8th November–

...I consider our progress very fair– last night we had a baffling squally night with rain, thunder & lightening & I am annoyed at the want of proper economy of the wind, for instance the Captain is called & without going on deck to get a little wet he undertakes to give orders, whereas he should either brave the weather or let the officer of the deck judge what is best, in the cabin no one can judge half so well what is best to be done & the consequence is a too careful taking in sail– I consider that a want of good management in this & some other respects has lost us a full week– I said before that we are getting heartily tired of each other– but when I feel ill natured I retire to my "state room" & take a book– however I am not often very savage for I keep constantly at work during the day & as I seldom take a nap except Sundays by day, I sleep well at night–...in Canton I used to be almost afraid to look in the glass & when I did it made me feel worse, but now I take pleasure in contemplating my face in the mirror particularly as Bob's picture is reflected in it, I am cultivating quite a pair of pepper & salt whiskers–...I do not allow myself to doubt for a moment that you & Bob are also well, tho' I can imagine how anxiously you must hear the wintry winds howl around your house & imagine I am suffering by them–...The Doctor almost annoys me by his cowardice respecting the weather & if he has no more courage in his missionary labours he will never be a shinning light among the heathen– he says he is determined to devote the whole of his life to China & that when he embarks again for that far distant land, he will take a last look at his native hills– *but I know better*–...I have dreamed twice lately of seeing Bob– once he appeared dark & manly not handsome, once surprisingly fair & beautiful– I expect a medium– it is now time to go to church so adios– I dare say you will pray for me to day at the chapel–

SUNDAY 15 NOV–
When I wrote last Sunday we were just going to hear the Dr– he began a very decent sermon on the atonement– but getting nervous at a little squall he broke off in the midst & dismissed his congregation– they ran off to their births & not a rag of sail was taken in– he has just given us the rest of the sermon left unfinished– the Doctor is not a fascinating preacher that is a fact–

We are now in the Latitude 21 N & Long 53 1/2 & ten days would easily carry us in– I fear however it will be more– we have not done so well as I expected this week– Yesterday the wind was variable & for several days it has acted very much as if the trade was about deserting us, but this morning it has again come from the right quarter (NE)

A brig passed near us this AM but too far off to speak her –...

THE ADVENTURES OF PEDRO

We had quite a startling occurrence a few nights since, we shipped a man named Pedro, a Manila man at Macao of late he has showed symptoms of insanity so much so that I feared he would make way with himself– the Dr gave him medicine & did not advise his being confined– so he was allowed to go about as he pleased, his disease showed itself in melancholy– a belief that he never should get home– he talked of going overboard with his chest &c– but as these facts were not made known at first I took no active part in advising respecting him– well, a few nights since it being very smooth & pleasant after prayers Pedro was missing & it was ascertained that, he had been last seen at 8 oclock going over the bows into the head, this (as all seamen know) was not calculated to excite any alarm– at the time– a search was instituted & continued all over the ship below & aloft & no Pedro could be found, even the hen coop & the paint locker were examined– after an hour he was given up for lost, & then several of the men said he had appeared anxious to leave the ship & he had asked some of them to assist him in getting his trunk on deck & he had once been persuaded to come in from over the bows– I felt sorry that I had not advised his being confined originally, not so much in his own a/c as on a/c of the safety of the rest as he might go overboard in the night & then get sorry of his folly & cry out to be saved, this would naturally cause great confusion & the chances would be that in trying to save him we might lose one or more valuable lives– however the Dr was attending to him, I thought it not my place to interfere, & poor Pedro being gone, it would not be worth while to cast my reproaches in any one even if deserved, I said nothing therefore– his bunk was brought aft & examined for papers or any thing which might lead to the knowledge of his place of birth &c –about 10 oclock the Drs servant Asung a Chinese came running aft as if he had seen a ghost & said Pedro was over the bows– we all ran forward & discovered him laying at full length on the lower knee of the

Cutwater, where a monkey could hardly go, I will show you on my little ship the place where he lay, a man went down in a rope & Mr Pedro was hauled in & after a great deal of persuasion he was made to swallow some medicine & at my earnest request & advice was put in confinement in the steerage, not tied or in irons, but merely shut down there with his trunk, the next morning when search was made for him he was found in a state of nudity shoved away in a hole where Flora could hardly go– he is very quiet & very unhappy & watched, but not strictly enough & I feel assured that he will yet give us the slip or make way with himself– he speaks but little English & he imagines that all are against him– he has been treated kindly always & I presume his insanity is constitutional–...

I feel that I owe John a debt of gratitude which though it will be difficult to pay, I shall bear up under with the conviction that few Brothers have ever been so attached & to few would the exertions he has made, & the risks he has taken give more pleasure– I feel somewhat doubtful about his health & mothers, & I think John has a good deal of anxiety in store for Sarahs health & that of his children– but about you and Bob– though I know you to be mortal, I have no doubts, I expect to find you both well, you in a state of excitement at my protracted arrival, particularly if the *Globe* gets in first & which I think will be the case by three or four days– My imagination is brought up to the highest pitch about Bob's looks & actions too– I sometimes imagine that you will send him to walk in Beacon Street every morning at 8 or 9 oclock so that, I may meet him in the street & know him– that would be *fat* & I think over how *cooly*, I should accost him & ask what his name is & if he knows me?

Let us go through with the whole scene– Imagine me getting out of the cars at 9 AM a fine cold day, call a hack & away I go with my small trunk– I go through Charles Street & into Beacon St– halfway up I meet a *gal* with a fine fit boy *leading her* or perhaps running ahead & picking up snow or ice to throw at some one, he has got a handsome jockey cap on & a short blue frock & white trousers– his cheeks red as *Roses* (used to be)– Thats him exclaim I– hullo hackman, stop! & undoing the door, out I jump & run to him, thus undoing my first attempt at being cool– I cast my eye at Nathan Appletons window & then seeing several familiar faces just looking out & recognizing me, I endeavour to be cool & running up to Bob & say "Hello my little man whats your name" he looks up with a roguish eye & says "I guess I know"– "your name is Bob" says I & "I am your Papa" he looks at me doubtingly & replies– "I guess I am Bob– But I guess you aint Papa, because his whiskers are not so long & they are not *all* grey– I then catch him to my heart & he begins to cry & wonder what it all means– we go into the carriage & home & then________

SUNDAY 22 NOVEMBER–

This has been a very tedious week & we have made only five or six hundred miles, & at noon shall be 950 from New York...I think if we are not in by the 29th we shall not be till after the first– On Wednesday we boarded the English Brig *Horatio* from Barbados for Glasgow 8 days out & from him we got intelligence from England to August & newspaper accounts from America to May– these are very old but still are several mos later than we have had & I was very glad to find there was no war of consequence existing among the civilized nations– I think I smell bad times at home however as in May the spring trade had been dull– last night I dreamed of tombs & coffins but of no ones in particular, & I dont think I am superstitious enough to feel at all anxious in consequence of my dream, but I record it for reference– We have just had a good sermon from Dr Parker & the weather is like summer still– we sat on deck with our heads uncovered as usual & our doors are all open, though a blanket at night is not objectionable–...I can hardly realize that I am so near home– it seems like a dream– I think you will get my *Globe* letters on Thursday & then wont you be in a fidget until I get in– Flora has had two good washings & is pretty clean– We have caught plenty of fresh water & are well supplied with every thing– Butter, Fowls, *last goose to day,* one pig more, Indian meal, pumpkins, potatoes we got out of the *Horatio*– Salmon, Sardines, currants, gooseberries, cherries, the most remarkable thing we have is a *pet hen* which was permitted to go about deck a long time– one day she was missed & I supposed the Steward had killed her, particularly as the mate said he saw her feathers at the cook house, well two or three days since the spars near the long boat were moved to clean– then poor Biddy was found jammed in where she could not move an inch, she was still alive but reduced to a mere skeleton, I took care of her, giving her Indian meal mush & water, & cleaned her, to day she is running about almost as well as ever, she had been *buried* nearly 3 weeks & could not have had a morsel to eat & only salt water & the drippings of one or two light showers to sustain life that is to be preserved & Capt Doty– has promised to take her home & after making him a visit she is to be sent to Boston to me for a pet for Bob–

Pedro has been better this week, but to day was fractious again & would not take medicine & he is confined, where I hope he will be kept until we get in–...

A STRONG SQUALL

FRIDAY 27 NOVEM–

Here we are with a gale of wind dead ahead & a prospect of its continuing several days– We are only about 500 miles from New York at the beginning of yesterday we had a splendid SW wind & I began to flatter myself that we were to have it all the way in & be safe home by Monday, but now alas & alack we may be three weeks– I feel that the winter is setting in early & I will make no more calculations till we see Sandy Hook–[185] I think of writing an ode to sleep & then reading myself to sleep over it– nothing but poetry of my own composing will I think act as an opiate–...We had a sudden change of wind night before last & a sudden North West Squall last night both caught us unprepared & the management in such cases is so execrable that I have conceived the idea of writing an account of a strong squall *well taken care of,* another account of the same as taken care of *it*–

Capt S– Mr Pike– send the Boys up to free the main Top Sail, be hardy lads & lay down quick –

The squall had now got almost to its strength, the ship sending before it intently blaring up a regular Nor West gale & no object in doing any thing but to make her all snug before its fury breaks on her–

Capt S– Haul up when you are ready Mr Tremor

Mr T– all ready Sir– start away– round him up boys; & up he come

Capt S– Mr T– close reef the main Top Sail set him & reef furl the fore sail– clap another reef in the fore Top Sail & furl him also–

In less than half an hour all this was done & the ship made snug– at day light

---

[185] Sandy Hook is a narrow sandy peninsula of Monmouth County, New Jersey, that extends north. Five miles long, it lies between the Atlantic Ocean and Sandy Hook Bay and is fifteen miles south of Manhattan. It and the Atlantic Highlands behind it have long been one of the landfalls for ships coming into New York.

the Royal yards were sent down, the main Mizen stay sail bent, the launch securely lashed, & wind very politely denied to blow & crack your cheeks– all hands were merry & eat their breakfasts with good appetite–

So ends the squall– taken care of as it should be– I had forgotten to mention that Jardine being awakened by Critic with a "good morning" & seven bells, it blows a regular siren– Jardine turns over for another nap & says "Let me know when it moderates, when I am hungry I will turn out" Critic also called Dr Bolus but he having perfect confidence in the Captain desired to be called when breakfast is ready he also takes another cat nap–

The squall as it was– mismanaged–

Capt S cried Mr F at the cabin door "Squally Sir" & before Capt S could get on deck– it was upon us– Capt S is in a hurried & incoherent voice– "hard up keep her off– let go Top sail halyards– call all hands, clear up this main Top reef sail, get the spinnaker down, haul in that weather main Top sail brace, send um along here, where are you all, all dead– steady"– by this time all hands, being at & about one thing, the main sail they had got it up, the main Rope gallant sail, flying & flapping, spinnaker half down, main Top sail & fore Top sail ditto– I got to the helm & friend Antone a green hand, a Portuguese speaking little English, I assured him, set Joe to work to get the spinnaker down & stopped & got the mizzen top sail yard square & endeavored to reply to the Capts orders about steering– he was in a rage because Jack had given up the helm at 4 oclock *before* the squall came, he sent him back & then sang out–

Mr Tremor– stand by to get– the– boo boo boom–

aye aye sir–

Why dont you swing her off so that we can get that jib down–

says Critic– please say port & starboard simply & I will man the wheel...[2 pages of squall follow with captain shouting nonsensical orders directions to his crew]

Critic savage as a bear to think how all things are managed & the Dr half scared to death thinking there must be some great danger at hand to make the Capt cry out so– sail ho & theres an end to my squall–

SUNDAY 29TH NOVEMBER

400 miles still from New york & no prospect of getting in for several days– patience– patience– no service to day tho' the wind was moderate & the weather fair, it is now about 1/2 past 3 PM at church time I imagined you at Mr Greenwoods praying for me & walking home from church with Bob– a fine sun shiny day & pleasant breeze at WSW– if we were now close to the land further West this would be a fair wind but we are in the edge of the gulf stream & the current is consequently unfavorable though the ship is making a good course– I doubt if you went to church to day, you had my *Globe* letters by Thursday or Friday & indulged the idea that I should get home by the rail road to day– & being disappointed are at home full of worry– Oh fie fie–

3 DEC

...At 7 AM to day rainy & cold which continued till the PM when it cleared off fine & this is a superlative evening which I dare say you are looking at anxiously somewhere, we have just sounded in 38 fathoms & are not over 80 miles from Sandy Hook & I expect to be awaken at 6 AM with the sound of Light-ho- or Land-ho- or ship ahoy– it would be funny if the *Sylph* should put a pilot on board of us– hey what? My emotions can be better imagined *by you* than described by *me*– are you all well or are you not– if well I shall be happy I dont doubt it much–

hope I may get into the Providence boat tomorrow & dont expect to find you in New York– Tho I do John

Friday evening 6 oclock

"Man proposes, God disposes"–

"There is many a slip between the cup & the lip"

& various other sayings true & just– I might adapt to our present situation–...

Last evening...I walked the deck till 9 PM not a cloud to be seen thinking of home & feeling quite confident that we should get a pilot early this morning & be within the hook before this time safe & sound– I lost– some warm Port wine sangria at 9 & went to bed not to rest, I retried in vain to sleep & at 11 oclock dressed myself & again went on deck, the sky still cloudless & the wind nearly fair, but freshening– at 12 took in some sail & sounded in 28 fathoms– went to bed again & tried to sleep but it was "no go"– I felt quite well but could not sleep, by 2 oclock the wind freshening to a brisk gale with good weather reefed top sails, I went aloft to try to see a light– asked the Capt why he did not make signals for a pilot to which he replied that we should get one at day light– at 4 AM the fine clear sky was all gone & it blew a gale, still at NE & being there in 13 fathoms water we stood away from the land, at early day light– stood in again & saw several small vessels which we flattered ourselves were pilots but no they proved to be coasters–

OFF THE JERSEY COAST

The weather exceedingly cold, the Thermometer but little above freezing point the clouds dense & bleak– but dry & as we could see a good way we stood in boldly under a press of sail towards the land, I went aloft many times & at 1/2 past 10 had the pleasure of crying out Land-ho– then came the doubts & the debates as to what point it was, these doubts continued until near noon when the mate who had been in a pilot boat a long time declared he saw two light houses & that it must be Sandy Hook– then we were all excitement– Capt Jauncy declared he saw the ships at anchor back of the low land, hurry boys, call all hands cries the Capt & get the anchors clear– but at a second glance it was evident that instead of being Sandy Hook it was Barnegat[186] 40 miles from the Hook!!! then came the disappointment–

The Dr turned in despair, Jauncy & I made merry with the mistake & laughed at the Capt & mate, but our merriment had a reservation– we stood in close to Barnegat Inlet & saw two small craft running in for shelter, we envied them & I was sorry I could not have got on board of one of them & landed *any where*– at noon we tacked off shore again within two miles of the land, the weather still cloudy & cold with a hard forced gale– dined on our last fresh mass of pork, Pumpkin fritters preserved fresh salmon & salt Beef– drank a glass of port to each others *speedy passage* smoked a cigar & then I got under the blankets with Flora laying on my feet to keep them or *her* warm, (no fleas) read myself to sleep & was awakened at 4 by the Dr with the unwelcome intelligence that it was hailing & snowing– turned out & recommended the mate to call the Captain– make more snug before dark, wind still NE & here we are under very snug canvass standing off shore within 40 miles of our haven & likely to remain as far off for a day or two to come– OH patience, patience–

[186] Barnegat is a large shallow bay behind a beach in New Jersey, and located below Sandy Hook and its large bay. In Sandy Hook Bay ships often anchored before going up to New York Harbor.

now all this no doubt sounds "*horrid*" to you– if you could realize where we are you would no doubt be worrying yourself more than you are now, which is quite enough, I dare say you were looking anxious at the moon last night & praying fervently that I might get in, as I did, today you are contemplating the snow sleet before your door & *sighing* for me, perhaps *crying* hey? but you need not worry yet– it only blows a stiff close reef gale, not a tempest, we have a good ship under us, our crew all well & the Captain is quite at home here– having made up my mind for a gale given up the idea of getting in for a day or two I am easy & shall sleep much sounder to night than I have for several nights– I have packed up Bob's picture & almost all my books & am more solitary– our only cause for anxiety is the fear of being run down by some happy man bound to the sunny south, but we have a moon though covered with clouds & the night is not very dark– I pity the sailors more than any one, but they are queer fellows– their "sweetening" is all gone & yesterday I sent them a box containing nearly 20 lbs of sweet chocolate enough to have lasted them, with due economy three days, well what think you they did with it eat it all up yesterday & last night, so that when the cook was called out at 4 this morning to make a fire & boil chocolate– it was all gone– so if I were to give one of them six pair of stockings he would no doubt put them all on at once–

Oh deary me, deary me, when are we to get in the other day we were so far off shore that a SW wind was not fair & now that we are close in a NE wind which then would have been fair, is now ahead– well– as Jacob Faithful says, "better luck next time"– we have plenty of salt beef, pork, water, bread & "small stores" & at a pinch we can eat Flora, the Cat– the Java sparrows & a monkey Curry would not be bad, there are two remaining– besides our pet hen–

Good Night and may the good Angels guide & guard us

Sunday 4 PM

Ever since my last epistle at 6 PM on Friday it has been blowing a hard gale at NE & we have been "laying too" drifting to leeward under very short sail– until 13 oclock to day, noon the wind shifted suddenly to the Southward & is now blowing moderately at SW & when the old NE ever get down a little we shall begin to go along again– The sun peeped out at noon & we got the latitude & find that we have drifted from 40 miles from NY on the 4th to 160 & if the gale had continued another day we might have drifted nearer to the shore than would have been agreeable– it blew very hard all night with a high sea & to aggravate the same I had one of my sick head aches last night & was forced to take an emetic which directly relieved me & I am now quite well again–...

I must confess that I am not sanguine, & I think the weather is not yet settled– I slept below last night in my cot as our hurricane house would not stand a very heavy sea– good bye for to day– I will get out of the ship– first chance–

6 oclock– went on deck & found the wind had already begun to come round to the Westward & now we have it nearly NW & blowing a gale, if the wind in this quarter should be moderate we might hope to get back to Barnegat where we were on Friday but as it is, we cannot expect to see NY until a change of wind–

Two hours since, we had a very good prospect of getting there in 24 hours now alas– we may be a week– four of our crew have given out & are useless however we must take it as it comes, as a man takes a wife, for better or for worse– I think a great deal more about you than about myself & I can imagine that you are very unhappy–

Monday 11 AM–

here we are after a blowy night with more moderate weather & sunshine, the wind at NW & sail made so that if the *Niantic* was a decent sailor & her copper good we might hope to make something, two or three days now appears to me a very small affair & if we do better we shall be delighted– our sugar is out– Rice ditto & we are reduced to Salt Beef & pork & Bread & our allowance of water– however the living is the least of my anxiety, arrow root, sage, bread & Tea sweetened with ginger syrup and appetite go a good way–

Dec 9

Tuesday evening 6 oclock

...at 2 oclock I went to bed to take a nap & about 4 I was awoke by the screeching of blocks & I immediately "smelt a rat" & opening my window saw that they were hauling up the main sail, out I jumped knowing well that the operation could be for no other purpose than to receive the pilot– I went on deck & there was the lovely pilot boat close to & putting my hands to my nose thus.

I looked at the Capt Jauncy & says I "no you dont catch old birds in the way"– they had intended very quietly to get the pilot on board without advising me but it was a decided failure– well the man came on board & pulled out a letter– Oh that moment of suspense– the blood rushed back to it source– Capt Doty read aloud RB Forbes Esq– I seized the letter– turned the seal side out & saw it was *red,* looked at the direction– the first words were "alls well"

I retired to my room of state & there I tore the seal read the most sensible pithy epistle that I ever received– it runs thus–

Boston 25 Nov 1840

Dear B–

Alls well, wife boy mother & all as when the *Panama* left, Teas high here & in Europe, *Ann McKim* just in

Yours ever JMF

Go to Astor House for letters–

I read this & rushed on deck, poked it into the Dr's face, & the Capts & Jauncys– I could not speak, my heart was full of gratitude & *haddock* for the pilot bought some on board & we have just done supper– God be praised–

The weather looks fair, but breezy yet I hope to get in early in the morning– I find by the papers that the late gale has been very severe, more so than we have had it– you must really have been *enraged* with fear– Oh God be praised & may I succeed on getting up to Town in time for tomorrows boat– this is even at most the happiest hour of my life– Good night & love to Bob– Flora is glad too–

AFTERMATH

As the opium trade moved from difficulty to controversy to war, Captain Charles Elliot received very exact orders from Lord Palmerston, England's Foreign Secretary. He was instructed how to use the force under his command and told what he should demand from the Chinese Government. But Elliot often used his own judgement and did what he thought needed doing. At the center of the drama, and with such a time lag of months before orders reached him from England, he felt he should have some discretion.

At the end of June, 1840, just before Robert Bennet Forbes sailed for home, an English fleet under Captain Elliot's command sailed north to deliver a letter from England's Foreign Secretary to the Chinese government. Among other details it demanded that the 20,283 chests of opium that the British merchants had surrendered to be destroyed be paid for in cash. Three hundred miles up the coast at Amoy an attempt was made to deliver the letter under a flag of truce. The Chinese had no idea what the flag signified and refused to allow the British to land. The fleet continued north another 400 miles to Chusan Island, located south of the estuary of the Yangtse River. Ting-hai, the island's chief city, was summoned to surrender on July 4. The Governor of the island refused. Elliot's troops landed and took over the island with no opposition from the Chinese.

Then the fleet sailed another 800 miles North to Pei-ho. The British were now only a hundred miles from Peking. From there the letter was finally delivered to Kishen, who was Grand Secretary. When the Emperor heard how the letter arrived, he realized that Lin's policy had agitated the barbarians and caused a fleet of their warships to sail almost to the gates of the capital. He was furious with Lin and sent him a violent letter of dismissal. The Emperor appointed Kishen to take Lin's place, with instructions to negotiate with the English. Kishen with flattery and promises got the English to return to Canton for peace talks. By November 20 the English fleet was back at Macao.

But the Chinese interpreted this retreat as weakness. The Emperor at this point had only lost Chusan Island to the barbarians. Only about a thousand troops had landed on the island and half the men were sick from fevers and dysentery. Kishen was instructed to draw out the talks in Canton as long as possible to allow the Emperor's forces to gather and launch a sudden attack to regain Chusan. By the beginning of January, 1841, Elliot was aware that he was being played with and decided to use force to get a settlement.

The opening salvos of the Opium Wars were fired on 7 January 1841. That day under Elliot's command a line of ships moved in to attack the two forts at the mouth of the Bogue–Chuenpee on the east and Tycocktow on the west. The battle lasted from 9:30 to 10:30 am. Five hundred Chinese were killed and 300 wounded. There were no fatalities on the British side. The English fleet could now enter the Bogue, capture the two inner forts, and sail right to Canton. But Elliot called off further action; it had been a convincing demonstration of British power and resolve. By January 20 an agreement, known as the Convention of Chuenpee, was drawn up and signed by Elliot and Kishen. Its terms were: cession of Hong Kong to the British Crown; payment of six million dollars for disruption of trade; and permission for trade to be opened again and continued at Canton until Hong Kong was ready. As valuable as Hong Kong became to the British, it was seen as "a barren rock" in 1841. Lord Palmerston described it as "a barren island with hardly a house upon it" in a despatch to Elliot, and predicted that it "will not be a Mart of Trade, any more than Macao is so."

The Convention of Chuenpee was declared unacceptable by both England and China. Palmerston was furious with Elliot and chastised him in letters that called him disloyal and neglectful. The young Queen Victoria expressed her indignation as well: "The Chinese business vexes us much...All we wanted might have been got, if it had not been for the unaccountable strange conduct of Charles Elliot...who completely disobeyed his instructions and tried to get the lowest terms he could." The British government repudiated the Convention of Chuenpee and sent out Henry Pottinger to replace Elliot.

Elliot was exiled by Queen Victoria to the Republic of Texas, where he was Consul-General for several years. After Texas, he became Governor of Bermuda, and later in his career served as Governor of Trinidad and Governor of St. Helena. He was 39 when he conducted the war against China. He was 74 when he died. On the Chinese side of the controversy, Kishen fared disastrously. He was removed from Canton in chains and taken to Peking for a trial in which he was found guilty and condemned to death for giving Hong Kong to the barbarians. All his possessions, valued at 10,000,000 pounds, were confiscated, and this contribution to the Imperial coffers helped to pay for the war. In the end Kishen was not executed, but exiled to Tibet.

A year later, after more skirmishes, the Treaty of Nanking officially ended the first of the Opium Wars. The terms were now far stricter than before. The Chinese were made to pay $21,000,000 in indemnities for the opium they had destroyed and for the cost to the British of carrying on the war. They had to open five new ports, and had to turn over Hong Kong to the British Crown. No mention of the opium problem was included in the terms, and so the trade quietly continued. With the addition of five new ports and the island of Hong Kong, the volume of opium actually increased. The number of chests of the drug coming into China rose from 20,000 at the time of seizure in 1839 to 52,000 in 1850.[1]

Two years later the Americans, through Caleb Cushing, negotiated their own agreement with China in the Treaty of Wanghia. It expressly declared the drug "contraband," but that did not stop the Yankee traders, including Russell & Co., from bringing in opium as they did before.

Robert Bennet Forbes, soon after his return from China, took a six-month trip to Europe with his benefactor and uncle Thomas Handasyd Perkins, who was now an old man of 76. Once again Rose was left at home. When RBF returned he remained close to Boston for the next nine years. In 1843 a daughter Edith was born, and two years later a son named James Murray.

In the middle of the 1840s the potato crop in Ireland was devastated by blight, and the result was famine. In the United States money was subscribed, a petition was presented to Congress, and two ships were placed at the disposal of the petitioners to carry corn, flour, and other provisions to the starving Irish people. The *Jamestown* was to leave from Boston and the *Macedonian* from New York in the spring of 1847. Robert Bennet Forbes took command of the *Jamestown* and sailed to Ireland with 800 tons of supplies. He made the transAtlantic passage in 15 days and three hours from Boston. When Forbes sailed for home he brought with him many tokens of respect and affection from the grateful Irish people.[2]

In 1849 Forbes once again left for China, this time on the steamer *Europa*. Shortly before reaching Liverpool, the steamer ran down the American bark *Charles Bartlett* with more than 160 passengers aboard. Forbes, who was resting in his cabin, rushed on deck and saw the sailing ship sinking with a great hole in her side. Her decks were swarming with screaming men, women, and children while the steamer still made way under sail. Without a thought for himself, RBF plunged overboard to try to save lives in the thick fog, and later in the rescue effort he pulled an oar in one of the boats lowered from the *Europa*. RBF's heroism was rewarded with medals and testimonials abroad and at home.

When Forbes reached China, he again became a partner in charge of Canton operations for Russell & Co., and spent a year trading. After he returned to Boston in 1851, RBF retained an interest in Russell & Co., with some intermissions, until 1857. In 1858 he sailed for Argentina in a vessel of his own with three friends, among them the anatomist and ethnologist, Dr. Jeffries Wyman. On the deck of the brig he carried a small iron steamer. His intention was to unite a commercial enterprise with the pleasure of exploring and hunting on the Rio de la Plata. The adventure nearly came to an end when the brig was dismasted and narrowly escaped sinking.

Despite such experiences, Forbes never ceased to love the sea and everything connected with it. He invested in shipbuilding and took a technical

All during his life, Robert Bennet Forbes made models of vessels. Here he is shown in his workshop in the 1880s with several in progress.

interest in the new steam engine and its applications in ships and boats. He was an early advocate of iron shipbuilding in America, and during his lifetime was part-owner or supervisor of construction in 68 vessels, sail and steam. He supervised the building of gunboats for the U.S. government and established a coastal patrol for defense against rebel raids during the Civil War. He created yacht and ship models, both large and small, complete with rigging and minute details, all through his life. In his later years he took a creative interest in improving the lives of seamen. He invented the famous "Forbes rig" for ships, which reduced the size of square sails and made them safer to handle, and was the author of many papers and pamphlets on nautical subjects. He was President of the Boston Marine Society, Trustee and President of Sailors' Snug Harbor, one of the Boston Pilot Commissioners, member of the Board of Trade, Trustee of the Massachusetts Humane Society, and a member of the Boston Port Society.

In 1867 Forbes visited the South of France and astonished the sportsmen at Pau with his vigor at the age of 63, following the hounds and riding boldly. He went to California in 1870 in the first Pullman train to cross the continent, and delivered a lecture in San Francisco comparing the small town he found on his first visit there in 1825 to the great city of 45 years later. At the age of 67 RBF hunted buffalo on the plains of Nebraska.[3]

In 1879 Robert Bennet Forbes published an autobiography entitled *Personal Reminiscences.* Three years later this text was enlarged and published by Little, Brown, & Co. At 75 RBF decided it would prove interesting to write a history of Russell & Co. using material contributed by the surviving partners. Delano did not cooperate and sent only a brief summary of his experience in China, carefully omitting any mention of opium. There were others who were reluctant to help such a book along, and in time Forbes gave up the notion of a Russell & Co. book, and instead added the material collected to the second and third editions of *Personal Reminiscences*, which appeared in 1882 and 1892. Writing to Delano he confessed that "The only thing I fear is that in giving a sketch of the causes and effects of the opium traffic...I may say too much."[4] When Rose Forbes died in 1885, RBF's health began to fail, although his mind was lively and lucid. RBF died on 23 November 1889 at the age of 85. He requested that this motto be placed on his gravestone: "He tried to do his duty."

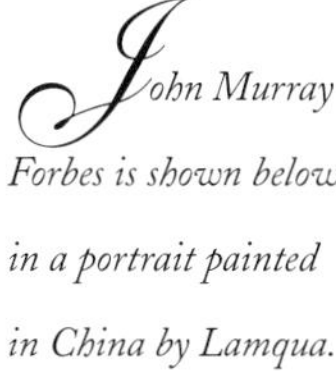

ohn Murray Forbes is shown below in a portrait painted in China by Lamqua.

John Murray Forbes never returned to China, but attended to the interests of Russell & Co. in the United States. He lived in Milton with his wife Sarah and their six children and commuted to Boston. Realizing that the China trade and the whaling industry were on the decline, in the last half of the nineteenth century he threw his energies into the development of the railroads and the possibilities of the expanding West, principally through his investments in the Michigan Central Railroad and other railroad enterprises in Illinois, Iowa and Missouri. During the Civil War he was an especially zealous supporter of the Union cause, organizing The Loyal Publication Society, advising President Lincoln and other officials, and helping to establish the black regiments of Massachusetts. In 1863 he was sent to England and successfully persuaded the British government to prevent certain ironclad vessels being built in British shipyards from reaching the Confederate government. These efforts were a significant service to the Union, and may even have helped to prevent war between England and the United States.

In *Letters and Social Aims*, Ralph Waldo Emerson paid a great tribute to JMF, citing his generosity, his social skills, and finally his modesty: "...How little this man suspects, with his sympathy for men and his respect for lettered and scientific people, that he is not likely, in any company, to meet a man superior to himself. And I think this is a good country that can bear such a creature as he is." Like his brother RBF, John Murray Forbes lived a productive life until the age of 85.

Robert Bennet Forbes Jr., or Bob as he was always called, did not turn out to be the success his parents had every reason to expect. Always fond of animals, he spent his time training horses, hunting, and racing trotters. He was a sportsman and boulevardier for whom dressing fashionably was important, and he spent a good bit of his money on clothes. His extravagant style of life was a continual frustration for his parents. Many of their letters to him and to each other deal with his over-spending. Bob never married and died at the age of 66 in 1891, three years after his father's death.[5]

Warren Delano remained in China until 1842, taking over RBF's position as head of Russell & Co. at the age of 33. In 1842 he returned to the U.S. for the first time in almost a decade, and during this vacation met and married Catherine Robbins Lyman of Northampton, Massachusetts. He returned to China with his 18-year-old bride and spent three more years as a trader. On relocating to the U.S., he invested the fortune he had accumulated in China in railroads, coal mines and shipbuilding. He was soon a millionaire; but much of his money was lost in the depression that began in 1857, causing him in 1860 to return to China to recoup his fortune. As head of Russell & Co., now located in Hong Kong, Delano again traded in tea and opium as successfully as he had done 20 years before. His wife and seven children sailed to China to join him in 1862. Warren and Catherine eventually had a family of 11 children. Sara, the seventh, was the mother of President Franklin Delano Roosevelt. Warren Delano retired to the family estate at Newburgh, New York, surrounded by Chinese porcelain, furniture and art, including a large portrait of Houqua which always hung in his parlor. Delano was 91 when he died in 1898.[6]

Captain Philip Dumaresq continued to sail the seas between the United States and China for many years and acquired a handsome fortune. In semi-retirement he passed several summers at his father's place on an island in the Kennebec River in Maine where, one morning in 1855, he returned from a shooting expedition to find that the river had flooded and drowned both his wife, Margaretta, and their eldest daughter, a beautiful girl of 17. Although there were six other children, Captain Dumaresq was so devastated by the tragedy that he returned to his profession and took solace in the sea. He was the first American captain to enter a Japanese port after the American treaty of commerce in 1858. Ironically this great mariner, who had braved the dangers of the oceans for forty years in all parts of the world, was lost overboard in Long Island Sound on a night in June of 1861 while traveling as a passenger on the steamer *Empire State*.[7]

John C. Green became an investor and a philanthropist after he returned from China. With the fortune earned as head of Russell & Co. he became one of the financial backers of the Michigan Central Railroad along with John Murray Forbes. He was a Director of the New York Bank of Commerce, and was one of the founders of the Home for Ruptured and Crippled. He was for many years Governor of New York Hospital. He donated half a million dollars to Princeton, where he had attended college, and was responsible for the construction of three buildings there, endowing three chairs in scientific subjects, and financing Princeton's school of civil engineering.

William C. Hunter retired to Macao after the Anglo-Chinese War of 1842 and looked after his business interests in the Far East. He lived with his Chinese mistress, who bore him several children. His love for her was such that at one point during his career in Canton, after departing on his first return visit to the United States in 18 years, he became so lonesome for her that he had the ship sail back to Macao halfway through the voyage home. He was a part owner with RBF in the *Midas*, which sailed from New York in 1844 and was the first American steamship in Chinese waters. In 1882 and 1885, respectively, he wrote and had published in London *The 'Fan Kwei' at Canton Before Treaty Days, 1825-1844* and *Bits of Old China*. Both books were written with the encouragement and assistance of RBF. His accounts of life in the Canton factories are considered the most intimate and accurate material on the subject. Writing decades after his experiences in Canton, Hunter was able to record them with a detachment that attempted an equal understanding of Chinese and Western viewpoints in the opium controversies and other events of the 1840s. He died at Nice, France, in 1891.[8]

RBF's colleague William C. Hunter is shown above in a portrait by George Chinnery.

Abiel Abbot Low left Canton for home in 1840, having been a successful partner in Russell & Co. since 1837. Part of his business in China had been a joint venture with Houqua which made him enough money to finance a business in New York with his brother Josiah, the famous A.A. Low & Brothers. The firm quickly gained a prominent position in the trade of China tea and Japanese silk with its fleet of clipper ships. Low participated in the financing of the first Atlantic cable, and the building of the Chesapeake & Ohio Railroad through West Virginia to the Ohio River, among other investments. He died in Brooklyn, New York, in 1893.

Dr. Peter Parker, on returning to the U.S. in 1840, briefed members of the administration about developments in China. In March of 1841 he married Harriet Colby Webster, a relative of Daniel Webster, confirming all his friends' suspicions that he had returned to the U.S. to find a wife. He sought financial support in both Europe and America for his hospital, and returned to Canton to resume his medical practice in June of 1842. In 1844 he served as one of the secretaries to Caleb Cushing in the negotiation of the Treaty of Wanghia. The next year he was appointed secretary to the American legation. In 1855 he became American commissioner and minister to China, where he remained until 1857. When he retired, he made his home in Washington, D.C., interesting himself in such enterprises as the American Evangelical Alliance and the Smithsonian Institution. He died at the age of 84 a year before RBF.

Russell Sturgis remained in the Far East for many years as a member of the firm of Russell Sturgis & Co. and of Russell & Co. In 1844 he retired from merchant adventures and came home to Boston to join his children, who attended school in the area. In the mid-1840s he married Julia Overing Boit, his third wife, but finding the cost of living in the United States too high he decided to return to Asia. He was to sail from Boston to London on the *Canada* and connect there with a vessel that would take him to China. The express man who brought Julia and Russell's luggage in from Jamaica Plain was delayed by an open drawbridge and did not make it to the wharf until the *Canada* was clear of the harbor. However, Sturgis had decided not to sail without the luggage. The Sturgises took the next ship for London, but missed their connections there and waited for several weeks to resume their trip to China. During their unplanned stay in England, the senior member of Baring Brothers & Co. asked Russell to become a partner in the firm. Sturgis accepted without hesitation. Thus, due to the delay of his luggage, Sturgis' life took a very different turn. Although he kept in touch with his family and friends in Boston, and gave large contributions to the new Boston Art Museum in Copley Square (designed by his son, John Hubbard Sturgis), he remained in England until his death in 1887.[9]

Houqua was 71 when Robert Bennet Forbes sailed for home in 1840. Although Forbes does not mention it in his journals, just before RBF left China Houqua gave him a portrait of himself in oil by Lamqua. The Houqua portrait now hangs in the Forbes House in Milton. With the abolition of the co-hong system, Houqua retired, and along with other Hong Merchants had to pay about a million dollars as his share of the debt owed to the English when the first Opium War was over. He declared himself opposed to the opium traffic even though he had profited so much by it. When they heard of his fate, John Murray Forbes and Robert Bennet Forbes encouraged Houqua to come to the United States for his retirement and settle in Florida where JMF owned land. However, the old merchant thought it better to stay in China; he died soon after in 1843 at the age of 75. He had outlived his wife and all his sons. In 1848 Houqua, in his lifetime perhaps the richest merchant in the world, had reached worldwide celebrity and was represented by a life-size wax statue at Madame Tussaud's in London.

*homas Handasyd Perkins is shown below in an engraving by W.H. Smith based on a portrait painted by Garebardella.*

William Jardine left China in January, 1839, and was given a lively going-away party that RBF described in his letters to Rose. His partner Matheson came to take his place. Sensing the trouble to come, and worrying that the firm of Jardine, Matheson was in jeopardy, Jardine did not go home to Scotland. Instead he sailed to London to see Lord Palmerston. His mission was to urge the Foreign Secretary to a vigorous policy of force against the Chinese for the purpose of opening more Chinese ports to trade and re-establishing the drug traffic on a sounder, safer basis. When the news of China's decree to stop all trade with England reached London in the autumn of 1839, Jardine had not yet met with Palmerston. He felt it best not to be too assertive, because he was aware of the negative opinion in England where the opium trade was concerned. But Jardine was soon joined by many English businessmen who depended on Chinese goods. They were demanding prompt action and reimbursement for losses they had suffered since the trade with China had been stopped. When Jardine finally got to see Palmerston, he provided him "a paper of hints" urging an effective show of force in China. Palmerston would later credit Jardine for giving the assistance and information needed to allow England to get exactly what it wished in the Treaty of Nanking. In 1841, at age 55, Jardine was elected to Parliament from the Borough of Ashburton. In the House of Commons, he sat behind Palmerston in the opposition until his untimely death just two years later.[10]

Colonel Thomas Handasyd Perkins died at 89 in 1854, long outliving his brother James who had died in 1822. The Colonel was survived by only two siblings, RBF's mother Margaret and his aunt Mary Abbot, and of T.H. Perkins's eleven children only six were left. His son, T.H. Perkins, Jr., had died of cancer at 53 in 1850. The Colonel's funeral was a grand affair. Both branches of the Massachusetts Legislature were closed early so that members could pay their final respects. Among other things, Perkins was praised for starting and generously supporting the Boston Anthenaeum, the Bunker Hill Monument, the Massachusetts General Hospital, and The Perkins Institution for the Blind.[11]

— PFK

NOTES:

[1] Collis, Maurice, *Foreign Mud* (London: Faber & Faber Ltd., 1952) 246-254.

[2] Forbes, H.A. Crosby, and Henry Lee, *Massachusetts Help to Ireland During the Great Famine* (Milton, Massachusetts: The Captain Robert Bennet Forbes House, 1967)..

[3] Forbes, Robert Bennet, *Personal Reminiscences* (Boston: Little, Brown, & Co., 1892).

[4] Ward, Geoffrey C., "A Fair, Honorable, and Legitimate Trade," *American Heritage* (August 1986).

[5] Forbes, Robert Bennet. The letter books of Robert Bennet Forbes, 1838. Reel 1, The Massachusetts Historical Society, Boston, Massachusetts.

[6] Ward, Geoffrey C., *Before the Trumpet* (New York: Harper & Row, 1985) 67-69, 199.

[7] Perkins, Augustus T., *A Sketch of the Family of Dumaresq* (Albany: J. Munsell, 1863) 6-7.

[8] Hunter, William C., *The "Fan Kwei" at Canton* (Shanghai: Kelly and Walsh Ltd., 1911).

[9] Crawford, Mary Caroline., *Famous Families of Massachusetts,* Volume I (Boston: Little, Brown, & Co., 1930) 322-323.

[10] Collis, Maurice, *Foreign Mud* (London: Faber & Faber Ltd., 1952) 250-256.

[11] Seaburg, Carl, and Stanley Paterson, *Merchant Prince of Boston* (Cambridge, Massachusetts: Harvard University Press, 1971) 416-419.

ACKNOWLEDGEMENTS

I first went to the Massachusetts Historical Society to find out what I could about my great-great grandfather Robert Bennet Forbes with the idea of writing a young adult novel. I began to decipher his journals and realized that what I was reading would be fascinating to adults but inappropriate for children. Each weekday afternoon for three years I faithfully typed the letters word for word into my laptop computer. Then I began the long process of researching and writing footnotes. Several more years were spent finding the right publisher for this book and then waiting for funding and publication. Quickly, seven years passed.

Many people helped me along the way. For their time and attention I am deeply grateful. My mother, Elizabeth McKean Bourneuf, helped me the most. She unfortunately did not live to see this culmination of our work. She was an enthusiastic assistant, reading sources to help educate us on the history of the American China Trade and helping to figure out the many mysterious references which had to be footnoted. She eagerly transcribed many of Rose Forbes' hard-to-read letters. This helped to answer many questions and gave us an idea of what Rose Forbes' life was like in Boston.

My cousin Elsie Youngman, whom I met for the first time while working on the project, was the granddaughter of RBF's daughter Edith. Sadly, she too is no longer alive to see the published book. She was able to supply me with a missing section of the journals that covered the departure from Boston and the 1838 ocean voyage ending at Macao. This had been handed down to her in typed form by some family member who must have thrown out the original. She also helped me locate family pictures and looked forward to seeing them in the finished book.

My brother Joe Bourneuf deserves a great deal of thanks for his wisdom and guidance, dispensed from the Widener Library at Harvard where he is head of the Reference Department. He helped me find sources, and answered many questions about footnotes with competence and assurance.

The Captain Robert Bennet Forbes House staff in Milton were always there to aid the project in any way they could–from supplying answers to my questions to taking the pictures off the museum walls so I could take initial photographs of them. In fact, Director Dana Ricciardi, eager to know all she could about the Forbes family, actually read the journals out loud to the staff for many months as they ate their lunch.

Crosby Forbes, my uncle, who has a combined interest in the China Trade and in Forbes family history, deserves acknowledgement for taking time from his busy schedule to pore over the letters, correcting and advising. Crosby also kindly agreed to write the book's Foreword.

Staff members of The Massachusetts Historical Society, which now houses a majority of the perishable Forbes papers, were very helpful to me during the three years I spent there with the RBF letters. Peter Drummey, Virginia Smith, Catherine Craven, and Chris Steel all made me feel very much at home and followed my progress with enthusiasm and patience.

Llewellyn Howland deserves credit for introducing me to Mystic Seaport Museum's publications program. He thought they might be interested in publishing several interesting excerpts from the RBF journals in the museum's quarterly magazine. Upon seeing the journal entries, Andrew German, recognizing their potential, asked to look at the entire collection of letters and offered to publish them. Thanks go to Andy and Joe Gribbins, who took over the project. With patience and persistence they worked with the journals and explanatory text, and then located all the paintings and photographs and obtained the necessary permissions to use them. The work was then handed over to Clare Cunningham who planned its final attractive format. It is interesting to note that this book went finally to Hong Kong to be printed, which seemed ironic and fitting since most of the letters were written very near by.

Finally thanks go to the two men in my life, my husband Andrew Pitman Kerr and my son Adam Forbes Kerr, for their devotion and unfailing support throughout this project.

Phyllis Forbes Kerr
Cambridge, Massachusetts
April 10, 1996

BIBLIOGRAPHY

Amory, Cleveland, *The Proper Bostonians.* Hyannis, Massachusetts: Parnassus Imprints, 1993.

Beeching, Jack. *The Chinese Opium Wars.* New York: Harcourt, Brace, Jovanovich, 1975.

Briggs, Vernon. *Cabot History and Genealogy, 1475-1927.* Boston: Privately printed by Charles F. Goodspeed Company, 1927.

Collis, Maurice. *Foreign Mud.* Oxford, U.K.: Oxford University Press, 1947.

Crawford, Mary Caroline. *Famous Families of Massachusetts,* Volumes I and II. Boston: Little, Brown & Company, 1930.

Crossman, Carl L. *The China Trade–Export Painting, Furniture, Silver, and Other Objects.* Princeton, New Jersey: The Pyne Press, 1972.

Dulles, Foster Rhea. *The Old China Trade.* Boston: Houghton Mifflin Company, 1930.

Fairbank, John King. *The Great Chinese Revolution.* New York: Harper & Row, 1986.

Forbes, H.A. Crosby, and Henry Lee. *Massachusetts Help to Ireland During the Great Famine.* Milton, Massachusetts: The Captain Robert Bennet Forbes House, 1967.

Forbes, Robert Bennet, The Letter Books of Robert Bennet Forbes 1838-1840, Reel 1:3-8. Boston: The Massachusetts Historical Society.

Forbes, Robert Bennet, *Personal Reminiscences.* Boston: Little, Brown & Company, 1892.

Goodwin, Jason. *A Time for Tea.* New York: Alfred A. Knopf, 1991.

Greenberg, Michael. *British Trade and the Opening of China.* Cambridge, U.K.: Cambridge University Press, 1951.

Hibbert, Christopher. *The Dragon Wakes* . London: The Longman Group, Ltd., 1970.

Hunter, William C. *The 'Fan Kwei' at Canton.* Shanghai: Kelly and Walsh Ltd., 1911.

Morse, Hosea Ballou, *The International Relations of the the Chinese Empire.* vol. 1:1834-60, vol. 2:1861-93. Oxford, U.K.: Oxford University Press, 1926.

Perkins, Augustus T. *A Sketch of the Family of Dumaresq.* Albany: J. Munsell, 1863.

Reischauer, Edwin O., and John K. Fairbank. *East Asia–The Great Tradition.* Boston: Houghton Mifflin Company, 1958.

Seaburg, Carl, and Stanley Paterson. *Merchant Prince of Boston.* Cambridge, Massachusetts: Harvard University Press, 1971.

Saltonstall, Leverett. *"Memoir of Robert Bennet Forbes."* Proceedings of the Massachusetts Historical Society, 2nd Series, Volume VI, 1890-91.

Spence, Jonathan D. *Chinese Roundabout.* New York: W.W. Norton Co., 1992.

Tamarin, Alfred, and Shirley Glubok. *Voyage to Cathay.* New York: The Viking Press, 1976.

Waley, Arthur. *The Opium War Through Chinese Eyes.* London: Allen & Unwin, 1958.

Ward, Geoffrey C. *Before the Trumpet.* New York: Harper & Row, 1985.

Ward, Geoffrey C. with F. Delano Grant, Jr. "A Fair, Honorable, and Legitimate Trade." *American Heritage.* (August, 1986).

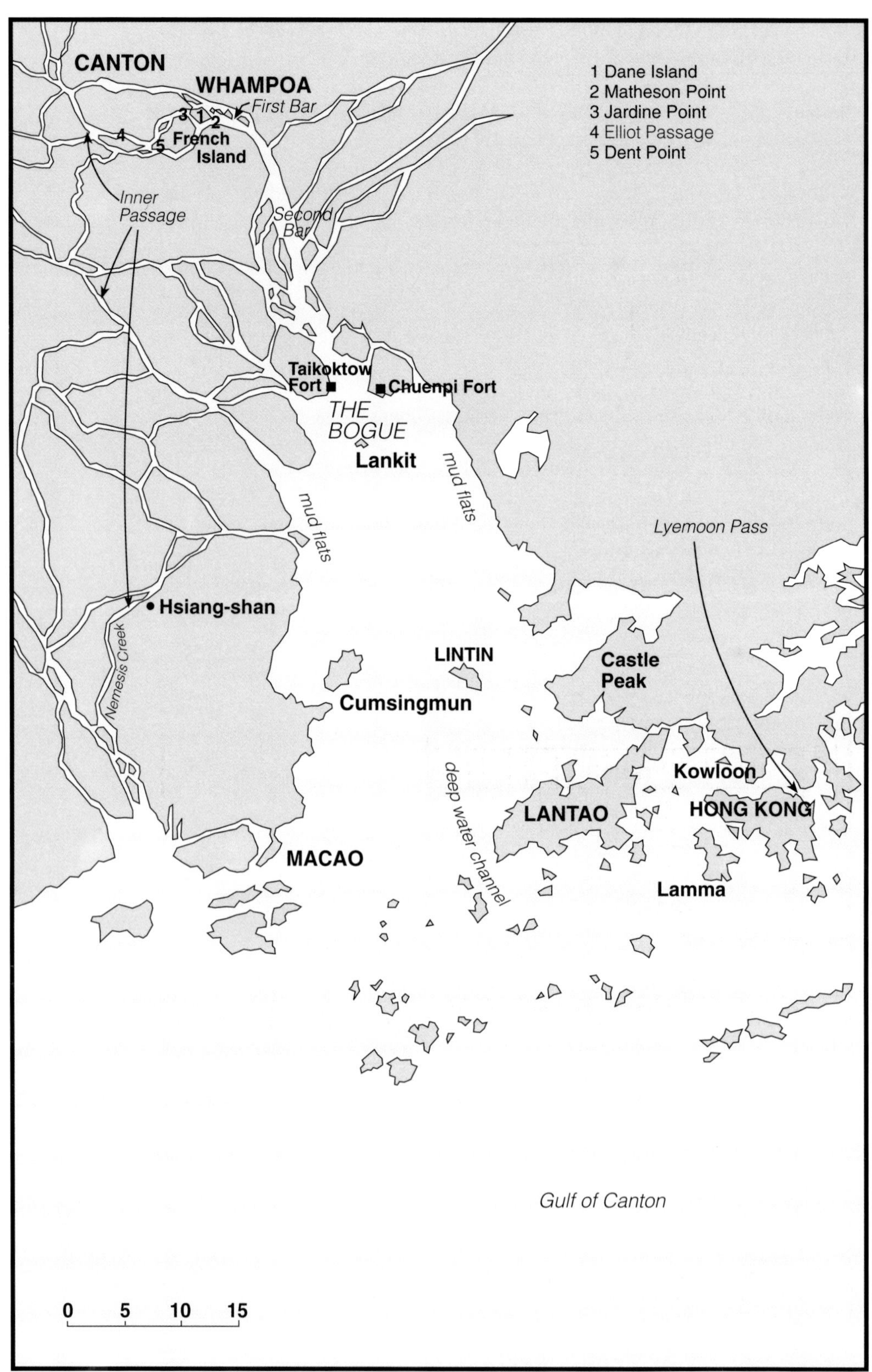

CANTON
WHAMPOA
First Bar
French Island
Inner Passage
Second Bar
1 Dane Island
2 Matheson Point
3 Jardine Point
4 Elliot Passage
5 Dent Point
Taikoktow Fort
Chuenpi Fort
THE BOGUE
Lankit
mud flats
mud flats
Lyemoon Pass
Hsiang-shan
Nemesis Creek
LINTIN
Castle Peak
Cumsingmun
deep water channel
Kowloon
LANTAO
HONG KONG
MACAO
Lamma
Gulf of Canton
0 5 10 15

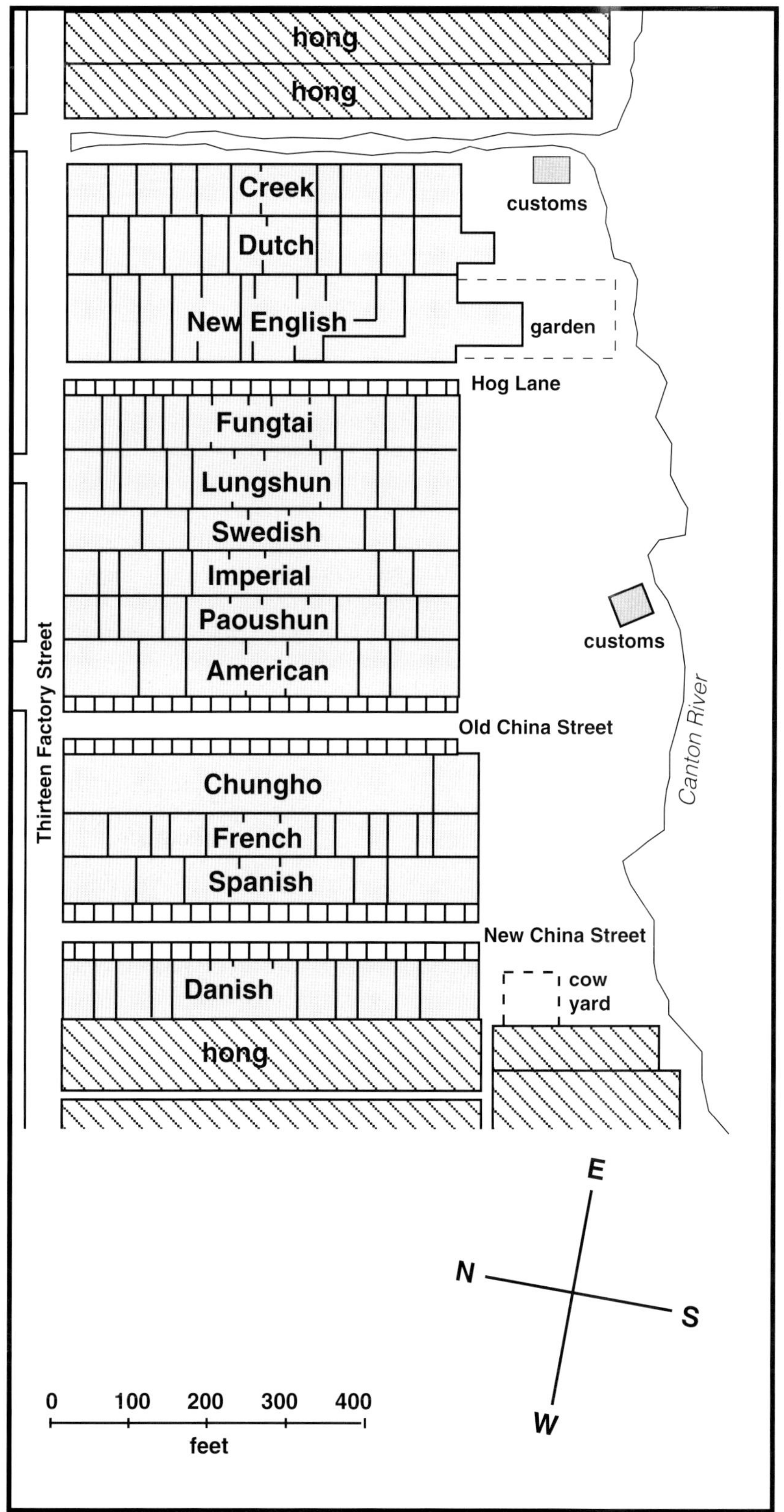

On page 278 is the Pearl River estuary with its many islands and waterways. On this page are the foreign and Chinese factories on the Canton waterfront, from the Creek Hong along the creek to the East down to the Danish Hong along New China Street.

C. W. KING'S ARTICLE ON THE OPIUM TRADE IN THE CHINESE REPOSITORY

(January, 1840)

Art. II. Progress of the difficulties between the English and Chinese; the position of the American
residents, &c. By C.R.

Could the new and beautiful invention, which is soon to furnish us with perfect pictures of all external things, painted by a pencil 'dipped in light,' be extended to abstract subjects, we know of no scenes, we would more gladly submit to the 'papiers sensibles' than those now being presented to us, in this part of the world, in connection with the opium-question. With such representations of our political scenery, there could be no disputing about proportions; no complaint of excessive or deficient coloring. The hand that sketched them, being above suspicion, could be charged with no omissions, no false lights, and no distortions. As the case is, the absent must be content to take and put together our partial and differing views; and as for the artist–he must be content to get, from one praise; from another, criticism; from a third abuse; as his sketch may suit the eyes and the interests of the frequenters of the exhibition. Still we shall not be deterred by the sense of imperfection, the desire of praise, or the fear of censure, from reverting to this interesting subject, as from time to time, new phases are presented to us. In this article, however, we shall do no more than state,–after a brief repetition of some opinions on the past stages of the controversy,–what we hope will be done for us and our cause, or rather, what, we trust, is already doing.

Our first opinion is–that the earliest prohibitions of the drug in 1800, and all the imperial action upon it, from that time downward, was and has been sincere, and that the neutralization of the national policy for so long a period, is to be ascribed to the combined connivance, corruption, and daring of the provincial government and the foreign residents.

2d. The local connivance, even if it could be proved to reach the highest provincial officers, never did convey any valid excuse or equitable protection to the foreign importer; for he knew, that the practical security he enjoyed, was derived by corrupt means and from a legally incompetent party.

3d. The proposition to legilize the import, made in 1836, did not convey any such protective right, because that motion was clearly negatived within four months of the proposal, and followed closely by a reenaction of the preexisting prohibitions. The right to move and discuss changes in existing regulations must be possessed under every government, and nowhere can such propositions be admitted to weaken the force of the laws, until a formal repeal is actually completed.

4th. The movement of the imperial government, up to the very act of confiscation of March 18th, was so slow and measured, that no one interested in the opium trade wanted opportunity to put himself and his property in safety, had be inclined to use that remedy. The actual appointment of a high officer with large powers and summary instructions, was formally notified to all parties more than two months before his arrival near the foreign residences, and this notice was coupled with the strongest persuasions and warnings to withdraw beyond the reach of his measures.

5th. The course taken by the commissioner before and in the act of confiscation, cannot be reconciled with European modes of procedure, or with our notions of personal justice. Yet, so far as the actual holders of the confiscated drug are concerned, the eastern mode was not more severe than the western. On them, the personal arrest, and armed seizure practiced under European writs, would have fallen at least as heavily as the demand of surrender, and the denial of passports. It is the non-holder who has the right to complain, that the confinement was made general instead of personal, and he and his property implicated without cause and without remedy.

6th. The position of the British superintendent under these circumstances was so embarrassing, as to claim and merit the utmost consideration and allowance. As a consular officer under the British government, he was bound by law and instruction to give no support to his countrymen in courses subversive of the fiscal regulations and general policy of the empire. On the other hand, as the agent of the government interested directly in the growth of the drug, and pledged, as it were, not to depreciate its value on its customer's hands, he was deterred from those timely explanations and disclaimers, which would have cleared the British flag, and the legal trade conducted under it, from implication with the illegal. All who know him, know that his personal feelings on the question are, and have ever been, pure and honorable; worthy of himself, his office, and his country. It was the anomalous position of his government, which embarrassed him. Had he been his own counsellor, or the free, unfettered representative of England, he would at once have disclaimed all connection with the opium. But as the coadjutor of the E. I. Company, as the correspondent of the governor-general, he hesitated, and compromised, and lost the invaluable opportunity.

7th. On the occasion of the first attempt to execute a criminal before the factories at Canton, the opposition of the residents to the act was as just, as it was successful. The ground so attempted to be employed, was a part of their own leased premises, and it was proper to guard their right by resistance, even if there had been no other reasons for their interference. The case was considerably altered, when the governor, in reply to the appeal of the Chamber of Commerce, declared the sole grounds of the offensive spectacle. We would have had the national representatives accept his paper as a disclaimer of all national bearings, in the humiliating act; and as to the importers of the drug, they should have so laid it to heart, as to have made impossible, the repetition which shortly followed.

8th. When the entire stoppage of the trade of Canton ensued, the interference of the superintendent, by order of Dec. 18th, to expel the smuggling boats, was right and necessary. Not so, his attempt to draw an imaginary line across the Bogue, and to confine the harm and guilt of smuggling to the waters of the river. The previous practice of the British government may have lent some support to such a discrimination; still, its futility is evident. The Chinese jurisdiction does extend over the shores beyond the Bogue, and to deny their right of domain over the outer anchorages, is to usurp a portion of their territory. Or, if the instructions of the superintendent made it necessary for him to treat the outer waters as the 'high seas,' and to claim exclusive jurisdiction over offenses committed thereon, by British subjects; then such pretensions should have been clearly explained to, and adjusted with, the provincial government. No doubt should have been suffered to rest on a point so important in itself, and so closely connected with the opening controversy.

9th. No such explanation having been made (that we know of); no such division line having been agreed on; no British claim to the outer anchorages having been admitted; the superintendent's order of March 22d requiring all British vessels to repair to Hongkong, and there prepare to resist every aggression on the part of the Chinese government, was wholly indefensible. To resist that government within the river, had been, three months before, declared penal, and homicide committed in such contest, to be murder. Unless therefore, some mutual demarcation was agreed on, the command to oppose the same authority, on the same business, without the river, was a solecism of the greatest magnitude. That the order to arm and resist did include the opium fleet, is manifest from its whole tenor, and especially from the fact, that the whole fleet, was officially placed, in case of the absence of H.M. sloop Larne, under the command of the senior captain of the storeships. Had the Chinese then, leaving their own forms, adopted the European mode of seizure, how could the bloody contest, which must have followed, been defended from the charge of breach of faith? What explanation could have been given, for thus defending by public authority, in ships without the river, an article which the same authority had given up to confiscation, in boats, within the Bogue? Had the acquaintance of the Chinese with European usages extended a little farther, they would at once have met the superintendent's notice by the withdrawal of his exequatur, and thus dissolved their obligations toward an officer, who had publicly declared, that he had lost, 'all confidence in their justice and moderation.

10th. The confinement of the foreign residents having taken place, it was a generous, a gallant thing for the superintendent to throw himself within the guard, and share with them their dangers and their humiliations. The policy of that act, we shall not question; the main error lying, to our view, in the use subsequently made of it. Communication with the authorities was prefaced by an interference which necessarily destroyed the just influence of the British representative. The withdrawal of the gentleman on whom the commissioner had fixed, as the representative of the opium dealers, from under the Chinese guard to the asylum of the British factory, identified the superintendent with the body whose part he thus took, and made him the object of strong suspicion. Of course his proffers to adjust the question at issue, on principles of equity, were suspected, for it was evident that the two officers differed in toto as to their interpretation of the word equity. The negotiation was soon at an end, the demand for passports followed, and the breach between two great nations was now made broad, if not irreparable.

11th. Although the Indian drug was the growth of the East I. Company, and bore their mark, we know by the declaration of the select committee in 1826, that they meant to denounce and disclaim it, the moment the tea-trade should be endangered on its account. They would have ordered off the opium fleet, that the superintendent sought to protect. Instead of giving Mr. Dent the protection of their factory, they would have deported him. It was a strange thing, therefore, to see a directly opposite course pursued, to behold the whole mass of the drug assumed for the service of the British government. Considering the origination of the article, and the close connection of that government with it, this was just as it should be. An unseen retribution seemed to control the act. But looking at the consular instructions, at the high tone of British policy, and at the deference due to a friendly nation, a greater official error than the assumption could scarcely be committed.

12th. The ardent temperament of the superintendent, his energetic character, his extreme sensitiveness to the honor of his flag, and that ever ready recourse to arms, which military training from youth up always engenders, scarcely account for his subsequent measures. The Baconian creed, 'let nations that pretend to greatness, have this, that they be sensible to wrongs, either upon borderers, merchants, or politic ministers, and that they sit not too long upon a provocation,' hardly authorises them. In fact it is not easy to avoid the conviction, that finding himself sinking into unpromising inactivity, the superintendent hailed the opportunity to fasten a quarrel on the Chinese people. His government had shown itself indifferent to points of honor, and matters of personal disrespect, in the cases of Mr. Marjoribanks and lord Napier. But here was an opportunity to touch 'that sensitive region, the breeches pocket,'–to vest in the Queen a quarrel worth £2,000,000 sterling.

13th. The breach once made, it was necessary to the same policy that it should not close again. It would not do, to sit down quietly under official protests, until the pleasure of the home government could be known. Because this clumsy government, once in motion, had trampled upon the illicit trade, it was necessary that the legal too should be trodden down along with it. This was the practical effect of the superintendent's injunctions on all British subjects, to quit their residences and their business, and to retire from Canton for an indefinite period. The American residents refused to follow this example for these reasons; because, to withdraw at that moment and on such grounds, was to stake their chances of sympathy and support on a hopeless throw–on an opium quarrel; and because the interests of the absent and the innocent were not lightly to be sacrificed; and because they had no representative able and willing to bear the responsibility of a similar order. Situated as they were, they seem to us to have made the wiser choice. At the same time it is to be granted that the semblance of generosity, the show of honor, the seeming of disinterested sacrifice, were on the side of the retiring party. The show, we say, for it was necessary to the reality, that the choice should have been made voluntarily, and when made, honestly and manfully abided by.

But in truth the obedience of the British residents to the orders to withdraw, seems ascribable only the peculiar circumstances of their case. They had given up £2,000,000 sterling, on the responsibility of the superintendent, and it would not do, to question his powers, or attack the authority for so important an act of alienation. This would have revived their personal responsibility for the surrender, and deprived their claims of his official advocacy. Had not the surrender preceded, the retirement had never taken place.

14th. As a public measure, the withdrawal seems to us impolitic and indefensible. It involved the innocent with the guilty, committed the legal traders to intolerable losses, drove them to evasions of the orders they dared not openly disobey, and at last destroyed their confidence in the superintendent and in each other. It completed the identification of the British government with the contraband trade, and converted the superintendent, from an influential mediator into an open enemy of the commissioner. Besides, the order to retire, like the prior order to arm and resist, seems to us to have been based on a geographical error. It assumed that it was necessary to withdraw from Canton, but not necessary to retire from China. It supposed that private life and property were unsafe within the Bogue, but safe in the outer anchorages. How did the result bear out these assumptions. Did the Chinese yield their claim over those waters? Could Macao afford any protection? Was Hongkong beyond annoyance? No. While on the one hand, the Chinese claims were successfully asserted; while the impression of the British fleet spreading its sails and seeking safer harbors, was not made; while the onus of every difficulty was thrown upon the superintendent; while the idea that trade was still expected and desired, was kept up by the presence of the merchant ships: on the other, more loss of comfort, life, and property were involved in the outset, than continued residence at Canton could by any possibility have endangered. These results are all so many attestations to the wisdom of those articles in modern treaties, by which it is provided, that, even in event of hostile rupture, the merchants of either party shall have a sufficient interval for the settlement of their affairs, and for a safe retirement from the enemy's dominions. For instance, by the 12th article of the treaty of 1826, between Great Britain and Mexico, 'it is agreed, that if at any time any interruption of friendly intercourse, or any rupture should unfortunately take place between the two contracting parties, the merchants residing upon the coasts shall be allowed six months, and those of the interior a whole year, to wind up their accounts, and dispose of their property, &c., &c.' Both the British and the American codes abound with specimens of the like considerate and humane negotiation. And in the view of these, we cannot but look upon the hasty injunctions of May last, as a measure becoming an enemy of British commerce, rather than its legally appointed superintendent and protector. Even had the conduct of the Chinese government been ten times worse than is was; had hostilities been sure to ensue; had it been absolutely necessary for all official correspondence to cease; still time was due to the legal trader for the settlement of his affairs, if negotiation could procure it; and had it been denied, the mere refusal would have consituted a further ground of just complaint against China. But the harsh requisition came from the British representative, not from the imperial commissioner. The guardian of British interests on this side the Pacific, inflicted with his own hands, the losses, from which the same commerce on the opposite shores, is sedulously guarded by solemn treaty.

15th. The signature of the first bond by the Americans was great error. To induce the English to remain at Canton, exemption from all bonds had been offered. In all probability therefore, a calm statement of the just objections of foreigners to such bonds, would, at that stage of affairs, have been successful. This release had been virtually promised to an American resident, who came a little before to look on at the destruction of the opium. Unhappily these fair prospects were clouded over; a bond was signed; and to make the matter worse–to add the character of meanness to error–it was arranged that the resident merchants should be screened, and the whole risk be thrown upon the commanders and crews of vessels. Why then were these last fastened on, and the former passed over? Had they been the authors of these troubles? Had they been the chief encouragers of the traffic, the means of its increase and the sharers of its largest profits? No; the resident merchants. Why then this unfair substitution? Because the wily head of the cohong knew whom he was dealing with, and that to subdue the opposition of hardy sailors; to have a victim forthcoming, when the time for sacrifice should arrive; it was necessary to bribe the resident agents.

16th. Unfair and objectionable as the first bond was, there were reasons for submitting to its signature, as a temporary measure, when it became unavoidable. After all that may be said of the law of honor, and of the duty of resistance to every unjust demand; the individual is fully authorized by the Christian code to adopt a less lofty, a humbler demeanor. To fight for every right, to resent to the last every despotic encroachment, may be the duty of governments; but the private man may and generally should submit under protest, waiving his just claims, until appeal can be had to national protection.

Again, at the time of the signature of the first bond, no law touching the case of foreigners, dealing in opium, was or had been promulgated. The new regulations; referred to in the bond itself, were silent as to capital penalties. The edicts of the commissioner, the sole ground of the dread of capital punishments, conveyed direct exemptions for a very long interval. On these grounds it was believed, that no conviction could legally take place under that bond, and hence, that its signature, though inexpedient and humiliating, involved no practical danger. This belief was strenously combatted, however, by some, and the submission of the Americans treated as a direct sacrifice of every security for life and property. The argument continued open until the receipt of the commissioner's edict of 20th October, requiring a new bond to be given by all vessels entering the river. The language of this paper was, 'the American ships having been the first to enter the port on the 11th of June, at which time the particulars of the new law had not been promulgated &c. But now the new law has already been made, wherein it is said, that any foreigners bringing opium to the inner land, shall be immediately executed, &c., all must therefore comply with the form prescribed. This declaration from the highest authority was decisive, that the first bond, though objectionable in itself and injurious as a precedent, was not an assent to a capitally penal law, for such had not then been promulgated.

17th. When the British residents had made their election, to quit Canton, and the Americans theirs to remain; one and only proper course remained for both parties. The former were bound to stand manfully by the injunctions of the superintendent, without flinching or evasion; and the latter, were bound not to interfere or temper with them. The views of the superintendent towards the Americans had been at all times, kind and friendly. He wished and invited them to leave Canton with him, but since this could not be, he had no disposition to molest them. They were bound, on their part, not to interfere with his policy or draw away his people from their professed submission to him. When therefore leading American houses at Canton began to look with an eager avidity on the profits of this forbidden agency, and to prepare for its active prosecution, no disinterested person, even of their friends, could regard it as anything less than a departure from all propriety, from all just deference to the representative of Great Britain. The American commodore, then in the Chinese waters, expressed himself thus on the subject,– 'The trade carried on under our flag between Canton and Hongkong appears to me pregnant with evil, and I regret to find that men who were considered prudent, are largely engaged it. The * * * has come down laden with a cargo for an English ship at Hongkong, and her master informs me, that two of the first American houses are about employing constantly two ships to supply the British shipping with cargoes. If any misunderstanding should grow out of this, our countrymen will have themselves alone to blame for it, and cannot expect the aid of men-of-war, to assist them in doing wrong, &c.' These opinions were the more correct, this claim of the superintendent to deference from the Americans was the more clear, because he had already, with a generous disavowal of all wish to annoy, sanctioned such purchases of British goods in exchange for their bills, as was necessary to carry on their usual trade without the smallest interruption. This important concession should have satisfied the Americans, and content with the undisturbed prosecution of their own business, they should have held themselves above the temptations presented, and thus given to the world a fine specimen of mercantile principle and moderation. As the merit and good effects of such a course would have been great, so the results of the opposite were lamentable. The friendly feelings of the superintendent were of course affected, and private merchants, as they yielded one by one to the pressure of losses, and sent their property within the river, felt anything but cordiality or respect towards their American agents. Thus the policy which dictated the retirement was gradually broken up, until all that was intended to be impressive and coercive upon the Chinese, fell with almost unmitigated weight on the shoulders of their generous opponents.

18th. While the commissioner was among us, as the impersonation of the temperance spirit in China, we were disposed to follow his movements with indulgence, if not with favor. We saw something of justice, as well as of severity, in his decree of confiscation. In following him through the details of the measure, we remembered how far the Chinese usages differ from our own, and excused in part his preference for his own national modes of procedure. As the officer of an Asiatic and pagan government, we were not surprised to find him somewhat wanting in that strict integrity, that undeviating veracity, which western nations owe solely to their Christianity. But when we stood by the spot where the opium was being destroyed, and passed on from the humiliating scene to an interview with his excellency, we conceived his work of punishment to be finished, and made it our earnest petition, that he would now change his course, and close his mission with revising and liberalising the laws regarding foreign intercourse with China.

Unhappily his excellency was already in an attitude of hostility towards the larger portion of the foreign residents, and the advice was not taken. The bloody affray of July soon followed, and the relations of the two nations were thrown into inextricable confusion. When this affair was carried to the commissioner, he reverted at once to the old Chinese law and precedents, and demanded the murderer. The terms he was then on with the superintendent, precluded any calm and friendly settlement, and irritated by the refusal to comply with his demand, by the lingering of the opium ships and dealers, and by the renewed sales of the drug, he suffered himself to be hurried on to those harsh and unjustifiable acts, which have left an indelible stain on his mission and character. Acting on the system of mutual responsibility, so interwoven with the Chinese polity, he proceeded to coerce the surrender of the guilty individual by oppressing the British residents at Macao, a place forty miles distant from the scene of the murder. The superintendent and most of his countrymen withdrew to Hongkong, where the denial of provisions, and other local annoyances brought on remonstrances, and finally a collision with the Chinese force at Kowlung, a small port in the vicinity. Of this affair, we believe the general opinion to be, that it was rash and 'untoward.' It threw upon the British flag the odium of being the first to aggress, the guilt of the first bloodshed.

19th. The right of blockade is confessedly a portion of international law, which belligerents and neutrals are far from being agreed on. But there are sufficient expositions extant, to show clearly, that the blockade of the port of Canton, announced the 11th of September and revoked the 16th, was defective in authority, as well as based upon misapprehension. The actual cutting off of certain British subjects by the Chinese, which had been assumed in the notice, proved incorrect, and even if it had not, no maritime nation would, we think have admitted the blockade as emanating from competent authority. That a British consul and a British post-captain can declare war, or assume certain acts of foreign powers to be a declaration of war, and thence proceed without any direct instructions, or any reference to superior authority, to exercise belligerent rights upon neutral flags, is a doctrine that would overthrow all the securities of commerce. Least of all could such principles be admitted in application to remote parts of the mercantile world, where incalculable losses would be inflicted, before such reference could be made or confirmation had, from the supreme governments. In the particular instance before us, the assumption maintained by the blockade party and derided by their opponents,–that war did actually exist–would have been even more disastrous to British than to neutral interests. Had it been true, the large amount of British property lying within the Bogue, would have been at the mercy of the Chinese, and almost the whole in the outer anchorages also, liable to capture and condemnation under charge of trading with the enemy. But in truth no war existed, and the revocation of the blockade, five days after its announcement, was coupled with a notification of negotiations pending with the enemy.

20th. We shall not attempt to analyse these negotiations, or to trace the causes which led to their failure. On this, as on the other prior matters, we want fuller copies of what passed between the contracting parties, to decide exactly. From the papers which have appeared, it would seem that the whole negotiation for a trade at Chuenpe, was carried on by the parties at cross purposes with each other. From the commissioner's edict of 9th October, ushering in the arrangements, and from the momorandum of propositions and replies published Oct. 26th, it is evident he contemplated as complete a subjection of British life to Chinese adjudication at Chuenpe, in case of the detection of opium, as could be conveyed by the subscription of any bonds whatever. At the same time, it is equally apparent from the whole course of the superintendent, that, on his part, no such submission was intended. Whether any further modifications took place, or whether the superintendent secretly relied on the presence of a sloop-of-war to rescue any British subject charged with smuggling, we know not; but so far as appears, no arrangement was at all practicable between parties so wide of each other. Bad faith on the commissioner's part may have existed, but it is unnecessary to call it in, to account for the subsequent failure. A frank and clear understanding, a full declaration of each one's meaning, was all that was needed to produce that result,–to break off a negotiation based wholly upon concealment or mutual misapprehension.

21st. The failure of the arrangements at Chuenpe gave a new impulse to the freighting business already going on in American and other bottoms. This last hope of renewed trade disappointed, the anxiety of the British ship-owners and consignees to clear their vessels, and the competition which followed, carried freights of cotton (from Hongkong to Whampoa) up to $6 per bale, while, for bringing down teas, &c., $10 per ton was given. The depreciation of the British flag and the enhancement of the value of others went on, until ship after ship was sold for nominal considerations, to supply the demand for neutral tonnage. This strange alteration of values was of course the legitimate fruit of the superintendent's measures. But whether he foresaw this result or not, we are not aware, and therefore make no comment on the official causes. As a concern of the merchants interested in these transfers, no commendation can be expressed either of the buyers or the sellers. The public and generous nature of the superintendent's contest, however impolitic, should have prevented any man of any other nation from this direct opposition to him. Still more wrong was it for British subjects, to evade their obligations to their own officer, laboring for their own protection. The former violated their neutrality; the latter, their consistence and their allegiance. The part taken by the American consul in these purchases is open to the same and even greater objections. By giving his sanction to such transfers, instead of checking them in the outset, he of course involved the consulate in the course so offensive to the British representative. By going further, and granting formal passes to vessels so bought, requesting all "princes, potentates, &c., to suffer said ships to pass, without let, hindrance, or molestation,' he exceeded, in the common opinion, his proper and legal functions. As the question here involved is an important one, we will briefly state the grounds of that judgment, as we understand them.

We learn from the consular instructions promulgated on the first of August, 1801, that 'our consuls had already originated the practice of providing with certificates foreign vessels purchased abroad by citizens of the United States.' 'To regulate a course of proceedings the tendency of which was to blend American with foreign property in appearance,' the consuls were instructed to require certain proofs of bonafide ownership, and thereon empowered to grant a certificate, after a form prescribed, which paper–it is added – 'must be limited to the vessel's return to the United States, and her destination to some port therein must be specified in it.' The form referred to, after reciting the evidences of property–closed thus– 'I have granted permission that the said ship may depart and proceed on her voyage to the port aforesaid. This permission to continue in force only during the said voyage.' If therefore this certificate were still authorized, it would appear to convey no protection to purchased vessels, plying on freighting trips between foreign anchorages, with no homeward destination, and no idea, in fact, of ever being sent to any port within the Union.

But after four years' experience of the workings of this permission, the department of state issued, July 12th, 1805, the following instructions. 'the multiplied abuses of the certificates which the consuls of the United States were, by the instructions of the 1st August, 1801, authorized to give, in the case of foreign vessels purchased by a citizen of the United States, notwithstanding the precautions taken against them, have led to the conslusion, that the discontinuance of the certificates altogether is the only effectual remedy. You will therefore forbear to grant any certificate whatever relative to such purchases, except to those who may satisfy you, that the purchase was made without knowing this alteration in your instructions. Accordingly, you will publicly advertise that you are restrained from issuing certificates in such cases, with the sole exception just mentioned; and from allowing the exception itself, after the expiration of two months from the date of the advertisement.' This is, so far as we know, the latest action of the American government, on the subject of these certificates. The revival of the practice in China, after so long an interval, is, we suppose, based on the general consular power to grant certificates, or on the silence of the general instructions of March 2d, 1833, or on the late receipt of new instructions. The first supposition, could not, in any case, we suppose, authorize more than a consular deposition, respecting the ownership of the vessel in question, even if this be not precluded, by the special exception recited. The second ground seems equally defective, because the object of Mr. Livingston in his digest, was–to guide the consul in his duties,–in the exercise of powers yet belonging to his office, not to recite repeals, or to authorize resumptions of those long taken from it. On the third point, the American consul is of course the best authority, and he certainly will not refuse to make known such instructions, nor indeed any reasons which have justified, to his own mind, this portion of his official conduct. In the absence of such explanations, our impression is–that while the United States will always extend to foreign built vessels purchased by Americans, the protection accorded by acts of Congress of 1802 and 1803, they yet confine all certification to the home authorities, because it cannot in their view be safely intrusted to the consuls.

22d. The failure of the Chuenpe negotiation led to other consequences of a much more serious nature. The commissioner renewing his commands to the British fleet ' to enter the port or leave the coast,' under pain of capture or destruction, the superintendent proceeded with two sloops-of-war to the Bogue, to demand the withdrawal of these offensive orders. No satisfaction being afforded, and the Chinese fleet showing signs of hostile preparation, the sloops began a fire which shortly disabled or destroyed several of the junks, with some scores or hundreds of their people. On this conflict, opinions are, we believe, much divided; some joining with the superintendent in lamenting the carnage; the most regretting that the complete destruction of the fleet was not effected. We do not hesitate in this diversity to take the side of the superintendent and of humanity. And we would further respectfully ask, was it, then, for the safety of life and property, that the retirement from Canton was ordered? And are these the fruits of that measure? With all allowance for difference of value between Chinese and British blood, could any consequences so costly have resulted from a continued residence at the factories? We know these questions will be answered with a show of triumph, by pointing to the violences of the commissioner. But the reference is not satisfactory. Had the orders to repair to Hongkong never been issued to the fleet, probably the homicide of July had never happened. Or if it had, the presence of the superintendent at Canton, had he preserved a position of impartial mediation, should have been at least as influential, to resist unjust demands, as was that of the E.I. Company's select committee. Or if the singular violence of the kinchae had brooked no terms and even extorted a victim to the law of retaliation, then how clear and unquestionable would have been the position of Great Britain. As the case now stands, it is not easy to say how much of these difficulties has proceeded from causes worthy of a nation's quarrel, or how much from subaltern error and exasperation. On the one hand, it is undeniable that the course of the commissioner has been harsh and even hostile. But on the other, the declaration of March 22d was hostile. The language and conduct of the British community during the confinement was openly hostile. The retirement was avowedly the precursor and preparation for hostilities. No more conference, no more papers–was the superintendent's language–a swift and heavy blow will be struck at the Chinese, without preface or explanation. The attack at Kowlung, the notice of blockade, the affair at Chuenpe, were all hostile. In short, the whole history of these troubles forms an admirable comment on the wisdom of those provisions against rash war-making with half civilized states, which fill up some of the brightest pages in western diplomacy. We quote for instance, the following from Art. 24 of the treaty of 1786, between the United States and Morocco. "If any differences shall arise by either party infringing on any of the articles of this treaty, peace and harmony shall remain notwithstanding in the fullest force, until a friendly application shall be made for an arrangement; and until that application shall be rejected, no appeal shall be made to arms." And again, from the 16th article of the treaty of 1816 with Algiers: "In case of any dispute arising from the violation of any of the articles of this treaty, no appeal shall be made to arms, nor shall war be declared on any pretext whatever; but if the consul, residing at the place where the dispute shall happen, shall not be able to settle the same, the government of that country shall state their grievance in writing, and transmit the same to the government of the other, and the period of three months shall be allowed for answers to be returned, during which time no act of hostility shall be permitted by either party."

These articles seem to us to embody the true spirit of an enlightened and pacific diplomacy; to treat the fearful power of making war,–of taking life,–in the only proper manner,–as an essential attribute of sovereignty, not to be trusted to subaltern hands in any case whatever.

23d. The collision at Chuenpe, as it threw an additional doubt on the safety of British property within the grasp of the Chinese, gave a new impulse to transhipments. Five or six ships of the British fleet were transferred by sale to American hands, and several more were placed under other neutral colors. How far these sales might have gone, is not to be told, had not the commissioner, seeing perhaps that his efforts to dislodge the British fleet were neutralized by the permission to tranship, withdrew by his edicts of Nov. 25th, the license he had previously given through the American consul. These important papers drew the more attention, because they put an official end to the British trade with China, from and after the 6th December. Whether they will be construed rigidly or loosely, whether the exclusion will be applied generally, or only to such vessels from Indian ports as refuse to give bonds against opium, remains to be gathered from the future course of the commissioner and his successors.

In this tangled and complicated state of affairs, it is our design now to express our views and wishes, as to the more immediate measures necessary to bring back these agitated elements to quiet and order. Beginning with the American community, we venture to offer some brief recommendations, first to the consul, and next to the private merchants. To the former, we propose that he reconsider his course on two points; the granting of passes to purchased vessels, and the mode of dealing with petitions placed in his hands by his fellow-citizens for presentation to the Chinese authorities.

Beside the objections to those grants, arising out of the consular instructions, he should consider their offensiveness to the superintendent, and their tendency to destroy our neutral character, by confounding all the distinctions between American and foreign property. When the transhipments first began, in American built vessels, commodore Read warned his countrymen–that, 'if they could not carry on their commerce without having their interests so completely and thoroughly blended with those of the English, it would have been better that ships-of-war had not appeared here.' Had he remained in the Chinese waters, until equal and even greater suspicion came to be thrown over the flag itself, his opinions on the point would surely have gained further strength, and thus placed the two American officers in the country, in direct collision with each other.

Again, we hope the consul will reconsider his course with respect to the receipt and forwarding of petitions. We must explain our views by saying–that when the British fleet had repaired to Hongkong, and it became absolutely necessary to the prosecution of the American trade, to exchange bills for goods, a strong objection was felt to any transhipments, by some parties, on account of their irregularity. These parties wished to bring the subject at once before the commissioner, that the practice might have his sanction, or if it were refused, that ships might repair for the purpose to ports beyond the Chinese territory. The hongs would not receive the petitions; and on application to the sub-prefect of Macao, he required that the petition be presented through the consul. The consul refused to transmit it, and thus for some months, the transhipments went on under an odious and hazardous singularity. But when the actual sale of ships, as well as of goods, brought the subject before the commissioner, and he demanded explanation, the consul was compelled to state what he had before declined, and the transhipments were admitted in reply 'to come within the limits of allowable business.'

Again, when the second bond was first presented to the American captains, it was the strong wish of parties that the just objections to that paper should be calmly and frankly stated. Memoranda were prepared for that purpose, but when on the refusal of the hongs to interpose, the consul was applied to, his answer was, that he should not petition himself, nor could he transmit any petition for others. We are fully aware how very low a rank the consular officer holds in the political system, and that the American especially has no right to approach any native government, at all, except in cases of emergency, and in the absence of an accredited minister. Still, in such circumstances as exist in China, we think it extremely desirable that the consul should not refuse to act upon points which intimately concern life, property, and honor. While we would not have him assume powers at variance with his instructions, and which if exercised, can only serve some private speculation; we would have him ever ready to interpose in behalf of those who are suffering for their fidelity to their principles and their country.

As respects the American merchants, if our opinions might have any influence, we would use it, to recall them to their own regular commerce, and to a more becoming position toward the Chinese government. It is to be hoped, that the prohibition of transhipments will do something to forward the former object; and as for the latter, though error has reached an almost irreparable point, yet something may be done to make it the less disastrous. The mistake we refer to is–the signature of the second bond, without protest, explanation, or remonstrance. The first bond was sufficiently objectionable. It was vague and without any expressed penalties. It looked like a studied attempt to combine apparent rigor with real immunity from punishment. The admissions with which it was coupled deprived it of any fatal power, until the lapse of a considerable interval. Yet, even in the signature of this bond, the American merchants went to the very verge of dishonor. They made a bad precedent, in the hope of discharging better, an important duty. In the attempt to give the Chinese government every possible proof of their sincere abjuration of the opium traffic, they had conceded all and perhaps more than society and governments could sanction. Still this was no inexcusable, no irreparable error. Yet, had no new bond been presented to them, they would have been bound on the expiration of the commissioner's limitations in December, to have brought the subject before him, and remonstrated against a longer signature. When therefore the new bond was presented, with all its offensive and fatal clauses, there should have been an unanimous refusal to accept its terms, and the grounds of this rejection submitted frankly to the commissioner. The quiet swallowing of such conditions, in silence, without an effort to effect an abatement, was a proceeding wholly inexcusable, and utterly beneath the American character. Enough had been already done, to evince a complete abandonment of the opium trade, and here was a fine opportunity to show, how satisfaction to the injured government of China, could be reconciled with every other duty. It was thrown away, as if of no value. Lamentable as this recklessness was in itself, and in its influence to confirm the Chinese in error as to foreign usages, something may yet be done, and certainly should be, before the departure of the commissioner. Taking advantage of his return to the provincial city, they may lay before him their petition in form something like the following.

The undersigned, American merchants, approach your excellency for the purpose of respectfully stating their views on the form of bond lately required, through the hong merchants–

When the British merchants withdrew from Canton in May last, we declined the invitation to follow them, because we were anxious to prove, that our abandonment of the opium trade was sincere and final. Your excellency having then specified four and eight months as the periods after which the new law should take effect, on vessels from India and from Europe, we were anxious to use this interval, to settle our affairs, and to give every reasonable satisfaction to your excellency. It was ever our intention, on the expiration of these periods, to come before your excellency with our frank petition against the full enforcement of those regulations. Now before the period has elapsed, we find ourselves called on to submit our vessels and crews to their full and unreserved operation. We take this occasion therefore to state the following objections.

1st. The bond now required is unnecessary. When your excellency arrived at Canton in March last, the opium trade was flourishing. With two weapons, the confiscation of the drug and the banishment of the importers, the traffic was driven from the factories. If then, these two means were sufficient to eradicate the evil, they are surely sufficient to prevent its springing up again within our residences. Where is the necessity for the confiscation of legal property, or for the use of capital punishments?

2d. The bond is misplaced. For the last eight months, not a chest of opium has been sold by the foreigners at Canton; while hundreds and perhaps thousands, have been delivered along the coasts of the empire. It is not, therefore, by new and severe regulations applicable to Canton alone, that the evil is to be reached, but by measures extended along the sea-frontier.

3d. The bond is fraught with danger to China. The confiscation of the drug, in March last, and still more, the shutting up of the foreign residents and consuls, have already endangered the peace of the empire. How then can war be avoided, if confiscations be extended to whole cargoes of licit property, and even life be taken away, for a catty of opium?

4th. The bond is framed an entire dereliction of the benevolent professions of the government towards foreigners. It is not only capitally severe toward the really guilty, but it involves all, having property on board the ship whence opium is landed, in common forfeitures. To use the language of Mencius, it converts the waters from the Ladrones to Whampoa into a vast pit for the ruin of foreigners.

5th. The bond manifests complete ignorance of the views and usages of foreign nations. All good men in the west regret the use of opium by your people. But it is their custom to check vice by pure examples, by clear instructions, &c., not by capital punishments. If such means are necessary to restrain your people from the use of opium, they leave you to apply them. Your people know the laws and language. If accused, they can defend themselves. They have friends to intercede for them. If wronged, they can appeal to the emperor. Not so the foreigner. He is an alien on your shores. He can with great difficulty prepare a short petition. He has no friends, no access by appeal to the emperor. Foreign states will give every guaranty against opium, but they will ever demand, either that their people be treated in all respects as natives, or suffered to live entirely under the jurisdiction of their consuls. This has always been granted to the Portuguese at Macao; why should it not be granted to all other foreigners?

6th. The bond, even if given, is of no value; no man signs it sincerely. He submits, because you are strong and he is weak, but he utterly denies the obligation. He neither means to give up his crew nor his vessel, nor his cargo. He has no right and no power to do either. He regards you as an oppressor, for demanding it, and is determined to act, just as if he had signed no bond whatever. His rulers too will disown the certificates so soon as they hear of them.

For these and other like reasons, we petition your excellency to desist from the demand of these bonds, and to revert to the means already so successful in your hands,–the confiscation of the drug wherever found, and the expulsion of all foreigners taking part in its introduction.

Objections like these are surely too well founded to be overlooked by the American residents; nor will their consul again refuse them his aid, when it is thus required–not for mercenary purposes, not in doubtful stretches of uncertain powers,–but for the preservation of life, property, and public honor. Even if such a petition should fail to change a policy now hardened by our own needless submissions, yet it is worth while to have placed it in the provincial archives, and in the hands of the commissioner. It is something to have told this government, that while it keeps the foreigner an alien on its shores, it must find some means to reconcile its own demands, with the allegiance he still owes to the laws of his native country.

To go on to the British community, we take the liberty to give our counsel to the mercantile residents with all the freedom of friendship and sympathy. Their choice seems to us to have been made, once for all, when they obeyed the superintendent's injunctions to retire from their factories. Or rather the surrender of the opium was the pledge, too heavy to be forfeited, staked upon the validity of his injunctions, which bound them to respect his command and support his authority. Deference to the superintendent, and unanimity among themselves, were henceforth their true policy. They should not have sent their property, as such, within the Bogue, nor should they have employed other flags, other covers, and other agencies. Evasions, jealousies, discords, only lowered their own stand, and weakened their hold on the home government. It is time that frankness, truth, unanimity, and loyalty, resume their empire. The act of this government, which now puts an official period to British commerce, is the act which should unite all minds in a firm, patient, undoubting expectation for the powerful interposition of their sovereign.

As regards the British superintendent, we trust it may not be inconsistent with the deference due his rank and superior information, to express our wishes on two points,–the armed possession of Chinese harbors, and the defense of such positions by hostile measures. We think he will admit the doctrine, though laid down by a transatlantic tribunal, that 'the jurisdiction of a nation within its own territory is exclusive and absolute. It is susceptible of no limitation not imposed on itself. Any restriction, deriving its validity from an external source, would imply a diminution of its sovereignty to the extent of that restriction, and an investment of that sovereignty to the same extent, in the power which could impose such restriction. All exceptions to the full and complete power of the nation within its own territories, must be traced up to the consent of the nation itself.' Candor and the maps further oblige us to admit, that the anchorages now and lately occupied by the British fleet are 'within the body of the country,' not 'the uninclosed water of the ocean on the seacoast, outside the fauces terra.' Under such premises, we would respectfully ask, if it be right for the officer of a foreign nation to occupy and hold by force, such harbors? Does this impose no 'limitation' on the Chinese sovereignty? And when this assumption is made, not in war but in peace, not by supreme but by inferior authority, is it justifiable; is it in short, the proper part of a peaceful, protective, trade-superintendency? We cannot see it to be so. The policy of the superintendent on this point,–the withdrawal from Canton to take up a position without the Bogue,–seems to us to have involved a common forgetfulness of precedents and of geography. It overlooked that favorite provision in modern treaties already quoted, by which a long interval (six to twelve months) is secured to merchants, &c., wherein to settle their affairs, before they shall come under the reach even of a declaration of war, and hurried them from their residences on a hasty and insufficient notice. It drew the same erroneous line across the Bogue, which had been drawn in reference to the opium smuggling, in the previous order of December. The superintendent's abandonment of this demarcation as concerns the drug, and his declaration (notice of 11th September) that 'H.M's. flag does not fly in countenance or protection of the traffic,' and requiring all British vessels engaged in it 'to depart immediately from the harbor and the coast,' go far to show that the distinction between inside and outside never was well founded, and should be given up entirely. The orders not to trade with the Chinese, have now been met by the orders of the commissioner not to trade with the English, and oaths, it is said, are about to be exacted, of all vessels entering, that they have not communicated with the British shipping. We trust therefore the necessity of a general evacuation will soon be admitted, and the fleet leave these waters for some more hospitable harbors.

If the armed occupation of Hongkong was indefensible, much more so were the bloody encounters of Kowlung and Chuenpe, by which it was sought to maintain possession. But the orders to repair thither being issued, it was next necessary to secure a supply of provisions for the fleet, as well as to guard it from molestation. The attack on Kowlung aimed to gain the first object, that on the Chuenpe fleet, the second. If the British relations with China were those of war, when the first action took place, it was surely too much to require the Chinese to furnish supplies–to commit the treason of 'aiding and comforting' the enemy. If they were peaceful on both occasions, then we must view these 'untoward' affairs, as humble, inglorious imitations of Copenhagen and Navarino. But there is a broader objection to these encounters, than any that arises out of the momentary relations of the contending parties. 'War,' to borrow again the language of a western statesman, 'is the ultimate and last resort; and much ought to be borne, before a nation, especially a commercial one, should appeal to arms.' It is the last resort to which humanity consents, even when the reluctant act of supreme authority after slow and solemn deliberation. How much more objectionable then, when the work of destruction is made to precede the declaration of hostilities; when the sovereign, in whose hands this awful power is constitutionally lodged, is not consulted, the counsel and deliberation are forgotten in the hurry of mutual exasperation. Hence the wisdom of that provision against rash hostilities already quoted; and hence the earnest wish we venture to express, that when the British fleet can no longer ride quietly in the Chinese waters, it will retire, until its safe and honorable and triumphant return can be provided for, as it should be, by orders under the sign-manual.

We now reach the last topic we design to touch, viz. the action, to be expected and desired, on the part of western governments. And here we look mainly to the interposition of G. Britain; not that we doubt that an American (and may be a French and a Dutch) envoy will soon be out; but because his appointment will probably be anticipated, and his measures outweighed, by the quicker and more powerful interference of England. Unquestionably the United States will exhaust every peaceful recourse, rather than leave their citizens resident in China longer exposed to loss and contumely. But all their efforts will be deliberate and pacific. Their neutral position, during the long wars of Europe, and the succeeding disturbances of the Spanish colonies, has taught them patience. The tardy and reluctant satisfaction granted to their claims, but granted at last, by almost every European power, attests their long-suffering, and at the same time, the steadiness with which, when wronged, they demand, and finally obtain justice. They will say of these troubles in China, as was said of the conduct of the South Americans, by the secretary of state in 1827, 'had we declared war upon every occasion of complaint like these, (and there is no disposition to underrate them,) the United States would have enjoyed scarcely a year of repose, since the establishment of their present constitution.' For this reason chiefly, we suppose the American action here will be set aside, and therefore direct our attention chiefly to the expected movements of Great Britain. The nature of the present troubles–of the crisis which calls for her interference–compels her, at the very first step, to take up the opium question.

The origination of that traffic by the British government, through its creature the E.I. Company, has given rise to two obligations on her part,–one, towards the Chinese government. The E.I. Company has trained up a class of men, and employed them to do its work and fill its coffers, by carrying on a contraband trade in China. These men have been overtaken in their sad service, by sudden and heavy losses. The character of their agency is such, that no armed protection can be afforded them, no claim for security or compensation can be put in, on their behalf, to the Chinese government. Their cause cannot be defended even in argument, much less espoused and borne out by warlike measures. There is only one thing upon earth, they can claim from their government, and that is money. The power which has raised them up, and taken care to secure the lion's share of their profits, in all the times of their safety, is now bound to bear a liberal share of their losses in their day of adversity. Great Britain stands obliged by sheer justice, to take upon herself a generous division of the late losses, and beyond this, she owes no respect to the traffic, its authors, or conductors, whatever. The money must be counted down, and then the drug, in all its connections, must be swept from her path, at once and for ever. Their claims, their pretensions, their existence, must not stand for a moment longer, between her and her honor.

A distinct satisfaction being done, apart and by itself, to the sufferers of March, in pounds, shillings, and pence, Great Britain approaches, unembarrassed, her obligations to China. Into these, nothing pecuniary enters. Inroads upon a people's virtue, life and happiness, cannot be calculated or paid for, either in sycee or sterling. The past is irrevocable. Frank explanation, manly bearing of just so much censure as is merited, only, can be given; the rest is all prospective. As we are charged, in common with other opponents of the opium trade, with holding all sorts of absurd opinions upon this point–the satisfaction due from England to China–we take this occasion to state our real sentiments the more freely.

As concerns the Chinese government, and especially its imperial head, we hold, that so far as its action upon the opium springs from and evinces a sincere determination to check the fearful progression of a popular vice, it merits respect and deference. Motives so honorable, even if they do not completely justify, yet should bar all hasty and hostile retaliations. At the same time, we are far from yielding to this government, unmingled commendation. Its merits are subject to some large deductions. It is evidently unenlighteded on the subject of 'inefficacious punishments.' It cannot be said 'to love mercy rather than sacrifice.' It clings as closely as ever, to the theory now nearly exploded in the west, that crime is best guarded against by unmeasured punishments. Hence it has already loaded its people with so many odius bonds and penalties, to repress the favorite vice, that nothing but conscience probably keeps down insurrection. Another deduction must yet be made, which should not be overlooked by the moralist and the Christian. The authority which commands a public reformation from a long-practiced vice–universal abstinence from a darling luxury–is the very same, that shuts its people up, from the strongest motives, the most essential helps, to purity and virtue. The imperial proscriber of the opium traffic is also the proscriber of Christianity. Equal sincerity may perhaps animate both acts, but this neither excuses them, nor helps the case of the people. There is no propriety in commanding them to resist seduction, and in denying them, at the same time, the faith that overcomes the world, and fortifies the heart against temptation. It is asserting what all history, all revelation disprove, that there can be popular virtue without Christian motive or private piety.

Unquestionably, all sincere reformation must spring from enlarged knowledge, deep convictions, sincere repentance, in the erring party. And with the aid of Christian motive and the awe of just penalties, such might have been the true and lasting recovery from the national vice of China. No trenching on the popular liberty, no odious bonds, no unjust responsibilities, no harsh and murderous enactments would have disfigured such a reformation. Its effects would have been purely good; not as now, largely mixed with evil. Indeed the imperfect suppression of the traffic at this moment, while the commissioner still lingers near the provincial capital, makes it an easy inference, that his departure will be the signal of fresh importations. If so, of all this costly movement, only two partial fruits will remain:–the moral lesson 'read to Europe,' and the impression made on Chinese society. The first will not soon be forgotten. For the last, the smoker will resume his pipe, for new pleasures are not, new nerves cannot be, given him. The young, the aspiring, the uncontaminated, only, will eschew a vice, once fashionable and flattering, but now odious, the mark of the informer, the surest disqualification for official honors.

The satisfaction due to the imperial author of this national movement, must, as we have said, be almost entirely prospective. He does not ask for any retroactive measures. Security against future importations is all that is demanded by China of Great Britain. The British government has not even an explanation to tender, unless so far as it deems them necessary to the vindication of its own honor. We hear it has already sanctioned that notice of Dec., 1838, by which the superintendent withdrew protection from the smuggling craft within the river. And when it comes to pronounce upon the notice of March 22d, by which the same officer, changing his ground, defended without the river, what he had denounced within, we cannot doubt, it will declare the distinction vain, and express regret that it was ever adopted. Indeed it has been, as we have said, already abandoned by its author; the notice of September 11th, being as full a disclaimer of the whole obnoxious traffic, outside and in, as could have come from the foreign office, or from the pencil of the commissioner. It remains only for the British government to sanction that official act, and to tender to the emperor such securities for the future abstinence of the E.I. Company and all private parties from growing or carrying the drug, as are consistent with the national usages.

The question then is, do British precedents permit the government to interfere to check the opium trade by making it penal for British subjects to carry the drug, and thus to satisfy the demands of China? We find an answer to this query, in the treaty, on the navigation of the Pacific, &c., concluded February, 1825, with Russia. After defining boundaries, granting free commerce,–&c., the 9th Article adds–'the abovementioned liberty of commerce shall not apply to the trade in spirituous liquors, in fire-arms, or other arms, gunpowder or other warlike stores; the high contracting parties reciprocally engaging not to permit the abovementioned articles to be sold or delivered in any manner whatever, to the natives of the country.' Nor is Great Britain alone in these humane provisions. The United States (beside its treaty with Siam, in which opium is specified as prohibited, and its traffic forbidden to their citizens) has a similar treaty with Russia, on the same subject, dated April, 1824. By its Article 4, 'all spirituous liquors, fire-arms, &co., are excepted from the commerce permitted by the preceding article; and the two powers engage reciprocally, neither to sell or suffer them to be sold to the natives, by their respective citizens and subjects, nor by any persons under their authority' Accordingly, congress acting on the right reserved under this treaty, to determine and inflict punishments for contravention of its articles, proceeded to fix, by act of May 19th, 1828, the penalties (fine and imprisonment) to be incurred by any persons so offending.

These remarkable compacts no doubt owe their existence to the working of mingled interest and compassion. And since they have been entered into, for the sake of the scattered tribes on the north Pacific, and their petty traffic; they may be, for the Chinese people and intercourse with China. If they have been made to include spirituous liquors in their list of prohibitions, they may take in the more deadly drug, which has been intoxicating this empire. If these stipulations–these limitations on a gainful traffic–have been granted on the demand of the czar, they cannot be denied to the demand of the emperor. We hazard little in predicting that they will be conceded; that within a very short period, provisions equally broad and just will be applied to the matter in controversy with this empire. One point of difference between the cases will then have to be provided for. The Indian tribes were too feeble to enforce the system devised for their protection. China is more civilized and more powerful. A fair division of jurisdiction would have therefore to be agreed on; such for instance, as the reserving all offenses on the 'high seas' to the foreign, and leaving all committed in harbors, to the native, tribunals.

Securities like these, tendered by foreign governments to the Chinese (with such modifications as circumstances might be found to require) would surely go far to satisfy the imperial mind, and settle the pending controversy. Until the tender is made, all retaliations and hostilities are, to say the least, premature; for it cannot be known that they are necessary. The offer involves no extermination of the poppy, as many would have us believe; no crusade against Turks, or Malwarrees; no breach of faith, law, or usage. Let the two great powers most interested in the matter, make the concession, and let time tell, if any other dare violate what they unite to respect, or refuse what they have conceded.

Supposing this satisfaction–these securities–once given, we close this article with a short reference to the further questions, most urgently claiming foreign interference. Taking the late occurrences as a guide, (and leaving out of sight the higher and ulterior privileges belonging to those cordial and equal relations, we are one day to have with China,) we confine our remarks to two points, the protection due to the foreign residents, and the security of the innocent among them, from implication with the guilty.

The protection due to the citizen while resident abroad, is one of the important and delicate parts of diplomatic provision. Three degrees of this may be noticed. One, where civilized nations, treating with each other, in mutual confidence, give up their citizens to each others municipal laws, without any reservation. This confidential footing is seen in the relation of the European states with the United States of America, and with each other. The second and almost opposite course is followed with respect to states half-civilized, whose police regulations are imperfect, and whose general administration of justice is not to be trusted. Thus the czar treating with the Ottoman Porte at Adrianople in 1829, stipulates, 'that Russian subjects shall live under the exclusive jurisdiction and police of the ministers and consuls of Russia:' and the United States, treating with the same power in May, 1830, make the only stipulation of the kind in their diplomatic code, that their citizens 'shall be tried by their minister or consul, and punished according to their offense, following in, this respect, the usage observed towards other Franks.

An intermediate degree of protection is sometimes secured, for examples of which, we may cite the treaties of the United States, with Morocco, Algiers, Tunis, and Tripoli. For instance the Article 21 of the treaty of 1786, with the first of these states provides: 'If a citizen of the United States should kill or wound a Moor; or on the contrary, if a Moor shall kill or wound a citizen of the United States, the law of the country shall take place, and equal justice shall be rendered, the consul assisting at the trial' And again, the 19th and 20th Arts. of the treaty of 1816 with Algiers provide, that 'any disputes that may take place, between the citizens of the United States, and the subjects of the regency of Algiers, shall be decided by the dey in person, and no other.'* * And– 'if a citizen of the United States kill, wound, or strike a subject of Algiers (or the contrary), the law of the country shall take place, and equal justice be rendered, the consul assisting at the trial; but the sentence against an American shall not be more severe than against a Turk in the same predicament.'

The second of these forms is, no doubt, that which all western governments will prefer, when once they address themselves to work of making their people safe in China. And as the Portuguese have long been permitted to make and apply their own laws at Macao, no insuperable difficulty seems to lie in the way of the extension of the privilege to other foreigners. It is, at all events, much more easy of concession than those full diplomatic relations, which equalize the native and the foreigner–and which alone will ever induce western governments to give up their citizens to the unmitigated operation of the laws of this empire. If, however, some difficulty should oppose the introduction of both these modes, the third is sufficiently substantiated to admit of being tendered to this government; though without a trial, it seems probable, that the Chinese would rather turn foreigners over entirely to their own officers, than admit a joint exercise of judicial authority.

We have every reason to believe that neither Great Britain, nor any other power, will attempt to screen their people from the course of a steady, a somewhat severe justice in this county. Late events, however, make it impossible that they should longer neglect a due provision for that very end–the attainment of a calm and discriminating justice. The homicide of July has been the means (at once atrocious in itself and fortunate in its connection) of reviving the odious pretensions of the Chinese on this point, at a moment when public attention cannot but be turned toward China. It is enough, that Great Britain and the United States have each suffered one such occasion to pass unimproved; that each once looked on unmoved, and saw a subject die unjustly under the hands of the Chinese executioner. It is due in great measure to the firmness of the superintendent that the same scene has not been lately reenacted, and we feel sure, his superiors, though they may regret that his hostile position interfered with the satisfactoriness of his trial, will fully support his exclusive jurisdiction over the homicide of July. It will be the unpardonable fault of the great powers in commerce with this country, if this long contested question be not now settled aright and for ever.

The second point, we have selected–the security of the innocent from implication with the guilty–touches on a remarkable feature of the Chinese polity–that of mutual responsibility. As a domestic question, we are not competent to argue upon it, much less to sit in judgment upon it. It is in theory capable of no defense, and all its justification even as a domestic affair, must arise solely out of the necessities of the government that enforces it, and of the social system, with which it is interwoven. In this point of view, the real question is–does the state of the administration and of the social system in this country, demand the mutual responsibility–or, in other words–is it the lesser of two evils–the only alternative from confusion and anarchy? The late Dr. Milne, commenting on this subject (translation of the Shing Yu p. 40), in connection with the atrocious severity of the Chinese statute of treasons, asks– 'may it not be, in a great degree owing to this singlarly severe feature of the Chinese law, that their government has continued for so many ages unchanged, as to the radical principles and great lines of it?' We venture no answer to the question. It is not with the home bearing of the subject that we have to do, and it is clear enough, in any event, that its extension to the foreigner is wholly inadmissible. He can be controlled, corrected, tried, punished, without such odious compromises of distributive justice. If the guilty man cannot be awed or punished, in his own person, for his own offenses, by Chinese law; he can be reached by his own country's pains and penalties. He needs not to be restrained, or made to suffer at second hand, through the medium of his unoffending relatives. It remains for the powers intrusted herein, to put a period to such unjust liabilities; tendering at the same time to the Chinese, such aid as may ensure the attainment in all cases, of the ends of substantial justice. We must not again see a community of innocent men and women, broken up and flying before edicts which hold them responsible for crimes committed at forty miles distance. The delicate female, the helpless child must not again expiate in flight and exposure, the atrocious brutalities of every drunken homicide. Unless Great Britain make the late proceedings, to which we refer, the occasion for procuring these securities, along with public and private satisfaction for the wrongs sustained, she will release all her absent subjects from any further confidence in her sympathy or her protection. If war be ever justifiable in this age and under the dispensation wherein we live, the denial of such reparation, of security against such injuries, surely goes far to sanction its declaration.

Our limits forbid our entering further into the catalogue of rights, civil, commercial, and diplomatic, which has often been made out of late, for presentation to the court of Peking, as an ultimatum. To one only will we advert, and that because every day gives painful experience of its value, viz. the possession of a true copy of the Chinese fiscal code and tariff, under the sanction of the supreme authority. For the private merchant to obtain this, is, and has always been, impossible. He has never been able to gain such a definition of his duty. Even now, no diligence of inquiry, no sincerity of obedience, no sacrifices, can satisfy his own sense of right, or raise him above the taunts of the malicious. The time of public interference is now at hand, and the longer sufferance of this great abuse, will convict western governments, to say the least, of small regard either for the happiness of their people, or for their own honor.

Finally, we repeat our opinions, formed long ago, as to the mode of acting on this empire. Every peaceful resort must be exhausted, before force is employed against China. The cause of peace, the enlightened sentiments of the age, demand this; it is enforced by the recollection of the vast usurpations, already pushed forward by Europeans upon the soil of Asia. Military movements here must awaken the worst suspicions, and arm all there is of love of country, and pride of independence against their authors. Such movements, if strong enough for irritation and yet too weak for success, tend directly to force this government, upon the stricter exclusive policy of its eastern neighbor. If powerful enough to shake the Mantchou dynasty, they endanger the disruption of the political tie, and may let loose again the very demons of confusion and anarchy. Every reader of Chinese history, remembering those long reigns of terror which abound in its ancient annals, will unite in warning western governments to be careful how they throw down a polity they cannot reconstruct, or seek to conquer what they cannot govern.

Here we have the Scylla and the Charybdis of foreign interference with China;–on the one hand–the introduction of an exclusion as rigorous as that of Japan; on the other–the overththrow of the dynasty, and the substitution of lawlessness and anarchy. The first cannot but be deprecated by the friend of peaceful intercourse; the second must awaken the far more serious alarms of every friend of humanity. Here is room for political wisdom to show itself, viz., in so steering, as to avoid these opposite dangers. The improbability that this degree of wisdom will be possessed by the conductors of ordinary military movements, or indeed by any single negotiator, sent hither, added to the love of peace, have made us long since feel and express a strong desire, that a combined mission from the western governments in commerce with China, should be the instrument selected for pressing their common suit at the bar of this empire. To this course, we have never heard an objection, except this, that western states cannot, and will not, move and work together. To this we reply, the cause is common; and peaceful unanimity in its pursuit cannot fail to make a deep impression. A joint guaranty against the violation of the Chinese territory, and a joint tender of a treaty like that we have already cited, are almost sure to disarm distrust and pave the way to confidence and freedom. Union is itself proof of disinterested aims, or at least, of aims resting on broad foundation, and not on the basis of national pride, cupidity or retaliation. If such union be not due to China, it is yet due, in our estimation, to western interest. Are these combined motives too abstruse, or too feeble to be felt and admitted by western cabinets? If they be, yet let generosity touch them, and while they exhaust every expedient for pacific success, they may rely, that if heaven will that the Ta Tsing dynasty be overthrown, it will provide a way for that end, in its haughty rejection of all advances; realising once more in the history of Taoukwang, the ancient saying, quem Deus vult perdere, prius dementat.

It remains once more to advert to those purer principles, which are just beginning, in our day, to be recognised, as laws for public, as well as private conduct. The time is fast drawing on, when 'the spear shall be cut in sunder, and the war chariot burned in the fire.' The best, the divinely appointed agent of amelioration upon earth, is the Bible, and not the bayonet. It is still left in part to us, however, to employ or reject the proper instrument. Or rather it is permitted to men to do the part assigned to them by Providence, under motives worthy or unworthy, disgraceful or meritorious. So will it be in this exigency, and in this country. Western states will be used, as the instruments of certain predicted changes here, and these they will work out, as their real characters may be, from lofty and pure respects, or from cupidity, revenge, and ambition. There is a pure influence, a commanding superiority, in their keeping; and if they are wise and good enough to use it, the work will be done, and done to their immortal honor in the sign of earth and heaven. But if these noble motives are thrust out by angry, selfish, and cruel passions, then however complete the success, no merit will attend, no blessing hallow, the instrumentality. As citizens of western states, as humble sharers in their failures or their triumphs, we earnestly hope and pray, that they will on this remarkable trial now before them, do their duty.

The representative is no doubt bound to interpose, promptly and fearlessly, the moment the safety of a fellow-citizen is endangered. But when (as in the case before us) the citizen stands charged with infraction of the laws, it is necessary so to interfere as evidently to secure, not obstruct; the course of justice. Hence we preferred, that the superintendent should stand by Mr. D. protesting against every injustice, demanding every security, &c., rather than remove him. The former course could not have been mistaken; the latter was immediately interpreted as an attempted abduction. The determination to protect was worthy of all praise, the mode only was objectionable. The British factory was no more safe than any other; and the alternative–the surrender of the confiscated drug–was noways altered.

This interval is extended to twelve months in the treaty with Tripoli.

The receipt of the imperial rescript published January 5th, now makes it nearly certain that the exclusion will for the present be acted on.

Supreme Court of the United States. (The Exchange vs. McFadden.)

It is under the same humane and intelligent system, that the Hudson's Bay Company and the American Fur Company have been concerting and carrying out together, the gradual withdrawal of spirits from their hunting tribes.

Compare, at least its influence with the present state of things, and the impressions thence resulting. The E.I. Company offering near 20,000 chests of opium for public sale, for export by sea only, and advancing on a further crop of the poppy;–2000 chests on its way from Bombay; 9000 to 10,000 more in store of the old crop; and more than 20,000 of the new, just gathered in Malwa.– Powerful vessels, British owned, plying on the Chinese coasts, showing such flags as they please, and to crown all, actively supplying their native associates with fire-arms and ammunition!! And with all this before the Chinese, with the E.I. Company's advertisements in the hands of the commissioner, we wonder, and resent his measures. It is said too that the governor-general will probably be empowered to coerce a settlement of the pending controversy. Can it be? Whatever chastisement China may deserve, are there none to adminster it, but the monopolist growers of the opium? What justice could be looked for, were the most criminal of all the parties concerned, to be transferred from the bar to the bench, to measure and dispense it? No: let nothing of our delicate and important cause be given over to the Calcutta council, until the time come, so long predicted, when "the child may put his hand on the cockatrice's den.

ROBERT BENNET FORBES' RESPONSE TO C.W. KING'S ARTICLE ON THE OPIUM TRADE

(February, 1840)

Art. VI. Reply to article second, in the Repository for January, in a letter addressed to the editor, dated Canton February 14, 1840. By Non Sine Causa.

[In the article by C.R. in our last, and in that here introduced, there is somewhat which might well have been modified, or omitted. Our pages are designed for a Repository of facts, rather than for forensic debate. Yet when great and difficult questions are pending, it is desirable they should be freely and fairly discussed. To this no one will object. But there is danger of making partial or erroneous statements, or of making them in objectionable terms, liable to be misunderstood. We express our unfeined regret that any such should ever appear in our columns. In future, we hope our correspondents will be more guarded in what they write. Having admitted C.R.'s paper, we feel bound to admit the reply. How to remove existing evils, extend and secure honorable commerce, and open and establish friendly relations–such commerce and such relations as shall be mutually beneficial and satisfactory–are great objects–now, more than ever before, demanding from all careful consideration.]

Dear Sir,–In the conclusion of the leading article in your number for January, I observe that you allude to a long communication which had "just been put into your hands," and you say that you "are encouraged to expect more from the same and other writers," and that you expect by a comparison of the views of different persons, the "due medium may be found out, and that, "order, peace, good will, and prosperity will be secured."

If you expect a comparison of the views of different persons, so that a "due medium" may be arrived at, you may be perfectly safe in putting the article by C.R. upon the very extreme line on one side; no one can go beyond his Utopian ideas, nor arrive nearer the confines of truth and honesty of purpose; no one *professing* a Christian spirit, far less any one *possessing* a particle thereof, can go beyond C.R. Even admitting his statements to be correct, there is a spirit of jealousy stamped in every line, there is a degree of self-esteem and arrogance in the language of the article, under notice, which renders it a harmless missive; its venom must recoil on the writer. The article would be entirely beneath my notice, or that of any American merchant in Canton, were your journal to stop its circulation here; but shall we endorse the cold blooded slanders of C.R. by permitting them to cross the ocean? Shall we see a respectable individual, like our consul, vilified, and shut our mouths? Forbid it, truth and justice! However, Mr. Editor, I shall confine my strictures, principally to the libels on the American merchants of Canton, leaving the consul and the superintendent to speak for themselves, if they consider C.R. worthy of flagellation. C.R. writes well; therefore he can claim no immunity from me on the score of ignorance; I need make no apologies for my style, for your readers will readly see that I am a plain man; and all who are acquainted with the subject, will say that the truths I write must put down error, however, homely the garb in which they are clothed.

I am quite amused at the temerity of C.R. in wishing to submit even the opium question, and the relation growing out of it, to the "papirs sensibles," for in close connection with that question, in some shape or another, would be found most transactions of the general trade, in which C.R. expects *praise* from one, *criticism* from another, and *abuse* from a third: he will be disappointed in the *first* most assuredly, and though he will have plenty of *criticism* he will be spared *abuse*,–for on looking into "Webster" I find that "*abuse*" means "improper treatment," "perversion of meaning," "rude speech," & c., all these definitions it will be difficult to apply to anything that the English language is susceptible of in relation to the article of C.R. If he considers his tirade of thirty pages, "a brief repetition of some opinions on the past stages of the controversy," spare us, I pray you, the infliction of his *full statements*.

In regard to the opinions of C.R., I would say briefly, in reply to his reasoning on paragraph 7th, that his position is a wrong one; for had the government been actuated by a sincere desire to put down the opium trade, it would have succeeded; this is amply proved by the fact, that the first sincere efforts for its suppression have been successful. In relation to paragraph 7th, I would say, that C.R. approves of the interference of the foreigners on the occasion of the first attempt to execute a Chinese in front of the factories, because he took an active part in that interference; the repetition of the act, or rather the carrying out of the attempt alluded to, was the *consequence* of that *very proper interference*, and not because the importers of the drug did not "lay the first lesson to their hearts." I pass over paragraphs 8, 9, and 10, leaving one of the many friends of the superintendent to notice them.

Paragraph 11th. C.R. says the honorable Company's committee would have ordered off the ships, and deported Mr. Dent. C.R. should remember that Mr. Dent was one of many, and was not particularly subject to the notice of the Chinese authorities until we were all prisoners; and then if the select committee had been here, it would have afforded him the same protection which Captain Elliot did, and the act would have been equally praiseworthy; and the individual who would hesitate, under similar circumstances, to do as he did would be subject to the censure of every honorable mind.

Par. 12th. All who know Captain Elliot, will be slow to believe, that he estimated for a moment the value of the surrendered drug in comparison with the safety of his countrymen; this last was his primary object, and he never dwelt on any other consideration.

Par. 13th. I agree entirely with C.R. that the Americans pursued the wisest course in remaining in Canton, instead of retreating with their English friends to the great prejudice of their own interests, and the interests of their constituents; but I had a different feeling at the time, and would have retired had others been so disposed; this, as matters have turned out, would have been a great error; I do not agree with C.R. as to the *motives* for remaining; not a man remained here because he was unwilling "to stake his chance of sympathy and support on an opium quarrel," but *every merchant* remained here, I believe, because he felt himself personally secure from danger, and because he expected to reap the reward of his continued partial imprisonment, to say nothing of his duty to his constituents.

Par. 14th. C.R. attempts to show that the English committed a geographical error in going outside the Bogue; or, in other words, that they were no more safe outside than in! Most assuredly they "assumed, that life and property were unsafe within the Bogue, and safe at the outer anchorages," and the result has borne out those assumptions; the Chinese *did not* yield their claim to the jurisdiction over the various anchorages; but they *did* no more, they *dared* do no more, than annoy the ships, causing them to move a few miles on or about the day that they had previously meditated retiring; and the sanction of the commissioner to the then trade, between British and Americans, was actually given, as also that of the superintendent, the *former* by chop to the United States consul, as C.R. tells us further on in paragraph 23d, and the *latter* by tacit consent, backed by the presence of the superintendent himself.

Par. 15th. The *bond*! The subject of the signature of the bond, has been publicly discussed before, and a *very near friend* of C.R.'s, has said, that the odium of first signing it, has been frankly assumed by the party to whom it justly belonged; but he forgot that the party assuming the responsibility at that time, did it only on one condition, namely, that if the sin thus committed should weigh too heavely, or rankle in the breast of C.R.'s *friend*, or any body else, that party would assume the responsibility; and as this said *friend* did endeavor to throw off what he considered an awful responsibility, he thereby admitted that his conscience pricked him. C.R. knows full well, and knew at the time he so "reluctantly assented to the bond," that no one declined signing it because the thought it a dangerous document, but because it was well known that to yield one step to the Chinese, would give them an advantage.

C.R. can rest assured that many calm statements, in reference to the signature of the bond, were made; it is true that these were made without the especial sanction, and approval of C.R.; the unpardonable error was committed, of not consulting this paragon of human excellence, "this second Daniel!" C.R. was probably the identical *American resident*," who had been promised a virtual immunity from the bond! We have his word for that, and nothing more; and it can easily be credited, that his vanity led him into the belief, that what he states was truth. In reference to this C.R. says, "unhappily these fair prospects were clouded over, a bond was signed, &c." I would ask him, what prospects? Did the *resident* publish, that if a little time could be gained, the bond would be quashed? No; he cherished the idea with characteristic vanity, equalled only by that of C.R., that *he individually* would be the favored one, all others might, from their *suspicious characters and knavish pursuits*, be compelled to sign bonds, but *he*, the *pure*, the *uncontaminated 'resident*,' would proudly hold up his head, and say, "Lin knows whom to trust," "my word is as good as my bond;" if he ever had any reason to expect such immunity, he fully expected to make a private use of it.

C.R. accuses the Americans, his neighbors, with meanness for making it necessary for the captains to sign the bonds, instead of themselves. He says, "were they the authors of these troubles?" "Had they been the chief encouragers of this traffic,&c." "No–the resident merchants." C.R. here assumes the false ground, that the resident merchants, then in Canton, were "*en masse*," engaged in the opium trade, and desired to carry it on, and shift the responsibility on the captains! I pronounce this to be neither more nor less than *most atrocious intimation*, conceived in malignity, and born with falsehood stamped upon its face. Surely, if there was any danger of opium being brought in, accidentally, or secretly, it must have been known to the captains; and C.R. with all his venom, will hardly go so far as to say, that the captains were to be inveigled into bringing in the drug by the residents, and afterwards be asked to sign the bond. The fact is, Mr. Editor, the captains knew the tenor of the bond before entering the port, and the captains under my control, as agent for their owners, were not (like C.R.'s captains,) servants of mine. C.R. knew perfectly well that his signature, or that of his agent in Canton, would satisfy the authorities as well as the name of the captain, and therefore if he considered it 'mean' to put the responsibility on the captains, *why did he do it*? And for the reason, why was it settled that the captains should sign the bond? "Because the wily head of the cohong knew whom he dealt with, and that, to subdue the opposition of hardy sailors, to have a victim forthcoming, when the time of sacrifice should arrive, it was necessary to *bribe the resident agents*." This is truly a most rancorous, unjust, and libelous sentence; but to any one acquainted with the Chinese character, it excites only laughter, and falls upon the too lofty head of C.R.

Par. 16th. C.R. tells you that there were reasons for signing the *first bond*, as a temporary measure: I presume one of the most urgent, was that he had a ship at that moment in port, which he was extremely anxious to dispatch; and I will take this occasion to remark that, C.R. finds a good excuse for going just so far, in the measures leading to the heinous offenses committed by his countrymen, *as suits his own interest*. No man who signed the bond thought for a moment that by doing so he would keep opium out of his ship, he signed it because he was perfectly sure that, from other considerations, none could come in her, and that by doing it, his cargo would certainly be on its way to its destination much sooner than if he declined. If, as C.R. says and attempts to prove by stating that "no conviction could legally take place under the bond, and that there were reasons for signing the bond,: why was it an act of meanness to ask the captains to do so? As to the *second bond*, C.R. knows perfectly well, that originated in the precedent established by the "Thomas Coutts," and not in any newly promulgated law; for it is clear, that the most lenient bond would have been quite enough, with the publication of the law; but I deny that there is any essential difference in the two bonds; if the Chinese are disposed to be sanguinary, we are equally at their mercy, bond or no bond.

Par. 17th. This has very little to do with the questions between C.R. and the Americans, whose course I am attempting to justify; but a very cursory survey of its contents affords me so good an opportunity to notice the inconsistency of C.R., that I cannot refrain from giving it a passing word. In paragraph 14th C.R. says, "The harsh requisition (to stop the British trade,) came from the British representative," "and the guardian of British interests, on this side the Pacific inflicted, with his own hands, the losses, &c.;" after this he tells you, in the article under review, that the English residents, having made their election to retire, were bound to stand manfully by the cruel injunctions of the superintendent, in one breath C.R. accuses him of "great official errors," and in the next, he gilds the pill, with a little flattery. Every American in Canton will readily assent to the sentiment of C.R., that the superintendent was particularly considerate to the Americans; thereby proving that he entertained for them a much better feeling than their fellow countryman. C.R. did, and notwithstanding the "eager avidity," with which, he says, they began to look on the profits of this illicit gain, they may rest assured that if, C.R. and his cant, were put into the scale against the most humble of the Americans, and Elliot should hold the scales, C.R. would be found wanting. The idea of abandoning the means of procuring cargoes for our American constituents, and of refusing consignments from our English friends, because Elliot had issued precautionary injunctions to keep the crown aloof from further responsibilities, is too supremely ridiculous to merit more than one of C.R.'s contemptuous sneers.

As to the opinions of the American commodore, if I had the desire, I would bring forward, at least as strong quotations, in favor of the trade, carried on in American ships as C.R. can against it. The worthy commodore was comparatively a stranger here, and did not profess, as C.R. does, to instruct his countrymen, and all the world besides, as to what was best to be done with their own affairs. In this paragraph the 'cloven foot' shews itself again. C.R. says, (what I must confess I never heard of before,) that the superintendent sanctioned the purchases of British goods, with bills! This is new to me, and I should as soon have thought of asking the superintendent's permission to do this, as of asking him to allow me to consume the produce of England at my table.

As to the feeling of the English towards their American agents, "after they had yielded to their losses, and sent their property within the river:" I am unconscious of any such feeling towards me, but I can easily conceive, the C.R., who had reviled every opium agent, should have imagined, and perhaps justly conceived, that his English friends, with whom he exchanged bills for cotton, should have had a most contemptuous opinion of his principles, which carried him, strait along an imaginary line of his own creating; to go on either side of which, he considered a deadly sin in any other man.

Par. 18th. Is only a register of the consummate vanity of C.R. and requires no notice.

Par. 19th. Is rather a good one, and treats of the blockade notice of the 11th September; the only good results of which, *to Americans* were the enhanced value of freights, and the opportunity of testing *principle versus profit,* in the person of an intimate friend of C.R. who on that trying occasion had a ship loading at Hongkong.

I pass over article 20th, and come to the 21st. C.R. asserts what he certainly can have no proof of, and thereby subjects himself to the just imputation of a perverted heart, that "ship after ship was sold for nominal considerations;" this, I fully believe to be false, though I would not charge C.R. with a deliberate intention of uttering so grave an untruth; *I do distinctly charge him with an acrimonious feeling, a petty meddling and jealous disposition*; after giving full vent to these feelings he pounces upon the American consul, and to him, I leave the reply, fully satisfied that he will get his deserts from that gentleman.

Par. 23d. C.R. says, the affair at Chuenpe, "as it threw an additional doubt on the safety of British property, within the grasp of the Chinese, gave a new impulse to transhipments;" the oracle has told you that British property, *only nominally covered,* was illicitly being carried to Whampoa; he must have very strange ideas of the sagacity of the British merchants to suppose, that the *greater the danger* to their property the *more anxious* they should be to put it in jeopardy. C.R. has told you that the superintendent consented to the transhipments, and he now tells you that the commissioner, had given his consent; wherein then (having the consent of both sides) was the sin of carrying British property to Whampoa? And what would have been the position of British and American trade at this moment, if the Americans had not committed these grievous sins, in the eyes of C.R., *sins only* when they passed the imaginary line drawn by himself. Having expressed his disapprobation of the course of his countrymen, having vilified them with no measured hand, having blended with his statements, just enough of facts, to give them the semblance of reason, he now comes out with his sage advice; beginning with the "American community," and at the head of this, the consul, and next the private residents.

I had determined to let the consul speak for himself, and I feel sure that he will; yet I should regret that his countrymen remain silent on a point involving the honor of that respectable gentleman, it is quite evident that C.R. has some covered and secret motive for decrying him, and this will be shown sooner or later; very probably he would accept the consulship himself, it it were *respectfully solicited of him by our government*; he has probably an eye to the :"loaves and fishes," or perhaps he thinks he would acquire more influence with *his friend Lin* were he to come out in the consular uniform; he could then sport the American flag before his own house, and if the commodores should dare to call on their private friends before they waited on him, he could haul down the flag at his pleasure, as a certain consular vice agent, did on a former occasion.

All I have to say in respect to the consul is, that his countrymen entertain the highest respect for his character, and they will doubtless be ready to resist any and all slanders and aspersions, when they are called upon; while he is at his post, this will be unnecessary, he is fully able to defend himself; and C.R. may consider it a compliment if he deigns to notice his late writings. If he ever refused to present petitions, it must have been because he felt sure they would contain matter offensive to the Americans generally; however, I say again, let the consul speak for himself; I do not profess to be encumbered with diffidence, at the same time, I enter on a few remarks in regard to C.R.'s advice to the American merchants, with some reluctance, feeling aware that there are others here who can much more readily do justice to the vanity and egotism of C.R. I have no authority to speak for the American community, no more right to give their opinions, than C.R. has to school them. I therefore speak for myself, and have only to hope that I peak the sentiment of the Americans generally.

The first grave and unfounded accusation is, that the Americans signed the second bond, "without protest, explanation or remonstrance;" *this is false*; the writer has some agency in the matter, and does not speak without book, as C.R. does. The second bond was objected to most decidedly, and orders went to the ships *expected* (in duplicate) by *dispatch boats*, enclosing the copies of the old bonds, and requesting the captains of the ships then expected, to sign none others; but unfortunately, the "Thomas Coutts" had assented to the new bond, a precedent was thereby established; and the Chinese, with their usual art, presented similar documents to the captains *outside*, and they signed them; finding the step could not be retraced, remonstrance was used without success, and then *protests* were made before the consul, and every captain which the writer has had any control over has been recommended to protest; some have done it, and some have thought it unnecessary. So much for the truth of C.R.'s assertion; and whether he made so grave a charge ignorantly, or maliciously, he deserves censure equally. I have already said that the Americans did not sign the first bond "*to prove their sincerity in abjuring* the opium traffic;" they signed it, to *facilitate their legal and proper business, and because their duty to their constituents and their own interests demanded it*; they gave proof enough to their sincerity in the abandonment of the opium traffic, by issuing circulars to that effect, and above all, by *remaining at Canton*. C.R. assented to the *first bond*, or through his agent precipitated the signature of it, because he had a ship to load; but when the *second bond* was to be signed, he had no ship unsecured. I hold that our remaining in Canton, bond or no bond, gave *a tacit assent to any and all the laws of China*; the statement of C.R., that the Americans quietly swallowed the new bond, whatever might have been their opinion of its severity, "without efforts to effect an abatement," *is false*.

C.R. next attempts to put a petition into the mouths of his countrymen, the only sensible clause in which is the 6th; "the wily head of the cohong," would have looked to his safety by refusing *at once* to present such a document' and if C.R. had carried it to the city gates, he might have been sent back with an endorsement of bamboo. I do not offer any very strong objections to his statements in this petition, but one would suppose, that C.R. had just landed in China: what he says would be very well for a *private* letter, in confidence *to his friend Lin*; but officially, it would not do, he would return it as he did certain globes and books unperused; he would no more assent to the terms of C.R.'s petition, than to the absurd idea, which a friend of "Lin's" endeavored to impose on him, namely, that the world is round and revolves on its axis. Then the idea of this rejected petition being placed in the archives of the province! I really begin to think as I go on, that I have misten my man, and that C.R. is just imported: however, I believe I am not mistaken, and that C.R. can be neither more nor less, than that person who shakes his best friend's hand with the tips of his fingers, as if he would say, with a regal air, "touch but pollute not, this is a hand that never was engaged in any illicit trade." But this is a digression.

C.R. goes on to school the British community, the superintendent, and I dare say, before I get through, I shall find him giving his sage advice to the queen herself, and to congress. I have heard that "whoso humbleth himself shall be exalted," and I hope it is equally true for C.R.'s future welfare, that whoso exalteth himself shall be humbled. C.R. gives his counsel to the British *community* "with all the freedom of friendship and sympathy;" they will doubltless say, in relation to this whole paragraph, "*preserve us from our friends*."

C.R.'s views of the superintendent's conduct, in respect to the armed occupation of Chinese harbors, is very logical; he is truly a most disinterested person, but I suppose he would not have had the superintendent remove his protection from Hongkong, until after the due "exchange of bills for British merchandise" had taken place. Then comes some Latin; here C.R. has the advantage of me; I disclaim all knowledge of the dead languages, yet I should like to put a spice of Latin or Greek into this long article. What shall I say? "*Non sine causa*" sounds well enough, and might afford an excuse for inflicting this penance on you. "*E pluribus unum*" looks pretty enough when seen on a golden eagle, and might express the feeling C.R. had of his own power! But to be serious, Mr. Editor, and who, let me ask you, would fail to be so, when noticing the rancorous absurdities of C.R. He tells you again, that the superintendent "hurried the residents from their homes without a sufficient notice," and yet he says just before, that they should manfully have supported him, or in other words "kissed the rod" which was inflicting heavy punishment on them.

I have nothing more to say in reference to Kowlung and the amusing "skrimish," which I had the pleasure of witnessing at a *most safe distance*, than that it is no affair of C.R. or mine. I now come to the last topic of C.R.'s article: he doubts not, that an American, and perhaps a French, and Dutch envoy, will be sent out, if he lives in China until he sees *either*, he will have had ample time to repent of his sins, be they few or many. He says, the United States "will exhaust every peaceful recourse rather than leave their citizens, resident in China, longer exposed to loss and *contumely*." I thank thee, C.R. for that last word, it is exactly what *the Americans have received at your hands*; may they never be exposed to more from others, than they reap from your well provided store.

I cannot trespass much longer on your valuable time and space, Mr. Editor, and I shall therefore overlook much of what C.R. says on the opium question, *as it once was*; it is quite sufficient *for me*, that the most enlightened company of merchants, chartered by the most enlightened Christian power, should have given its sanction to the opium trade, to acquit my conscience for having once dealt in the drug. C.R. says truly, that, "all the merchants who gave up their drug last March can ask for, is money," *this is all they want*!

Some of C.R.'s remarks on page 470 are very sane and proper, but as I have not taken up my pen to praise, but to punish, I will not say a word in favor of the sentiments I allude to; my praise would afford him little more satisfaction than my censure. I now come to page 473, where a hope is held out, like a beacon light on a vast desert, that the end of C.R.'s article is close by; this fills me with pleasure, until I turn over, and find, that there are several pages more of sage and learned matter; have a little patience, my good sir, for I will not keep you long. I find nothing in particular upon which to offer a remark, until the first paragraph on page 476 meets my eye. C.R. wants a true copy of the code of laws which govern this empire, and particularly (I presume) that part relating to commerce; he says, that "no diligence of inquiry, no sincerity of obedience, no sacrifices, can satisfy his own sense of right, or raise him *above the taunt of the malicious*."

I am not aware of what he alludes to in the last part of this quotation, unless he means to say, that it has been intimated, that he, in common with all American merchants at Canton, has evaded (innocently of course) the laws in regard to duties; it has been "maliciously" said perhaps that he has transhipped cargo to Whampoa, with intent to save the duty: or the more heinous crime may have been attributed to him of shipping goods through Macao, for the same illicit end; or the still more unjustifiable accusation may have been brought against him, of having landed goods by night in Canton, for the same purpose, and I am by no means sure that he may not have been unjustly accused of bringing in a much smaller quantity of rice than the law allows. That he has ever given the "malicious" any grounds for saying thus much, I am not personally aware. I have now come to the last page, and I dare say you are equally glad, Mr. Editor. I pass over the first part merely observing, that, if the queen, the superintendent, the American consul, the Dutch, and French envoys, the yumchae, the hong merchants, and last not least the British and American merchants, will only consent to put their business into C.R.'s hands, they cannot fail to come out well; notwithstanding it is somewhere said "put not your trust in *princes*." I finish by requesting C.R. to look into his own heart, and his own motives, and to refrain in future from casting the first stone, or courting attack by holding his head too high. Let him, if he sincerely desires the good will of good men, or if he desires to bring "the stray sheep into his fold," put off a little of his lofty tone, and endeavor to assume a respectful lenity towards the faults and foibles of his fellow men. I now take leave of C.R., and offer no apologies for the length, or quality, of my writing; if what I say is not acceptable to my friends here, I shall sincerely regret it; that it will be so to C.R., I cannot hope or wish. I am, &c., &c. *Non Sine Causa*

ILLUSTRATION CREDITS:

Cover:	Peabody Essex Museum, M3793;
2 & 140:	Peabody Essex Museum, M3870-8;
4 & 55:	Peabody Essex Museum, E46,494;
13:	Courtesy of The Captain Robert Bennet Forbes House, Milton, Massachusetts;
17:	The Boston Public Library;
18:	Courtesy of The Vallejo Gallery, Newport Beach, California;
19 & 20:	Courtesy of The Captain Robert Bennet Forbes House, Milton, Massachusetts;
53:	Peabody Essex Museum, M11693;
54:	Peabody Essex Museum, M3793;
55:	Peabody Essex Museum, E46,494;
56:	Peabody Essex Museum, M217;
58:	Peabody Essex Museum, M11510;
60-61	The Boston Public Library;
70:	Courtesy of Yale University;
80-81:	The Boston Public Library;
87:	The Boston Public Library;
97:	Mystic Seaport Museum, MSM 70.50;
102-103:	The Boston Public Library;
104:	Mystic Seaport Museum, MSM 96-1-6;
106:	Peabody Essex Museum, 19611;
137:	The Metropolitan Museum of Art, New York, Bequest of W. Gedney Beatty, 1941;
138-139:	Peabody Essex Museum, M3870-8;
154:	Peabody Essex Museum, M212;
172-173:	Mystic Seaport Museum, MSM 54.591;
200-201:	Mystic Seaport Museum, MSM 70.39;
208:	The Boston Public Library;
226-227:	The Boston Public Library;
242:	Peabody Essex Museum, M9195;
250-251:	Peabody Essex Museum, M7316;
268:	Peabody Essex Museum, M4947;
269:	Courtesy of The Captain Robert Bennet Forbes House, Milton, Massachusetts;
271:	Peabody Essex Museum, M17226;
272:	Mystic Seaport Museum, MSM 96-5-3;

Maps in Appendix drawn by Karen Kratzer.

INDEX

A

Abbott, Mary Perkins, 91, 94
Acqui (cooly), 235
Adelaide, 23
Aho(o), 75, 142, 150, 215
Akbar, 220, 222, 229
Albion, 118, 170, 174, 188
Alligator, 232
Allom, Thomas (artist), 17, 61, 87, 210, 227
Alpha, 76
American trade
  no opium interest, 117
  gains from British departure, 128, 129, 147, 162, 164, 174, 183
  Tingqua painting **140**
  edict against transhipment with British, 188
Amoo (comprador), 73, 74, 75
Amory, James, 160
Amory, Martha, 149, 188
Anglo-Chinese War
  Battle of Cowloon, 167
Anjier Point, **250-251**
Ann McKim, 195, 198, 199
Apthorp, 167, 179
Arabella, 76
Ariel, 43
Ashburton, Lord, 237
Asia, 65, 187, 193, 219
Aurelius, 159

B

Bacon, Daniel C., 24, 35, 66, 69
Baring, 193
Baring Brothers, 13, 59, 105, 145, 172
Barnegat Bay, NJ, 262
Bashaw, 15
Bates, Joshua, 145, 185, 234
Battle of Cowloon, 167
Benjamin, Capt., 235-236
Benjamin, Mary, 158
Bigelow, Dr., 150, 203
Bocca Tigris, 114, 120, 125, 184, 185
Bradford, Mr., 79
Breeze, 20
Bridges, Capt., 186, 187
British trade *See* English trade
Bryant, John, 213
Buddhist Temple of Longevity, 73
burial at sea, 50-51

C

Cabot, Elizabeth Perkins, 37
Cabot, George, 36
Cabot, Samuel, 14, 36, 37, 45, 48, 202
Cabot, Thomas Handasyd, 67
Canton, **60-61**
  port center of trade, 8-10
  imprisonment, 111-122
  British to leave, 124
  port blockade, 167, 168
Canton bargemen, **17**
Canton Packet, 12, 147, 156, 158, 166
Canton Regatta Club, 69
  not half so green, 64, 65
  RBF member, 65
  RBF wins cup, 67
Cap-Sing-Moon Bay, 229-230
Caravan, 91
Cary, Thomas Graves, 146
Cashmere, 129
Cassador, 189, 193
Champlin, Capt., 35
Chariot, 35, 47, 84, 94, 99, 109
Charles Forbes, 177
Chesapeake, 198
China
  attitude to foreigners, 8
  supresses opium trade, 73-74, 98
  and Americans, 162
  and murdered Chinese, 161-163
  British sink three junks, 184, 185
  and shipwreck victims, 189, 192
China trade
  and Americans, 9, 105, 221
  principal exports, 10
  regulations for foreigners, 8-10
Chinese house and garden, **87**
Chinese New year, 95
Chinese Repository, 84-85, 142, 213
Chinnery, George, 58, **58,** 77, 157, 271
  Houqua portrait, **137**
"chop boats"
  definition, 9, 225
Churchill, John, 230, 232
Clark, Alvin, 144, 229
Clarke, Mr., 131
Cleveland, Sarah (Sally), 178, 216
Codman, John, 182
Co-hong
  association of Chinese merchants, 9
Cole, Capt./Mrs., 76, 219
Columbia, 121, 126
compradors
  definition, 9, 72
  Amoo, 73, 74, 75

Consoo House, 74, 109, 116, 196
Coolidge, Joseph, 59, 62, 83, 172, 173
and RBF, 145, 181-182, 189-196, 192, 237
and Russell & Co., 96, 177, 181-182, 234,
Coolidge, Mrs., 194, 195, 228
Cox, Dr., 92, 158
cumshaw, 95
Cunningham, Francis, 120
Cunningham, John, 182, 183
Cunningham, Mary Forbes, 120
Cushing, Caleb, 267
Cushing, John Perkins, 12,59, 69, 100, 143, 144, 146, 175, 216
and Perkins & Co., 14-15
Cynthia, 175, 179

D

David, 232
Delano, Warren, 59, 62, 66, 71, 73, 75, 76, 79, 100, 101, 113, 119, 132, 134, 144, 162, 169, 170, 173, 177, 183, 186, 198, 200, 204, 218
and opium, 16
to join R&Co., 72
at Hong Kong and Macao, 76-77
sailing with RBF, 95
indespensable, 214
and RBF's China departure, 221, 225
RBF to Singapore, 231
in Canton, 237
background, 270
Delhi, 210, 234
Dent & Co., 63, 71
Mr. Dent, hostage, 109-110
Dickinson, Mr.
sermons, 86, 93, 95
dinner party, Chinese, 79-83, **80-81**
Doty, Capt., 238, 252
sick, 239, 240, 241, 244, 245
RBF critical, 253
Downies, Capt., 229
Drew, Capt., 23, 27, 28, 32
Druid, 230
Dumaresq(ue), Philip, 22, 48, 57, 143, 149, 213, 220, 229
letters, 236-237
background, 270
D.W.C. Olyphant & Co., 16, 113, 142

E

East India Company
leased the largest hong, 10
and opium, 14, 101
Eben Preble, 170, 172, 180, 183, 202
Eckley, David, 127, 141
Edmonton, 129, 162
Elliot, Admiral George, 237
Elliot, Capt. Charles, 16, 58, 77, 113, 129, 159
arrives in Canton, 110-111
and opium, 112-116
British to leave Canton, 124
meets RBF, 124
and Commissioner Lin, 161-165, 185
Battle of Cowloon, 167
at Hong Kong, 167-169
Thos Coutts violates injunctions, 178
aftermath, 266-267
Empress of China, 9
Engle, Capt., 48
English
and opium trade, 104, 105, 109-112, 116, 117, 119, 128
depart Canton, 129
fire at a war junk, 128-129
leave Macao, 161-165
sink three Chinese junks, 184, 185
vessels of war, 238
English trade
and Commissioner Lin, 161-165, 181
in American ships, 178
Thos Coutts violates injunction, 180
at Chuenpee, 181
transhipment with Americans, 188
Everet, Mr. (American merchant), 62, 79

F

factories. *See* hongs
"fast boat," 9, 196
definition, 8
description, 156
Fati(ee) Gardens, 8, 93
Flora (pet dog), 20, 22, 24, 28, 30, 31, 31, 47, 64, 91, 99, 164
and pups, 38, 40, 147
herds pigs on deck, 34
portrait, 65, 66
Macao, 129
pup for Rose, 156, 175, 179
on board *Niantic,* 238-264
Forbes, Charles, 22, 164, 234
Forbes, John Murray, 20, 57, 67, 91, 99, 100, 122-123, 124, 173, 192, 259
background, 11, 13, 269-270
advanced RBF $60,000, 144
twin daughters, 123, 133
and Joseph Coolidge, 185
Lamqua portrait, **269**
Forbes, Margaret Perkins, 11
Forbes, Paul Seiman, 30
Forbes, Ralph Bennett, 11
Forbes, Robert Bennet, **19**, **268**
background, 11-13, 267-270
house, **13**
Mary Chilton at sea

cabin, 20-21
reading, 21, 26, 29, 37, 38, 40, 41, 42, 43, 44, 45, 46, 47, 49
woodworking, 21, 22-23, 24
exercise, 22
Rose at promised time, 23, 28,
health and diet, 26
ship's doctor, 28, 39, 40, 42, 43, 44, 45, 46, 49-50, 52, 150
Rose's birthday, 31
"History of a Portrait," 34, 62
Chariot, 35
and creation, 36
"The Escape,", 39
and Capt., 42
bird shooting, 45, 48
prayer/burial at sea, 51
arrives at Lintin, 56-57
and Russell & Co., 59-62, 130, 140
living with Mr. Snow, 63
health and diet, 64, 92, 95, 120, 135, 145, 158, 180, 189, 211, 228
sailing, 67, 69, 84, 85, 95, 165
smoking, 67, 136, 175
surgery, 70-71, 86
dinner party, 79-83, 86-90
earnings, 84, 125, 131, 183, 197, 210, 216, 234-235
acquisitions, 85, 91, 95, 130, 147, 182, 187, 219, 223, 224, 234
coffee pot, 85, 94
at Macao, 75-76, 225, 228
miniature, 77, 83, 85, 176-177
imprisonment, 111-122
speculates Opium war, 113, 119, 204-205
and Chinese people, 114, 115
child rearing, 129, 179
room in Canton, 132
midshipmen meet Houqua, 136
horseback riding, 144, 157, 162, 163, 164, 217-218
at Hong Kong, 166-179
birthdays, 168, 249
wedding anniversary, 199
departure plans, 220-221, 232
leaves Canton, 224
Niantic at sea
Skipper, 238-245
stateroom, 239
reading, 240, 248, 249
woodworking, 241, 246, 247, 249, 253, 254, 257
storms, 244, 252, 260-261, 262-263
at Anjier, 248
meals, 249, 262
Tamerlaine, 252
and marriage, 255-257
Forbes, Robert Bennet, Jr. 25
China dress, 66, 69
portrait, 123, 140, 144-145, 187
miniature, 146, 147, 148
verse, 233
background, 270
Forbes, Rose Greene Smith, 13, **20**
RBF business affairs, 59, 125, 140
saleable items, 85, 94, 95, 182, 185, 202
Forbes, Sarah Hathaway, 13, 123
Forbes, Thomas Tunno, 11, 37
drowns in China, 12, 157
RBF visits grave, 239
Forbes, William, 46
Francis Stanton, 43, 64, 65, 66, 75, 105, 109

G

Gardner, John L., 170, 175, 203
Gilman, Capt., 58, 115, 131, 143, 162, 229
Gilpin, 124
Globe, 238, 259
Green, J. C., 48, 59, 62, 63, 64, 66, 73, 75, 79, 83, 115, 121, 122, 222
RBF critical, 120-121
leaves China, 128, 130
aftermath, 270
Green, Sam, 222
Green, Sarah, 222
Greene, Charles (C.W.), 94, 95, 108, 124, 231
Greene, Copley, 30, 94, 170, 174
Greene, Lizzy, 149, 174
Greenwood, John, 24
Gribble, Capt., 196, 197, 199
Gribble, Mrs., 234
Gutzlaff, Charles, 16, 119

H

Hathaway, Frank, 62, 66, 95, 132
Heard, Augustine, 91, 96, 172, 177, 184
and Joseph Coolidge, 193, 196
Hercules, 177
Hillard, George Stillman, 64, 93, 94, 95
Hillard, Susan, 160
Holbrook, Dr., 48
Holland, Gordie, 99
Holland, Susan, 99
Hong Kong, **172-173**
Hong merchant
definition, 9
opium trade, 14-15, 73, 77, 109-111
responsible for foreigners behavior, 74-75, 109-111
Hongs, **54-55**
definition, 10, 59
barricaded, 111-122

Hooper, Samuel, 35
Hoppo
Chinese customs official, 9
Horatio, 57, 58, 127
Houqua (hong merchant), 21, 59, 112, 114, 118, 130
most distinguished Hong merchant, 9
deals with Russell & Co., 13
Green interest in Russell & Co., 63-64
Amoo's arrest, 73
and opium, 74-75, 98, 105, 109-110
Father's burial, 100
Hunan visit, 136
portrait, **137**
gardens, **138-139**
and Coolidge, 181
and Commissioner Lin, 185
and RBF, 186, 218, 225
aftermath, 272
Howland, Capt., 56-57, 58, 62, 76, 79
Howland, Mrs., 126, 127, 132
Hubbard, Lizzy, 212
Hunan (Honam), 136
Hunter, William, 36, 59, 89, 115, 132, 146, 147, 162, 169, 170, 177, 218
aftermath, 270-271, **271**
Hyacinth
fires on Chinese war junks, 184, 185

I

Inglis, Mr., 105, 110
Innes, James, 73-74, 75, 77

J

Jackson, James, 40, 135, 175, 203
Jardine, Matheson & Co., 57, 86, 109
and opium, 16
Jardine, William
farewell party, 86-90
aftermath, 272
Jauncy, Capt., 245, 255, 262, 264
eye wound, 238, 239, 240
John Adams, 122, 126, 136
Joseph Peabody, 229

K

"keang," 73
King, C. W., 113, 116
King, Charles, 213
King, Edward, 130, 142, 143, 147, 164, 186, 204, 218
health, 186

L

Lamqua, 269
Larne, 111, 121, 237
Lee, Elizabeth Cabot, 36
Lee, Joseph, 36, 47
Lehigh, 180, 183, 187
Lerna, 186, 230
letters,
overland, 63, 132
save RBF's, 78
delivery process, 95, 97
Rose's arrive, 66, 90-91, 92-93, 94, 99, 122-124, 133, 143, 149-153, 159, 170, 205=207, 221, 222, 236
Levant, 12, **53,** 170, 171, 174, 189, 197
Lewis, S. W., 224-225
Lin, Imperial Commissioner, **106**
end to opium trade, 16, 101
opium destroyed, 108, 109-111
blockades hongs, 111-122
visits Macoa, 161-163
and British Merchant ships, 184, 185
Lindsey, Mr., 105
linguists, 114, 115
definition, 9
misinterpret, 117
Lintin, 30, 58, 76, 125, 129, 164, 167, 183, 186, 198, 229
storage ship at Lintin station, 12-13
at Whampoa, 185, 186
Lintin Island, 12, 53
and opium, 15
Lion, 170
Lockwood, Capt., 220
London, 100, 101, 210
lorcha, 76
Lotos, 193
Low, Abiel Abbott, 111, 115, 142, 143, 144, 147, 186, 199, 203
Lund, Capt., 148
Lyce, Mr., 156
Lyman, Joe, 94, 123, 151, 175, 210

M

Macao, 56
mouth of the Pearl River, 8
western women, 8, 78
Portuguese, 161, 162-163, 165
British evacuation, 186
waterfront, **226-227**
Macartney, Lord, 231
Macondray, Capt. F. W., 58, 73, 84, 86, 171
MacPherson, Mr.and Mrs., 191, 192-193
Magee, Mary, 170, 175, 176, 178
Mary Chilton, 118
meals, 23, 24, 25, 33, 41, 49
sights land, 38, 45
RBF's stateroom, 41-42
livestock, 47
at Anjier, 48
arrives Lintin Island, 56
departs China, 68
Matheson, James, 165

McClane, Mrs., 57
McDougal, Capt.
  wife and children, 162, 166, 167, 168, 169, 179, 180
Milo, **53**
Milton Academy, 12, 187
Mingqua (hong merchant), 72
  dinner party, 79-83
  hostage for opium, 109-110
Morea, 182, 183, 184
Moroccan, 96
Morrison, 94, 97, 98, 99
Motley, Mary, 84, 90, 149, 159, 160, 174, 212, 216, 222
Motley, Tim, 170
Mount Vernon St. (Boston), 26

N

N. Gossler, 48
Nabob, 23
Nahant, Massachusetts, 27, 35, 156
Nanking, Treaty of, 172
  ends Opium Wars, 267
Nantasket, 211
Nantasket, 114, 127, 129, 144, 146
Napier, Lord, 111, 114
Naushon Island, 27, 35, 37, 91, 99, 128, 134, 211
Navigator, 171, 176, 186
Niantic, *See also* Forbes, Robert Bennet, 90, 101, 109, 217, 221
  RBF sails home, 237-264
Nile, 16
Nivison, Eliza, 211
Nye, Mr. (American merchant), 62, 66

O

Omega, 48, 65, 115
Oneida, 140, 141, 143, 171, 174, 175, 178
Opium chests, **104**
Opium smokers, **102-103**
Opium trade, 267
  importation laws, 14-15
  smuggling, 15-16, 75, 79, 98
  seizure of, 73-74
  government measures, 73-74
  dealer execution and riot, 76, 98
  explanation, 101-105
  prohibition, 108-111
  foreigners imprisoned, 111-122
  20,000 chests of opium to Yumchi, 113, 143
  Captains and Parsees continue, 161
Opium Wars, 266-267
  RBF speculates, 113, 119, 204-205
Osage, 136, 188
Osgood, Capt., 166, 180

P

Paine, Frederick W., 14
Panama, 95, 96, 98, 99, 128, 129, 236
Papanti's, 143
Paris, 129
Parker, Daniel P., 186
Parker, Peter, **70**, 124, 133, 197, 198, 225, 253
  American missionary and doctor, 70-71
  aftermath, 271-272
  hospital, 79, 115
  sermons, 83, 222
  RBF's health, 135
  leaves China, 237-238
  as sailor, 248-249
  and marriage, 255-257
Parker, Stanton, 135
Pearce, Capt., 22
Pearce, Mrs., 127
Pearl River
  open for pleasure boating, 10
Pearson, Charles, 33, 48, 57
Pedro, 258-259, 260
Perkins & Co., 11, 12
  joins Russell & Co., 12
  J.&T.H. Perkins & Sons, 14
  and opium trade, 14-16
Perkins, Gustus, 164
Perkins, James, 11
Perkins, Sally, 92
Perkins, Sarah Elliot, 11
Perkins, Thomas Handasyd, 11, 12
  aftermath, 272, **272**
Perry, Capt., 57
Porcia, 129, 147, 220
Portugese
  at Macao, 161, 162-163, 165
Pottinger, Henry, 267
Price, James, 66, 79
Prince Louise, 203
Puankhequa (hong merchant), 65, 73

Q

Queen Victoria, 121, 230, 267
  guarantees for losses, 117
Qunghing (hong merchant), 79

R

Rambler, 118, 119, 146
Reed, George, 121, 122, 126
Respondentia Walk, 10, **54-55**
Richard Althorp, 48
Ritchie, Mr., 170, 180, 204, 210, 229
Ritchie, Mrs., 194, 228
Robbins, Anna, 151, 223
Robert Fulton, 92, 94, 170
Robertson, Sandy, 76
Roman, 90, 91, 92

Rose, 36, 126, 162, 166, 167, 220, 230
Royal Saxon, 196, 203
Russell & Co., 59
joins Perkins & Co., 12
and opium, 15-16, 104, 104-105, 108, 108, 113, 131, 267
RBF joins, 59, 62
family, 143
Macao house, 145, 157-158, 162
fourteen vessels consigned, 178, 180
business grows, 186, 193, 203-204, 207, 212, 213, 214, 215
sells ship to Chinese, 204
loads fleet, 219

S

samshu(e), 16, 82
definition, 8
distilled, 93
Sandy Hook, NJ, 262
shipwrecks, 189, 192-193
Smith, Capt., 230
Smith, Rebecca Greene, 25
Smith, Sarah, 25
Smith, Thomas H., 48, 59
Smith, W. W., 27
Snow, Peter W., 59, 63, 69, 85, 98, 116, 177
daughter dies, 231, 232
Splendid, 144, 146, 147, 148
Spooner, Mr., 143
St. Helena, 193
Stackpole, Susan, 212
Stanton, George, 231
Stetson, Mr., 84
Sturgis, James, 57, 162, 225, 234
gifts for Rose, 239
house in Macao, 163
Sturgis, Lucy Lyman Paine, 41
Sturgis, Mary Greene Hubbard, 41
Sturgis, Russell, 41, 57, 62, 66, 67, 69, 71, 76, 95, 100, 101, 119
children Lucy and John, 57, 130, 132
leaves Canton, 105
Sumarang, 193
Sunda, 189, 192, 193, 193
supercargo
definition, 9
Surat,210
Sylph, 35

T

Talbot, 183
Tarquin, 229, 230
Tea cultivation
painting, **200-201**
Tea trade, **97**
prices, 65, 86, 97
market, 95
Teanur, Mr., 116
Temple Place (Boston), 20, 26, 78, 91, 178
Tenobia, 170, 180, 183, 186, 199, 201, 203
Thames, 196
Tho Perkins, 73-74
Thos Coutts, 178, 180, 183, 198
at Whampoa, 184, 185
Tingqua (artist)
Houqua's gardens, **138-139**
tea merchants, **140**
tea cultivation, **200-201**
Tingqua (deceased hong merchant), house, 72-73
Tonkoo Island, 193
Trenton, 170, 171, 186, 186
Turner, Mr., 115

U

Union, 133
Union Club
RBF joins, 85

V

Valparaiso, 170, 180, 186, 198, 220
Van Barel, Mr., 116
Vancouver, 84, 105, 109
Varnhem, Warner, 227
Volage H.M.S., 166, 167, 230
fires on Chinese war junks, 184, 185

W

Wanghia, Treaty of, 267
War of 1812, 11, 14
Warner, Capt.
Thos Coutts, 185
Warren, John Collins, 79
Wells, F. Boots, 234
Westminister, 90
Wetmore & Co., 59, 96, 129, 156, 236
Wetmore, Mr., 74, 116
wife dies, 95
Whampoa
as seaport of Canton, 8-9, 58
anchorage, **56**
Wilhelm Lording, 186
Winslow, George, 21, 22, 43, 45, 143

Y

"Yellow Pagoda Fort," **208-209**
York, 84, 85
Yumchi
definition, 109

Z

Zion's Corner, 113

tent when this morning
from the Francis Stanton
appearance I greedily
your three letters one da
week after I sailed & on
realise that only a few d
only the state of feeling
at you were alive &
the well being of our de
ps — I will make a s
you have no copies y
note — now I have the a
journal & see what
were doing day by
I find you were doing pr
ith the boy Arthur of Tom —